CO… ADULTS
…ANSITION

Mary L. Anderson, PhD, is an associate professor emerita in the Department of Counselor Education and Counseling Psychology at Western Michigan University (WMU) in Kalamazoo, Michigan. She earned her master's and doctoral degrees from Oakland University in Rochester, Michigan. She has served on the faculty at three different universities in Council for Accreditation of Counseling and Related Educational Programs (CACREP)-accredited counselor education programs. Dr. Anderson's publications and presentations focus on topics relevant to international issues in counseling, professional development, supervision, school counseling, spirituality and transitions, and group work. Dr. Anderson has served in numerous roles in professional organizations, both at the state and national levels. She enjoyed working closely with former First Lady Michelle Obama's Reach Higher Initiative developing coursework specializing in career and college readiness and providing professional development for school counselors in the field. Dr. Anderson was an active participant at several White House Convenings focused on university/community/K-12 partnership initiatives and advocating for marginalized populations. Awards include recognition for strengthening community connections, creating college access, and meritorious service, along with an appreciation award from the American Counseling Association.

Jane Goodman, PhD, is a professor emerita of counseling in the Department of Counseling, School of Education and Human Services Education, Oakland University, Rochester, Michigan. She received her master's and doctoral degrees in guidance and counseling from Wayne State University, Detroit, Michigan. She formerly worked as a consultant and trainer for the Continuum Center, Oakland University, Rochester, Michigan, and served on the counseling faculty of Eastern Michigan University. She was the 2001 to 2002 president of the American Counseling Association, the 2005 to 2007 chair of the American Counseling Association Foundation, and the 1994 to 1995 president of the National Career Development Association, and is a past president of the Counselors for Social Justice. Dr. Goodman is a fellow of the American Counseling Association and the National Career Development Association. Dr. Goodman's awards include the Eminent Career Award from the National Career Development Association, the Distinguished Service Award from the Michigan Counseling Association, the Group Worker of the Year Award from the Michigan Association for Specialists in Group Work, and the Champion of Career Development award from the Michigan Career Development Association. She is currently a vice president of the International Association of Educational and Vocational Guidance and is retired member-elect of the Counselors for Social Justice.

Nancy K. Schlossberg, EdD, professor emerita at the University of Maryland, College Park, in the Department of Counseling and Personnel Services, College of Education, was a tenured full professor for 27 years. She received her doctorate in counseling from Teachers College, Columbia University. She also served on the faculties of Wayne State University, Howard University, and Pratt Institute and was the first woman executive at the American Council on Education (ACE), where she established the Office of Women in Higher Education. Dr. Schlossberg's awards include Fellow of three divisions of the American Psychological Association (APA), Fellow of the Gerontological Association, the 1983 APA G. Stanley Hall Lecturer on Adult Development, and Distinguished Scholar at the University of Maryland (1983). She was named one of the Eminent Women in Psychology by the APA and was listed in *Who's Who of American Women* in 1993. She received the 2016 Teachers College Columbia University Distinguished Alumni Award and the 2018 APA Citizen Psychologist Presidential Citation. She received awards from The National Career Development Association, National Association of Student Personnel Administrators, and American College Personnel Association. She has written 10 books, the most recent of which is *Too Young to Be Old*.

COUNSELING ADULTS IN TRANSITION

Linking Schlossberg's Theory With Practice in a Diverse World

FIFTH EDITION

Mary L. Anderson, PhD

Jane Goodman, PhD

Nancy K. Schlossberg, EdD

SPRINGER PUBLISHING

First Springer Publishing edition 1984; subsequent editions 1995, 2006, 2011

Springer Publishing Company, LLC
11 West 42nd Street, New York, NY 10036

www.springerpub.com
connect.springerpub.com/

Acquisitions Editor: Rhonda Dearborn
Compositor: Transforma

ISBN: 978-0-8261-3546-9
ebook ISBN: 978-0-8261-3547-6
DOI: 10.1891/9780826135476

21 22 23 24 25 / 5 4 3 2 1

Library of Congress Cataloging-in-Publication Data
Names: Anderson, Mary Louise, author. | Goodman, Jane, 1942- author. |
Schlossberg, Nancy K., 1929- author.
Title: Counseling adults in transition : linking Schlossberg's theory with
practice in a diverse world / Mary L. Anderson, PhD, Jane Goodman, PhD,
Nancy K. Schlossberg, EdD.
Description: Fifth edition. | New York, NY : Springer Publishing Company, [2022] | Includes bibliographical references and index. | Summary: "We now have a fifth edition, by Mary L. Anderson, Jane Goodman, and Nancy K. Schlossberg, updated with new, evolving theories, and providing an increased focus on specific practical applications for meeting our clients' needs in an increasingly diverse and ever-changing socio-cultural landscape. It also attempts to address the dramatic changes mentioned above, including the Pandemic, economic instability, Black Lives Matter and climate change. The dramatic and unprecedented changes in our environment challenge us to adapt our theoretical conceptualizations, methods, and strategies for working with clients. The goal of this edition is to provide an updated vision for working with transitions, with the integration of new theories, along with Schlossberg's timeless model. This book is predicated on several assumptions"-- Provided by publisher.
Identifiers: LCCN 2021017073 | ISBN 9780826135469 (paperback) | ISBN 9780826135476 (ebook)
Subjects: LCSH: Counseling. | Adulthood. | Middle age--Psychological
aspects. | Middle-aged persons--Counseling of.
Classification: LCC BF636.6 .A53 2022 | DDC 158.3--dc23
LC record available at https://lccn.loc.gov/2021017073

Contact sales@springerpub.com to receive discount rates on bulk purchases.

Printed in the United States of America.

Since the last edition, each of us has experienced a number of transitions in our lives. The tapestry is rich with love, loss, joy, and meaning.

To all who have enriched our lives, and especially to our partners, children, and grandchildren, we dedicate this book.

CONTENTS

PREFACE

The 20th century was termed *the century of the refugee* due to the vast numbers of people uprooted from their homes and accustomed lives by war and politics (Bateson, 1990). This rings even more true in the 21st century, with adults across all nationalities, socioeconomic statuses, and cultures experiencing the dramatic impact of change on their lives. Since the publication of the fourth edition of this book, we have witnessed social, political, and economic upheavals that could not have been predicted. These included the Covid-19 pandemic and the worldwide economic hardships that occurred as a result. There was also an upsurge of outrage in the United States that arose from the police killings of Black Americans, giving rise to an intensified Black Lives Matter movement, and the ongoing issue of climate change with its ever-increasing and intensifying storms. These events continue to shake people to their core, and the need for coping and adaptation has become increasingly evident. Technology continues to affect lives as well, with information now instantaneous via tweeting, blogging, and social networking. Most cell phones have email and video capabilities, and events are shared as they take place across the world community.

Adults need coping strategies to face the challenges of this complicated world. It is also imperative for counselors and other helping professionals to continue to increase our focus on the many aspects of cultural diversity. There is an increasing appreciation in the field regarding the profound effects of culture, especially as this relates to the manifestation of resilience and coping with traumatic events. We cannot underestimate the importance of the sociocultural context in shaping the coping process, and it is key that we continue to take seriously the need for advocacy on behalf of our clients, particularly those whose options are limited by discrimination and oppression. While we implement ways of advocating, we also need to be mindful of our clients' own coping and self-advocacy skills, whether learned in the counseling setting or elsewhere, perhaps within our clients' unique culture.

Nancy Schlossberg presented her transition theory in the first edition of this book, placing it in the context of other theoretical work on adult development. The second edition, with Elinor Waters and Jane Goodman, added more focus on what counselors hear and included practical suggestions for what to do with what they hear. The third edition, with Jane Goodman, Nancy Schlossberg, and Mary L. Anderson, affirmed our belief that the model is still an excellent basis for conceptualizing what we do to help adults cope with transitions. We now have a fifth edition, by Mary L. Anderson, Jane Goodman, and Nancy K. Schlossberg, updated with new, evolving theories, and providing an increased focus on specific practical applications for meeting our clients' needs in an increasingly diverse and ever-changing sociocultural landscape. The dramatic and unprecedented changes in our environment challenge us to adapt our theoretical conceptualizations, methods, and strategies for working with clients. The goal of this edition is to provide an updated vision for working with transitions, with the integration of new theories, along with Schlossberg's timeless model. This book is predicated on several assumptions.

ASSUMPTION 1: PRACTICE MUST BE TIED TO THEORY

The scientist-practitioner model, so prevalent in counseling, is based on the notion that practice stems from research and theory, and theory learns from practice. In this book, we present a theory of individuals in transition—a theory that lays the groundwork for the many practices, programs, and strategies suggested. We also describe how the theory was influenced by practical experiences.

Transition theory posits a structure for viewing *any* change, whether it is anticipated or unanticipated, positive or negative, a success or a failure, or an event or a nonevent. The persons and issues vary; the structure remains the same.

Transition theory states that individuals manage transitions differently. The variability stems largely from differences in people's resources and deficits as they approach transitions. The theory categorizes potential resources such as the individual's *situation, self, support,* and *strategies*—the components of the 4 S system. The practice details what can be done to assess these resources and compensate for deficits that may exist.

An example of the interface between theory and practice relates to coping. It was found that people cope by either changing a situation, changing the meaning of a situation, or managing their own reactions to it. Knowledge and understanding of these categories can guide counselors as they work with clients in an individual or group setting.

ASSUMPTION 2: WE CAN TAKE THE MYSTERY—IF NOT THE MISERY—OUT OF CHANGE

Change is not as mysterious as it seems. By looking at the degree to which a transition changes one's roles, relationships, routines, and assumptions, counselors can help clients gauge how traumatic a transition will be. Then, counselors can help clients examine their potential resources for coping and identify deficits and can then jointly plan ways of compensating for those deficits by deciding whether to change them, change their meaning, or manage the resultant stress. One can also better understand a client's stress by looking at where they are in the transition process.

ASSUMPTION 3: COUNSELORS CAN FOLLOW THE THEORY-TO-PRACTICE MODEL BY ORGANIZING THEIR THINKING AROUND THREE QUESTIONS

1. What do counselors need to know?
2. What are counselors likely to hear?
3. What can counselors do with what they know and hear?

The first section of the book addresses what counselors need to know by presenting an overview of established and emerging theories, along with an in-depth description of Schlossberg's transition model. The second section is rich with the issues that clients often bring to counseling, along with case examples of specific clients. The final section focuses on specific strategies and interventions that incorporate the knowledge counselors have about transitions with their counseling skills. These strategies may be used in either individual or group counseling. Counselors will also use this knowledge when they work as consultants or advocates to best meet their clients' needs.

We hope that this theory-to-practice book is useful as you help clients become better able to navigate the transitions that challenge their coping abilities and their lives.

Mary L. Anderson, PhD
Jane Goodman, PhD
Nancy K. Schlossberg, EdD

ACKNOWLEDGMENTS

We would like to express our gratitude to the editors at Springer, Rhonda Dearborn and Mehak Massand, who encouraged us to write this fifth edition and provided their ongoing support along the way. We thank the graduate students who helped us with each of the editions of this book, with research and feedback, along with their questions and life stories. For this latest edition, we would like to make special mention of doctoral graduate assistant, Zari Carpenter, who was very insightful, dedicated, and helpful with our process.

I

WHAT DO WE NEED TO KNOW?

To set the stage for what counselors need to know, the reader is introduced to an overview of theories that lay a foundation for working with adult clients. We provide a discussion of theoretical perspectives that relate to both individual development and contextual factors. To capture this intersection of influence, we highlight Erik Erikson's (1950, 1963) psychosocial stage model, along with contextual and life-span perspectives of adult development. The reader is then introduced to the transition perspective, delving into the transition process itself. Understanding transitions is more crucial than ever before, and the focus on working with adults in transition continues throughout the following chapters.

1

Adult Development in Context

INTRODUCTION

Adults face times that are increasingly challenging. A central theme in our current social context is *change,* reflecting the dynamic impact of forces across demographic, social, cultural, technological, political, and historical domains. Today, many adults find themselves charting unfamiliar and unexpected waters while striving to cope with this uncertainty for themselves and their families. Discontinuities are created by a number of factors, including personal life events, both anticipated and unanticipated, along with events that are shared by the world community. Although larger issues may be shared, these may be experienced at the most personal levels. As we discuss, the intersection of the individual, cultural, and contextual influences cannot be overestimated. For example, the most recent global pandemic continues to directly influence relationships and public health, along with the changes it has wrought in the structure of the world of work, which include job loss and economic uncertainty for so many. These profound upheavals have been compounded by unprecedented natural disasters related to global warming, along with a referendum on racism and political unrest. As escalating and sweeping changes have become the norm, life can feel increasingly complex and unsettling (Bright & Pryor, 2008, 2019). Traditional assumptions and expectations about adulthood continue to be reshaped and questioned. Indeed, today, continuity is the exception, and adjusting to discontinuity has become the norm of our era (Feiler, 2020). Whether people accept the changes around them or not, they may find that their old coping strategies no longer work.

As counselors, we see clients struggle with their feelings of grief and anger regarding their often unexpected losses and their anxieties about an uncertain future. Our goal is to help adults explore, understand, and cope with what is happening in their lives. We help them increase, or at least maintain, their capacity for love, work, and play—goals that are often conceptualized in terms of increased competency, maturity, and mental health. As we assist clients in recreating their lives, we often ask, "How can we, as counselors, most effectively assist adults as they strive to cope with the transitions—or the meaning of the transitions—that they encounter in their lives? How can we find the best way to support them in handling the stresses that accompany the changes confronting them?" It is our hope that, as counselors, we will help with an exploration of the issues, expand possible options, and facilitate movement into positive, hopeful directions. As we work with our clients to cope with the transitions of their lives, we help them to uncover their own sources of strength and adaptation as well as increase their ability for coping across the many roles they play in their lives and careers.

One of the best ways of achieving these goals is to integrate theoretical perspectives with our already-acquired helping skills. The more we, as practitioners, keep informed about adult development, the more effective we can make our responses and interventions. It is imperative that counselors keep current with newer, emerging theories and perspectives, especially as our world continues to be enriched and challenged by ever-increasing complexity and diversity.

THEORETICAL APPROACHES TO UNDERSTANDING ADULTHOOD

A theory is a set of abstract principles that can be used to predict facts and to organize them within a particular body of knowledge. A theory of adult development would thus suggest how cognition, personality, and other characteristics might evolve over an adult's life course. Ideally, theory should go beyond predicting the different aspects of adult development by offering new ideas that relate to things that are already understood. A current challenge for counselors is meeting the needs of increasingly diverse clients and formulating interventions that are culturally sensitive. This requires an intentional approach that is attuned to the cultural values and worldviews of our clients. As we consider these theoretical perspectives, it is imperative that we are invested in developing multicultural competence through continued acquisition of knowledge and skills, along with the cultural humility needed to advocate and develop new theories that are more responsive to all groups (Sue et al., 2019). So while we lay a foundation, we are continually challenged to expand our knowledge and cultural sensitivity with theoretical applications.

The Developmental Perspective

The developmental perspective emphasizes the sequential nature of adult development and is a scientific approach that is very familiar to both counselors and the general public. At its essence, human development entails "a process of change that occurs over time, extends across the lifespan, and involves both gains and losses for the individual" (Juntunen & Schwartz, 2016, p. 2). Developmental theory proposes a twofold conceptualization of human lives; the first one describes the social roles that define the various life stages, "each with distinct activities, opportunities, constraints and rewards" (Eliason et al., 2020, p. 205). The second conceptualization refers to the person's recognition, interpretation, and evaluation of their experiences associated with these life stages. When working with clients, we often explore issues that concern their perspectives on their progress along life trajectories. These subjective understandings include the inevitable comparisons of where one stands compared to others, along with the ambiguity and ambivalence that often comes with living in a context with increasing diversity, individualization, and variation across life stages (Eliason et al., 2020). People's observations of their lives often stand in contrast with the traditional models of adulthood and expectations based on a mapping of the stages of adulthood. This contrast continues to pose questions that remain a focus for research, especially regarding the timing and sequencing of the traditional markers of adulthood (Hall & Walls, 2016; Gersstorf, 2020; Hall & Walls, 2016).

Although developmental theory provides an important foundation for our understanding of life stages, a key consideration is that while people pass through a sequence of stages, these stages are not necessarily linked exactly with chronological age. Erik Erikson (1950, 1968) addressed this in his original writings, which postulated a broad view of development and took into account the influence of historical conditions. According to Joan Erikson (1997), the original theory made clear that "an individual life cycle cannot be adequately understood apart from the social context in which it comes to fruition. Individual and society are intricately woven, dynamically interrelated in continual exchange" (p. 114). Although increasingly less predictable, each of the stages can be understood as a progression of psychosocial development. Some people move through the stages faster than others do, some may experience the stages that seem to be out of order, and other people may become arrested at one stage and never successfully move on. Within the developmental approach, each stage is associated with a crucial task and a crisis that must be resolved. The transition poses both the opportunity for growth and the vulnerability of a poor resolution. This was defined as *ego qualities* with a description for each stage, including both a positive and negative outcome. According to Joan Erikson (1997), the positive outcome "support[s] growth and expansion, offers goals, celebrates self-respect and commitment of the very finest," stating that these qualities "sustain us as we are challenged by the more dystonic elements with which life confronts us all" (p. 106). She reminded us that although conflict and tension are a part of moving through the stages, this very struggle has the potential to be a source of growth and strength. The eight stages begin at birth and build on one another: trust (vs. mistrust), autonomy (vs. shame and doubt), initiative (vs. guilt,) industry (vs. inferiority), identity (vs. confusion), intimacy (vs.

isolation), generativity (vs. stagnation), and ego integrity (vs. despair). After the original conception of the eight life stages, Joan Erikson (1997) extended the cycle to include a ninth stage that is based on the experiences of the oldest old. She offered a rich reconceptualization of each of the stages as these relate to people encountering the challenges of moving through their 80s and 90s, with the crucial issue continuing to be integrity versus despair. She discussed the challenges of old age, along with the influential factors of community and transcendence. A key concept that has been coined by gerontologists is the term *gerotranscendence.* She chose to reword this as *gerotranscendance,* to capture the meaning of the need to *rise above* independent of the universe and time. For Joan Erikson (1997), the theory is much richer than simply a series of stages, as she stated, "In truth we are called to become more and more human; we must discover the freedom to go beyond limits imposed on us by our world and seek fulfilment" (p. 126).

This relates to a core focus of Erik Erikson's (1950, 1968) original theory, which conceptualized identity as a sense of self-sameness that continues over time. He described three interacting elements that shape one's sense of identity: biological characteristics, psychological factors (needs, interests, and defenses), and cultural contexts that serve to shape identity. Marcia (1966, 1980) proposed that identity in adulthood relates to four distinct stages: diffusion, foreclosure, moratorium, and achievement. These stages were termed *identity statuses* and can be understood with the concepts of exploration and commitment. According to Marcia, when a person's identity is diffused, no active exploration or commitments are made. In foreclosure, individuals make commitments without exploration, usually by identifying with authorities and/or parents. Those in moratorium continue to explore alternative identities without making any commitments. Those who achieve identity make commitments after a period of exploration.

Gender-specific identity models have been applied in a broad way to women (Downing & Roush, 1985). These conceptualizations describe women's identity development as a process, moving from passive acceptance of patriarchal, external definitions of womanhood to a more personalized, internally organized definition. These models have come under criticism because they do not capture the diversity and the complexity of women's self-concepts or address the experiences of racial/ethnic minority women. Moradi (2005) proposed a *womanist identity* development model that aims to move beyond the focus on a specific aspect of identity (gender), to capture women's multiple personal and group identities (e.g., race/ethnicity, class, and sexual orientation) that shape their identities. According to Moradi (2005), the term *statuses* seems warranted as a replacement for *stages* to bring attention to the fact that women may exhibit multiple identity development attitudes at the same time; these attitudes could well vary across time or contexts, especially relative to the level of work–family conflicts experienced. This concept has become more recently known as *intersectionality;* however, the intention was to highlight the experiences of Black, transgender women with a focus on power and oppression (Moradi & Grzanka, 2017).

The issues of career choice, identity, and transition experienced by women are strongly affected by family influences along with social gender role expectations. This relates to relational models of development, which highlight the central importance of relationships as relevant to women's identities and values (Gilligan, 1982). In a qualitative study, Kim (2012) examined how international students' spouses perceive and cope with the challenges of acculturation. Participants were Korean women and the most distinctive themes that emerged from the data were associated with life challenges and barriers, specifically language barriers, limited social supports/networks, and cultural differences. Another predominant theme concerned the psychological distress associated with acculturation and adaption, along with the negative emotions and the underutilization of mental health services. These women described altered family structures that resulted in limited interactions with their husbands, who were facing their own numerous challenges related to their studies and careers. However, positive implications related to the strengths gained throughout the process of adaptation, with participants becoming more independent and adapting to a new gender role. For these women, the newfound personal strengths were developed through meaningful cross-cultural friendships and community activities, such as volunteerism. Also, culturally meaningful activities, such as cultural events and language classes, helped them find meaning and happiness in their lives. In the discussion of the results, the researcher contextualized the key findings from this study referring to the work of Csikszentmihalyi and Seligman (2000), and their discussion of positive qualities as coping resources, especially as these relate to courage, optimism, emotional intelligence, and a sense of purpose.

Although strides have been made to explore the development of women in general, very few studies have been conducted on lesbian adult development. Wheeler-Scruggs (2008) conducted a qualitative study to analyze how self-identified lesbians fit into Levinson's developmental model. Overall, women in this study were similar to heterosexual women in other studies regarding developmental tasks. However, the primary difference was the issue of coming out (identifying as a lesbian to self and others). For the women in this study, coming out during the early adult transition added a new dimension to their life structures. According to the results of this study, coming out resulted in feelings of confidence, assurance, and a sense of self and helped define who they were as adults. Those who did not come out seemed to have a lack of identity as adults and also lacked the confidence and assurance expressed by those who had come out. Some participants experienced a "giving up of self" during the entering-the-adult-world phase. This involved going against personal thoughts, feelings, and ideas and, for some, involved dishonesty about their lesbianism. This was difficult, especially if honesty was a closely held value. Some advantages of coming out were also described by participants in this study, including individuation, increased intimacy, moving away from family of origin, a recognition of "faulty thinking," understanding one's anger, self-acceptance of one's lesbianism and femaleness, and seeking a spiritual life.

Identity issues are considered central to the theories discussed in this section, and it is important to note that these dominant theories have been criticized for defining identities in terms of the individual rather than a collectivist orientation (Blume, 2010). Blume (2002) proposed an alternative identity theory, termed *identity renegotiation,* that is applicable in a variety of cultural contexts. His theory incorporates ideas from current, emerging theories, such as narrative, social construction, dialogical self-theory, and liberation psychology. In essence, this theory views behavioral and emotional problems as having narrative *social understandings,* which are multiple, temporary, and situational. Blume (2010) proposed that identity is, in fact, the answer to the question, "Who can I be in this relationship?" In other words, significant others are considered to be *cocreators of identities,* through shared identity stories. At a larger, system level, Blume (2010) stated that identities are "less a result of direct interaction and more a result of membership in a group or category" (p. 9). The implications of this, according to Blume, are that group identities, when negative, can make it difficult to achieve validation for identity change, and positive group identities can be restrictive in order to remain a socially useful identity. When working from this theoretical orientation, counselors help clients in their awareness of the fluid and changing nature of self in relationships, along with recognizing the effect of social influences on their experiences. In this way, identity renegotiation can take place when clients are able to focus on the relevant discourses, related behaviors, and strategies for desired change (Blume, 2010).

Development Based on Age

Although early developmental theorists recognized the importance of the adult-life phase, the demographic changes that have occurred over the past half century have changed the shape, timing, and structure of adulthood. Thus, additional specific segments of the adult life span continue to be defined, including emerging adulthood as a distinct life stage, midlife as a crossroads between growth and decline, and the later years of adulthood that extend to the oldest old (Mehta et al., 2020). Each of these stages has been described in terms of common issues, themes, and characteristics For example, *emerging adulthood,* was coined to describe a period spanning the ages between 18 and the late 20s, in which the young person prepares for adulthood through exploration and experimentation. Although this stage offers excellent opportunities for self-exploration, it is also demanding regarding identity development due to the cultural changes that occur (Arnett, 2000, 2004). For example, the current pandemic has resulted in many young adults moving back in with their parents as they lose entry-level jobs or are unable to land that first posteducation job, thus complicating this stage of life.

An overlooked period of adulthood has been recently addressed by Mehta et al. (2020), with a focus on what they have termed *established adulthood.* They describe this stage, roughly ages 30 to 45 years, as "the most demanding and rewarding years of adult life," a period that has not been integrated within developmental theory. They pointed out a problem with this stage of life; that is, this phase of life may be blended with other stages, such as *young adulthood* on one hand, and as part of the *midlife* years on the other. The authors make a strong point that they are not proposing established adulthood as universal, one-size-fits-all theory, which, they agree, relates to "the unfortunate history of proposing universal life theories based on a tiny segment of the human population" (p. 432). They underscore that there is, in fact, much variation in the timing of and experience of established adulthood and that it is crucial to consider race, ethnicity, gender, social class, and cultural context as having a strong influence, which should be a focus for additional research in the field. While creating a theory of this stage, these authors stress that this period is when obligations are high in both work and family domains and that the resolution of developmental tasks has the potential to profoundly influence the rest of an adult's life.

The Contextual Perspective

The contextual perspective views adulthood primarily in relation to the context within which it occurs. People live, grow, and experience changes within the social context around them. Individuals experience career transitions, choices, and stability, as these are all incorporated into the daily contextual issues of everyday life. For example, although old, the study of bakery workers in France (Bertaux, 1982) illustrated the importance of context. According to this study, the individual life stories of bakers and their wives were a direct result of the structure and nature of the world of work in which they participated. Most bakery workers worked at least six nights a week, from 3 a.m., or earlier, until noon, totaling at least nine hours per night. This meant that whether "they were from rural or urban backgrounds, Catholic or agnostic, fat or thin, married or single, they worked at least 54 hours a week." As Bertaux stated, this fact "determined most of the rest of their lives ... weekly time budget, family life ... health (which declines after age 40 because of long hours and working in front of an oven), [and] activities outside work" (p. 133). This pattern of living, this same life story recurred over and over, "as a direct consequence of the structure of relations of production" (p. 134). Bertaux's findings are relevant to those working with adults because they suggest ways to help people identify the social factors that may lie at the root of some of their personal concerns.

Researchers (Shoon et al., 2007) analyzed data from two longitudinal studies following the lives and careers of over 20,000 individuals born in the United Kingdom 12 years apart. Analysis of the data included examining the antecedents and outcomes of educational and occupational aspirations of both men and women, especially during the transition from dependent childhood to independent adulthood. Shoon et al. (2007) assessed the processes by which family background and the wider sociohistorical context influence both work- and family-related careers. Their findings demonstrated the role of gender, social origin, and individual agency as they interact with a changing sociohistorical context. Although the teenage girls in the study demonstrated higher occupational aspirations than boys of the same age, they were less likely than men to achieve the same occupational level. The authors hypothesized that the earlier step into parenthood was an influential factor in the girls' lives and that young people from socially disadvantaged family backgrounds were more likely to become a parent early in life and less likely to climb the occupational ladder. Shoon et al. (2007) concluded that adult occupational status is influenced by a number of factors: parenting histories, occupational aspirations, and academic attainment. They stated that their study confirmed the vital role of teenage aspirations and academic performance in delaying parenthood. They also noted the differences between cohorts, in that the earlier cohort, born in 1958, entered the labor market during a period of economic growth, whereas the 1970 cohort left school at the height of the economic recession. The predominant pattern of the earlier cohort was to leave school to take jobs, and as the demand for skilled workers increased, education took on a more important role, thus influencing transition patterns and adult occupational status. The massive unemployment rate caused by the 2020 pandemic will surely affect the development of today's young adults.

Environmental factors, such as poverty and racial discrimination, are influential aspects relating to career development, occupational attainment, and access to work opportunities. For Black and Latinx young adults, the transition to the world of work can be influenced by a number of internal and external contexts, including educational experiences, cultural and family influences, and perceived and real barriers to educational and vocational goals (Constantine et al., 2007). Many Black and Latinx students are confronted with expectations that they will not succeed and may feel anxiety around contradicting this stereotype while they also anticipate the potential impacts of racism and discrimination. Challenges for Latinx adolescents may include psychosocial factors, such as acculturation stress, language barriers, incongruity between cultural values and the values of educational institutions, academic isolation, and socioeconomic inequities. Yet individual differences may also play a role. Exposure to positive racial messages and possessing high cultural self-esteem can influence perceived barriers and career-related outcomes. Contextual factors, such as formal and informal mentorships and learning experiences, have been shown to improve career-related and academic self-efficacy and may be helpful in dealing with the profound social costs that can be experienced when pursuing higher education. In other words, for some Blacks and Latinos, pursuing college could result in changing contextual factors, such as physical and emotional distance from their families and communities (Niemann et al., 2000). When discussing cultural influences, it is important to consider how Whites tend to hold values based on individualism, whereaspeople of color align more with values grounded in collectivism, placing the needs of the group/family/community as paramount. Although these tendencies are stereotypes not applicable to all members of the described group, understanding these underlying values can enhance working with cultural protective factors, such as resourcefulness and coping skills to deal with societal issues, and finding strength in familial and community support systems (Sue et al., 2019).

Environment also has an impact on such transition problems as the popularly accepted *midlife crisis.* This concept emerged with Levinson's (1978) Seasons of Life model in which he defined the period of the early 40s to be a time of intense psychological turmoil. Although this became a general expectation about midlife, research findings do not support this idea. Although midlife is viewed as a pivotal period of life, the chronological age boundaries are commonly viewed to range across the ages of 40 to 60 years, and individuals may subjectively consider themselves to be middle-aged anywhere from the age of 30 to 75 (Lachman, 2004). As described by Erik Erikson (1950, 1963), generativity is a key component of this life stage, and a central aspect of midlife is balancing multiple roles, social networks, and connectedness across generations (Infuma et al., 2020). The term *midlife* continues to be fraught with misconceptions, and this period of adulthood may be best described as *an intersection* of social context and inner struggles (Cohen, 2012). We often meet midlife adults presenting for counseling as they grapple with the aspects of self while also needing to make meaning and cope with their changing relationships. For some, this may entail making some adjustments to a current life situation, and others may require recreating their lives and redefining themselves in substantial ways (Anderson, 2016). The midlife years have been characterized by the interplay of multiple roles, and although changes in relationships may be stressful, it is important to remember that these relationships also provide a source of support. Relationship challenges may include becoming caregivers for aging parents, supporting adult children, and managing grandparenting responsibilities. An area for future research is understanding midlife experiences across cultures and within different aspects of diversity (Infuma et al., 2020). This is especially imperative today, with ongoing changes in family structures and challenges within the environmental context, along with increasing disparities experienced by marginalized populations. The term *midlife* was originally associated with the baby-boomer generation; however, it is a mistake to assume homogeneity with any age cohort. Rather, each generation is composed of a group of diverse individuals who have grown up in a shared historical time frame. According to Hudson (1999), however, each generation shares cultural reference points and historical events that influence their values throughout the life cycle. Generational identity greatly influences how individuals view their world and how they age and develop as human beings. Although midlife adults today continue to expand their expectations for their lives and their options, increasingly they are experiencing a wide gap between their dreams and reality. Hudson (1999) stated that the challenge is one of courage, and rather than mourning the premature death of the "American dream," adults need to explore their new personal depths and discover their own visionary capacities.

Neugarten and Neugarten (1987) emphasized that to understand a particular life history, one must view it in its appropriate historical context. Clearly, as historical times change, social prescriptions for age-appropriate behavior may also change. For example, people are living longer, and the postparental period has consequently lengthened considerably. At the same time, economic maturity for many young people is being delayed while a larger proportion of them attend college and go on to graduate or professional schools. In addition, what has been humorously called the *boomerang generation* has developed; that is, adult children who return home for a time, or several times, while getting situated in the world. Patterns for women have also changed radically, with most women now combining work and child-rearing. In many families, child-rearing practices are changing as partners increasingly share responsibilities. However, the recent challenges of the pandemic have disproportionally impacted women, with many women leaving the workforce: Factors driving this trend directly affect the types of positions women tend to hold in the workplace; added to this are the compromises that must be made when childcare is not available and schools are closed with children learning from home (NPR, personal communication, October 2, 2020).

These kinds of historical trends have a definite impact on the chronological and social norms for age-appropriate behavior, norms that were already being blurred and loosened in society (Neugarten & Neugarten, 1987). In adulthood, there seems to be little biological necessity for such norms; the most dramatic biological change after puberty is menopause, which itself has become surrounded by many emotional myths. Research, however, suggests that responses to menopause are closely tied to other midlife events (such as children leaving home), which in turn are very much influenced by environmental, cultural, and historical contexts.

This blurring of age-defined roles and tasks, often referred to as the *fluid life cycle*, represents flexibility and freedom for many. Others, however, some of whom may appear in counselors' offices, find it difficult to adjust their timetables. For example, some young people may feel inadequate if they have not met their achievement and family goals by the age of 35, even though they are likely to live into their 80s. When people maintain traditionally defined internal timetables that are rigid and at odds with their actual situations, they are susceptible to anxiety and conflict (Neugarten & Neugarten, 1987). This anxiety continues to be heightened, with unpredictability becoming a hallmark of our time. Increasingly, life is becoming less linear, which can explain why people are feeling so overwhelmed. It can be helpful to acknowledge that the *linear life* is begin replaced by the *nonlinear life*, especially with the current reality of everyday events that continue to disrupt and reshape people's lives (Feiler, 2020).

In addition, in a pluralistic society such as ours, subgroups may have their own age-normative systems. Factors, such as race, socioeconomic status, disability, sexual orientation, and geographic location, may determine differences in age-defined behavior. For example, the length of the "coming out" process for lesbian and gay people (Fassinger, 1991) may delay the establishment of permanent relationships and the creation of families. This process may be even more complicated for individuals who are bisexual or transgender. Similarly, occupational prejudice and discrimination may impede and delay career attainment for specific minority groups. For example, it is still legal to fire someone for their gender and orientation identity in many states. These contextual factors become especially obvious when we attempt to apply general normative theories to our intervention efforts.

Another source of change and challenge is *history-graded* changes. Researchers who propose a *life-course* perspective view development as an intersection of chronological age, family-related roles, and membership in a particular birth cohort experiencing historical events. This is an especially salient issue in the context of fewer or weaker social bonds combined with expanding and heightened threats and a pervasive sense of vulnerability in what has been termed an *age of anxiety* (Broderick & Blewitt, 2003). We need not look far to see many examples of profound historical events and can only imagine the impact these are having for the different age cohorts experiencing them. The historical events of recent times have only served to heighten the meaning of living in an *age of anxiety*, which is being experienced at personal, family, community, and global levels.

It is evident then that a body of literature is now accumulating in which researchers explain behavior by analyzing the social context in which it occurs. For example, an alternative theoretical approach, the *constructivist* perspective, has emerged in response to our postmodern, multicultural age. The postmodern worldview offers an alternative to modernism, which is based on an objectivist, reductionist quest for truth and knowledge. This positivist worldview dominated the first half of the 20th century, with most scientific methods of study designed to explore some behavior of social patterns of current interest. A problem, however, is that because of the rapid rate of social change, the phenomena of interest are transformed before the study is complete (Gergen, 2000). Another limitation to modernism is that scientific truth is culturally dependent and value laden. Within the postmodern perspective, people are actively constructing their mental realities rather than simply coping with an objective "truth." This approach emphasizes that people develop as they construct meaning and make choices within their social/cultural context. According to White (1996), "The constructivist approaches are based on the assumption that we are constructive—that we are engaged in a process of actively building our reality or world view, instead of there being an "objective" world that can be known independent of the knower" (p. 8).

The constructivist perspective has an established usefulness for understanding how people make sense of their experience. Although the modern emphasis on the objective dimension served to give recognition to the dominant culture's voice, the constructivist approach focuses on a person's private sense (Savickas, 2015, 2019). Yet social constructions are often developed within institutional contexts. Understanding the process of constructions is fundamental, especially when one is looking at race/ethnicity, social class, sex/gender, and sexuality. Understanding these systems involves the recognition of the inequality and domination that have an impact on people's development (Orr, 2000). It is also imperative to accept the premise that "race, ethnicity, and culture are powerful variables in influencing how people think, make decisions, behave, and define events" (Sue et al., 2019, p. 37). The constructivist approach is thus compatible with system-based theories while being relevant to the lives of women and non-Eurocentric worldviews (Brott, 2001; Brown, 1996). The preferred technique of constructive therapies is the exploration of personal narratives with the therapeutic goal of meaning-making and personal development (White, 1996).

Regardless of the focus of investigative attention, the result is to examine individuals by also accounting for the sociological and ecological factors that affect them and the meanings that are constructed out of this experience. As counselors, we must be aware of these perspectives of adult development. When appropriate, these theoretical lenses can help us to recommend interventions designed to change the environment of clients or to alter the way the clients cope with their environment. It is crucial to understand that the different theories of counseling represent different worldviews and that each racial, ethnic, or cultural group has its own perspective on the nature of people and healthy development (Sue et al., 2019) This relates not only to critically evaluating the underlying assumptions of our theories but also to the issues of social justice. We discuss the important role of counselors as advocates in the last chapter of the book.

The Life-Span Perspective

The third perspective on our continuum—the life-span perspective—focuses on individuality and issues of continuity and change. Development is viewed as a process of adaptation taking place within multiple contexts that vary for individuals, thus leading to very different pathways through the life span. Some theorists see continuity among individuals over the course of life, whereas others see so many individual pathways that variability becomes the cornerstone of adulthood. Kagan (1980, 1998), for example, wondered why social scientists have invested so much effort in a search for stability and continuity. He questioned the premise that information about a growing child is sufficient to explain the life course of the child. In examining conclusions about a Berkeley longitudinal study in which 166 people were observed from birth through adulthood, he noted: "When the subjects were seen at age 30, 12 years after their previous interviews, the researchers were shocked by the inaccuracy of their expectations. They were wrong in two-thirds of the cases, mainly because they had overestimated the damaging effects of early troubles" (1980, p. 64). Counselors who are aware of the findings of this study can caution adults against using early problems as a rationale for being "stuck" and not taking responsibility for their actions as adults.

Neugarten (1982) also emphasized variability, which she called *individual fanning out*. She pointed out, for example, that 10-year-olds are more similar to each other than are 60-year-olds and emphasized that the most consistent finding was that people grow old in very different ways. He stated that there are striking variations among groups that reach old age, among ethnic, urban and rural, and socioecomic groups, along with idiosyncratic sequences that "widen the divergence among individuals. The result is that 60-year-olds or 80-year-olds are extremely heterogeneous groups" (p. 6). And Pearlin (1882), in his work on strain and coping, echoed Neugarten's emphasis on individuality and variation. He maintained that human variety is as rich as people's historic conditions and current circumstances and that even within the same cohort, the impact of conditions may differ because of variations in coping resources. Thus, in his view, it was untenable to speak of either ages or life stages as though undifferentiated people were following a uniform life course.

There is agrowing interest in considering diversity as a source of strength, and it has been suggested that adaptive cultural strengths are central in promoting resiliency and adaptive coping throughout the life span. Cultural strengths have been considered to be protective forces in maintaining a sense of hope, vitality, and persistence to excel against discouraging odds. A life-span perspective is necessary when considering the unique challenges faced by African American or other individuals living in distressed urban ecologies. These may include (a) chronic role strain and resiliency challenges, (b) risky psychosocial coping strategies, and (c) protective emic cultural strengths (Bowman, 2006). Bowman (2006) stated that empowerment strategies are crucial, and three types of goals must be implemented: therapeutic, resiliency, and systemic change. Strategies in these areas are imperative, especially as marginalized people face alarming risk for chronic strain in major life roles by systemic racial, class, ethnic, and/or gender role barriers. Specific empowerment strategies may be helpful in facilitating adaptive coping at the personal, family, and community levels (Bowman, 2006). The recent emphasis on Black Lives Matter arose from racially motivated police brutality and has multiracial support, but it also can be useful in encouraging the adaptive coping mentioned earlier.

A key aspect of life-span developmental theory is the role of adaptation as a continuous influence on people's lives. Adaptation can take different forms, including growth, maintenance/resilience, and regulation of loss. *Growth* involves adding new characteristics, understandings, and skills, whereas *maintenance/resilience* involves finding ways to continue functioning when facing challenges or suffering a loss. *Regulation of loss* involves adjusting expectations and accepting a lower level of functioning. All of these adaptive processes occur throughout the life span, and it is through these adaptive processes that successful development unfolds (Broderick &

Blewitt, 2003). Whitbourne (1996) addressed coping and adaptation over the life span and saw adaptation as the continuous evaluation of life experiences rather than reactions to discrete events. An individual's life-span construct is subject to change as the individual meets experiences that contradict it or are totally incongruent with it. For instance, the act of coping itself may result in an altered life story as individuals distort the meaning of events toward the maintenance of their self-esteem. Coping may also alter an individual's aspiration levels toward greater congruence with their environment when it is clear that failure to achieve aspirations does not stem from the individual's inadequacy. Thus, in this model, the adaptation process takes on different configurations, depending on whether an event is consistent or inconsistent with an individual scenario.

The reality of adults' lives today is characterized by variety and diversity, influenced not only by gender and culture and the roles people have but also by the timing of the stages they move through. For example, some people marry and have children at relatively young ages, whereas others wait until their 40s to pursue family life. Others may never marry or live with a partner yet may choose to be a parent. These changes in the social context have challenged models that relate stages to age (Barnett & Hyde, 2001; Fraenkel, 2003). Subsequent models conceptualize development based on particular events in an adult's life. These models, called *life events models*, propose that the events in adults' lives, not age, determine the course of their development (Helson & Srivastava, 2001; Roberts et al., 2002). In other words, rather than looking at critical periods in adults' lives, they are looking at life events that are specific to the individual. The implication of this is that two people of very different ages may share commonalities in significant life events and thus in their personality development.

Feiler (2020) created a Life Story Project and interviewed 225 people from various backgrounds across all 50 states in the United States. After compiling these interviews, he discovered that, although people tend to believe that their lives will progress on an upward trajectory, many are shocked to realize that their lives "oscillate instead" (p. 7). He stated that unprecedented forces continue to reshape contemporary life, bringing about more tumultuous transitions. As he emphasized, navigating transitions became an overriding theme in the current context. His overall observation was that people's lives today are filled with chaos and complexity and that we experience life "as a complex swirl of celebrations, setbacks, triumphs, and rebirths across the full span of our years" (p. 15). He stressed that the key obligation facing people is to "navigate an almost overwhelming array of life transitions" (p. 15). Feiler's research defies the concept that life generally unfolds with mostly stable periods, interrupted by transitions that occur between developmental stages. Rather, current forces are bringing about an increasing number of challenges that occur across the entire life span.

An emerging consensus among researchers is that the next decades will be characterized by increasing shifts in the population, cultural diversity and disparity, changes in work, and further extensions of digital and information technologies. All of these factors will continue to shape and reshape adult development and aging (Gerstorf et al., 2020). A rethinking of adulthood includes consideration of historical changes and the rapid changes occurring in adult development worldwide, and serves as a call to further research that is creative and intentionally diverse (Arnett, 2020).

Bringing us back to our foundational developmental perspective, life entails a series of stages, events, and crises to manage. It is in the transitions where we meet both the challenges and opportunities to grow and thrive. The experience of transition can feel like a crisis. The Chinese ideogram for crises involves two characters: danger and opportunity. The literal translation is *opportunity riding on a dangerous wind* (Corlett & Millner, 1993). This is where we often meet our clients, in the transitions.

The Transition Perspective

The fourth theoretical perspective in adulthood—the transition perspective—focuses on life events entailing change. Schlossberg (1981, 1991) presented a transitional model that incorporated both anticipated transitions—the scheduled, expected events that are likely to occur for the individual and that can be anticipated and rehearsed—and unanticipated transitions—the nonscheduled events that are not predictable. That model, described in detail in Chapters 2 and 3, is the cornerstone of this book.

Transitions are often experienced as frightening or traumatic. Hudson (1999) characterized life for adults as being "on a raft floating down a commanding river" and the transitions as "the white waters of the river" that test every skill we have as "we slide over rocks and rapids and swirl about in unforeseen directions" (p. 51). He stated that the river metaphor captures two aspects of dealing with transitions. One is a sense of chaotic power beyond our control, and the other is a sense of adventure requiring our continual readiness and vigilance.

Theorists have positioned transitions within a developmental framework, defining them as *turning points* or as a period between two periods of stability (Levinson, 1986). Moving through a transition requires letting go of aspects of the self, letting go of former roles, and learning new roles. People moving through transitions inevitably must take stock as they renegotiate these roles. Transitions often involve significant life events that require coping with what is perceived to be a crisis situation. Innate growth and potential may be realized through addressing and coping with these significant life events (Brown & Lent, 2008).

Within a developmental framework, the transitions themselves are viewed as occurring in stages, with each stage relating to the next for adaptation and successful adjustment. Within this perspective, a transition occurs over a period of time between life phases or life stages. Whether viewed as a time of crisis or as a developmental adjustment, transitions present a unique opportunity for growth and transformation (Bridges, 1980; Hudson, 1999; Schlossberg et al., 1995). According to Bridges (2001), "renewal is possible only by going into and through transition, and transition always has at least as much to do with what we let go of as it has with whatever we end up gaining in its place" (p. 43).

Research regarding the role of positive emotions and coping with stress has been prompted by evidence regarding both negative and positive emotions that co-occur throughout the stress process (Folkman & Moskowitz, 2004). According to Folkman and Moskowitz (2004), coping is a complex, multidimensional process that is sensitive to both the environment and to personality dispositions, which influence the appraisal of stress and the resources for coping. They stated that, despite gains that have been made in understanding coping, researchers have only begun to understand the concept. They maintained that much of the problem is that coping is not a standalone phenomenon, as it is embedded in a process that involves the person, the environment, and the complex relationship between them. A related area of knowledge relates to what has been termed *posttraumatic growth,* defined as *the experience of positive change* resulting from the struggle with major life crises (Calhoun & Tedeschi, 1999, 2006). This line of research began as a response to the universal experience of trauma and coping, with a focus on adaptation to stressful events. This perspective considers that, although negative consequences are associated with stressful events, there are also benefits and growth. Crucial applications of this approach include understanding posttraumatic growth across cultures, especially the influence of culture on the meaning and manifestation of resilience and coping (Weiss & Berger, 2010).

SUMMARY

Examining our theories is important because it helps us to clarify our views and assumptions of adult development. Our aim here was to provide a quick overview of different theories and to set the stage for showing how theory affects practice. As we develop the transition perspective, we will see how all the theories described so far feed into it, making it an eclectic theory that looks at context, development, life span, and the construction of meaning.

REFERENCES

Anderson, M. L. (2016). Supporting adaptation to new family roles in middle age. In C. L. Juntunen & J. P. Schwartz (Eds.). (2016). *Counseling across the lifespan: Prevention and treatment* (2nd Ed.). Sage.

Arnett, J. J. (2000). Emerging adulthood: A theory of development from the late teens through the twenties. *American Psychologist, 55*(5), 469.

Arnett, J. J., Robinson, O., & Lachman, M. E. (2020). Rethinking adult development: Introduction to the special issue. *American Psychologist, 75*(4), 425–430.

Arnett, J. J. (2004). *Emerging adulthood: The winding road from the late teens through the twenties.* University Press.

Barnett, R. C., & Hyde, J. S. (2001). Women, men, work, and family. *American Psychologist, 56*, 781–796.

Bertaux D. (1982). The life course approach as a challenge to the social sciences. In T. K. Hareven & K. J. Adams (Eds.), *Aging and life course transitions: An interdisciplinary perspective* (pp. 127–150). Guilford Press.

Blume, T. W. (2002). Negotiating identity in couple sexuality. In L. Burlew & D. Capuzzi (Eds.), *Sexuality counseling* (pp. 89–109). Nova Science Publishers.

Blume, T. W. (2010). Counseling for identity renegotiation. *International Journal of Theory and Research, 10*, 92–105.

Bowman, P. J. (2006). Role strain and adaption issues in the strength-based model: Diversity, multilevel, and life-span considerations. *Counseling Psychologist, 34*, 118–133.

Bridges, W. (1980). *Transitions: Making sense of life's changes*. Addison-Wesley.

Bridges, W. (2001). *The way of transition: Embracing life's most difficult moments*. Perseus Publishing.

Bright, J. E. H., & Pryor, G. L. (2008). Shiftwork: A chaos theory of careers agenda for change in career counseling. *Australian Journal of Career Development, 17*, 63–72.

Bright, J. H., & Pryor, G. I. (2019). The chaos theory of careers: Emerging from simplification to complexity, certainty to uncertainty. *Asia Pacific Career Development Journal, 2*(1), 1–15.

Broderick, P., & Blewitt, P. (2003). *The life span: Human development for helping professionals*. Merrill Prentice Hall.

Brott, P. E. (2001). The storied approach: A postmodern perspective for career counseling. *Career Development Quarterly, 49*, 304–313.

Brown, D. (1996). Status of career development theories. In D. Brown L. Brooks, & Associates (Eds.) *Career choice and development* (3rd ed., pp. 1–13). Jossey-Bass.

Brown, S., & Lent, R. (2008). *Handbook of counseling psychology* (4th ed.). Wiley.

Calhoun, I. G., & Tedeschi, R. G. (1999). *Facilitating posttraumatic growth: A clinician's guide*. Erlbaum.

Calhoun, I. G., & Tedeschi, R. G. (2006). The foundations of posttraumatic growth: An expanded framework. In L. G. Calhoune & R. G. Tedeschi (Eds.), *Handbook of posttraumtic growth* (pp. 1–23). Erlbaum.

Constantine, M., Kindaichi, M., & Miville, M. (2007). Factors influencing the educational and vocational transitions of Black and Latino high school students. *Professional School Counseling, 10*, 261–265.

Corlett, E., & Millner, N. (1993). *Navigating midlife*. Davies-Black.

Csikszentmihalyi, M., & Seligman, M. E. (2000). Positive psychology: An introduction. *American Psychologist, 55*(1), 5–14.

Downing, N. E., & Roush, K. L. (1985). From passive acceptance to active commitment: A model of feminist identity development for women. *The Counseling Psychologist, 13*, 695–709.

Eliason, S. R., Mortimer, J. T., & Vuolo, M. (2015). The transition to adulthood: Life course structures and subjective perceptions. *Social Psychology Quarterly, 78*(3), 205–227.

Erikson, E. H. (1950). *Childhood and society*. Norton.

Erikson E. (1963). *Childhood and society* (2nd ed.). Norton.

Erikson, E. H. (1968). *Identity, youth, and crisis*. Norton.

Erikson, J. M. (1997). *The life cycle completed*. Norton.

Fassinger, R. E. (1991). The hidden minority: Issues and challenges in working with lesbian women and gay men. *Counseling Psychologist, 19*, 157–176.

Feiler, B. (2000). *Life is in the transitions: Mastering change at any age*. Penguin.
Folkman, S., & Moskowitz, J. (2004). Coping: Pitfalls and promise. *Annual Review of Psychology, 55*, 745–774.
Fraenkel, P. (2003). *Contemporary two-parent families: Navigating work and family challenges*. In Walsh, F. (Ed.), Normal family processes: Growing diversity and complexity (pp. 61–95). Guilford Press.
Gergen, K. J. (2000). *An invitation to social construction*. Sage.
Gerstorf, D., Hulur, G., Drewelies, J., Willis, S., & Schaie, W. (2020). *Adult development and aging in historical context. American Psychologist, 75*(4), 525–539.
Gilligan, C. (1982). *In a different voice*. Harvard University Press.
Hall, S. H., & Walls, J. K. (2016). Exploring family-oriented markers of adulthood: Political and personal variations among emerging adults. *Society for the Study of Emerging Adulthood and Sage Publications, 4*(3), 192–199. https://doi.org/10.117/2167696815579827
Helson, R., & Srivastava, S. (2001). Three paths of adult development: Conservers, seekers, and achievers. *Journal of Personality and Social Psychology, 80*, 995–1010.
Hudson, F. M. (1999). *The adult years: Mastering the art of self-renewal*. Jossey-Bass.
Infuma, F. J., Gerstorf, D., & Lachman, M. E. (2020). Midlife in the 2020s: Opportunities and challenges. *American Psychologist, 75*(4), 470–485.
Juntunen, C. L., & Schwartz, J. P. (2016). *Counseling across the lifespan: Prevention and treatment*. Sage.
Kagan, J. (1980). Perspectives on continuity. In O. G. Brim, Jr. & J. Kagan (Eds.), *Constancy and change in human development*. Harvard University Press.
Kagan, J. (1998). Biology and the child. In W. Damon (Series Ed.) & N. Eisenberg (Vol. Ed.), *Handbook of child psychology: Vol. 3. Social, emotional, and personality development* (5th ed., pp. 177–236). Wiley.
Kim, J. (2012). Acculturation phenomena experienced by the spouses of Korean international students in the United States. *Qualitative Health Research, 22*(6), 755–767.
Lachman, M. (2004). Development at midlife. *Annual Review of Psychology, 55*, 305–331.
Levinson, D. J. (1978). *The seasons of a man's life*. Ballantine.
Levinson, D. J. (1986). A conception of adult development. *American Psychologist, 41*, 3–13.
Marcia, J. E. (1966). Development and validation of ego-identity status. *Journal of Personality and Social Psychology, 3*, 551–558.
Marcia, J. E. (1980). Identity in adolescence. In J. Adelson (Ed.), *Handbook of adolescent psychology* (pp. 159–187). Wiley.
Mehta, C. M., Arenett, J. J., Palmer, C. G., & Nelson, L. J. (2020). Established adulthood: A new conception of ages 30 to 45. *American Psychologist, 75*(4), 431–444.
Moradi, B. (2005). Advancing womanist identity development: Where we are and where we need to go. *Counseling Psychologist, 33*, 225–253.
Moradi, B., & Grzanka, P. R. (2017). Using intersectionality responsibly: Toward critical epistemology, structural analysis, and social justice activism. *Journal of counseling psychology, 64*(5), 500.
Neugarten, B. L. (1982, August). *Successful aging*. Paper presented at the 90th Annual Meeting of the American Psychological Association, Washington, DC.
Neugarten, B. L., & Neugarten, D. A. (1987). The changing meanings of age. *Psychology Today, 21*, 29–33.

Niemann, Y. F., Romero, A., & Arbona, C. (2000). Effects of cultural orientation on the perception of conflict between relationship and educational goals for Mexican American college students. *Hispanic Journal of Behavioral Sciences, 22*, 46–63.

Orr, T. E. (2000). *The social construction of difference and inequality: Race, class, gender, and sexuality*. Mayfield Publishing.

Pearlin, L. I. (1982). Discontinuities in the study of aging. In T. K. Hareven & K. J. Adams (Eds.), *Aging and life course transitions: An interdisciplinary perspective* (pp. 55–79). Guilford Press.

Roberts, B., Helson, R., & Klohnen, E. (2002). Personality development and growth in women across 30 years: Three perspectives. *Journal of Personality, 70*, 79–102.

Savickas, M. L. (2015). *Life-design counseling manual*. Mark L. Savickas.

Savickas, M. L. (2019). *Career counseling* (2nd ed.). American Psychological Association.

Schlossberg, N. K. (1981). A model for analyzing human adaptation to transition. *Counseling Psychologist, 9*, 2–18.

Schlossberg, N. K. (1991). *Overwhelmed: Coping with life's ups and downs*. Lexington Books.

Schlossberg, N. K., Waters, E. B., & Goodman, J. (1995). *Counseling adults in transition* (2nd ed.). Springer publishing Company.

Shoon, I., Martin, P., & Ross, A. (2007). Career transitions in times of social change. His and her story. *Journal of Vocational Behavior, 70*, 78–96.

Sue, D. W., Sue, D., Neville, H. A., & Smith, L. (2019). *Counseling the culturally diverse*. Wiley.

Weiss, T., & Beger, R. (2010). *Posttraumatic growth and culturally competent practice: Lessons learned from around the globe*. Wiley.

Wheeler-Scruggs, K. S. (2008). Do lesbians differ from heterosexual men and women in levinsonian phases of adult development? *Journal of Counseling and Development, 86*, 39–46.

Whitbourne, S. K. (1996). *The aging individual: Physical and psychological perspectives*. Springer Publishing Company.

White, M. F. (1996). *Constructive therapies*. Guilford Press.

2

The Transition Framework

INTRODUCTION

Adults experience many transitions over the course of a lifetime, some of which are planned for and some others that are unexpected. Although the types of transitions and reactions vary from person to person, some common elements include a sense of leaving what was once familiar, having to find one's way, and the sense of loss associated with what has been left behind. Classic literature is full of examples of heroes' journeys, moving into the unknown and encountering the unexpected challenges that present themselves along the way. Metaphors of change and transformation are abundant in nature, which include the changing seasons, migration of birds, and the transformation of a caterpillar into a butterfly through the process of metamorphosis. These metaphors each imply a *process*; navigating transitions most often requires courage, tapping into one's inner resources, and seeking sources of support. This is where we often meet our clients, as they are in the struggle and process of coping with changes in their lives. The purpose of this chapter is to provide helpers with a framework for understanding the transition process itself and informing our interventions.

The transition model and theory was originally developed by Nancy K. Schlossberg (1981, 1984) and offers a conceptual framework for assessing clients' assets and liabilities, along with designing interventions and strategies for adults in transition. Her model is universal and useful for various types of transitions, for diverse populations, and for designing interventions sensitive to individuals' unique situations and experiences.

Adults in transition often experience a mix of reactions and find themselves in need of assistance to sort through the losses, challenges, and opportunities that transitions present. To capture the experience of a transition, we often describe the experience of a trapeze artist. Standing on a solid platform can feel secure, at least until it is time to "go over there" to the other platform. This requires swinging out, turning and "letting go," and then experiencing a free fall through the air before grabbing onto the approaching swing and landing on the other platform. When describing transitions, we are likely to act out this scenario and then ask participants, "What is it like to be in the free fall," to experience the "in between"? Answers inevitably vary; however, some themes are consistent:Answers include feeling groundless and scared, along with some individuals describing a sense of exhilaration and excitement. The free fall is the transition, and reactions illustrate that no one can assume what a client is experiencing, as every person's experience is unique . When clients are able to explore their issues more fully and understand the underlying meanings, they are likely to move forward to cope more effectively and creatively.

To help adults explore, understand, and cope, helpers need to be able to weave together their skills and knowledge at each phase of the helping process—whether by exploring our clients' contextual situation, understanding the issues at a deeper level, or developing strategies to help enhance coping and growth through the transition process. Transitions can be disorientating, yet they can lead to new thresholds for personal growth. Although it is natural to resist transitions, helpers can serve as guides for letting go of what has been lost and claiming what remains to be discovered. Often, this involves "being with" in the midst of uncertainty and ambiguity, and working phenomenologically, seeing the transition through the perspective of the client. And it cannot be overstated that ongoing education, training, and sensitivity regarding culture and diversity are crucial in working with clients to promote their optimal development and coping. This is especially important in order to understand the cultural norms and expectations and to tap into culture as a source of belonging, support, and resources.

OVERVIEW OF THE TRANSITION MODEL

The transition model provides a systematic framework for counselors, psychologists, social workers, and other helpers to consider as they listen to the many stories—each one unique—of colleagues, friends, and clients. The transitions differ and the individuals differ, but the structure for understanding individuals in transition is stable. The transition model has three major parts:

1. Approaching transitions: Transition identification and transition process
2. Taking stock of coping resources: The 4 S System
3. Taking charge: Strengthening resources

To summarize, approaching transitions identifies the nature of the transition and provides an understanding of which perspective is best for dealing with it. Transition identification asks what change is impending—a new baby, a job change, an intrapersonal change, a relationship change?

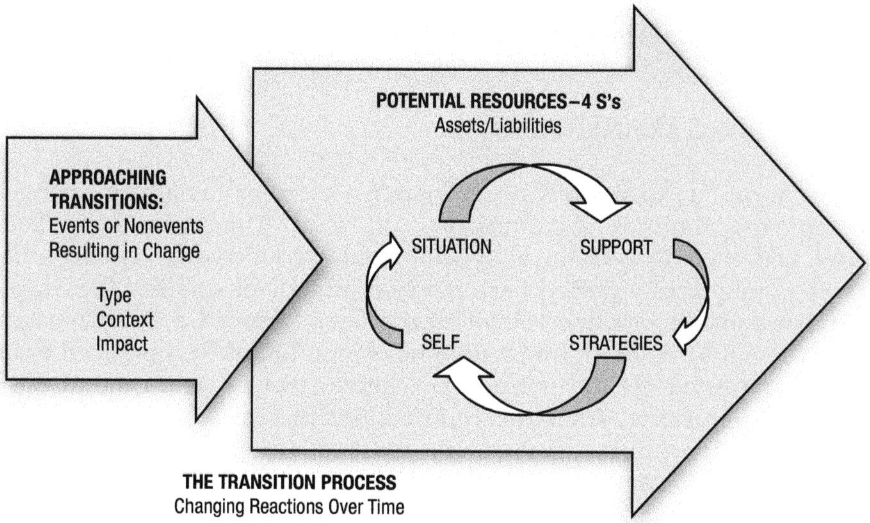

FIGURE 2.1 The individual in transition.

Is it anticipated, unanticipated, or a nonevent? Knowing more about it and being able to describe it helps get the discussion moving about what is troubling or challenging a client. Even more important than the mere identification of the change is specifying the degree to which the particular transition changes the client's life or the perceptions of how their life is being affected. Three people describing a similar transition, for example, the loss of a loved one, are not talking about the same event. To understand its significance, the counselor needs to see how this loss has changed each individual's roles, relationships, routines, and assumptions.

The transition process locates where the adult is in the transition. Did the client just learn of an impending illness? Is the person newly coping with a loss, or has it been some time since the loss occurred? Reactions to any transition change over time, depending on whether one is *moving in, through,* or *out of* the transition.

Taking stock of coping resources: The 4 S System provides a way to identify the potential resources someone possesses to cope with the transition. The 4 S's refer to the person's *situation, self, support,* and *strategies.* No matter where one is in the transition process, no matter what the transition is, one deals with it differently depending on the availability of these resources.

Taking charge: Strengthening resources demonstrates the use of new strategies. Even though some transitions are out of our control, we can control the way we manage them—we can strengthen our resources, our 4 S's. Figure 2.1 depicts the model. Part 1, approaching transitions: transition identification and transition process, is detailed in this chapter. Taking stock of coping resources: The 4 S System is described in Chapter 3.

APPROACHING TRANSITIONS

In broad terms, a transition is any event or nonevent that results in changed relationships, routines, assumptions, and roles. Transitions have been placed conceptually within a developmental framework, described as *turning* points or as a period between two periods of stability (Levinson, 1986). For some clients, the transition may be perceived as a crisis situation. Others may be grappling with a nonevent, the often unspoken event that was expected yet did not occur. Whether viewed as a time of crisis or as a developmental adjustment, transitions present unique challenges, along with opportunities for growth and transformation (Bridges, 1980; Hudson, 1999; Schlossberg et al., 1995). Whether an obvious, more dramatic life change (such as high school graduation or the birth of a child) or more subtle changes (such as the loss of aspirations for a promotion or a marriage proposal that never happened), a transition can be defined as an event or nonevent resulting in change.

Regardless of the specific nature of the changes involved, transitions require coping. Moving through a transition requires letting go of aspects of the self, letting go of former roles, and learning new ones. People moving through transitions inevitably must take stock as they negotiate the changes in their lives, and these changes may involve gains as well as losses. As practitioners, it is key to be mindful of the meaning that people attribute to their transitions and that experiences of meaning are embedded within a sociohistorical context. Therefore, cultural values must be considered, keeping in mind that within collectivist cultures, individuals may prefer to develop their meanings in a social way rather than individualistically. Also, helpers need to be aware of their own subjective biases as we may attribute our own meaning to the events and experiences shared by our clients (Vos, 2018). Culture, social marginalization, and economic status all exert critical roles in shaping people's experiences. These are key influences on how people attribute meaning, along with the dynamics of work, family, and community, and opportunities regarding outcomes (Kenny et al., 2018). This is a crucial lens to keep in mind as we discuss the different types of transitions, and how people may cope and view the opportunities (real and/or perceived) that are available to them.

Types of Transitions

The first step in approaching a transition is to identify the type of transition that has happened or is happening: Was it anticipated or unanticipated? Or is it a nonevent?

Anticipated Transitions

These transitions comprise normative and expected events and may include marriage, the birth of a first child, starting a first job, or retiring. Many adults find that having an opportunity for role rehearsal, whether mental, vicarious, or real, can ease an anticipated transition. Examples include premarriage counseling, birth classes, and recommended job shadowing and/or internships before formally entering a field of work. However, it is best to keep in mind that in the current context, life is not as predictable as it once was. Although adjusting to anticipated transitions may be more manageable, increasingly there are more unexpected twists and turns in people's realities and the events that impact their lives.

Unanticipated Transitions

Unanticipated transitions present unique challenges that can be very different from anticipated transitions. When transitions are anticipated and planned, they are often self-initiated and made with ample time to consider multiple options. However, when confronted with unanticipated transitions, individuals do not have the opportunity to prepare and may make decisions in a less-than-ideal context (Fouad & Bynner, 2008). Many theoretical perspectives about transitions make assumptions that individuals are making transitions in optimal circumstances and that people have the capabilities and resources to make the transition. However, for many individuals, transitions are navigated in a time of turmoil, and it is important to understand how culture influences the perceptions and options that are available (Fouad, 2019). Culture, social marginalization, and economic status all exert critical roles in shaping people's experiences, their meaning, and the dynamics among work, family, and community, along with opportunities and outcomes (Kenny et al., 2018). These are key considerations for working with clients and their perceptions of the barriers that challenge them, along with potential options available to them. This can be particularly salient when working with people encountering unanticipated transitions.

According to Feiler (2020), life today can be best described as *nonlinear*, which explains why people can feel so overwhelmed, especially when they have been brought up to expect their lives will unfold on a linear path. He stated that acknowledging this reality rebukes conventional thinking about life trajectories and also provides an invitation to recognize the randomness of events that reshape our lives. He termed unanticipated transitions as *disrupters* and shared that unanticipated transitions are far more prevalent than anyone expects, based on results from 225 life-story interviews. He defined a *disrupter* as "an event or experience that interrupts the everyday flow of one's life" (p. 52). The experiences of his participants ranged across the various types of events, from caring for aging parents, being fired, to going from overnight fame to public humiliation. He stressed that although disrupters may be viewed as negative life events, these may also become the catalysts for reinvention. Many of us know people who have reinvented themselves after an unexpected transition, for example, starting a new business after losing a job, or pursuing passions that were formerly put aside. There are many layers when working with clients who are coping with unanticipated life events, especially when their expectations for their lives have been challenged by unexpected realities.

As counselors, we must develop sensitivity to our clients' needs in dealing with the unexpected events of their lives, along with the ability to assess the many factors involved in coping with the transition. These often include the emotional, social, or financial support to adjust to the transition. Barriers can also be environmental, such as racism, sexism, or ageism, a slow economy, high unemployment, or the unpredictable timing of opportunities. Another consideration is that external resources are often shaped by social and institutional policies of the context in which they are made. These policies vary from country to country; for example, some cultures in Western Europe believe that society is responsible for helping individuals with transitions, whereas in more individualistic societies, such as the United Kingdom and the United States, the assumption is that people are supported by their families and are responsible for managing their own transitions (Fouad & Bynner, 2008). These policies relate to a key part of our counselor role, that of advocacy, which is discussed in more detail in Chapter 10.

Nonevent Transitions

These transitions are the ones that an individual had *expected* but that did not occur, thereby altering their life—the marriage that never occurred, the promotion that never materialized, the child who was never born, or the false-positive cancer diagnosis. For example, a couple who had counted on having children may finally, in their late-40s, realize that this will not occur. The realization that the expected transition did not and will likely never occur alters the way they see themselves and might also alter the way they behave. Generally, four types of nonevents can be identified: personal, ripple, resultant, and delayed. These circumstances are discussed in detail in Chapter 8.

Let us use having a child as an example to summarize the types of transitions—anticipated, unanticipated, and nonevent. A planned pregnancy is anticipated. An unexpected pregnancy when you are 15 years old is unanticipated. For those who wish to have a child but are unable to conceive, a baby is a wished-for but nonoccurring nonevent. Sometimes, a transition may change from anticipated to unanticipated or even become a nonevent, depending on the circumstances. Such is the case with miscarriage, when what was anticipated is interrupted by an unanticipated event with the miscarriage. Moving forward, this becomes a nonevent, and it can be difficult to process the feelings of grief when there are no rituals to acknowledge the loss. Thus, it is not the transition itself that determines its meaning for the individual, but rather how this is experienced as expected, unexpected, or never occurring.

Several other points about the types of transitions need to be mentioned. These involve the concepts of perspective, context, and impact.

Perspective

An anticipated change for one person—for example, retirement—might be unanticipated for another. For example, a high school teacher had carefully planned for retirement and was on track to follow his plan when he reached the age of 65. For another teacher, retirement was considered as a possibility in the future when, during the pandemic, she elected to retire earlier than expected, something that she never anticipated. Several factors influenced this decision, including an underlying health condition and the urging of her adult children, who were concerned about her continued exposure working in the schools. For another individual, this was a nonevent—not retiring—which was driven by financial circumstances resulting in a decision not to transition or consider retirement as a viable option.

The individual's appraisal of the transition is key. Does the individual see it as positive, negative, or benign? One person might define retirement as positive, with an opportunity to spend more time with family. Others may view this as a challenge: How to figure out how to meaningfully fill their days and/or meet their basic needs? Another might see it as the next step before dying, the end of a productive life. One's appraisal clearly influences how one feels and copes with the transition, whether anticipated, unanticipated, or a nonevent.

To illustrate perspective, we use an example from a workshop conducted by one of the authors, during which a question was posed to the participants. The individuals were asked to consider the transitions of their lives and, if willing, to share a challenging and/or painful transition they had experienced. Responses were varied and, of course, were from the individual perspectives of those who chose to share. It was interesting that for one woman, the most difficult transition was the unexpected death of her parents in a car accident when she was eight years old. She shared how different aunts and uncles adopted each of her brothers and sisters and herself. The room was hushed and reverent as she shared what was obviously a dramatic and painful life event. The next person shared her experience of going to college and receiving a "terrible haircut" as a freshman; from her perspective, this was a very difficult event in her life. As counselors, we are often challenged to remember that it is the client's appraisal that determines the impact of the transition, the perceived challenges and meaning this holds, and the specific needs for coping.

Context

It is important to consider the contextual factors that influence people's lives, and as mentioned earlier, these include factors such as gender, socioeconomic status, ethnicity, and geographical location (Fouad, 2019). Contextual factors may have both direct and indirect influences on a transition, and Bronfenbrenner's ecological theory (1977) offers a helpful conceptual framework. This theory began with a focus on childhood development and has expanded to applications across a variety of settings and populations. Bronfenbrenner described context in terms of systems that are in closer or further proximity to the individual, and how they interact and influence one another. The closest system, the microsystem, includes the immediate environment around a person and refers to the activities, roles, and relationships that exist within the home, school, family, and workplace. The mesosystem refers to the connections that take place among these systems, such as home, school, peer groups, and community. The exosystem is composed of environmental systems that interact, and thus indirectly exert influence; and the macrosystem encompasses a person's culture and the broader social context. The chronosystem was later added to represent the dimension of time, to reflect how changes within the person and environment may influence one's patterns and behaviors. It is interesting that Bronfenbrenner emphasized the importance of *ecological transitions* that people undergo, such as starting school, getting a sibling, marriage, or divorce (Eriksson et al., 2018). Another key application of this theory is understanding that people's lives are embedded in and shaped by broader societal and historical contexts (Buhler & Niktin, 2020). Although beyond the scope of this chapter, utilizing an ecological systems approach provides a way to conceptualize our clients' transitions in context, along with a framework for where to focus interventions.

Another consideration with context is that each generation is subject to a combination of historical events that influence their life course. Age cohorts experience different historical events and cultural climates. Each generation experiences shared events that may have repercussions on their lives as they progress from childhood through adulthood. For example, a young person may have been influenced by 9/11 when in elementary school, the 2008 economic recession as a young adult, and the COVID-19 pandemic at a crucial time of emerging adulthood. Although generations share commonalities, a key consideration regarding the transitions that people are navigating is that we must be sensitive to the fact that everyone does not start on a level playing field. The differentiation in opportunities and obstacles continues to shape people's potential, across backgrounds, locations, birth eras, and countries (Fouad & Bynner, 2008).

When addressing context, the relationship of the individual to the event or nonevent resulting in change is also central to our understanding of transitions. Does the primary event start with the individual (their illness) or with some other person (their family member's unemployment)? Is the transition personal (the individual has lost their job) or interpersonal (the individual has experienced sexual harassment in their workplace)? Is the transition involved with the public or the community (does the individual feel disgraced by having to go on unemployment or stand in a food line)?

Often if something is happening to an individual, resources can be mobilized. For example, after the initial shock of becoming disabled, a client became proactive in working through her limitations and beginning a new life requiring accommodations. But if something is happening to someone else, for example, the divorce of an adult child, the individual often can only sit by, suffer, and offer support. We need to note that many parents and grandparents as well, feel the tragedies and excitements happening to their children/grandchildren as if they were happening to themselves. Often, as counselors, we help people sort through a mix of feelings regarding the context of the transition and their relationship to what is happening.

A key question to ask is, "What is the arena in which the transition occurs?" In today's society, people are trying to balance multiple roles, and this inevitably leads to what has been referred to as *role* strain. It is helpful to consider the context of life strains across various roles, and the anticipated or unexpected events impacting one role may often spill into another. For example, adjusting to midlife may encompass coming to terms with aspects of self while also trying to cope with the changing roles across work and family relationships. Sorting out these changes can involve addressing an array of complex and interconnected issues (Anderson, 2016). Today, multigenerational families are common, and people in midlife can find themselves in what has been termed *the sandwich generation;* as people live longer with three or four generations in the family, this term has evolved to *super sandwich generation* (Grundy & Henretta, 2006). To continue with this example, a 65-year-old grandmother may be considering retirement to assist with her grandchildren while also being the primary caregiver for her elderly parents. This illustrates how her roles may interact and change across relationships, along with work, routines, and financial contexts.

To summarize, the context for a transition affects our reactions. The transition may involve clients' roles across the areas of self, friends, family, work, health, or economics. The context also includes the larger socioeconomic and political arenas along with issues around cultural diversity. We, as practitioners, have an obligation to consider these larger contextual factors in working sensitively with our clients and facilitating them in reaching their full potential. Bright and Pryor (2005), writing about the application of chaos theory to career counseling, reminded us that "reality as individuals experience it … [is] richly complex, nonlinear, and serendipitous" (p. 302). Coping with change involves the person, the environment, and the complex relationship between them.

Impact

For an individual undergoing a transition, it is not the event or nonevent that is most important but its impact, that is, the degree to which the transition alters one's daily life. When an event, such as a company's financial collapse and subsequent layoffs, creates problems for an individual, we need to look not only at the type and context but also at the impact of the event on the individual's relationships, routines, assumptions about self and the world, and roles. We may assume that the more the transition alters the individual's life, the more coping resources it requires and the longer it will take for assimilation or adaptation. As aspect of impact considers concurrent stressors, such as adapting to working from home during a pandemic while also schooling children from home and worrying about the welfare of vulnerable parents. Addressing the impact requires practical strategies; however, our work often begins with processing our clients' reactions and exploring their feelings and concerns as they come to terms with a new reality. Feelings may encompass losing what was familiar and known, a loss of opportunities, and a loss of personal history with what *used to be.* Sometimes, especially painful transitions can also bring a loss of a sense of self, a loss of perspective, and a loss of hope (DiMarco, 1999). Even when transitions are viewed as positive, coming to terms with loss can still be in play and require coping. For example, receiving a promotion may also come with a required move to another location, which involves leaving much behind in the process.

While conducting his Life Story Project, Feiler (2020) found that five story lines emerged that reflect the impact on people's lives across the following realms: *love, identity, beliefs, work,* and *body.* He compared his list of themes to an earlier life stress assessment, the Holmes–Rahe Life Stress Inventory (1967). This earlier assessment identified 43 *life change units* that were weighted according to the impact and associated stress of each of these life events. The highest stress score was given to death of a spouse, and the lowest scores were assigned to major holidays and minor violations of the law. Feiler pointed out that his own list, developed 50 years later, shared some similarities and also key differences. An example he discussed was one of the categories on the Holmes–Rahe inventory, *change in church activity.* In Feiler's data, this change was determined to be three categories: *change in religious observance, change in religious affiliation,* and *personal calling.* He noted categories regarding *work* shared similarities, with his categories reflecting the rise of entrepreneurship. Another example is *divorce,* which was included on both lists; however, Feiler's research also included custody battles, which are now more common than 50 years ago. His focus on current life disrupters included some key categories that were missing from the earlier inventory: sexual harassment, domestic violence, mental illness, suicide, addiction, and public humiliation. He noted that all of these were dominant themes of the Life Story Project. In his final data, Feiler provided what he termed a *Deck of Disrupters,* with 52 life changes that emerged across his interviews, with these falling under the major themes listed previously: love, identity, beliefs, work, and body. As practitioners, we explore the impact across each of these life arenas with our clients, which are discussed throughout the subsequent chapters of this book.

To summarize impact, assessment of a transition's impact on relationships, routines, assumptions, and roles is probably the most important consideration in understanding an individual's reactions. This is a key point. Sometimes, the changes are profound. For example, Naomi left her position at a hospital to move from Botswana, Africa, to San Francisco, California, to pursue her education. Her relationships with colleagues changed; her daily routines changed—not just regarding work and school, but learning her way around in a new city and culture; and her assumptions about herself also changed as she became an immigrant, far from her country of origin. Some of her roles, however, remained intact. She was still a daughter, sister, aunt, and engaged to be married, although the nature of these roles changed with the distance between herself and her significant others. Years before, Naomi had changed positions to work in a hospital and moved to a new location that was 20 miles from her home. She clearly had made a change, but it was not nearly as extensive. This new move and the associated changes had an impact across Naomi's relationships, routines, assumptions, and roles, thus requiring extensive coping skills as well.

Or let us look at divorce. Clearly with this event, there are changed relationships, routines, assumptions, and roles. For many, changed assumptions about themselves and their world become paramount. To illustrate, Jill said, "I am no longer part of a couple. Am I deficient in some way since I cannot keep a marriage together?" She stayed in the same house with her two small children but began to think about ways to get more training so that she could earn a decent salary to raise her children. The changes involved in this transition could include multiple factors for Jill, including coping with the turmoil of the divorce, anxieties about her ability to perform in the work world, and fears concerning her children's adjustment to the divorce and her return to work. A key aspect of working with Jill would be helping her sort through the impact of the divorce across her roles as a mother and single adult, her new routines as a working mother, and her assumptions about being a woman and a mother to her children.

Summary

To understand the meaning a transition has for a particular individual, we need to examine the *type* of transition (anticipated, unanticipated, or nonevent), the *perspective* of the individual regarding the transition, the *context* of the transition (relationship of the person to the transition and cultural/social/political context in which the transition occurs), and the *impact* of the transition on the individual's life (on relationships, routines, assumptions, and roles). This point needs to be further underscored. Often people in the midst of one transition experience other transitions, which makes coping especially difficult.

THE TRANSITION PROCESS

Within a developmental framework, transitions occur in stages, with each stage relating to the next for adaptation and successful adjustment (Bridges, 1980; Hudson, 1999; Schlossberg et al., 1995). Although the onset of a transition may be linked to one identifiable event or nonevent, transitions are really a process over time. Six months, 1 year, and sometimes 2 years pass before one moves fully through a major transition. For example, if you interview a person before a move, during the move, 6 months after the move, and again 2 years later, you will get entirely different responses. Reactions continually change. The only way to understand people in transition is to study them at several points in time. At first, people are consumed by their new role, such as being a new graduate, a new widow, an unemployed worker, or a recent retiree. Gradually, they begin to separate from the past and move toward the new role, for a while teetering between the two. The process of leaving one set of roles, relationships, routines, and assumptions and establishing new ones evolves over time, and people's reactions to transitions change—for better or worse.

When working with clients, it is clear that transitions may provide both opportunities for psychological growth and dangers of psychological decline. And this often relates to people's unique reactions, lived experience, and the way they view the changes in their lives. Brammer (1991) defined transitions as both ordinary changes and extraordinary changes that occur continually throughout people's lives. He described a transition as *a journey through,* usually to something unknown, requiring the courage to take risks and the ability to cope with fear. Brammer conceptualized the levels of adaptation to transitions: *adaptation,* when one adjusts to change; *renewal,* when one sets goals; *transformation,* when one experiences rebirth; and *transcendence,* when one reaches the ultimate level for meaning-making of both the transition itself and one's whole life as well. This reflects a deeper focus of our work with clients, by exploring their assumptions and perspectives, and facilitating meaningful responses to life events.

In systemic literature review and meta-analysis, Vos and Vitali (2018) examined the types of meaning-centered treatments available across different populations, including those with chronic physical illness, transition moments in life, and clients with psychological problems. They found significantly large improvements with these clients compared to others in the control groups. Improvements related to quality of life, meaning in life, hope and optimism, self-efficacy, and social well-being. According to Vos (2018), when individuals are capable of living a meaningful life, they may experience flow, mindfulness, peak experience, and happiness and find that their lives can be lived with authenticity.

These findings relate to a growing recognition in the field for the possibility of benefits and growth after highly stressful events. The term *posttraumatic growth* (PTG) first emerged in response to working with victims of trauma worldwide (Tedeschi & Calhoun, 1995). The assumption of this approach is that facing and struggling through difficulties can bring about positive changes, which can also include radical transformations. Although a thorough discussion of this topic is beyond the scope of this chapter, the concept of PTG has been applied internationally and emphasizes the positive effects of culture and meaning on people's potential for resilience and coping (Weiss & Berger, 2010).

An Example of the Transition Process

To continue with the example of retirement, incorporating retirement transitions into your life takes time. At first, people are consumed by exiting from their past role and figuring out a new life. The change is consuming, and then, gradually, people begin to separate from the past and move toward a new life. According to Schlossberg (2017), retirement entails a series of transitions, which may take from 6months up to 2 years to move through, and typically includes an initial period of disruption and confusion. She described the experience of retiring as leaving the structured world of work and not yet entering into a new life. She highlighted that it may take some trial and error to find the right combination of activities and that with time the change becomes integrated into a person's life, with new relationships, routines, and emerging assumptions about self and the world.

In Schlossberg's (2004) studies of retirees, she found that they followed many paths during this process: Some *continued* in a modified way what they once did; others experimented and *adventured* into new activities like the researcher turned massage therapist; others glided easily, taking each day as it came; others *searched* for their place in the sun; some stayed as *involved spectators* like the former lobbyist who was now a news junkie; and others unfortunately *retreated.* Many, of course, combined paths. Each retiree has a psychological portfolio, which is the bridge that connects past work and future retirement. The portfolio consists of one's identity, relationships, and meaningful involvements.

Identity

This is key to the psychological portfolio. What do you put on a business card? How do you identify yourself when you meet someone? As one man said sadly, "When people ask what do you do? I don't know how to answer. Should I say, 'Nothing?'" Miriam, a skilled dentist, could not wait to retire so that she could do carpentry. She had her workshop ready the day she retired. Yet it took her 2 years to say to herself and to others that she was a professional carpenter. Incorporating a new identity takes time.

Relationships

Relationships play a critical role in one's psychological portfolio. Schlossberg (2017) stated that replacing work relationships takes time and requires effort. Also, readjusting family relationships can be challenging, especially with spending more time with a spouse or partner. For example, Cal, a retired professor, claimed that what he missed most was "schmoozing." He was having difficulty replacing work relationships—a must to keep your psychological portfolio strong. Cal amazed himself when he heard himself arguing with his wife at the checkout counter about the brand of cereal she had bought. Now that he was no longer working full time he went grocery shopping with her. Adjusting to being at home with her after 50 years of spending days apart takes time.

Meaningful Involvement

Meaningful involvement is a necessary component of one's psychological portfolio. Sociologists Moen and Fields (2002) concluded that peoples' work provides social as well as financial capital. After retirement, participation in volunteer or part-time work is an effective way to build up your social capital (Schlossberg, 2017). Many studies point to the relationship of volunteering and mental health and even longevity. Working often leads persons to feel competent, useful, and, most of all, that they "matter." If you feel that you matter and that your life has meaning and purpose, then clearly you have the necessary assets in your psychological portfolio.

THE RESOLUTION

At some point, transitions are assimilated into one's life. For example, a woman hearing that she has been diagnosed with breast cancer will be totally absorbed in her reactions, her search for the right treatment, and by facing the many decisions to be made. The process of hearing the initial diagnosis, dealing with the treatment plan, and seeing herself and her body in a new way takes time. Eventually she is someone who had cancer. She is no longer absorbed; she has dealt with the medical and psychological treatment. She incorporated her new sense of herself, aware that this is now part of her reality, she has regained her sense of well-being.

A man who was forced to relocate will at first be totally absorbed in the logistics of moving himself and his family—selling his house and buying another. He will be focused on his wife's search for a job in the community and his children's registration in and adjustment to a new school. He will then be able to focus on his emotions about the move, positive and negative, and the learning curve required to be up to speed in his new position. And all of these reactions will be mediated by his explanatory style.

SUMMARY

The transition framework is based on the following premises:

- Adults continuously experience transitions.
- Adults' reactions to transitions depend on the type of transition, their perceptions of the transition, the context in which it occurs, and its impact on their lives.

- A transition has no end point; rather, a transition is a process over time that includes phases of assimilation and continuous appraisal as people move in, through, and out of it.

These primary elements apply to nonevent transitions as well as to those triggered by specific events. Those events we thought might happen that do not are often of critical importance in the lives of adults and are often underplayed or ignored. Yet they can have a profound influence on a person's well-being and may require an intentional response with meaning-making to move forward in life with hope and optimism. Nonevent transitions are described further in a special chapter that includes theoretical and descriptive material as well as exercises for helping adults navigate nonevent transitions.

REFERENCES

Anderson, M. L. (2016). Supporting adaptation to new family roles in middle age. In C. L. Juntunen & J. P. Schwartz (Eds.), *Counseling adults across the lifespan: Prevention and treatment* (2nd ed.). Sage.

Brammer, L. (1991). *How to cope with life transitions: The challenge of personal change.* Hemisphere.

Bridges, W. (1980). *Transitions: Making sense of life's changes.* Addison-Wesley.

Bright, J. E. H., & Pryor, G. L. (2005). The chaos theory of careers: A user's guide. *Career Development Quarterly, 53,* 291–305.

Bronfenbrenner, U. (1977). Toward an experimental ecology of human development. *American Psychologist, 32*(7), 513–531.

Buhler, J. L., & Nikitin, J. (2020). Sociohistorical context and adult social development: New directions for the 21st century. *American Psychologist, 74*(4), 457–476.

DiMarco, C. (1999). *Moving through life transitions with power and purpose.* Pearson College Division.

Eriksson, M., Ghazinour, M., & Hammarstrom, A. (2018). Different uses of Bronfenbrenner's ecological theory in public mental health research: What is their value for guiding public mental health policy and practice? *Social Theory & Health, 16*(4), 414–433. https://doi.org/10.1057/s41285-018-0065-6

Feiler, B. (2020). *Life is in the transitions: Mastering change at any age.* Penguin.

Fouad, N. A. (2019). Three strands, one braid: My life in counselling psychology. *Counseling Psychologist, 47*(4), 658–673. https://doi.org.libproxy.library.wmich.edu/10.1177%2F0011000019873241

Fouad, N. A., & Bynner, J. (2008). Work transitions. *American Psychologist, 63,* 241–251.

Grundy, E., & Henretta, J. C. (2006). Between elderly parents and adult children: A new look at the intergenerational care provided by the "sandwich generation." *Aging and Society, 26,* 707–722.

Holmes, T. (1967). The Holmes-Rahe Life Stress Scale. *Journal of Psychosomatic Research,* 2.

Hudson, F. M. (1999). *The adult years: Mastering the art of self-renewal.* Jossey-Bass.

Kenny, M. E., Bluestein, D. L., & Meerkins, T. M. (2018). Integrating relational perspectives in career counseling practice. *Career Development Quarterly, 66*(2), 135–148. https://doi.org/10.1002/cdq.12128

Levinson, D. J. (1986). A conception of adult development. *American Psychologist, 41,* 3–13.
Schlossberg, N. K. (1981). A model for analyzing human adaptation to transition. *Counseling Psychologist, 9,* 2–18.
Schlossberg, N. K. (1984). *Counseling adults in transition.* Springer Publishing Company.
Schlossberg, N. K. (2004). *Retire smart, retire happy: Finding your true path in life.* American Psychological Association.
Schlossberg, N. K. (2017). *Too young to be old: Learn, work, and play as you age.* American Psychological Association.
Schlossberg, N. K., Waters, E. B., & Goodman, J. (1995). Counseling adults in transition (2nd ed.). Springer Publishing Company.
Tedeschi, R. G., & Calhoun, L. G. (1995). *Growing in the aftermath of suffering.* Sage.
Vos, J. (2018). *Meaning in life: An evidenced-based handbook for practitioners.* Springer Nature.
Vos, J., & Vitali, D. (2018). The effects of psychological meaning-centered therapies on quality of life and psychological stress: A meta-analysis. *Palliative & supportive care, 16*(5), 608–632.
Weiss, T., & Berger, R. (2010). Posttraumatic growth around the globe. In T. Weiss & R. Berger (Eds.), *Posttraumatic growth and culturally competent practice: Lessons learned from around the globe* (pp. 189–197). Wiley.

3

Factors That Influence Transitions

INTRODUCTION

The transition framework presented in Chapter 2 and here in Chapter 3 is designed to depict the extraordinarily complex reality that accompanies and defines the human capacity to cope with change. Four major sets of factors (Figure 3.1) influence the ability of the individual to cope during a transition:

1. The *situation* variable—What is happening? Does the transition come at a time of multiple stressors? For example, the transition to a new job is different from the transition to a new job while coping with a dying parent.
2. The *self* variable—To whom is it happening? Each individual is different in terms of life issues, personality, and inner resources.
3. The *support* variable—What help is available? Supports and available options vary for each individual.
4. The *strategies* variable—How does the person cope? People navigate transitions in different ways. We call these factors the 4 S's.

THE 4 S SYSTEM: SOME CONSIDERATIONS

The 4 S System—situation, self, support, and strategies—describes the factors that make a difference in how one copes with change. These four sets of variables can be regarded as potential assets and/or liabilities. To understand how these assets and liabilities work, first, we need to examine their interrelationship and how one goes about appraising them, but it is equally significant to examine the options faced by different individuals and groups

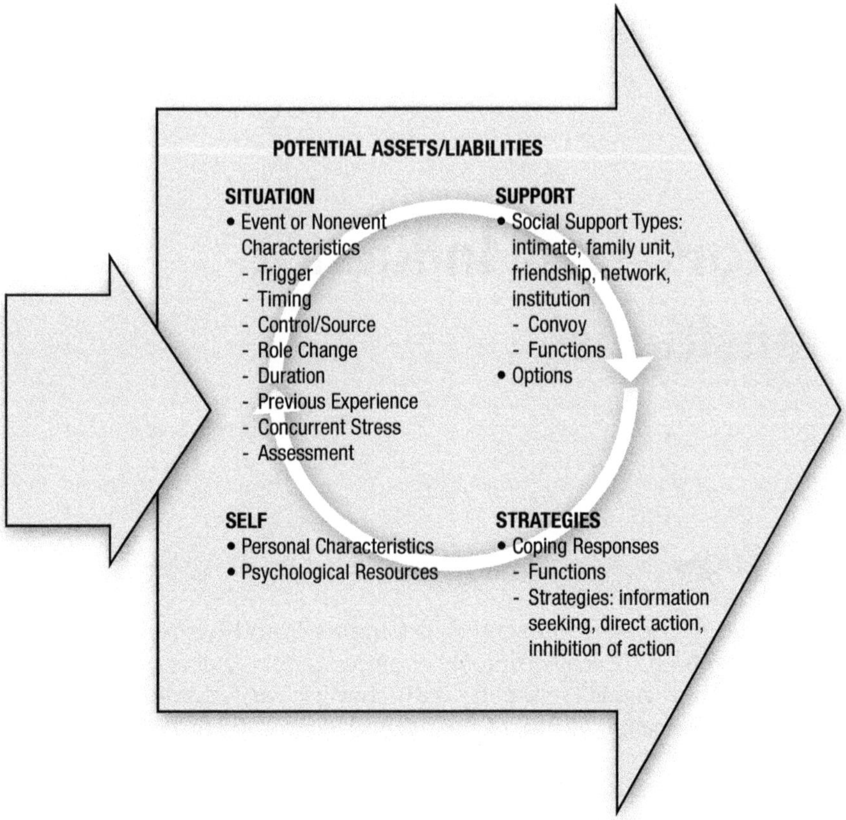

FIGURE 3.1 Coping resources—the 4 S's.

in our society. As noted previously, context is a key consideration and relates to one's relationship to the transition and to the setting in which the transition takes place.

Balancing Assets and Liabilities

Coping effectiveness is best examined and explained by using a model that balances opposing forces. Individuals have both assets and liabilities as well as resources and deficits as they experience transitions. A key aspect of working with clients is facilitating a meaningful exploration of their strengths and limitations, with the goal of increased ability to cope and better well-being. Thus, a model that incorporates both resources and deficits is meaningful, both with ongoing assessment and for designing interventions tailored to our individual clients.

To clarify this mix of resources and deficits, we look at two people who were diagnosed with Parkinson's disease. For both, the experience is painful, incapacitating, and psychologically distressing because of the inevitable progression of the condition. One of the individuals has important assets to balance this deficit in her physical condition, which include a highly supportive family as well as friends and colleagues who rally around her, and a coping personality. The other woman is low on assets at this particular point in her life. She has just recently gone through a divorce, which suggests that part of her support system has crumbled. In addition, this particular disability threatens her very economic survival by making it impossible for her to work as a day-care worker, a job that requires physical stamina. Moreover, she has a tendency to self-isolate with no close friends or family nearby, and her ability to cope has never been better than average. At this benchmark, her liabilities outweigh her assets, making her life especially difficult.

The 4 S System then, rather than assessing a person's mental condition in terms of health or sickness, employs an assets-to-liabilities ratio and allows for changes in this balance as an individual's situation changes. This approach partially answers the question of why individual reactions vary when experiencing similar types of transitions and why an individual may respond differently at different times. An influential factor is the assets–liabilities balance: Assets may outweigh liabilities, making adjustment relatively easy, or liabilities may outweigh assets, making the assimilation of the transition correspondingly more difficult. It is important that helping professionals must give careful consideration when diagnosing someone as "ill," which may be less helpful than addressing a necessary shift in the balance of assets to liabilities.

It is crucial, as well, to take into account the factors related to multiculturalism and diversity when considering both assets and liabilities of a person and their coping resources. For example, persons of color and other marginalized groups live in a society where institutional and cultural forces continue to demean them, disadvantage them, and deny them access to opportunities (Toporek & Worthington, 2014). These factors relate directly to liabilities when experiencing transitions; it has been well documented that African Americans experience disparities across many indicators of quality of life, being more likely to live in poverty, experience prolonged unemployment, live in more high-crime neighborhoods, and have fewer financial resources. However, when considering assets, empirical evidence indicates that cultural factors relate to preferred coping behaviors used by African Americans to manage adversity. Researchers report that African Americans' coping resources include forming affiliations with others and seeking guidance from elders in the community. Also, spirituality is a predominant aspect of African American culture that permeates many aspects of an individual's life and serves as a mediating factor for coping, health, well-being, and life satisfaction (Utsey et al., 2007). This emphasizes the importance of understanding clients' lived experiences, along with perceived and real limitations and strengths to combat sociocultural barriers and implement strategies for coping across contexts.

Appraisal of Transitions

The individual's appraisal of the transition is key, and perceptions can be influenced by cultural views and narratives, especially as these are reflected within the individualistic or collectivist worldviews. Calhoun et al. (2010) discussed the effect of cultural influences when people are confronting a traumatic event. They stated that Westerners tend to assume personal responsibility and may more likely identify their personal strengths as a result. They emphasized that those from Eastern cultures may be more inclined to adjust themselves to traumatic events and come to see the world differently as a result. Cultural factors also shape the ways that individuals see themselves and their relationships with others. Individualistic cultures encourage people to define themselves in terms of their uniqueness and accomplishments; people in these cultures tend to prefer individual action and striving to meet personal goals. In contrast, collectivist cultures encourage interdependent relationships, not standing out from the crowd, and seeking harmony with others (Calhoun et al., 2010). These factors underscore the importance of counselors' self-awareness and cultural humility, and not overlaying their own appraisal and approach to transitions, but rather working within the clients' worldviews. One of the authors once worked with a person from Japan, and she shared that in her culture, if you are a nail that sticks out farther from the other nails in a board, then you will be hammered down. This example illustrates the harm that could be done using an individualistic approach rather than being sensitive to the client's worldview and options that fit within their worldview and cultural values.

As we pointed out in Chapter 2, the transition process consists of various reactions that occur over a period of time. As reactions change, an individual's perspective of a transition can shift from what may initially be viewed as a devastating event, to recognizing this experience as a catalyst to positive outcomes and growth. One woman who was reeling from the unexpected loss of her husband later acknowledged the strengths that she had gained since having to navigate life on her own. Another participant in a workshop presented by one of the authors shared a renewed sense of hope and optimism as she reflected on her lifeline. She came to the realization that although she had experienced many lows during her life, the lows were always followed by highs. When discussing a client's appraisal of their current transition, it can be very helpful to reevaluate their previous transitions. This encourages a change in perspective that can allow for hope and formulating steps to move forward. This can be facilitated when clients learn about the process of transitions and gain a fresh perspective on how they have managed and coped with earlier transitions in their lives. An individual's appraisal and reappraisal of a transition can be examined in light of the 4 S's.

Options and Diversity

The history of oppressed groups in this country reflects a shift from a time when many individuals accepted that there were no options for their group to a time when the groups have organized to fight for change. Challenging existing structures, such as institutional racism, has become predominant in recent times with the Black Lives Matter movement. Creating new options for people is a key part of the counselor's role, and this ranges from how we work with our clients to political action and advocacy, which we discuss further in Chapter 10. A *social justice* counseling approach addresses the quality of life for all and works to end the "isms" that deny equal rights to everyone (racism, classism, sexism, ableism, agism, etc.). This often involves working across the levels of Bronfennbrener's (1977) model: the micro level, with a focus on individuals, families, and small groups; the meso level, with a focus on communities and organizations; and the macro level, with a focus on larger society and social policies (Sue et al., 2019).

As we have discussed, it is important to consider a person's worldview, which may be strongly influenced by sociocultural factors. Although we cannot assume that our clients share the worldview of their collective identity, it is important to be mindful of the potential to overlay our own values on the client's situation. Our goal is to empower our clients, and to do this effectively, we must work within our client's worldview and values. To provide another example of this, one of the authors led a group for women, and one of the participants was an Arab American woman. Group members were encouraging this woman to make steps toward coming to a decision, assuming that this decision was hers alone to make. After one particularly intense session, the Arab American woman approached the author for an individual consultation regarding the group. She shared that, for her and her culture, no decision was made by an individual alone, that decisions were made collectively. This information was brought back to the group and provided a valuable learning opportunity, that even with the best intentions, we may unintentionally allow Western values to influence the flow and focus of our work.

By looking at various groups' experiences regarding domination, oppression, and coexistence, we can begin to understand the amount of control that individuals have over the circumstances in their lives or the limited choices they may have in their assets, liabilities, and resources. Although the theory leaves room to explore the sense of control one has over one's transitions, unless sociopolitical constraints are boldly articulated, counselors from privileged classes can too easily overlook them. Everyone uses coping strategies, everyone has some kind of support system, everyone has a personal way of being in the world, and everyone has a unique situation. Yet there is an overriding concern. Some individuals' situation, self, support, and strategies are qualitatively so restricted that one cannot consider the 4 S's alone. For example, if people's concerns relate to feeding their families or dealing with ill children without health insurance, their resources are qualitatively different than those of middle-class professionals.

THE 4 S SYSTEM: A DETAILED VIEW

Situation

Every individual's situation varies according to the following factors:

- Trigger—What set off the transition?
- Timing—How does the transition relate to one's life situation?
- Control—What aspects of the transition are within one's control?
- Role change—Does the transition involve role change?
- Duration—Is the transition sudden or drawn out? Is it seen as permanent or temporary?
- Previous experience with a similar transition—How has the individual met similar transitions? What have they learned about themselves from previous experiences?
- Concurrent stress—What and how significant are the stresses facing the individual across their different life arenas?
- Assessment—Does the individual view the situation positively, negatively, or as benign? How has their assessment of previous transitions evolved over time?

Trigger

A transition, as we have defined it, can be anticipated or unanticipated, an event or a nonevent, and can vary with clients' experiences and perceptions. Triggers can be external, such as a decade-marking birthday, and have internal consequences, such as an awareness that time is running out. Triggers stimulate individuals to look at themselves and their lives in a new way. For example, a change in health—a heart attack or cancer—can act as a trigger for rethinking work and relationships. Job changes, especially job losses, trigger reevaluation. For one person, the trigger was the death of several of his close friends over a short period of time, which highlighted his awareness of his own mortality. For another, the *coming out* of her son brought about the realization that she may never become a grandparent. For another individual, a sudden change in disability status and the need for a walker was a jarring recognition of his failing capacities.

A transition can also be triggered by something that happens to someone close to the person: A husband's retirement may trigger a fear of aging in his wife; a wife's cancer diagnosis may trigger fears of death in her husband. Other triggers can be brought on by marker events, such as a class reunion or significant anniversary.

Timing

As noted, many adults have built-in social clocks that are the barometers they use to judge whether they are "on time" or "off time" with respect to family, career, and self issues. To be off time, whether early or late, can make individuals feel uncomfortable. Certain transitions, for example, getting married, having children, going to college, taking a job, and retiring, used to be linked in people's minds to a certain age range. Today, rigid timetables continue to loosen as people's lives follow more irregular paths. However, despite the more fluid life span, many still use age to define how they are doing. It is not unusual for clients to share concerns related to where they are *supposed* to be in life. Many times, this is a presenting concern and can relate to both the individual and to dealing with others' expectations of them.

Transition events or nonevents are also experienced as happening at "good" or "bad" times. For example, an emerging adult who recently claimed independence has to move back home during the pandemic, due to a loss of job opportunities. Another example relates to some newlywed couples who may define a job-required move away from parents and in-laws as happening at a good time, while others whose culture expects them to stay close to home may have a mix of feelings and reactions. The current pandemic has been exceptionally challenging for parents whose grown children live far away, with little opportunity to see them. Both flying and driving feel too risky. The timing of restrictions can be even more challenging with the birth of a new baby and/or key milestone events happening in their grandchildren's lives. This example, we hope, demonstrates the complexity and variation of timing with transitions that occur across both personal and broader contexts. Thus, events, both anticipated and unanticipated, can occur at better or worse times, making it easier or more difficult for individuals to go through the transition process.

Control

The source of some transitions is internal, a deliberate decision on the part of the individual, whereas the source of others is external, and the transition is forced upon the individual by other people or by circumstances. For example, the spouse who is suddenly informed of their partner's desire for a divorce may find this more difficult than if it was their decision to leave the marriage. Also, couples may experience considerable negative stress in connection with residential moves when the move is forced upon them by job requirements. Although they may maintain some sense of control over their decision to make the move, this choice could be complicated by other factors that are out of their control, such as the health of family members living nearby or concerns about how their children may adjust to a new school setting. The issue here is that individuals may perceive control or lack of control over their lives as they navigate transitions.

It is important to consider aspects of diversity that may influence having a sense of control, For example, in several studies examining *optimism* versus *pessimism*, boys and men scored higher on optimism than girls and women did, and a significant finding was that males also scored significantly higher on measures of *personal control* (Helweg-Larsen et al., 2011). According to

Lopez et al. (2015), the fact that women have historically had less control over their lives, with less social power and privilege, may affect their beliefs regarding what their futures may hold. They emphasized that the variability of beliefs and expectations for women across cultures could be further investigated. This highlights aspects of diversity when exploring our clients' beliefs and sense of control over their situation. Also, it is imperative to consider areas of intersectionality, for example, culture and gender-role expectations. However, it is crucial not to make presumptions. To illustrate exceptions to the study sited previously, one of the authors has worked with a number of female international graduate students. Some of these women have had a strong determination and the intentional courage to take control of their futures. This often required going against cultural norms and expectations, and navigating transitions without role models or sources of support from their culture. This example highlights how two sources of control—internal and external—interact. It is important to consider existential issues, such as loss and meaning-making, that emerge through transitions, and to discuss them in terms of the client's cultural context, beliefs, and their ability to respond.

Role Change

Many, but not all, transitions involve role change. As we noted earlier, role changes are an important aspect in determining the impact of a transition. Regardless of whether a transition involves positive gains or painful losses, some degree of stress accompanies it. To illustrate, although an individual may look forward with pleasurable anticipation to retiring from employment or seeing the last child launched into the world, the actual event may carry with it feelings of loss. Again, any role change, whether primarily positive or negative, involves adaptation and some degree of stress.

A given role change can be more or less difficult (and have greater or lesser impact) depending on whether the role change is viewed as positive or negative, or has explicit norms and expectations attached. An example is a young woman grappling with her decision to attend graduate school out of state while learning of her parents' impending divorce. As an only child, she had always been very close to her mother, and her father's decision to initiate a divorce came as an unexpected shock. To follow her plans to move away directly intersected with her role of daughter and the expectations she placed on herself around her role to her mother. Often, we sort through these types of value conflicts attached to client's roles, something that can necessitate exploration at deeper levels.

Duration

The expected duration of the transition affects the ease or difficulty of assimilating the transition. A change that is regarded as permanent will be perceived differently from one that is viewed as temporary. A transition that is painful and unpleasant may be more easily borne if the individual is assured that it is of limited duration, for example, when someone enters the hospital for surgery knowing that the discomfort and recovery are temporary. Conversely, if the change is desired, then the certainty that it represents a more or less permanent state may be reassuring. Uncertainty about duration, however, is connected with perhaps the greatest degree of stress and negative effect. For example, placing a spouse or parent in an assisted living facility can be initially difficult and even more challenging when witnessing their decline. Especially when the access to visitation is limited due to a situation, such as the pandemic, the duration can seem unbearable. A client shared her distress that she placed her spouse in a facility when she was encouraged to do so by her children, only to realize that she would not be able to visit him for an extended time. When she was finally able to visit him again, his sharp decline was evident, and he also had trouble remembering her. To continue with this situation over a duration of time involves summing up both internal resources and external sources of support. Another example of duration is being diagnosed with an illness with an uncertain prognosis, which may be more stressful and unsettling for an individual than to know for sure that their disease is terminal.

Previous Experience With a Similar Transition

It is generally assumed that the individual who has successfully weathered a difficult transition in the past will probably be successful at assimilating another transition of a similar nature. Conversely, the person who has been defeated by a situation may become more vulnerable and less able to cope in the future. Past experiences, to some extent, determine the person's mental set, and if that past experience was unfavorable, then coping with the current transition may be something of a self-confirming prophecy. Of course, given possible changes in the balance of assets and liabilities (discussed earlier), the correlation between successful assimilation in the past and at a later point in time is by no means perfect. It is also important to consider vicarious past experiences. If others in one's referent group have had negative experiences with a certain transition, one might anticipate having a similar outcome, even if one has no personal experience. An example is the decision to "come out" to a person's parents, which may be negatively influenced by others' stories of their experiences with this, even when their own relationship with their parents has been more positive.

Concurrent Stress

People are sometimes challenged to navigate several transition at once. A question that is often asked is how many transitions can adults be expected to face simultaneously? In his research, Feiler (2020) took some time to calculate this number. He concluded that people can expect to experience an average of 30 or 40 disrupters over their lives. He discussed these results in both negative and positive terms. The bad news, he stated, is that life can be more difficult, and the good news is that people are being freed from "the shackles of expectations, whether they come from our parents, our neighbors, or ourselves" (p. 73). He discussed his own situation, with being diagnosed with a pediatric cancer as a 43-year-old new dad. He concluded that the difference between a life of fulfilment or a life of frustration is how well we can manage the meaning of our lives. Working with adults in transition involves assessing for concurrent stress, along with helping them tap into their inner resources and support to achieve optimal coping.

Often transitions in one area stimulate other stresses and transitions. Consider the decision of a same-sex couple to adopt a child. Before the adoption was final, this upcoming event precluded informing their families of the true nature of their partnership. In this case, the transition of adoption rippled across transitions in family relationships. Understanding the nature of transitions is a multifaceted process, as is illustrated across the intersecting and overlapping areas of exploration of the 4 S's.

Assessment

As we have discussed, people's appraisal of their situation may relate to various factors, including culture, timing, control, role changes, and general perception of the positive or negative impact of the transition. In the current context, we must also consider both personal transitions, along with those that are experienced as a collective experience. According to Feiler (2020), for his participants, 87% of tumultuous life events were personal, whereas 13% were collective. An individual's assessment of a transition could be influenced by this factor, for example, a personal decision to change jobs versus a natural disaster that is shared by a community that comes together in response to rebuild.

Another key factor to consider in evaluating a person's assessment is whether the transition is voluntary or involuntary. Feiler (2020) noted from his research that 43% of changes initiated were voluntary and 57% were involuntary. An individual's view of who or what is responsible for the transition affects their appraisal of the transition, themselves, and the environment. The individual's attributions about self and situation are salient areas when assessing transitions from the client's perspective while also keeping in mind cultural norms and expectations.

Situation Review

Each transitional event or nonevent is different. The same individual can get divorced, become a grandparent, lose a job, inherit a million dollars, or not have a baby. Each of these transitions will be different in terms of the following:

- What triggered it?
- Was it at a good time in the individual's life?

- Did the individual initiate the transition or did it happen to them?
- Did the individual experience a role change? Is the transition permanent or temporary?
- Has the individual had previous experience with similar transitions?
- Is the individual experiencing stress in other areas of life?
- Does the individual assess the transition as positive, negative, or benign?

Self

We stated earlier that every individual has both assets and liabilities as well as resources and deficits. In addition to the situation itself, we now look at what the individual brings to the transition. We all hear clients who state, "I'm a pessimist and always see the glass as half empty" or "I'm usually up for change but this one has really knocked me out." It is complex to get a handle on the self, but we have identified the following characteristics that are particularly relevant for individuals as they cope with change:

- Socioeconomic status
- Gender and sexual orientation
- Age and stage of life
- State of health
- Ethnicity/culture
- Psychological resources
- Ego development
- Outlook—Optimism and self-efficacy beliefs
- Commitment and values
- Spirituality and resilience

Psychological Resources

A key aspect of our work with clients is promoting coping and wellness, especially as people are faced with life's challenges. This leads us to focus on psychological resources, such as optimism and self-efficacy beliefs as well as inner resources such as spirituality and resilience. As with other aspects of the 4 S's, we must acknowledge that cultural influences are integral to people's understanding of psychological strengths, and this extends to what may be viewed as positive behaviors or traits within particular cultural contexts. To emphasize this point, even the definition of strengths may vary across cultural groups (Lopez et al., 2015). When working with our clients, it is important to encourage conversations about how strengths are viewed within their cultural framework.

People also approach the same transition from different frames of reference. For example, another way to understand clients is though their preferred *outlook,* itself a result of the complex interplay of many factors that color the way change is viewed. Optimism and self-efficacy are two critical aspects of one's outlook. Seligman (2006) studied the qualities that enable people to rise above life's challenges, overcome adversity, resist illness and depression, and lead happier and more successful lives. His work focused on different ways that people react, especially to negative, uncontrollable, or bad events. According to Seligman, life inflicts similar setbacks and tragedies on optimists and pessimists, and optimists tend to weather them better. Although Seligman was careful to point out that optimism is not a panacea, his findings supported its positive impact on achievement, physical well-being, and overall mental state. He stated that optimists actually age better and experience fewer of the usual physical illnesses of middle age.

Seligman (2006) suggested that the individual's explanatory style, the way a person thinks about an event or transition, can explain how some people weather transitions without becoming depressed or giving up. As many transitions are neither bad nor good but a mixture, a person's explanatory style becomes a critical aspect of coping. A person with a positive explanatory style is an optimist, whereas one with a negative style is basically a pessimist. Another relevant concept is *learned optimism,* which Forgeard and Seligman (2012) described as the use of adaptive attributions to explain negative experiences or events. They concluded that optimists tend to make external and specific attributions for negative and/or failure events, whereas pessimists are more likely to make more internal and global explanations. Forgeard and Seligman indicate that responses can be learned, especially within childhood environments and from parents' explanations of events that enable children to continue to feel good about themselves. However, they also make an interesting point regarding the overuse of an optimistic explanatory style, with the potential to disregard potential problems and consequences. This relates to how people can overuse their strengths, which can then become liabilities.

For example, we can ask a client, Robert, who failed to receive a promotion, to explain what happened. Did he blame himself and say he was inadequate? Did he conclude that he would always be inadequate at work? People who blame themselves for everything that happens and then generalize to think that they always "foul things up" have a good chance of being depressed and passive. On the other hand, if Robert saw this as a learning opportunity and that, in general, he handled complex situations well, he has a good chance of coping effectively with this nonevent transition.

A related concept and one that predicts how one will negotiate transitions is self-efficacy. Bandura (1977) defined *self-efficacy* as a person's capacity to produce effects by their actions. He also addressed what he termed as *outcome expectations,* related to people's expectations regarding their ability to carry out what needs to be done to meet their goals. Extensive research has concluded that Bandura's theory has played an important role in promoting a strengths-based approach and understanding self-efficacy as a protective factor, both psychologically and in terms of physical health (Lopez et al., 2015).

The transition model intends to show the interrelatedness of situation, self, support, and strategies. So yes, self-efficacy and optimism are crucial, but they are not the entire story. For instance, the style one uses to process the world is important. Some rely on intuition, doing what feels right to them. Others use their senses to gather data on the world and then process these data in a logical, systematic way, arriving at reasoned decisions. People differentiate themselves along these lines, and many counselors spend time helping their clients recognize that their styles might be different from that of their partner, boss, or friends. Acknowledging these differences can be helpful in building collaboration rather than conflict. Administering the Myers–Briggs Type Indicator (1977) is one way of identifying one's style, which relates to preferences in how a person is energized, ways they take in information, makedecisions, and relate to others.

Another concept to consider is spirituality, which is closely related to religion yet can be understood as a distinct phenomenon (Young et al., 2000). Although religion can be part of spirituality and serve as an expression of spirituality for people, it does not encompass the broader concept of spirituality that runs through all religions and cultures. Religion generally refers to an integrated set of beliefs and activities, whereas spirituality is central to a sense of meaning and purpose and has been conceptualized as the meaning gained from life experiences (May, 1982; Myers et al., 2000). Spirituality is an especially important area of exploration in working with clients and may be an area that is overlooked. We are most likely to hear spirituality expressed through our clients' subjective, personal experiences and through their need for connectedness, meaning, and transcendence. Exploration of meaning can include contemplating one's life purpose and what gives life significance as well as answering more specific questions, such as what values does the client live by? What projects, relationships, and activities bring fulfillment? What are the next steps that need to be taken on their path (Smith, 2017)? By delving into questions regarding how our clients find meaning and purpose in their lives, we may also tap into hidden resources for coping with transitions.

A growing body of research has documented spirituality's relationship to both physical and mental health as well as to coping ability. For example, studies have found that people with a positive religious identity cope more efficiently with stress and experience better overall health and well-being overall (Steffen, 2012). Peres et al. (2007) provided a summary of studies regarding the benefits of spiritual and religious beliefs, especially as these relate to coping with traumatic events. They stated that "when people become traumatized they often look for a new sense of meaning and purpose in their life" (p. 346) and concluded that the role of spirituality may advance our understanding of adaptation to trauma. They also highlighted that spiritual or religious beliefs and practices are important components across cultures.

When counseling adults in transition, it is also important to look at resilience. Resilient people have been described as those "who are able to weather a storm in their lives, bounce back from adversity, or grow stronger in the face of adversity" (Bosworth & Walz, 2005, p. 1). The term *resilience* is related to its use in physics as the ability to return to an original form after being "bent, compressed or stretched" (p. 1). An interesting analogy was made by these authors in their description of why they once chose a blooming cactus for the cover of their book. They state that the cactus "is noted for its ability to overcome extreme environmental deprivation (i.e., drought) for extended periods of time and still display both beauty and strength.... This ability parallels what the resilient person is able to do" (p. ii).

In the literature, resilience is not narrowed down to a specific characteristic but rather includes a blend of characteristics in an individual. These may include characteristics such as being positive, focused, organized, proactive, and flexible (Barrett, 2004). A related concept is hardiness, which has become an established aspect of counseling psychology. When considering hardiness, we might look at individual differences, for example, how stressful changes may be debilitating for some people but developmentally provocative for others (Maddi, 2002). According to Maddi (2002), three attitudes combine to form hardiness: commitment, control, and challenge. Through these attitudes, people may learn to exemplify what he termed *existential courage* when facing difficult situations. Like wisdom, courage is appreciated and valued in many cultures, although it may be defined and manifested in different ways (Lopez et al., 2015).

When working with clients, we proactively tap into our clients' strengths to both uncover and enhance their psychological strengths and inner resources.

Review of the Self

Every person brings different assets to a transition. The following are some ways to assess clients.

- Are they able to approach transitions in a proactive manner? Can they tolerate ambiguity?
- Are they optimists? Do they see the glass as half full or half empty?
- Do they blame themselves for what happens?
- Do they feel in control of their responses to the transition?
- Do they believe that their efforts will affect the outcome of a particular course of action?
- Do they have a sense of meaning and purpose?
- Do they have characteristics that contribute to resiliency?

Support

When counseling clients in transition, we begin by assessing assets and liabilities across the *situation* and *self* through exploring the context and issues, and working with our clients' beliefs, sense of purpose, and inner resources. As we move through the process, our focus most often shifts to supporting clients in their efforts to move forward. The ultimate goal is to promote coping with transitions while understanding that taking steps forward most often requires courage and sources of support. Support, however, needs to be defined operationally, along with being tailored to the needs of our individual clients. The counseling relationship is ultimately a balance of support and challenge, and this can vary for each client across the process. Although the therapeutic alliance and helping relationship provide necessary support, other types of support are also crucial.

Types of Support

Types of support can be classified according to their sources, which most often occur through relationships (intimate relationships, family units, networks of friends), along with community organizations and institutions.

The family unit has long been a subject for research, especially those qualities of the family that contribute to its ability to adapt to a crisis or to ease the process of adaptation for one of its members. However, family relationships can be a source of support and/or increased stress. For example, an overcontrolling parent may inhibit a young adult in making decisions about their future. An individual's network of friends is also an important social support system. And while although a valued source of support, friendship losses may come with transitions. We often see this with people seeking sobriety, which necessitates a new friendship network. Another example of a loss of a network occurs when leaving the military for civilian life. A challenging aspect of this transition is losing a network of *brothers*, who were there day in and day out and are now out of sight (Anderson & Goodman, 2014). Loss of a network of friends and/or colleagues is commonly experienced with various life changes, thus exacerbating the difficulties of those transitions. Conversely, the presence of friends can cushion the shock of unanticipated transitions and also sustain a sense of history and point of reference, with both context and identity.

Other sources of support can come through organizations individuals can turn to for help, such as religious institutions, political groups, social welfare or community support groups, and other more-or-less formal agencies. As discussed in Part III of this book, the need for such agencies has become more widely recognized. There has been a proliferation of programs, which may take the form of seminars, lectures, workshops, or simply discussion groups, aimed at people experiencing particular transitions: midcareer change, divorce, retirement, or a return to school. Support systems have recently evolved to include both *in-person* and *virtual* connections, which continue to inform us of the power of connection, with relationships forming in various formats.

Functions of Support

Kahn and Antonucci (1980) identified the functions of social support as an incorporation of one or more of the following key elements: affect, affirmation, and aid. *Affect* refers to expressions of liking, admiration, respect, or love; *affirmation* refers to expressions of agreement or acknowledgment of the appropriateness or rightness of some act or statement of another person; and *aid* (or assistance) includes the exchange of things, money, information, time, and entitlements.

In addition to the functions of affect, affirmation, and aid, we include another—honest feedback. This refers to reactions offered that might be negative as well as positive. It refers back to the concepts of support and challenge; even with the best intentions, change can be hard. As counselors, we offer our authenticity and presence yet also confront what may be holding our clients back from achieving their desired goals and outcomes. Although confrontation is not always a favored counseling technique, it is sometimes necessary in the best interest of our clients.

Support Summary

In summary, to take stock of their clients' supports, counselors can ask the following:

- Is this client getting what they need for this transition in terms of affect, affirmation, and aid?
- Does the client have a range of types of support—spouse or partner, other close family or friends, coworkers, colleagues, neighbors, organizations, affiliations, and institutions?
- Has the client's support system been interrupted by this transition?
- Does the client view their support system for this transition as a low or a high resource?

Strategies

Strategies are tailored to our individual clients, based on their assets and liabilities and with regard to their situation, aspects of self, and available supports and resources. Pearlin and Schooler (1978) discussed major life strains and the coping strategies people use to deal with them. The researchers distinguished three types of coping: responses that modify the situation, responses that address the meaning of the problem, and responses that help to manage stress after it has occurred. More recently, researchers have discussed the concept of *coping flexibility*, which refers to a person's ability to modify coping strategies in response to their levels of stress. This type of flexibility is dependent on how well an individual is able to draw on coping strategies for positive outcomes, which can also be compromised by relying on negative coping strategies (Heffer & Willoughby, 2017). People may employ a mix of both positive and negative coping mechanisms when under stress, which ultimately influence their ability to implement adaptive responses to transitions.

When considering strategies, we consider the different contexts, such as Bronfenbrenner's ecological model as discussed in Chapter 2. At a personal level, strategies can include stress-relieving activities, such as contemplative practices, including mindfulness, creative pursuits, and using humor to lighten a situation. When moving to the family unit, strategies could include couple's counseling and family therapy, along with individualized strategies to enhance a sense of balance between family and work roles. At the community level, strategies can include connecting people to resources in their community, along with collaborating with faith leaders in the local churches.

In some cases, collective coping—that is, helping people share in a problem they cannot undo individually—is essential. Structural unemployment is just such a case, for it needs to be addressed collectively and politically. Another example is collective groups coming together to address larger issues, such as climate change and the impact of natural disasters. Some people, however, are clearly going to cope more effectively than others, and those with a repertoire of responses relating to their various roles will most likely handle the strains of life more effectively.

According to Lazarus and Folkman (1984), the coping strategies a person uses are more relevant than the stress experienced, and the person's appraisal of the situation is more central than the actual event. As we described earlier, the key is how the person views the strain, stressor, or event—whether it is perceived as harmful, benign, or challenging. Lazarus and Folkman classified coping in two major ways: instrumental, or problem-focused behavior, that aims to change the situation and palliative, or emotion-focused behavior, that aims to help minimize emotional distress. Again, as emphasized throughout, cultural considerations must be applied when working sensitively with our clients, and coping strategies are best designed collaboratively. The efficacy can be assessed collaboratively as well as to what is working and what could be further fine-tuned or modified. Lazarus emphasized that "the stress relationship is not static but is constantly changing as a result of the continual interplay between the person and the environment" (Lazarus, 1990, p. 4).

An important point for helpers to remember is that people who effectively cope are flexible and use a number of methods. Ability to cope is not a trait but is a dynamic process constantly in flux throughout the continuing process of appraisal. How effective such strategies are overall is a complex question. For example, some theorists and counselors focus on outcomes. Was the client accepted into an apprentice training program? By focusing only on outcome, however, we may overlook a client's coping effectiveness. A client may employ many strategies flexibly but still not be able to achieve the stated goals. Just as being assertive doesn't guarantee "winning," using flexible coping strategies does not always guarantee the desired outcome.

Summary of Coping Responses

In the preceding section, we described the ways several researchers have conceptualized and studied coping. According to Pearlin and Schooler (1978), most individuals when faced with a transition, most individuals try to control the situation (for example, by publishing a great deal to ensure promotion), control the meaning of the situation (by seeing promotion as irrelevant), or control the stress (by jogging to release tension caused by promotion worries). Lazarus and Folkman (1984) identified two major coping orientations—changing the situation (instrumental) or emotion-focused behavior (palliative). Thus, sometimes, strategies are designed for use at the individual level, and others relate to community resources and collective coping with larger events. Depending on the client, their self-factors, and cultural context, a variety of strategies can be implemented and continually assessed along the way through a transition. Strategies are best formulated collaboratively, between the counselor and client, who are engaging in what can be the most creative and innovative stage of the process.

Often clients ask, "Should I initiate a change?" "Should I go back to school?" "Should I get a divorce?" "Should I move?" Or they may wonder, "How can I weather the transition imposed upon me?" To answer these questions, one rates the client's 4 S's—the variables characterizing the situation, the self, the support, and the strategies. From these ratings, a balance score can be derived that will indicate whether or not the client has many or few resources. Further, the client can determine where their liabilities lie (Kay & Schlossberg, 2006).

SUMMARY

The focus of this chapter was on the 4 S framework, which conceptualizes the way we can assess and work with individuals coping with transitions. Different aspects of situation, self, support, and strategies were introduced, and in Part II, we move to a discussion of different types of transitions and applications. Although transitions often overlap across areas of people's lives, we share case examples of what we hear from clients regarding their balance of liabilities and assets. Then, in Part III of the book, we consider how that balance suggests to helpers the areas in which they can be most effective in providing motivation, support, and resources to help adults who are striving to navigate and find their way through transitions.

REFERENCES

Anderson, M. L., & Goodman, J. (2014). From military to civilian life: Applications of Schlossberg's model for veterans in transition. In R. Miles, M. Buzzetta & K. Kurzynski (Eds.), *Career Planning & Adult Development Journal, 30*(3), 40–51.

Bandura, A. (1977). Self-efficacy: Toward a unifying theory of behavior change. *Psychological Review, 84*, 191–215.

Barrett, F. (2004). Coaching for resiliency. *Organization Development Journal, 22*, 93–96.

Bosworth, K., & Walz, G. R. (2005). *Promoting student resiliency*. American Counseling Association Foundation.

Bronfenbrenner, U. (1977). Toward an experimental ecology of human development. *American Psychologist, 32*(7), 513–531.

Calhoun, L. G., Cann, A., & Tedeschi, R. G. (2010). The posttraumatic growth model: Sociocultural considerations. In T. Weiss & R. Berger (Eds.), *Posttraumatic growth and culturally competent practice: Lessons learned from around the globe.* Wiley.

Forgeard, M. J. C., & Seligman, M. E. P. (2012). Seeing the glass as half full: A review of the causes and consequences of optimism. *Pratuques Psychologies, 18,* 102–120.

Heffer, T., & Willoughby, T. (2017). A count of coping strategies: A longitudinal study investigating an alternative method to understanding coping and adjustment. *PLoS ONE, 12*(10), e0186057. https://doi.org/10.1371/journal.pone.0186057

Helweg-Larsen, M., Harding, H. G., & Klein, W. P. (2011). Will I divorce or have a happy marriage? Gender differences in comparative optimism and estimation of personal chances among U.S. college students. *Basic and Applied Social Psychology, 33,* 157–166.

Kahn, R. L., & Antonucci, T. E. (1980). Convoys over the life course: Attachment, roles, and social support. In P. B. Baltes & O. G. Brim, Jr. (Eds.), *Life-span development and behavior* (pp. 383–405). Academic Press.

Lazarus, R. S. (1990). Theory-based stress measurement. *Psychological Inquiry, 1*(1), 3–13.

Lazarus, R. S., & Folkman, S. (1984). *Stress, appraisal, and coping.* Springer Publishing Company.

Lopez, S. J., Pedrotti, J. T., & Snyder, C. R. (2015). *Positive psychology: The scientific and practical explorations of human strengths.* Sage.

Maddi, S. R. (2002). The story of hardiness: Twenty years of theorizing, research, and practice. *Consulting Psychology Journal: Practice and Research, 54*(3), 173.

May, G. G. (1982). *Will and spirit: A contemplative psychology.* Harper Collins.

Myers, I. B., & Briggs, K. C. (1977). *Myers-Briggs type indicator: Supplementary Manual: Development of Form G.* Consulting Psychologists Press.

Myers, J. E., Sweeney, T. J., & Witmer, M. (2000). The wheel of wellness, counseling for wellness: A holistic model for treatment planning. *Journal of Counseling and Development, 78*(3), 251–266.

Pearlin, L. I., & Schooler, C. (1978). The structure of coping. *Journal of Health and Social Behavior, 19,* 2–21.

Peres, F. P., Moreira-Amleida, A., Nasello, A. G., & Hoenig, H. G. (2007). Spirituality and resilience in trauma victims. *Journal of Religious Health, 46*(3), 343–350. https://doi.org/10.1007/s10943-006-9103-0

Seligman, M. E. (2006). *Learned optimism: How to change your mind and your life.* Vintage Books.

Smith, E. E. (2017). *The power of meaning: Crafting a life that matters.* Crown.

Steffen, P. R. (2012). Approaching religiosity/sprituality and health from the Eudaimonic perspective. *Social and Personality Psychology Compass, 6*(1), 70–82.

Sue, D. W., Sue, D., Neville, H. A., & Smith, L. (2019). *Counseling the culturally diverse.* Wiley.

Toporek, R. L., & Worthington, R. L. (2014). Integrating service learning and difficult dialogues pedagogy to advance social justice training. *Counseling Psychologist, 46,* 919–945.

Utsey, S. O., Bolden, M. A., Williams, O., Lee, A., Lanier, Y., & Newsome, C. (2007). Spiritual well-being as a mediator of the relation between culture-specific coping and quality of life in a community sample of African Americans. *Journal of Cross-cultural Psychology, 38*(2), 123–136. https://doi.org/10.1177/0022022106297296

Young, J., Cashwell, C., & Shcherbakova, J. (2000). The moderating relationship of spirituality on negative life events and psychological adjustment. *Counseling and Values, 45*, 49–57.

II

WHAT ARE WE LIKELY TO HEAR?

4

Individual Transitions

In this chapter, we focus on what we hear from clients about intrapersonal transitions, interweaving our case study with illustrative literature. We show how individuals experience their transitions in a unique manner, depending on their particular situation, the aspects of self that come into play, the support they have available, and the strategies they are currently using.

Case Study

Miguel Suarez, a man in his mid-40s, tells you the following:

> *First, please call me Mike. I am a second-generation American. My family likes to use the old names, but I find it easier to sound like everyone else.*
>
> *My wife has just told me that she wants a divorce. I know I haven't been the best husband or father. When we were first married, I worked two jobs to get by and even as we haven't been quite as poor, I have been working most of the time. That left her to raise the kids mostly alone. I kind of got in the habit of doing my own thing. Maybe a drink at the bar after work rather than coming right home. My father was rarely home, and I guess I just thought that was normal family life.*
>
> *I am totally surprised. She never said anything about being unhappy. She says there is no one else, but I am not sure I believe her. Our kids are 15 and 17. They are in high school and not home much either; it seems this has made her notice even more that I am not there. She wants us to go to counseling together and see whether we can salvage our 20-year-old marriage, but I told her I wanted to go by myself first. So I am here seeing you.*
>
> *I think I am still in shock. It seems I have taken my wife and my marriage for granted. I thought things were okay and I am really blind-sided by her unhappiness. Now I am wondering whether I am just*

totally unfeeling. I work in an auto parts factory; I have moved up to be a foreman and I am the building rep for our union. I finished only high school, so I am proud of my accomplishments. My wife has more education than I do—she has a two-year degree in bookkeeping. She stayed home when our children were small but now works half-time for a local business keeping their books. She is confident that she can get a full-time job if she needs to support herself. She likes her work and finds it satisfying to be useful and to be using her training and education.

I'll be honest. I am actually happy to be kind of forced to talk to someone. I feel like I have been drifting for a while. Everything is okay but nothing is great; you know what I mean? I am good at my job, but it is not challenging; my marriage, as I said, is okay, but not thrilling. Even the passion we once had seems to be dwindling. I have a long-lived family, but even at that, 45 is past the middle. I know it sounds like a cliché, but I am asking if this is all there is? Maybe that is what my wife is also feeling—we don't actually talk about our feelings. It seems like every part of my life is unsatisfying—work, my marriage, and even my feelings about myself.

Mike Suarez's poignant story describes his confrontation with several event and nonevent transitions. He is facing a potential major change in the relationship part of his life. He is asking himself existential questions about the meaning of life. The contentment he expected to find in his middle years has not happened. He is being forced to consider an unwanted transition—the ending of his marriage, and this has precipitated an examination of his life as a whole. His insistence on being called Mike, practically the first sentence out of his mouth, makes us suspect an uneasy relationship with his parents' and grandparent's immigrant identity. Clearly, it is a rare individual who lives in a vacuum; relationships and work are almost always an important part of life. But in this chapter, we use Mike's story to clarify transitions—events and nonevents—that pertain primarily to the individual.

We focus on what counselors *hear* from their adult clients about intrapersonal transitions, interweaving Mike's story with illustrative literature. We show how individuals experience their transitions in a unique manner, depending on their particular situation, the aspects of self that come into play, the support they have available, and the strategies they are currently using.

SITUATION

What makes Mike's situation similar to and different from other people's transitions? In this section, we first discuss the triggers to internal transitions, some of which may come from internal awareness and some of which may be stimulated by external events. We then turn our attention to the timing of these transitions. Are they off time or on time? Do they come at a time of relative peace in the person's life or at a time of turmoil? Next, we talk about the duration of the transition, and, finally, we address the source of control—or perceived control. As we discuss these general questions, remember that as people's answers differ, their experiences are unique.

Maslow's (1954) hierarchy indicates that basic needs for physiological and psychological safety precede the need for belongingness and self-esteem, and later, the search for self-actualization. The internal transition of meaning-making seems to be such a search. This would indicate that this sort of midlife transition is a phenomenon of the comfortable. It seems unlikely that the homeless or others desperately struggling to survive have time or energy to ask meaning-making questions. But there is little research on the psychological aspects of that population.

Triggers

Mike has come to see a counselor to talk about his wife's divorce request and the trigger of his reflection on his life as a whole. And he is also ready to talk about other aspects of his life that are creating discomfort for him. What has triggered this transition? On the surface, it is the possibility of divorce. He is also aware of his age and of the passage of time—perhaps exacerbated by his children's growth and the fact that they will probably leave home in the not-too-distant future. Mike seems to be confronting a change in perspective from seeing life as time spent to seeing life as time left. He acknowledges that he has been an inadequate husband and father, but he seems to think that he could still change. He is open to joint counseling but also committed to working on his own feelings and plans.

Whitbourne et al. (2009) stated that during the stage of middle adulthood, people continue to face and manage psychosocial tasks, particularly industry and intimacy (Erikson, 1950). They also found cohort differences in individuals' resolution of Erikson's so-called crises, leading credence to the concept of midlife as an evolving concept. And as life expectancy increases, the definitions and attitudes about midlife continue to change. When one of the authors of this volume did a workshop for women in midlife, the self-selected participants ranged in age from their early 30s to their late 60s. Clearly, there is not general agreement about what constitutes midlife. According to Sheehy's classic work (2006), there is a revolution going on in the life cycle. She stated that there has been a fundamental shift regarding the stages of adulthood, as age continues to be pushed forward and life spans continue to increase. More recently, Feiler (2020) concluded that Sheehy was wrong about predictable life stages. His conclusion after conducting many interviews was that lives are not linear and that they do not unfold in "passages, stages, phases, or cycles" (p. 47). And research suggests that people grow older in very different ways, with striking variations among people as they age, which is the fanning-out phenomenon described earlier (Neugarten, 1996).

Many people have compared life to the progress of a river. Sometimes it is slow moving and placid; at other times, it runs over swift rapids, with rocks and strong currents to be dodged. At other times, there are unexpected submerged logs or whirlpools, ready to trap the unwary traveler;the river is also clear, beautiful, and sometimes flows at exactly the pace one desires. Mike seems to be struggling right now with how to navigate the river of his life. Indeed, he seems often unsure whether he is the raft or the river. His perspective of both the present and the future has changed.

This change in perspective can be brought on by an external event, such as being called *sir* or *ma'am* for the first time; it can be caused by a consciousness of the changing physical self, such as a twinge in the knees, needing bifocals, or that first gray hair. For people whose self-esteem is closely tied to their appearance, the awareness of aging may be very painful. For people whose work roles require a youthful appearance, for example, modeling, this transition may be an important one. In the American culture, women are affected by aging more often than men. We are more accepting of aging actors than actresses. Gray sideburns make a man look distinguished, but graying hair is seen as making a woman look less desirable.

For some women, the onset of menopause is the trigger that begins their internal transition. For some, this is frightening and causes great concern. It inspires some women to ask, "Who am I now that I am no longer fertile?" Others see menopause as freeing them from needing birth control and having monthly periods, for some, an uncomfortable or painful time. Views of menopause are clearly tied to life satisfaction and with a woman's feelings about aging in general.

Clients describe many triggers, including an impending high school reunion; eligibility for AARP, formerly called the *American Association of Retired Persons,* or senior discounts; ineligibility for a management training program or the junior league; being offered a seat on the bus or being presented with a face cream for mature skin. The death of one's last parent creates an awareness for many of now being "the older generation."

Whether internally or externally triggered, sudden or gradual, the realization that one is aging can be disturbing. In Mike's case, the triggers included his wife's request for a divorce, his children's growth, and his own growing dissatisfaction with his work. Furthermore, awareness of time left often includes for the first time a personalization of death. The author William Saroyan is reported to have said on his deathbed, "I knew everyone had to die sometime, but I always thought I'd be the exception." Decade-marking birthdays often stimulate this kind of awareness. Card shops sell a variety of paraphernalia with the theme, "over the hill." Although meant to be humorous, this message implies that one is on the downside of the hill—with death at the bottom of the slope. Consider this line from a middle-aged character in the play *Change of Life* (Dubin, 1994), "People always said, 'You have your whole life ahead of you.' Well, my life isn't ahead of me anymore." Even the daily comic strips show an awareness of this phenomenon. The following conversation took place in *For Better or Worse* (Johnston, 1994):

You know, Connie ... I thought I'd never get old. Other people got old, but not me.

Connie: *Yeah.*

Then suddenly you realize that it is happening. I **am** *following my parents, as my parents followed their parents. The laws of nature apply to* **me** *too! ... It's scary.*

Connie: *Yeah ... we're on the great conveyer belt of life, and from this point you can look up and see the end.*

For some, the realization of the finiteness of life can lead to a determination to live life fully, to appreciate existence, to, in the words of the cliché, pick more daisies. For others, the awareness can lead to depression or panic, occasioned by a sense of urgency to "do it now!" The pandemic that began in 2020 created a heightened sense of awareness of personal mortality. Many survivors considered the question, "Why me?" with a determination to use the life they still have to make a difference in the lives of others. There has also been a spate of "bucket-list" type books recently—places to see or things to do before you "kick the bucket." We seem to be in a societal place of realizing that life is finite. As will be discussed in Part III, the challenge for counselors is to help reframe this awareness into appropriate goal setting.

Mike's transition is a complex one. It was triggered by another event, rather than internally, but Mike is also dealing with his own aging and what he sees as unknown opportunities for himself. While he is becoming aware that he has little sense of what he wants out of life, he has a vague sense that he wants more. He describes himself as a person who has never been introspective, and this new sense of internality is unsettling for him.

Timing

In Mike's case, his transition is created by the stage in his life in which it is happening. He was established in his career, in his community, and in his family. Now these interwoven areas of his life are being shaken up. His work is less satisfying than it once was. And that jeopardizes his place in his community. His children are beginning to rebel, to signal their growth toward independence. So his family life is beginning to look and feel different. He is past the statistical midpoint of life. He is seeing his parents age, his friends' parents die, and is thinking about his own death. Mike describes himself as having been shallow, and we now have the impression that he feels instead, in T. S. Eliot's (2010) words, hollow. Mike is trying to figure out how to fill in his hollow places—and choosing a healthy way to do it—by seeking counseling, rather than by alcohol, drugs, spending money he can't afford, or sexual promiscuity, other ways people often "fill up" hollow spaces.

Chronological age is important, but is not the sole determinant of a typical adult's midlife awareness. Internal or external triggers may precipitate this awareness at a variety of ages and invite the existential question, "Is this all there is?" And age may also have an effect on how an individual reacts to a transition event. A classic example comes from a study of men aged 37 to 67 years who were hospitalized following heart attacks (Rosen & Bibring, 1968). Whereas the younger men were generally cheerful and the 60-year-olds fatherly and easygoing, the 50-year-olds were hostile, withdrawn, depressed, and difficult as patients. The authors interpret these age differences as follows: Those younger than 50 simply denied the seriousness of their condition, those in their 60s accepted it as an on-time event, but those in their 50s experienced "open conflict from the active orientation of youth. ... A heart attack theoretically accentuates the very issues with which the [middle-aged man] has been actively struggling" (p. 207), that is, with his anxiety about aging and his reluctance about shifting from an active to a passive role. This finding was replicated in a similar study by Wurm et al. (2008). They found that "the incidence of a serious health event caused greater changes in subjective health and life satisfaction in middle compared to older age. This was as expected because serious health events are less common in middle age and are correspondingly experienced more often as an 'off-time event.'

Different cultures may have differing systems for recognizing aging. Some East African tribal societies organize their population into age groups. "Men in their prime may resist initiating a new cohort of young warriors. The entry of a new cohort automatically advances those above it by one grade and so places the senior men into the respected—but terminal—grade of elder" (Plath, 1980, p. 117). Or they may attach different meanings to certain ages. The definition of *old* is changing as today's generation ages with greater health and longevity than previous generations. Gloria Steinem's classic statement, on being told she looked young for 40, "This is how 40 looks!" reflects this. Yet, in American culture, there is also the paradox of the worship of youth. For women, this is particularly poignant. Fashion magazines rarely portray older women in either editorial or advertising photographs. Television advertisers consistently use young models to sell their wares, and it is rare to see older women star in television shows or movies.

Counselors need to be alert for client comments that demonstrate concern about aging, fear of future limitations, or more positive, excitement about future possibilities. We need to be alert for artificial barriers to change that may be revealed by statements such as "You can't teach an old dog new tricks." Clients who feel hopeless about their abilities to manage a transition may say things like, "It's too late for me to change; I'm too old." Sometimes a humorous interchange like the following may help break that cycle:

Client: *I can't train for a new job; it would take me 5 years and I'll be 55 by then.*

Counselor: *How old will you be in 5 years if you don't take the training?*

Client: *Fifty-five.... Oh ...*

The insight represented by that "Oh" can be the beginning of a new view of life's possibilities.

Similarly, older actresses, no longer able to secure ingénue roles, or actors, forced to change from leading man to character actor, must, because of an *external* trigger, change *internal* assumptions as they change roles. The performer who tries to retain a youthful appearance by cosmetic surgery and excessive makeup has become a commonplace butt of comedians' put-downs. But the real limitations in possible roles created by aging are no joke to the performer.

Duration

The duration of an individual transition is not always obvious. The time it takes for the new self to be accepted and integrated varies widely from individual to individual. The menopause process, for example, can last for 10 years. Some questions that may help a client gain a better understanding of duration are: Is it perceived as permanent, temporary, or unknown? Does the individual assess it as positive, negative, or mixed? Is it of great salience to the individual? For example, waiting 1 year to take one last class to complete a degree may be agonizing to person A and a minor nuisance to person B.

Health crises are an example of internal events that have varying durations. A person may be temporarily immobilized by back surgery or permanently disabled due to a spinal injury. Someone may have to restrict activities owing to a bout of pneumonia; another may have to lead a permanently quiet life because of a heart condition. The pandemic that began in 2020 resulted in most countries imposing varying levels of lockdowns or stay-at-home orders. Schools were closed, and many people lost jobs or began working from home. For many, the Covid-19 virus caused serious health conditions or death. For others, the loss of livelihood led to food and shelter uncertainty. But for others, less threatened, we have heard that the most difficult part of the experience was the uncertainty about its duration. "I could take anything if I knew if would end in 6 weeks, or 3 months." Ambiguity is not a comfortable state of mind, and uncertainty about the duration of a transition is an example of ambiguity. We have written earlier in this book about liminality, being on the threshold, being betwixt and between. Uncertainty and ambiguity are often associated with this uncomfortable place. George (2015) puts it poignantly, "there is a halfway world between each ending and each new beginning.... Don't underestimate the transition ... between farewell and new departure. Give yourself the time you need. Some thresholds are too wide to be taken in one stride."

Even health events of temporary duration can trigger a more lasting transition. If the health crisis leads to a redefinition of self or a sense of vulnerability or frailty, it may affect future goals and plans or lead to a different lifestyle. Of course, some non–pandemic-related health events may be also of unknown duration, for example, knee surgery or cancer treatment.

Counselors will hear some people with orthopedic problems complain that the athletic side of their lives is over; they will hear others investigate what kinds of braces to wear as they resume their sport or look into what sports they can play with their new deficit. Some tennis players, as their knees and backs give out, make the move from playing singles on a hard court to playing doubles on a clay court or to learning pickleball; others, with the same level of deficit, quit the game entirely or abandon all athletic pursuits.

Although some cancer treatments are so devastating that one can barely manage one's daily life, others allow more freedom. Helpers hear adults in similar circumstances describe their health transitions in widely different ways. The duration, uncertain, is the same for all; the interpretation is again quite different. Some of the reasons for these different interpretations are discussed later in the sections on hope and selective denial.

The duration of nonevents is even more difficult to assess. As one woman, bemoaning what she saw as a static life, said, "I thought this was to be the 'Change of Life,' but nothing has changed!" Perhaps the duration of nonevents is more appropriately considered as the length of time it takes people to accept as permanent a condition they thought was temporary. When concern about the nonevent ceases to take center stage, the transition can be thought of as integrated into one's life.

Individuals often come to counseling without a specific complaint, problem, or issue. They may describe a vague malaise, the sensealluded to earlier, of "is this all there is?" Although Mike came to counseling because of his wife's request for a divorce, his primary hope for the experience related to his concern about his life's trajectory. Once depression is ruled out, a sensitive counselor should be on the alert for a nonevent type of transition. One woman we saw came to counseling complaining that her marriage was "just not fulfilling" anymore. She was 45, had two children in college, and had worked as an accountant for a large firm for 15 years, since her children started school. On further investigation, it became clear that she had recently been passed over for promotion for the second time and that she and her husband had been forced to sell the house they inherited from her husband's mother for much less money than they had hoped. They had anticipated that the sale of the house would allow them to travel and enjoy some other luxuries even while supporting two college-age children. These two nonevents had been unacknowledged, and it appeared that the woman was displacing her feelings of disappointment onto her marriage.

Source of Control

The source of Mike's transition is internal as well as external. Having a sense of control is often critical to success in managing transitions. Many self-related transitions have an internal genesis and therefore an internal locus of control. Some, however, are a combination of internal and external factors. Health problems are a good example. If your asthma is aggravated by smoking, you have some control over the course of the disease. If you have a bad back, it may be improved by appropriate exercise. Careful management can allow a person to control diseases such as diabetes or high blood pressure. Many believe that our minds have great influence over the state of our health in general (e.g., Myers et al., 2012; Mayer et al., 2020; Wurm et al., 2008).

Garrett and Carroll (2000) described the mind–body connection as seen from a traditional Native American perspective. They describe life as being made up of four concentric circles: They include that which is within us, our spirit, our family/clan, the natural environment, and the spirit world. "In all we each have a circle of self, ...a circle of immediate family, extended family, tribal family, community, and nation; ...all of our relations in the natural environment, and a circle of our universal surroundings" (pp. 380–381).

The concept of wellness is increasingly accepted in medicine, psychology, and religion. This concept centers on a holistic view of human functioning, and the focus is on improving human functioning through the integration of body, mind, and spirit (Mayer et al., 2020). The goal of current wellness models is to maximize the potential through which people make choices for a successful existence. Models of wellness address the myriad factors that create healthy functions (Hattie et al., 2004). A paradigm of wellness has evolved as an alternative to the traditional medical model for the treatment of physical and mental disorders (Hattie et al., 2004; Myers & Sweeney, 2008). These models represent new directions in healthcare and have come out of the physical health professions that focus on the physiological aspects of development (Myers & Williard, 2003).

Myers and Sweeney (2007) and Myers et al. (2000) developed a Wheel of Wellness, which is a holistic model, in which "spirituality is depicted as the center of the wheel and most important characteristic of well-being. The components of spirituality include having a sense of meaning in life, in addition to religious or spiritual beliefs and practices. Surrounding the center are a series of 12 spokes in the life task of self-direction: sense of worth; sense of control; realistic beliefs; emotional responsiveness and management; intellectual stimulation, problem solving, and creativity; sense of humor; exercise; nutrition; self-care; stress management; gender identity; and cultural identity" (p. 1). They based their model on cross-disciplinary research that identified healthy behaviors that contribute to longevity, quality of life, and well-being. They concluded that spirituality is the core characteristic of healthy people.

These researchers emphasized the characteristics of healthy functioning as a major component of wellness and outlined five major life tasks that can be identified with each component of the Wheel of Wellness. Life Task 1 relates to spirituality, which they define broadly as "an awareness of a being or force that transcends the material aspects of live and gives a deep sense of wholeness or connection to the universe" (Myers et al., 2000, p. 253). They refer to specific components of spirituality as resources: positive thoughts, hardiness, generalized self-efficacy, and optimism. All of these factors have been strongly correlated with well-being and resistance to stress in the literature relating to the relationship between psychological resources and wellness (Lightsey, 1996). They point out that a clear correlation between subjective well-being and optimism is related to spirituality and the mediation of stress. They also relate the concept of tasks to Adler's (1927/1954) major life tasks of work, friendship, and love and concluded that spirituality is central to achieving these tasks. Sweeney (1998) expanded Adler's tasks by adding the task of *self-direction*, which relates to how people regulate and direct their daily activities in pursuit of their long-term goals. As we help people navigate transitions, we may want to consider these concepts and how they may influence decisions. The resistance to social distancing mandated in most places during the Covid-19 pandemic underlines how closely individuals' sense of well-being is tied to connection with others. Although many complained that isolation created financial havoc, many others complained that seeing friends and family on a screen, for example, through apps such as FaceTime or Zoom, was no substitute for a hug. And being forbidden to attend a place of worship seemed particularly galling when people sought that comfort.

A difficult decision for many gay, lesbian, or bisexual persons is whether or when to "come out" to family, friends, or work colleagues. Although individuals control the decision, they cannot control others' reactions. Sometimes a partner forces a revelation; sometimes a person is "found out" by being seen in a gay environment or by contracting AIDS or having a "roommate" contract AIDS. Some people make an active decision to let those close to them know about their sexual orientation but not to tell the world in general. Regardless of the etiology, the transition from secret to public is an important one to the individual and those close to that individual. Despite the activist call in the movie *Milk* to "come out, come out, wherever you are!" the decision may be a difficult one for an individual. A mystery novel by Alison Gordon (1990) dramatized the pain and loss of privacy when teammates and press responded with great hostility to a baseball star's coming out. The shock of his teammates and the sports world that an athlete could be gay provided a dramatic illustration of the misconceptions of many about homosexuality. The coming out process and other issues related to the gay, lesbian, bisexual. transgendered identity are discussed extensively in Croteau et al. (2005).

SELF

In this section, as we focus on the issues of the self as related to internal transitions, we look at issues of identity, autonomy, meaning-making, and self-efficacy. These add to the personal, demographic, and psychological characteristics of the individual presented in Chapter 3.

Identity

It is tempting to assume that most self-transition issues relate to identity. The answer to "who am I?" changes as life situations change. For Mike Garcia, the old answers no longer satisfy. For a person with a chronic illness, "I" has changed. Perhaps even more important, people often ask, "Who will I be?" With help, they may find the answers to be different than in the past. Many young adults believe that they will find out who they are one of these days. They see older people seemingly knowing this and make an assumption that this kind of wisdom comes with age. They retain the childhood wish of someday being and feeling "grown up," with its attendant assumption of self-knowledge. Perhaps one of the triggers to a midlife self-transition is the recognition that this "grownupness" may never happen, that it is a myth. Perhaps at the same time comes recognition of ultimate aloneness—the so-called existential awareness that we have mentioned earlier.

Older people, on the other hand, may be asking themselves, "Who was I?" Counselors hear older clients reviewing their lives, looking at the past as a way of assessing the present. Erik Erikson (1950) discussed the developmental crisis of old age as being one of integrity versus despair. Integrity is found by assessing one's life as having been meaningful. To continue this further, as mentioned in Chapter 1, Joan Erikson (1997) extended the last stages to include a ninth stage, with insight into the very old and the transitions inherent in older adulthood. Key tasks from this vantage point rely on the role of wisdom and investing in what is most relevant, enduring, and nourishing. Butler (1963) theorized that an internal life review was a universal occurrence. Counselors often hear older clients asking questions such as "Was I successful as a parent, spouse, worker, citizen, friend?" and "All in all, has it been a good life?" They may also be making summary statements such as "Given where I started, I've done OK" or "Nothing I've done has worked out. I guess you could say my life has been a failure." Counselors need to be alert for these types of statements so they can foster appropriate follow-up exploration.

For some, issues of identity are nonevents. If my dreams of being a spouse and parent, or grandparent, chair of the board, or chief steward do not happen, identity changes. Although Erik Erikson (1950) talked of identity formation as a task of young adulthood, midlife adults often recapitulate this issue. Counselors may hear people simultaneously grieving for the loss of a planned identity and questioning how they can reshape their dreams (Schlossberg & Robinson, 1993). If my desire to be a parent, as it often does, comes out of my need to be nurturing to the next generation, I may talk about volunteering in a childcare center, being a Big Brother or Big Sister, spending more time with my nieces and nephews, or becoming a foster grandparent. A bachelor of our acquaintance describes his brother's children as his "nephlings." This term is not only gender neutral, unlike niece or nephew, but implies a closer relationship with its connection to the word sibling.

Sometimes people use humor to help in their struggle to accept the nonevent. Tom Lehrer, mathematician, satirist, pianist, and folk singer, once said, "It's a sobering thought to think that when Mozart was my age, he had been dead for 10 years" (Lehrer, 1959). Judith Viorst's (1976) poem, "Facing the Facts," lists all the things she would probably never do, such as cure the cold, paint a Picasso, or advise presidents, and ends with, "I must still face the fact that they'll never be able to say, 'and she did it so young'" (p. 53).

One's past experience is clearly a central component of identity and often determines how a person approaches a current transition. Counselors may hear, if they ask the right questions, stories of previous challenges faced by their clients. When these stories describe a track record of successful coping, clients are usually more prepared to take risks and confront their current transition with verve. When these stories are largely descriptive of negative outcomes, clients may be afraid to trust their own instincts and will ask for solutions from the counselor. Counselors can help people recall positive coping experiences and look for the skills they used in making them positive.

Autonomy

Autonomy is defined as independence or self-directed freedom. A great deal of research substantiates the fact that life satisfaction depends on the perception of autonomy. Whether you believe the autonomy is real or an illusion may not matter. People who feel in control of their lives tend to describe their lives as happier. Autonomy is generally considered to be a Western value and is, in fact, a meaningless concept in many cultures. Happiness is culturally embedded. We must remember, in addition, Gilligan's (1982) work on women's development. She states that "Illuminating life as a web rather than a succession of relationships, women portray autonomy rather than attachment as the illusory and dangerous quest" (p. 48). She poses autonomy as an aim in conflict with compassion and connection, a narrower definition than the one we are using. We suggest that personal autonomy can include the choice, but not the compulsion, to be compassionate and connect. We take the androgynous position that intimacy and autonomy are desirable for men *and* women to lead satisfying adult lives.

Kincade (1987) suggested that individuals develop along the following lines: (a) The young child is *dependent* for all its needs on a nurturing parent. With growth comes a period of (b) *counterdependence*, a time of rebellion during which individuation and autonomy take place and then a period of (c) *independence* during which the individual leads or attempts to lead a completely separate life. Many individuals stop developing at this point, but Kincade suggests that fully mature individuals move to (d) *interdependence*, during which there is a recognition of the connections and mutuality suggested by Gilligan (1982). It is the authors' position that this interdependence expresses a true autonomy. One cannot fully participate in an interdependent relationship without being at first an independent, autonomous person. Adults who believe that they are able to function independently can willingly join with another in true mutuality. Adults who believe that they need another to survive will not be able to be a true full partner in the relationship—the risks are too great.

Levinson (1986) supported this position. He stated:

> One developmental task of this [midlife] transition is to begin a new step in individuation. ... We can become more compassionate, more reflective and judicious, less tyrannized by inner conflicts and external demands, and more genuinely loving of ourselves and others. (p. 5)

Clients may talk about fears related to loss of autonomy or expectations of increases in autonomy. People may be afraid that changes in relationships, such as marriage or childbearing, or changes in work, such as joining a large corporation, may have a deleterious effect on their autonomy. They may see other transitions, for example, getting divorced or having children leave home, becoming self-employed or retiring, as leading to more autonomy. And to further complicate matters, some people may *fear* increased autonomy. (We never promised you this would be simple.)

Many faced with retirement feel that they have lost control of their lives. A CEO who was forced into retirement was asked who he was by a passport clerk. The man said, "I know who I was. I don't know who I am" (Schlossberg, 2004, p. 29). He had had one identity—a top executive and father. All that had changed.

An important element of many midlife transitions is the need to make meaning of the transition and of life itself. Certainly, Mike is questioning his values and his purpose in life. And surely his hope and optimism are shaky. Transitions often shake spiritual sureties as well. We heard nothing about Mike's spirituality. We need to find out more about this aspect of his life. Does it include involvement in organized religion? In meditation? In other spiritual pursuits? These are important areas for his counselor to pursue. Counselors frequently hear that middle-aged clients are moving away from organized religion, particularly if they have been involved "for the children" who are now grown up. But they also often hear a commitment or recommitment to spirituality, defined more broadly than when the adult was younger. It now often includes belief in a higher power; hope and optimism, worship, prayer and meditation, purpose in life, love, and moral values. Other clients describe finding kinship in enhanced involvement with their religious community. The permutations are endless; the importance of counselors is to pursue the place of spirituality in an individual's life.

Spirituality

Jung (1933) integrated the spiritual dimension with human development in his theory and conceptualized spirituality as a process of *achieving wholeness.* According to Jung, life is a journey and, particularly in the second half of life, it can become a spiritual process. Jung viewed the spiritual search for meaning as an integral part of midlife. He believed that, as people reach this stage of development, they become increasingly centered and more deeply connected to their spiritual selves.

Howell's (2001) research supported the idea that midlife can involve a powerful spiritual awakening. According to Howell, a central influence on quality of life at midlife is an awareness of one's own values and motives, along with achieving agreement of these unique values with circumstances and behaviors. Hudson (1991) stated that as individuals move through midlife, their sense of purpose is likely to shift from ego-driven issues to more spiritual ones. For midlife adults, meaning and purpose become concerns as they address issues around mortal limits, death, and time left to live. This is not a morbid preoccupation; this awareness prompts adults to consider their deepest values.

Gerzon (1996) provided a metaphor for midlife. He stated that as people approach the second half of life, their old compasses no longer work, and the new compass must be read, not with their minds alone, but with their souls. At this time of life, according to Gerzon, people yearn for wholeness, and each must find his or her own way. Campbell (1988) believed that the quest for wholeness in the second half of life is ancient and universal, with the world's myths describing a quest for meaning and transcendence in adulthood. Although the word *midlife* often produces an adverse reaction in our culture, the crisis is in fact a spiritual one and can actually be a process of transformation (Gerzon, 1996). This is congruent with Bloch's (2004) ideas on phase transitions. According to Bloch, living beings are in a dynamic state, moving between order and chaos. She compared these phase transitions to the movement of water among the three phases: liquid; solid, or ice; and gas, or steam. She stated that phase transitions, whether sought or not, present the opportunity for creativity and the emergence of new forms (Bloch, 2004). According to Hudson (1991), as adults move through midlife, meaning and purpose become central concerns. This theory resonates with Campbell's (1988) conceptualization of the second half of life as a process of questing for meaning and transcendence.

A central theme in the literature on spirituality is its association with healthy development and functioning, along with increased adaptive capacities for dealing with distressingl situations (e.g., Hodge, 2001; Larson & Larson, 2003). Levin (2009) argued that faith can assist mental and physical healing. Graham et al. (2001) concluded that spirituality may involve resources that include finding meaning and purpose in life. According to Myers and Williard (2003), spirituality is an essential component of wellness, acting as an integrative force that motivates and shapes the physical, psychological, and emotional functioning of human beings. Savickas (1997) asserted that it is meaning that breathes life into a situation, energizing and orientating people toward self-completion. He described spirituality as facilitating movement forward, thus increasing adaptive capacity.

Anderson (2005) looked at the concepts of spirituality and coping in her study of midlife adults experiencing a work transition. She found that levels of spirituality were significantly associated with the levels of coping for people experiencing a work transition. Existential spirituality, in particular, as distinguished from religion per se played a role for midlife adults in coping with stressful work transitions. The existential aspect of spirituality relates to meaning and a sense of purpose.

Finding one's life mission often relates to spirituality. This can involve finding work that is meaningful in a deeper sense, but many people seek their life mission in other arenas of life. For example, one woman's search for meaning stemmed from a divorce. She took a 6-month leave from her job and spent time on an island near Singapore where she worked with a United Nations team providing mental health services to Southeast Asian refugees. While there, she met two young Vietnamese refugees. After her return to the United States, she became their sponsor and in the process changed her views about what was important in her life. This example illustrates the intertwining of internal and external triggers that invited one adult to search for life's meaning in a new way. Her divorce and her children becoming adults and leaving home provided both the spur and the possibility of a creative way to look for "more" out of life.

There is no right way to find meaning. Another woman quit a good professional job to spend a year in South America, doing things she had always wanted to such as swimming with dolphins and exploring more fully her own inner life. These "quests" are another way that some, whose life circumstances and financial means allow, seek to find meaning in midlife. Quests have a long tradition in many cultures. Sometimes relegated solely to the young, many cultures encourage the middle-aged or old among them to seek meaning in exploration, for example, American Indian vision quests. Many Catholics experience a visit to a shrine, for example, Lourdes in France, Fatima in Portugal, or Guadeloupe in Mexico, as fulfilling a lifetime dream. A Moslem's trip to Mecca is considered an important component of spiritual health. It is important to consider cultural diversity in finding meaning as in so many things. Quests are a long tradition for Native Americans. But we are reminded that there is no such thing as a global American Indian culture, just as most identifiable cultures are more diverse than they are monolithic.

Weenolsen (1986, p. 2) conducted a study to investigate empirically some of the ideas contained in existential philosophy, fiction, and psychology. Using the concept of transcendence, she stated that human beings are in "a continuous process of creating our lives and our selves." She asserted that loss and transcendence are the impetus to this recreation. Loss is defined more broadly than just the death of another or of a job but can include "a loss of will, freedom, control, plans, expectations, hopes, ideals, or illusions." She defined transcendence as "the overcoming of loss and the re-creation of the life-self."

Weenolsen interviewed 48 women aged 25 to 67 years, asking open-ended questions related to the meaning of life. Although she found that 38 of the 48 women in her study believed that life has meaning, there was a distinction between those oriented to loss and those oriented to transcendence.

In telling their stories, "The loss oriented answered in terms of what they did not have, whereas the transcendence oriented replied in terms of losses overcome" (p. 6).

Most women found meaning through conducting a life review. Although usually discussed as a later life phenomenon (cf. Butler, 1963), Weenolsen (1986) found that 71% of her middle-aged interviewees reported frequent or occasional life reviews, and only one individual reported that she never engaged in such an activity. Clearly then, counselors can encourage life-review activities for clients at all ages. This strategy can be encouraged or expanded upon as clients face new challenges. Weenolsen found four primary ways in which people find meaning: (a) as being preordained and coming from God, (b) as part of a process of personal and spiritual growth, (c) as a specific individual purpose such as being productive or helping others, and (d) as a more general personal purpose such as being loving or sharing joy. The women who believed that God has a divine plan for them believed that they would find life's meaning in that plan. The majority of subjects, however, believed that meaning could be created.

Weenolsen's proposed process of creation and renewal includes the stages of grieving, searching, replacing, and reintegrating. As counselors, we want to listen for statements that reveal where a person is in this process and how a particular client makes meaning. We can then plan interventions to help individuals find meaning as they manage their transitions.

This process of meaning-making can be new for some people. Palmer (2018) describes this process as a "reaching in" and "staying engaged with your soul" (p. 145). According to Palmer, the search for meaning is most salient when we experience diminishment and defeats, which can come at any age and are inevitable when we get old. He describes this as a process of reflection to help us reclaim "the ground of our being" and thus gain perspective, embrace our shadow and light, and transcend the regrets and fears that come with age. He describes the spiritual journey as "an endless process" of engaging life as it is and stripping away our illusions about ourselves, our world, and the relationship between the two. As counselors, we embark on this inward journey with our clients, something we must be also be willing to do for ourselves. Sometimes there are global events, such as the Covid-19 pandemic, through which we journey with our clients as we navigate the difficult waters of life. Providing a safe space for reflection and review can help our clients and ourselves to reclaim "the ground of our being," our core sense of purpose and meaning.

An interesting example of using the life-review process to find life meaning is found in *Inscape: A Search for Meaning* (Young, 1983). This memoir "records the backward look over a personal journey, a search to discover in the changing circumstances of my life, over a period of eight decades, my own meaning" (p. 1). Young comments near the end of the book that "the voyage of discovery consists in seeing with new eyes all that has woven the tapestry of one's life" (p. 98). Not everyone will write a book, but many can benefit from the introspective process used by Young.

Past Experience

One might make the case that having a past is the only universal experience of adulthood. All adults have both successful and unsuccessful coping experiences "under their belts." Past experience often determines how a person approaches a current transition. It is closely related to an optimistic or pessimistic viewpoint, transcendence, and self-efficacy. Exploring past experiences can be like "mining for gold" for the strengths developed through life's challenges. Sometimes a "problem-saturated" story can seem discouraging, both for the client and counselor; however, there are often "glimmers of hope" that emerge through exploration of past experiences with transitions.

Self-Efficacy

Counselors hear self-descriptions that run the gamut from confident to inadequate. Bandura (1982) coined the term *self-efficacy* to describe the belief that one can make a difference in one's own life and have an impact on one's environment. Self-efficacy enables a person to tackle a new problem with an optimistic expectation that it will be solvable, in other words, that one can cope effectively with it. Folkman et al. (1991) created an intervention strategy that included the person in the context of the environment. Two aspects are central to this model: (a) individuals' appraisal of the situation (Does it exceed or is it within their resources?) and (b) the coping response "through which the person alters or manages the person–environment relationship" (p. 240).

Lazarus and Folkman (1984) stated that an individual's appraisal of every encounter is shaped by the perceived harm, threat, or challenge found therein. And both the quality and intensity of people's appraisal are affected by their self-efficacy beliefs. Newer research regarding the role of positive emotions and coping with stress has been prompted by evidence that both positive and negative appraisals/emotions co-occur throughout the process (Folkman & Moskowitz, 2004). As counselors, we hear a mix of feelings and cognitions, and it is imperative to listen for the positive as well as the problematic when working to increase self-efficacy in our clients.

Consider Sylvia, a 55-year-old, divorced, teacher who had been offered an early-retirement package from her school district. She sought counseling help to decide whether or not to accept the offer. In describing her dilemma, she discussed her fears that she will be bored, that she will have no social life, which currently is made up mostly of school-related events, and that she will "wither away." She also talked about opportunities for visiting her children and grandchildren who live in distant states and for spending more time on her crafts and hobbies. She explained that she has made many bad decisions in her life, has no confidence in her ability to make this one, and is feeling panicky over its irrevocable nature. Clearly, her appraisal of the situation includes both present threat and fear of future harm, as well as possible challenge. This mixed bag, common to stressful situations, is coupled with low self-efficacy estimates.

Counselors can intervene in each of these arenas—evaluating the harm and threat, reinforcing the challenge, and changing the client's beliefs in her self-efficacy by helping her to explore past successes and current resources. As we get to know about the balance of Sylvia's assets to deficits, we need to consider not only the situation she faces and the areas of her self that impinge on that situation but also where else she can get assistance to face her current challenges.

SUPPORT

When individuals hear the word *support*, they usually think of other people. Counselors, with judicious questioning, can find out the shape, size, and range of a person's support system—who is in it and what function each person plays in the system. During times of transition, we often hear of great disruptions to a support system. The Covid-19 pandemic upended many, if not most, people's support systems. The inability to see friends and family with whom you are not living created a vacuum that was not totally fulfilled via Zoom, Skype, and the like. For many, however, the pandemic led to reconnecting with people not seen for a while, as old or distant friends feel the need to reach out and touch base.

Helping clients explore various ways to nurture their support networks is especially crucial with the increased challenges being experienced with changing roles, routines, and relationships. An important first step in planning ways to enhance a system is to learn about its present status. We discuss methods for improving support systems with individuals in Chapter 7 and with groups in Chapter 9. In this section, we describe what counselors may hear as clients describe their "people" supports. As with all of the discussions in this section of the book, our purpose here is to heighten readers' awareness of issues brought to counseling by people in transition. It is our hope that this heightened awareness will enable you to listen more productively as you help your clients explore their lives.

Types of Support

Waters and Samson (1993) used Pearson's (1990) research to provide a list of typical support needs. They included (a) acceptance, (b) self-esteem, (c) love and physical intimacy, (d) personal and work connections, (e) peers (particularly one in a particular arena, for example, other parents of adolescents), (f) stimulation and challenge, (g) role models, (h) guidance (mentors or sponsors), and (i) comfort and assistance.

Let us look at one of the needs listed: role models. In Mike's case, his parents are role models of self-sacrifice, striving, and putting their own hopes into their children. His wife is a role model in her satisfaction with her work, and we don't hear of any others. Mike has followed his parents in that he has seen his career as solely a pursuit done to support the family. But now he is looking for some more personal satisfaction. Mike seems to accept, reluctantly, his children's growing independence and sounds as if he does not see them as providing the vicarious achievements he gave his parents. Mike's counselor will want to help him think about who else have been or could be role models for him. The counselor and Mike may also want to think together about which aspects of his parents' lives he could use as a pattern for his own adult life.

As you elicit the stories of your clients in transition, listen for support issues such as having very few people filling many functions, having areas with little or no support, or statements such as "I don't need support" or "grown men don't depend on others." Often you can help people to feel more comfortable accepting support if you remind them of the times that they have supported others and encourage them to think of times in the future when they will again be able to be givers. It may also help to remind them of the pleasure they get in giving to others. When they do not let others assist them, they deprive the people they care about of the opportunity to be of support.

A man attending a party saw a list of emergency numbers next to a friend's telephone and asked, with some dismay, why he wasn't on the list. The unstated messages of "I thought you knew you could count on me in an emergency" and "I want to be able to help you out when you need it" were expressive of this desire to give. Many clients do not recognize the supportive function played by people in their lives. Sometimes, a delightful serendipitous outcome of exploring support systems is that clients share this awareness with those closest to them—who are generally very flattered and pleased.

People often receive support by belonging to a group designed specifically for its supportive functions. A plethora of groups have arisen, both self-help and professionally led, to provide a forum for adults with specific problems. These include support groups for people who have lost breasts or colons, groups for people who are newly divorced or widowed, or groups for new parents or those who have decided not to have children. These groups, which are discussed more fully in Chapter 9, have the potential to offer information and support and, with luck, help individuals to both acquire and perceive more control over their situation.

STRATEGIES

Part III is dedicated to counseling interventions—things we can do to help our clients develop strategies that will help them move forward in their lives. The goal of the strategies section of this chapter is to help you identify what you may hear from clients about strategies that they currently use. It is obvious that it is usually easier for clients to do more of what they already know than to learn new things. Thus, finding out in some detail what successful strategies clients already use is a productive aim of counseling.

Reframing

Hackney and Cormier (2005) suggest that reframing helps develop an alternative meaning that is "totally credible and believable" (p. 200). Counselors need to listen for statements that can be reframed. One woman we know, in the depths of despair over a painful divorce, talked about her pride in being able to care so deeply. In doing so, she reframed at least some of her pain into hope for a future deep relationship. Another woman described her graying hair as a "free frosting."

Two men were forced into early retirement by companies that were "rightsizing." One reframed it as an opportunity to spend more time with his family and to pursue several hobbies. Another overgeneralized and saw it as a total condemnation of his worth. He felt that if he was not valuable enough for the company to keep, then he was valuable to no one. He gave up his volunteer activities, quit his golf league, and retreated to his den where he watched television and generally exhibited symptoms of depression. He was not able to separate the causes of his layoff—economics, not a comment on his work performance—from his total worth as a person.

Bandler and Grinder (1975) discussed this process from the perspective of linguistics as well as psychology. They describe three processes through which we narrow the real world into our perceptive world. They are (a) *generalization*, in which we apply learning from one situation or experience to others we deem similar; (b) *distortion*, in which we change what we think, see, and feel about the world to match our internal perceptions; and (c) *deletion*, in which we selectively screen out parts of our perception, again often to match some internal sense. Counselors need to listen to their clients' uses of each of these processes to determine whether the use is self-enhancing or self-destructive.

Let us look in more detail at the case of the depressed laid-off man described earlier. He extended his negative feelings about his work abilities to include his feelings about all of his abilities—*overgeneralization*. It is likely that he distorted what he heard from the personnel office. Perhaps he was told that they had to let a certain number of people go and chose everyone earning above a certain amount. Or perhaps he was told that his department was being absorbed by another and that all the managers in his department had to be let go. But our hypothetical man probably already had fairly low self-esteem, perhaps based on a lifetime of negative thinking, so he *distorted* what he heard to match his internal perception of his value. Perhaps he was even told by the personnel office that the company was sorry to lose a good worker and would be glad to give him excellent references. Because he did not, deep down, believe that he was worthy; he "didn't hear" or *deleted* the positive message. Whenever any of these processes become evident to a counselor, the stage is set for reframing.

The adage that "every cloud has a silver lining" is well known. Another view of this situation is found in the Japanese word, *mono-no-aware*, defined as appreciating the sadness of existence. An example of the use of this word is, "You see the cherry blossoms on the trees in Kyoto in April and you love them, but you love them most of all because you appreciate, so sadly, that soon they will all be gone (Moore, 2004, p. 9). A negative example might be the so-called Murphy's law: If anything can go wrong, it will. Counselors can listen to a client's abilities to reframe positively so they can reinforce, modify, or teach this coping strategy. The idea behind Seligman's (2006) learned optimism, discussed later in this chapter, is that this trait is not inborn and fixed but can be acquired. Age is also seen as a determinant of positive coping. Leland (2020) cites Gary M. Kennedy, director of geriatric psychiatry at Montefiore Medical Center, speaking about older adults: "The reality is that older adults as a group have a positivity bias....Their pessimism and anxiety tend to abate with age. They're no longer striving for material achievements so what matters to them is what's emotionally satisfying" (p. 350).

According to Palmer (2018), one of the most important words he has ever used is *enough*, which speaks to the clarity of focusing on what matters most:

> [Enough] can safeguard the soul, and saying it comes more easily with age. ...I say "enough" without hesitation to anything that's not life-giving—whether it's frenzy and overwork, a personal prejudice, an unhealthy relationship, a societal cruelty or injustice. (p. 25)

As emphasized throughout this section, reframing can be useful for both enhancing optimism and for creating boundaries around unhealthy patterns and responses. A key consideration is what gives life meaning and what no longer serves a person well. Sometimes, it is the questions themselves that can facilitate this process. Palmer asked himself, "What do I want to let go of, and what do I want to *give myself to?*" (p. 27).

Selective Denial

The technique of selective denial is closely allied to reframing. Counselors can listen for the ways that people "forget" parts of their situations. A 60-year-old man had surgery for cancer. Although his odds for recovery were about 50–50, he believed that his cancer was all gone. He took the recommended chemotherapy and followed other medical recommendations, although he believed they were unnecessary. His selective denial allowed him to enjoy life during this unpleasant time and, if we believe researchers, such as Siegel (1986), increased his chances of complete recovery. The difference between healthy and unhealthy denial in this situation is that an unhealthy denier might refuse treatments. People can deny facts, as in this example, deny the meaning of a situation, deny the fact that the situation applies to them, or deny that the situation is pervasive or will be long lasting.

A client moved across the country by herself to a place where she knew nobody. She stated that she didn't consider herself alone or lonely. She enjoyed her own company, she said, and knew that eventually she would meet people and form new friendships. This denial of the possible ill effects of her move might have gotten her in trouble if she did not then reach out to others in her new community. But at the moment it gave her the energy to focus on settling into her apartment and finding a job.

People who deny that their own aging means slowing down, even if it means so for others, may be the same people we see competing in the "over 80" field in a marathon, triathlon, or swim meet. Selective denial for these athletes creates a true change in the reality, one that could generally be seen as positive. The humorous statement that, "I am the queen of de Nile," encapsulates denial at its most useful. Unhealthy deniers might continue to compete when it is causing permanent harm to their knees or even their hearts.

Denying the pervasiveness of the situation is the last type of selective denial. Counselors will hear people making pronouncements such as "It was only my job, not my life," "This will feel like home in a few weeks," and "I may look old on the outside, but inside I'm still a boy of 21." Counselors can be alert to the coping strategies related to selective denial currently being used by their clients. They can then support the ones that are functional and help to redirect those that are less so.

Hope and Optimism

It has been said that *hope* is the passion for the possible. According to the dictionary, *hope* is "the feeling that what is desired is also possible and that events may turn out for the best." According to the same dictionary, *optimism* is "a disposition or tendency to look on the more favorable side of happenings and to anticipate the most favorable result." Hope exists only when there is also doubt—otherwise, it is expectation. Another definition, given by Michael J. Fox, well known for his upbeat approach to his Parkinson's diagnosis, is that "optimism is informed hope" (Egan, 2020). Take the case of Marie, who had two adult children. She expected that her children would marry, and she would become a grandparent. However, one daughter became emotionally unstable and was in and out of hospitals, and the other daughter married but postponed having children. As the possibility emerged that she might not have grandchildren, her hope increased. In other words, when she fully expected to be a grandmother, there was no need for hope. As the possibility became ambiguous, hope became her "powerful ally." After her daughter announced that she and her husband had decided never to have children, hope went out the window. She became despondent, and she gave herself time to grieve over the loss of what might have been. Finally, she modified her dream by becoming a foster grandparent.

As mentioned earlier, Seligman (2006) addressed this issue in his book *Learned Optimism*. After much research, he concluded, "the remarkable attribute of resilience in the face of defeat need not remain a mystery. It was not an inborn trait; it could be acquired" (p. 30).

According to Hof (1993), hope is an important and often overlooked aspect of the therapy process. Reviewing the literature in family–couple counseling from 1975 to 1992, he found only two mentions of hope. He says that "One of the first tasks of the therapist is to uncover hope, to help create hope, or to instill hope" (p. 223). Counselors often find that people in transition can be divided among those with hope, those without, and even some, those he calls Paul or Paula Pollyanna, who may have so much that they fail to appropriately avoid danger. Some people come to counseling as a last hope. The December 2009 issue of the *Career Development Quarterly* provides a summary of research related to career development in the past year. Not once is hope mentioned explicitly. Niles et al. (2010) approached this issue in their book about hope in career counseling. In *Career Flow,* they propose that hope needs to be at the center of career planning. Niles et al. (2019) further describe their Hope-Action theory as "developing essential competencies as a road map for creating hope for, and engaging effectively in, education and career planning ... based on the essentiality of developing career adaptability" (p. 283).

What is it about hope that is so important in a transition? Again, we see the intertwining of experience and emotional state. Naturally hopeful individuals can lose this worldview during times of crisis but can regain it afterward. Naturally gloomy individuals may struggle even harder to cope with difficult times. We recall an experienced school counselor who found himself stultified in a job he did easily and had done for a long time. He returned to school for an advanced degree solely to energize himself in his profession. He described the experience with enthusiasm, both for his own learning and renewal, and for the renewed empathy he had for his students' academic tribulations. This man clearly believed that he had the ability to change his life through his own efforts—an optimist. We recall another man, also bored with his work in education, who counted the days to retirement for several years and withdrew more and more into a cocoon. He felt helpless to change his situation and believed that he had to suffer in silence—a pessimist.

As we discussed in Chapter 3, Seligman (2006) described several components of optimism–pessimism. Counselors can listen for the following aspects of their clients' explanatory style: their habitual way of explaining both bad and good events. Explanatory style has three dimensions:

1. *Permanence*: This indicates whether you believe causes are permanent or transitory. Optimists believe that causes of good things are permanent and bad things are transitory; pessimists believe just the opposite—that causes of bad things are permanent and good things are transitory. Counselors need to be alert for words such as *always* and *never* and the contexts in which they are used.
2. *Pervasiveness*: "The optimist believes that bad events have specific causes, while good events will enhance everything he does; the pessimist believes that bad events have universal causes and that good events are caused by specific factors" (Seligman, 2006, pp. 47–48). Pervasiveness can determine whether people who experience a painful transition will allow that event to spill into all areas of their lives or whether they will contain the event into its own "box." Counselors need to listen for "catastrophizing" statements

as they listen for the pervasiveness dimension. The same process holds for positive transitions. Counselors need to listen for whether people will allow the event to permeate their entire sense of self. Transitions relating to the self are particularly subject to pervasiveness *because* of their internality. It is hard to see "angst" or joy as anything but pervasive. A person who declares "I really seem to have a new sense of who I am and what matters to me" is unlikely to keep that feeling in a small box.

3. *Personalization*: The third dimension of explanatory style refers to whether one takes responsibility for one's own successes and failures or attributes them to others. Optimists take responsibility for their successes and blame others for their failures. A middle-aged optimistic man with healthy teeth said he had worked hard all of his life to keep them that way—flossing, brushing, getting regular checkups, and so forth. A pessimistic man with similar dental health said it was because his parents and then his employer made him go to the dentist regularly and that his dentist was a genius. The middle-aged optimist with bad teeth absolved himself from responsibility saying that it was because his employer had not provided dental insurance and his parents had not taken him to the dentist as a child. The middle-aged pessimist, also with poor dental health, said it was his own fault for not paying attention to oral hygiene and being lazy about visiting his dentist. This dimension of explanatory style is closely related to locus of control.

Researchers Kobasa and Maddi have been studying what they call *hardiness* and others call *stamina* for several years. They questioned the oft-quoted connection between stress and illness and found that hardy people handled stress better and were healthier than the nonhardy during stressful transitions. In an article written with Kahn (Kobasa et al., 1982), they defined *hardiness* to include commitment, control, and challenge. According to these researchers, commitment is "a tendency to involve oneself in (rather than experience alienation from) whatever one is doing or encounters." They define *control* as "a tendency to feel and act as if one is influential (rather than helpless) in the face of the varied contingencies of life." And they define the *challenge disposition* as "expressed as the belief that change rather than stability is normal in life" (pp. 169–170).

Sholk (1983) described bamboo in a poem, saying

> There is a stamina within that somehow has been transferred to me.
> Boughs will bend before they break.
> Stability in a swaying mobile grassland.
> Versatility.

The hardiness model provides counselors with additional clues to their clients' state of mind. One person may describe his or her awareness of life's finiteness as a time to fulfill dreams, experience more, set new goals, or make more careful choices about how time is spent. This person may come to seek help in implementing these plans or in managing other's reactions to new lifestyle choices. A person at the other end of the commitment continuum may describe group self-hatred, saying things like "I don't want to spend time with all those old people." Still another person may cling to the past by dressing in the clothing of his or her youth, reading nothing written after a certain date, or refusing to acknowledge changes in the world and its customs.

Listening for the control dimension may help counselors be alert to statements such as "I've handled other tough situations, I'm sure with a little help I'll be able to handle this one, too," or "There's nothing anyone can do. I guess I just have to suffer." Kobasa et al. (1982) stated that control "does not imply the naive expectation of complete determination of events and outcomes but rather implies the perception of oneself as having a definite influence through the exercise of imagination, knowledge, skill, and choice" (p. 169). In addition to managing transitions better, people who perceive that they have more control over their lives experience fewer of the deleterious effects of stress. In popular culture, the challenge disposition is described with adages such as "If life gives you lemons, make lemonade," or "When you get to the end of your rope, make a knot and hang on."

We are reminded of the man who saw turning 60 as an opportunity to increase his chances of winning tennis tournaments as he would then be one of the youngest in his new age group. A similar positive view is expressed in a poem found in a book with the delightful title: *When I Am an Old Woman, I Shall Wear Purple*. In the poem from which the title is drawn, "Warning" (Joseph, 1987), a woman describes how her age gives her the freedom to be nonconforming.

Counselors will hear statements from clients in transition that give clues to their optimistic or pessimistic outlook on life. Perhaps one of the most important interventions we can apply is to help a person establish or reestablish hope.

SUMMARY

In this chapter, we examined what counselors hear about individual transitions. We followed the transition model described in the previous chapters by first looking at the situation, including the triggers to the transition and the source of control. We next focused on the individuals themselves as we examined their identity, as well as their sense of autonomy, their spirituality, their past experiences, and their sense of self-efficacy. Support came next in this summary of what we hear as we discuss types of support with clients. Finally, we looked at strategies individuals use, including reframing and hope and optimism.

EXERCISES

1. Develop your own metaphor for your life and the transitions you have thus far experienced. Think about all the modalities—sight, sound,

sensation, touch, and taste. For example, you might say your life has been like an orchestra tuning up or an impressionist painting that only becomes clear when viewed from a distance.

2. Make a list of major adult life transitions, for example, developing a committed relationship with a partner, having children, completing one's education, and so forth, and note the age range you think society sees as appropriate for each of these events. Then note what age range you see as appropriate. What do you learn from this comparison?
3. Think about a client or someone else that you know. (You can use yourself if you wish.) List the intrapersonal (family and other people) and institutional or other nonhuman supports in that person's life space. For example, you might list a sense of optimism, close relations with a sister, and faith. What supports might be added to this person's life to make it more robust?

REFERENCES

Adler, A. (1954). *Understanding human nature*. Fawcett Premier. (Original work published 1927).

Anderson, M. L. (2005). *Spirituality and coping with work transitions* [Unpublished doctoral dissertation]. Oakland University.

Bandler, R., & Grinder, J. (1975). *The structure of magic*. Behavior Books.

Bandura, A. (1982). Self-efficacy: Mechanism in human agency. *American Psychologist, 37*(2), 122–147.

Bloch, D. (2004). Religion, spirituality, and health: A topic not so new. *American Psychologist, 59*, 52.

Butler, R. (1963). The life review: An interpretation of reminiscence in the aged. *Psychiatry, 26*, 65–76.

Campbell, J. (1988). *The power of myth*. Doubleday.

Croteau, J. M., Lark, J. S., Lidderdale, M. A., & Chung, Y. B. (2005). *Deconstructing heterosexism in the counseling professions: A narrative approach*. Sage.

Dubin, K. (1994). *Change of life* [Unpublished manuscript.]

Egan, E. (2020, November 13). When it comes to living with uncertainty, Michael J. Fox is a pro (Review of the book *No time like the future*, by M. J. Fox). *The New York Times*. https://www.nytimes.com/2020/11/13/books/michael-j-fox-no-time-like-the-future

Eliot, T. S. (1930). *The complete poems and plays*. Harcourt, Brace.

Erikson, E. H. (1950). *Childhood and society*. Norton.

Erikson, J. (1997). *The life cycle completed*. Norton.

Feiler, B. (2020). *Life is in the transitions: Mastering change at any age*. Penguin Press.

Folkman, S., Chesney, M., McKusick, L., Ironson, G., Johnson, D. S., & Coates, T. J. (1991). Translating coping theory into an intervention. In J. Eckenrode (Ed.), *The social context of coping* (pp. 239–260). Plenum.

Folkman, S., & Moskowitz, J. (2004). Coping: Pitfalls and promise. *Annual Review of Psychology, 55*, 745–774.

Garrett, M. T., & Carroll, J. J. (2000). Mending the broken circle. *Journal of Counseling & Development, 78*, 379–388.

George, N. (2015). *The little Paris bookshop* (S. Pare, trans.). Broadway Books.

Gerzon, M. (1996). *Listening to midlife*. Shambhala.

Gilligan, C. (1982). *In a different voice.* Harvard University Press.
Gordon, A. (1990). *Safe at home.* McClelland & Stewart.
Graham, S., Furr, S., Flowers, C., & Burke, M. T. (2001). Religion and spirituality in coping with stress. *Counseling and Values, 46,* 2–13.
Hackney, H., & Cormier, S. (2005). *The professional counselor: A process guide to helping* (5th ed.). Pearson.
Hattie, J., Myers, J., & Sweeney, T. (2004). A factor structure of wellness: Theory, assessment, analysis, and practice. *Journal of Counseling & Development, 82,* 354–364.
Hodge, D. (2001). Spiritual assessment: A review of major qualitative methods and a new framework for assessing spirituality. *Social Work, 46,* 203–214.
Hof, L. (1993). The elusive elixir of hope. *The Family Journal: Counseling and Therapy for Couples and Families, 1,* 220–227.
Howell, L. (2001). Spirituality and women's midlife development. *Adultspan,* 3, 51–60.
Hudson, F. M. (1991). *The adult years: Mastering the art of self renewal.* Jossey Bass.
Hudson, F. M. (1999). *The adult years: Mastering the art of self renewal* (rev. ed.). Jossey Bass.
Johnston, L. (1994, February 17). For better or worse. Detroit Free Press, 6F.
Joseph, J. (1987). Warning. In S. Martz (Ed.), *When I am an old woman I shall wear purple* (2nd ed.). Papier-Mache.
Jung, C. J. (1933). *Modern man in search of a soul.* Harcourt Brace.
Kincade, S. (1987). *A delegation workshop* [Unpublished manuscript].
Kobasa, S. C., Maddi, S. R., & Kahn, S. (1982). Hardiness and health: A prospective study. *Journal of Personality and Social Psychology, 42,* 168–177.
Larson, D., & Larson, S. (2003). Spirituality's potential relevance to physical and emotional health: A brief overview of quantitative research. *Journal of Psychology and Theology, 31,* 37–51.
Lazarus, R. S., & Folkman, S. (1984). *Stress, appraisal, and coping.* Springer Publishing Company.
Lehrer, T. (Speaker). (1959). *An evening wasted with Tom Lehrer.* Reprise/Warner Records.
Leland, J. (2020, May 3). Cooped up but upbeat. *The New York Times,* p. 35.
Levin, J. (2009). How faith heals: A theoretical model. *Explore, 5*(2), 77–96.
Levinson, D. J. (1986). A conception of adult development. *American Psychologist, 41,* 3–13.
Maslow, A. (1954). *Motivations and personality.* Harper & Row.
Moore, C. J. (2004). *In other words: A language lover's guide to the most intriguing words around the world.* Walker.
Myers, J. E., & Sweeney, T. J. (2007). *Wellness in counseling: An overview* (ACAPCD-09). American Counseling Association.
Myers, J. E., & Williard, K. (2003). Integrating spirituality into counselor preparation: A developmental, wellness approach. *Counseling and Values, 47,* 142–153.
Neugarten, B. L. (1996). *The meanings of age: Selected papers.* University of Chicago Press.
Niles, S. G., Amundson, N. E., & Neault, R. A. (2010). *Career flow: A hope-centered approach to career development.* Pearson Education.
Niles, S. G., Amundson, N. E., & Yoon, H. J. (2019). Hope-action theory: Creating and sustaining hope in career development. In N. Arthur, R. Neault, & M. McMahon (Eds.), *Career theories and models at work: Ideas for practice* (pp. 283–291). CERIC.
Palmer, P. J. (2018). *On the brink of everything: Grace, gravity & getting old.* Berett-Koehler.

Pearson, R. E. (1990). *Counseling and social support: Perspectives and practice.* Sage.

Plath, D. W. (1980). Contours of consociation: Lessons from a Japanese narrative. *Life-span Development and Behavior, 3,* 287–305.

Rosen, J. L., & Bibring, G. L. (1968). Psychological reactions of hospitalized male patients to a heart attack: Age and social class differences. In B. L. Neugarten (Ed.), *Middle age and aging* (pp. 201–211). University of Chicago Press.

Schlossberg, N. K. (2004). *Retire smart, retire happy: Finding your true path in life.* American Psychological Association.

Schlossberg, N. K., & Robinson, S. P. (1993). Non-events: Another name for heartbreak. *American Counselor, 2,* 21–25.

Schmidtke, C. (2016). *American Indian workforce education: Trends and issues.* Routledge.

Seligman, M. (2006). *Learned optimism.* Knopf.

Sheehy, G. (2006). *New passages: Predictable crises of adult life.* Ballantine.

Siegel, B. S. (1986). *Love, medicine, and miracles: Lessons learned about self healing from a surgeon's experience with exceptional patients.* Harper & Row.

Sweeney, T. J. (1998). *Adlerian counseling: A practitioner's approach.* Accelerated Development.

Viorst, J. (1976). *How did I get to be forty . . . and other atrocities.* Simon & Schuster.

Waters, E. B., & Samson, J. (1993). *Strengthening your team: A training program for volunteers and staff who work with older adults.* Continuum Center, Oakland University.

Weenolsen, P. (1986, August). *Life and self meaning: The process of their creation.* Paper presented at the 94th annual convention of the American Psychological Association, Washington, DC.

Whitbourne, S. K., Sneed, J. R., & Sayer, A. (2009). Psychosocial development from college through midlife: A 34-year sequential study. *Developmental Psychology, 45*(5), 1328–1340. https://doi.org/10.1037/a0016550

Wurm, S., Tomasik, M. T., & Tesch-Römer (2008). Serious health events and their impact on changes in subjective health and life satisfaction: The role of age and a positive view on aging. *European Journal of Ageing: Social, Behavioural and Health Perspectives, 5*(2), 117–127. https://doi.org/10.1007/s10433-008-0077-5

Young, C. L. (1983). *Inscape: A search for meaning.* Continuum Center, Oakland University.

5

Relationship Transitions

In this chapter, we use our case example and current literature to understand the transition model when working with relationship transitions. We discuss different types of transitions involving changes in family and other interpersonal relationships. Across relationship transitions, recurring issues include intimacy, belonging, and mattering. Changes involve role gains and role losses, and culture is a key consideration when working intentionally with our clients. Discussion includes issues and examples related to situation, self, support, and strategies. A "Coping Keys Worksheet" is included as an informal assessment regarding coping strategies that may modify the situation, change the meaning of a situation, and/or manage reactions to stressful relationship transitions.

Case Study

The first client you are seeing today is Cassandra Mitchell. All you know about Ms. Mitchell from the intake interviewer is that she is 48 years old, divorced, and has been a small-business owner for many years. Her shop, currently closed, offered unique gifts for decorating, specializing in high-end glassware and products from Sweden and Norway. She appears downcast, although she is dressed nicely, in slacks and a matching sweater set, with a brightly colored scarf draped around her shoulders. As soon as you introduce yourself and explain a little bit about how you work, Ms. Mitchell insists that you call her Cassie and launches into the following story:

It is difficult to come here today, to have to admit that I need help. I have been so proud of my independence and have also been so invested in "running my own show" with my shop for so many years. I was once married and managed to carve out a new path after an excruciating divorce. I took the opportunity to establish my shop, and through this venture, I gained many meaningful relationships from within the community—other business owners, community organizations, and my customers.

I have worked all my life, beginning with a teaching career. I enjoyed teaching music and also providing private music lessons out of my home. Opening the store was the perfect path for a "fresh start" after the divorce. Over the years, I built a base of regular customers, many who became friends. I also collaborated with the local Humane Society to raise money with seasonal-giving events in my store and by participating in their fundraising efforts. While I have experienced some ups and downs with the store over the years, the most recent downturn was just too much to take. Although a painful decision, I moved forward with a "going out of business" sale and closed my store for good. Although this has been financially manageable because I have good retirement savings, the loss of connections has been very painful. I have a wonderful church community, but during the pandemic, parishioners have not been attending in person. I live a distance outside of town, and because we are socially distancing, I have not seen most of my friends in months. I tend to be on the "more careful" end of the spectrum, due to my asthma and being older, I have not been anywhere other than the grocery store and outdoor church services on occasion. Also, I am very concerned about my mother, who just turned 93 years old. She lives in an assisted living facility, and keeping myself free of Covid-19 is the only way I can stay ready to possibly see her if and when they allow visitors again. I have always been very close to her, and she has experienced a noticeable decline since the shutdowns. This has created a well of grief that I sometimes try to avoid by working on my home projects and focusing on being with my two rescue dogs and my cat.

I recently learned that a close relative has died from Covid-19, and this leaves me feeling at loose ends, with no funeral or way to say goodbye with my family. My two siblings live out of state, and there is no way they would have risked coming in, even if there were a funeral. My aunt's death has hit me harder than I would have expected. While she was very dear to me, it seems like "something bigger" with all the suffering in the world today. Like I said, it is hard to ask for help, but I have been struggling and haven't really shared any of this inner turmoil with anyone. Everything just feels so unsettling. I am hoping you can help me sort through some of these feelings and feel better. I want the old upbeat me back!

Although Cassie is describing both a work and an internal transition, it seems clear to the counselor that her primary issue has to do with changes in her relationships. It is often the case with adults that transitions in work and relationships can overlap and happen concurrently. Given what we know about adult development, it it is understandable that Cassie is feeling unsettled. She has experienced a number of transitions in recent years—being divorced, opening and then later closing her business, and giving up her accustomed roles and routines. The transition she is currently grappling with encompasses existential loss, combined with changes in the world at large. The most salient issues seem to be changes in her identity, her relationships, as well as the recent death of her aunt. We would take note of her describing her "well of grief" about her elderly mother, indicating that she may be experiencing profound sadness about her mother, along with changes in her ability to maintain a caregiving relationship with her. In working with Cassie, it would be important to explore these issues at deeper levels and also address her isolation and resistance to seeking out help. This would include discussing sources of support to meet her needs, especially being a single, older woman living alone. If she were our client, we would help her to process her losses, make meaning of her situation, and develop strategies using the transition model to assess her resources and deficits across the 4 S's (situation, self, support, and strategies).

In terms of the situation, Cassie's transition decision to close her store was made in response to the economic downturn due to the Covid-19 pandemic. The connections that she describe are mostly related to her former work setting and are now on hold. With respect to self, we could help her explore her feelings and core values, tapping into her internal resources. On the surface, she seems to be relatively healthy and insightful, and she has demonstrated resilience in overcoming difficult times in the past. She mentioned her church family and we could discuss her spirituality and sense of belonging, especially as these relate to her future aspirations and sense of purpose.

In this chapter, we first discuss various types of relationship transitions, of which Cassie's is only one example, that bring adults to counseling. We then review the major recurring issues relevant to relationship transitions: intimacy, belonging, and mattering. In the final section, we consider ways to use the transition model to help us evaluate Cassie's case and those of other adults navigating relationship transitions. Throughout this chapter, it is important to remember Howard's (1978) statement: "The trouble we take to arrange ourselves in some semblance of families is one of the most imperishable habits of the human race" (p. 15). Although definitions of what constitutes a family change over time, differ from one culture to another, or can be a *family of choice,* family units are the basic units of society.

TYPES OF TRANSITIONS

One of the most common reasons adults seek counseling is that they are contemplating, experiencing, or having trouble adapting to transitions involving family or other close relationships. Often clients lend support to Bridges's (2004) view that transitions begin with endings, as we are more apt to hear about relationships that are in peril, needing to be renegotiated or already over, than about new loves.

As counselors, we may be asked to help our clients sort out their feelings about the unpredictability of family relationships today. Families come in many different shapes and sizes; there is no longer a "typical" family. For example, young girls, some married, many not, have babies during their teenage years, while other women delay childbearing until their late 30s or 40s. Therefore, first-time grandparents can be in their 40s or 70s. An increasing number of adults, most often but not always women, are responsible for parent care. But, once again, there is no specified age at which this occurs, no designated length of time that pinpoints how long parent care is necessary.

Today, multigenerational families are common, and the current pandemic has made moving in with family an economic necessity for many. As people live longer and the number of generations is extended, the potential also increases for many years of closeness and changes across relationships. The following is a discussion of some of the more common transitions involving close interpersonal relationships.

Partnering Relationships

Most people yearn for and value an intimate relationship, and whether marital, cohabitating, or romantic union, these relationships become a defining feature of our lives. Relationships inevitably go through ups and down, sometimes stressful, sometimes supportive, often both (Umberson et al., 2015). For many adults, having a committed relationship is a primary life goal. This relationship, if obtained, may be marked by satisfaction and/or conflict requiring continuous renegotiation.

For other individuals who seek counseling, a basic concern is, "Will I ever find the kind of partner I want?" and more significant, "What will happen to me if I don't?" As adults contemplate marriage or other committed relationships, they may ask transition-related questions such as, "How will my life change?" or "He wants me to move across the country, but how do I know if I can manage without all the supports I have here?" "We both have good jobs, but in different cities. Can we manage a commuter relationship?" One of the authors worked with a midlife woman whose daughter had recently married. Although married over a year, the daughter was still living at home with her parents; she had not yet lived with her husband because he was immediately shipped out to Afghanistan following their wedding. This mother was tearful as she said that her daughter would be leaving soon for Germany, where her husband would now be stationed. This example points to how transitions related to marriage and committed relationships may involve other family members as well.

Different value systems can create serious problems around the decision to marry. A woman recently said, "I think we should live together for a while before we marry, but he says his family will disown him if we do." Her desire for a trial period reflects her concern about not wanting to make a decision without being really sure, while his reluctance may stem from family or religious scruples about living together "out of wedlock." Cohabitation is increasingly being viewed as an option for couples in the United States, and regardless of how these arrangements are defined, cohabitating is a decision that involves many factors, including values and goals for the future. Research, however, indicates that many of these relationships end before marriage, although the reasons for this are unclear. Marriage is recognized legally by the state, and cohabitation is not. Another significant difference is that cohabiting individuals may hold different views regarding their relationship (Qu et al., 2009). A client of one of the authors was a single woman in her 60s who determined that she needed a prenuptial agreement before marrying for the second time. When she consulted an attorney, he encouraged her to just "live with the man" to reduce her financial risks if she should ever be admitted to a nursing home. Her attorney could have seen this possibility as a valid risk, considering the man was also in his 60s and dealing with an illness. This client, however, could not see herself doing this, especially with her adult children, their spouses, and her grandchildren involved. Counselors must remember to consider clients' values when assisting with decision-making around marriage, cohabitation, and other partnering relationships. Same-sex couples have somewhat recently obtained the right to marry in the United States and in many, but not all, other countries. The same issues being discussed apply whether or not the couple is of the same or different genders. Increasing awareness of and acceptance of nonbinary and transgender individuals has led to a greater understanding of the manifold variations of couples and families.

Various problems within marriage have been attributed to differing values between partners, and some scholars have hypothesized that couples who experience greater between-spouse dissimilarity could expect a reasonable amount of "trouble" in their intimate relationship (Collins, 2000). This view of partner dissimilarities emphasizes the potential for cognitive dissonance, with individuals feeling that they might be wrong in their beliefs or that something is amiss in their partner. Another concern is that these couples may experience incongruence regarding their differing expectations (Clarkwest, 2007). Issues of dissimilarity may be a salient issue for couples who come for counseling, and this is especially relevant for diverse couples. Examples of dissimilarities include differences in gender-role expectations, religiosity, educational attainment, age, and socioeconomic status.

Couples most often present for counseling when they are experiencing problems in their relationship and "usually indicate a desire for reconciliation, renewal, and a rebirth of their relationship" (Ferloiro et al., 2010, p. 16). According to Ferloiro et al. (2010), it takes courage and strength to reconstruct a wounded relationship, and positive psychology can provide useful strategies to install hope and work toward a more positive future. These authors discuss the integration of five approaches: positive psychology, solution-focused brief therapy, circular questioning, reflexive questioning, and appreciative inquiry. Although a thorough discussion of marriage counseling approaches is beyond the scope of this chapter, much has been written about each of these approaches. Across these perspectives, the emphasis includes a positive and future-oriented foundation for therapeutic interventions.

Another relevant theoretical lens used with partners is attachment theory, which was first put forward by Bowlby (1973). Although attachment theory was initially applied with children, the basic assumptions apply to adult relationships as well. A key concept of Bowlby's theory relates to attachment styles (secure, avoidant, anxious-ambivalent) that organize people's interpersonal decisions and actions. Attachment styles also influence an individual's expectations, perceptions, thoughts, feelings, and behaviors that play out within their relationships. In a review of six studies, Mikulincer et al. (2010) concluded that attachment-anxious individuals tend to exhibit attitudinal ambivalence toward a romantic partner, along with ambivalence regarding closeness. Their findings also supported previous studies that suggest that people with an anxious attachment orientation tend to hold dichotomous views of their partners rather than having more integrated and realistic perceptions. When working with couples experiencing transitions, it is helpful to combine theoretical approaches to assess for assets and liabilities, both as individuals and as a partners in a committed relationship.

Divorce

Coping with divorce is one of life's most difficult transitions, and although statistics may paint a picture of the rising or falling of divorce rates, we meet our clients in their own unique situations. Divorce rates in America have been falling and hit a record low in 2019, with 14.9 marriages ending in divorce out of every 1,000 marriages. This drop in the divorce rate has become a persistent trend; however, so has the overall lower marriage rate (Institute for Family Studies, 2019). Although broad statistics can be helpful, a nuanced approach to discussing divorce is more meaningful. When considering both marriage and divorce rates, it is important to take into account generational differences and aspects of diversity. For example, millennials (age 24–39) are now the largest generation, and more racially and ethnically diverse than previous generations. Just less than half of millennials are married (46%), which is different from baby boomers (67%) at the same stage of life. They are taking a very different path than previous generations did, by delaying marriage or perhaps never marrying. Also, more married millennials have a spouse who is of a different racial or ethnic background than do members of other generations (Pew Research Center, 2019). A concerning factor is an emerging "marriage divide," with college-educated and economically better-off Americans more likely to marry and stay married and working-class and poor Americans facing more instability and high levels of singleness. According to 2018 Census data, 64% of those in the top third income bracket are in an intact marriage, compared to just 24% of Americans in the lower third income bracket (Institute for Family Studies, 2019).

Although overall rates are decreasing, divorce remains among the most painful of life's experiences. However, it is important to keep in mind that moving through this transition can also be a time for growth and renewal for adults as they reevaluate their lives, roles, and relationships. When working with our clients, we address gender-role expectations, which can be a powerful influence within families and cultures; internalized gender roles may be difficult to manage after the dissolution of a marriage (Anderson, 2016). While in what has been described as "the throes of divorce," clients are likely to describe a sense of failure. For some, the pain of rejection is uppermost in their minds; for others, the guilt over what they are doing to other people is paramount. What clients tell you may also depend on where they are in the process of the divorce transition. As noted, cultural beliefs, family history, and gender-role expectations are also important aspects of the client's experience of divorce, especially if the client is from a culture with few divorces. As an example, a woman living in the United States made the difficult decision to pursue divorce from her husband who remained in India. This had been an arranged marriage, and her dissatisfaction had deepened over the years, including her distress at her husband's unfaithfulness and physical abuse. Although it is not permitted in India for a woman to initiate a divorce, she was able to proceed with it in the United States. Her key concerns were how her immediate and extended family members would accept her decision.

Sometimes, we meet with clients grappling with the decision to divorce, and a relevant concept is the need for self-efficacy to navigate this transition (Mahmoodabadi & Zarei, 2018). One woman in her late 40s recently told a counselor, "My marriage is not fulfilling, and I yearn for the courage to leave. However, I worry about him, and how will I be able to cope with starting life all over again? Our children and grandchildren could also be heartbroken by this decision, and holidays will be so complicated." Another woman in her early 30s shared, "I think my husband is having an affair. Shall I confront him or just pretend that I don't know? Other men in our family have cheated, but no one has gotten a divorce. I am afraid the extended family will reject me if I cause any disruption." Both these women are grappling with a major decision as to whether to initiate a divorce, a transition that would ripple out to affect other family members. Both of these women could benefit from exploring their family relationships and examining their resources for coping, regardless of the decision they make.

Many studies have been conducted to examine people's reactions to separation and divorce. Montenegro (2004) investigated the experience of divorce and the impact of divorce on midlife adults. Although most of the participants were coping fairly well overall, many described the difficulties associated with their divorces. These difficulties included uncertainty (40%), loneliness or depression (29%), feelings of desertion or betrayal (25%), and a sense of failure (23%). Common fears included failing again, having financial troubles, and not finding someone to marry. Yet most of these participants seemed to be coping better than expected overall. A growing trend is what has been termed *gray divorce.* Men and women older than 70 years getting divorced presents its own unique set of challenges, psychological and financial, as well as those of relationships with children, grandchildren, and other family.

McDaniel and Coleman (2003) studied the impact of divorce on midlife women, examining the women's reactions across the different areas of their lives. The participants in the study were 45 to 51 years old and represented a variety of situational and contextual experiences. All had been divorced within the previous 13 months from a long-term (at least 14 years) first marriage. The researchers concluded that, for these women, resolving the emotional aspects of divorce was directly related to movement toward an autonomous identity. However, they also concluded that completing the psychic divorce is especially difficult for midlife women, as they tend to be emotionally attached to their husbands and their former roles. The employment histories of these women were also influential factors, not because of how much these women worked, but because of how much they had invested in their work as a career. Most of the children of these women were young adults, and although some women found support from their children, others experienced disapproval or estrangement from their children. Community aspects of the divorce varied as well, with some women losing much of their social networks and others finding support in their friends. These findings illustrate the various contexts and issues we may hear about from our clients. As we listen, it is important to be mindful of the influence of culture, internalized family messages, and values as well. For example, one of the women in this study was having a particularly difficult time adjusting to herself as a single woman. She identified as a woman of strong Catholic faith and expressed that her religious beliefs were making it nearly impossible to see herself as both Catholic and divorced. Another client shared that she went to consult with her parish priest regarding her divorce from an abusive husband. Although the priest expressed compassion regarding her situation, he also made it clear that, while she was welcome to continue to be active in the church, she would "no longer be welcome to receive communion." She had since stopped attending mass and stated that she felt "unmoored without a faith community." As we help clients sort through their feelings, beliefs, and values, we also explore the resources available to our clients as they make the decision or adjust to the reality of a divorce. This client found another denomination where she felt welcome, yet her mixed feelings remained. This example provides a nuanced view of assets (new connections and resources) and liabilities (feeling adrift from her primary faith community).

A key area related to resources includes the real and perceived risks associated with a decision. Light and Ahn (2010) examined the decision to divorce and the levels of risk tolerance of the participants. Findings supported that divorce entails a greater risk for women, especially with the potential risk of economic loss of income. The researchers stated that risk tolerance is an important determinant of women's decision to divorce, with the most risk-tolerant women being more likely to divorce. As we explore the potential risks to our clients, cognizant that the risks may be higher for women in general, we cannot assume this to be the case. Clients will often talk about potential risks in terms of fears. A thoughtful exploration of our client's perceptions of the risks and resources required for coping, regardless of gender, is important for clients as they sort out a decision that will affect their lives across many of their life/career roles.

As counselors, we see more couples in interracial marriages, an aforementioned trend that continues to increase dramatically. When clients come in individually and discuss their marriage, we cannot make assumptions regarding the race and/or culture of their partner. One client talked at length about her partner without discussing his race. Later, in the interview, she discussed the issues her daughter was having at school as a biracial child. Although the number of interracial marriages is a relatively new phenomenon, few studies have provided theory and guidance on this issue. However, Zhang and Van Hook (2009) conducted a study to examine the stability of interracial marriages involving Whites with Blacks, Asians, and Hispanics, and their results supported that as a whole, interracial marriages are less stable than endogamous marriages. The Black husband–White wife pairings in their study were found to be the least stable and, according to these researchers, this could be a reflection of racism and distrust that is directed toward Black men in the United States. They cited Yancey (2007), who indicated that Whites who married Blacks experienced more firsthand racism as compared to Whites who married other non-Black minorities. The issues facing our clients as individuals and as partners in an interracial marriage may involve feeling marginalized and experiencing discrimination. This is an important area of awareness for helping professionals, especially in challenging their own biases and pushing themselves beyond their own cultural encapsulation. Counseling interracial couples requires knowledge of potential strengths and risk factors and also great sensitivity when working with the unique couple seeking help.

Widowhood

Much has been written about the major life transition of widowhood. The authors of books for the bereaved person, such as *Living with an Empty Chair* (Ternes, 1984) and *How to Survive the Loss of a Love* (Colgrove et al., 1991), as well as books for professionals (e.g., Worden, 2009) discuss the devastation and mix of intense feelings that may be experienced and of the fear felt by many that they must be going crazy, the pain they feel is so intense. According to Worden (2009), although not everyone experiences the same intensity of pain in the same way, the newly bereaved often feel unprepared to deal with the sheer force of their emotions following a loss. Didion's (2005) especially moving memoir of grief, *The Year of Magical Thinking*, provides an intensely personal experience of loss following the death of her husband of

40 years. She describes a life-changing event occurring on an "ordinary day." She was mixing a salad at one moment, lighting the candles, and moments later found her husband sitting motionless in a chair. He was pronounced dead shortly after. She was suddenly propelled into a grief that came in waves, along with what she termed *magical thinking*, which she described as a dislocation of "body and mind" that brings a sense of alienation and disorientation. For example, she couldn't get rid of his shoes, because he needed them to come back to her. Didion's honest portrayal of her grief process was her way of giving meaning to the experience and provides us with a personal account of the impact of grief.

Well-known English author C. S. Lewis (1976) wrote a poignant and insightful commentary on his experience of grief when his wife died of cancer. Lewis had been a confirmed bachelor until he married Joy Davidman, an American divorced woman with two small children. They shared four years of marriage before her death. The book is actually his journal, a personal expression of his journey through the process of grief. At an early point in his grieving, he wrote that "her absence is like the sky, spread over everything" (p. 11). He also described the meaning of his marriage when he wrote that most precious gift marriage gave him was the constant impact of "something very close and intimate yet all the time unmistakably other, resistant—in a word, real" (p. 20). This relates to how close relationships can make us feel "real" as we are invested in the process of discovering and defining ourselves within these relationships. This could also speak to how "unreal" life can seem when we lose someone very close, especially a partner who has shared so many aspects of our lives. Lewis also described grief as a process and compared it to a long, winding valley, where "any bend may reveal a totally new landscape," which speaks to the experience of grief and how moving through it is like navigating a new terrain.

When William Bridges wrote his book, *The Way of Transition: Embracing Life's Most Difficult Moments,* he had just lost his wife of 35 years to cancer. While he has spent his lifelong work helping others navigate transitions, this loss propelled him into the profound sorrow of loss. He described the difficult task of letting go, stating that "we don't let go of anything important until we have exhausted all possible ways that we might keep holding on to it" (2001, p. 58). With the loss of a spouse, he stated that as he moved through the grief, it became clear to him that what had been lost was "not just our relationship, but also all the hopes, fears, dreams and beliefs that had been connected with our relationship" (p. 58). He described his life in retrospect with his wife, stating "*that life* was the dream and her death the waking" (p. 157). He described the trigger as her diagnosis, and he gave voice to the nuances of grief, touching on areas that we may explore with our clients.

Counselors hear statements such as "I don't think I can live without him" or "We always thought I'd die first." This is not an unusual reaction on the part of widowers as both demographics and conventional wisdom show that wives usually outlive their husbands. A review of research supports the belief that generally men suffer more than women following bereavement (Stroebe et al., 2001). Early studies by Neugarten (1968) indicated that a major difference between the sexes is that women are more likely to rehearse for widowhood. This has been attributed both to differences in life expectancies and to the greater emphasis women put on connectedness in their thinking about and planning their lives (Gilligan, 1982). However, Elwert and Christakis (2006) discussed the *Widowhood Effect*, which refers to a postmarriage state entailing both benefits and losses. Positive lasting effects of marriage may include financial contributions from the husband, whereas the transition to widowhood requires adjustment to losses around changed social roles. An interesting finding by Bennett (2005), however, disputed the emphasis on gender, reporting that the more recent the widowhood, the more reduced the morale, social engagement, and psychological well-being of the bereaved. Another key influence was age at the time of bereavement, with increased age also associated with poorer psychological well-being.

It is clear that widowhood is experienced differently by individuals depending on context and impact, and sometimes this begins before the death of a spouse. Clients whose spouses are suffering from a long-term serious disability are clearly grieving but may be unclear about "how to do it." One woman whose husband had a serious stroke and was unable to talk said, "I know I'm grieving, but I'm not sure for what." There are no clear rituals, such as funerals, to assist people in this limbo status, so counselors may want to help clients develop their own. Bonanno et al. (2004) suggested that the factors surrounding one's loss are crucial to how people grieve over the death of their spouse. An unexpected finding was that participants evidenced depression before the loss followed by marked improvement after the spouse's death. For these caregivers of chronically ill partners, the death was experienced as the end of a chronic stressor. *Chronic sorrow* is a term created to describe a distinct grief reaction that occurs when loss is not final but continues to be present in the life of the griever. This type of chronic sorrow has become characteristic of a growing number of older individuals who provide long-term care for a spouse or partner with progressive disability. One woman in this situation described herself as a "widow in waiting." Widowed clients come with unique reactions of grief, depression, and anxiety associated with chronic sorrow, and interventions for these clients require sensitivity (Rossheim & McAdams, 2010).

For many, grief has been exaggerated by Covid-19. Often family have not been able to be with the dying person; in addition, normal funeral rituals have been cancelled or postponed. This can add to regrets about the passing of a spouse or other loved one, becoming an aspect of "unfinished business" around the sense that something was left unsaid or undone. It is important to periodically reassess bereavement-related regrets, along with other aspects of the continued relationship with the deceased and design interventions designed to facilitate resolution of these issues (Holland et al., 2013).

A principal role of counselors in working with widowed persons and people whose spouses are severely disabled is to assure them of the normality of their intense and often vacillating feelings. A wise counselor we know advised one of the authors regarding her recent widowhood, "Anything you feel is normal." However, it is also important to assess the grief reactions of our clients, especially in terms of complicated grief. The term *complicated grief* refers to grief-related symptoms that persist beyond a time frame that is considered adaptive. These symptoms may include chronic separation distress, loneliness, preoccupation with thoughts of the deceased, and symptoms of traumatic distress, such as feelings of disbelief, mistrust, anger, shock, and detachment from others (Lobb et al., 2010). When working with grief reactions, it can be helpful to facilitate the process of meaning reconstruction, which includes sensemaking, benefit finding, and progressive identity change. Currier et al. (2006) found that although objective facts regarding a death make a difference, the survivor's interpretation of the loss is the more influential factor in grief responses. Making sense of the loss can be done in personal, practical, existential, and/or spiritual terms, depending on the client (Neimeyer et al., 2010).

Some widowed persons complain that they are being ignored, or they hesitantly express resentment that everybody else seems to be just going along with their lives. At the approach of one holiday season, a widow asked with much pathos, "Will I ever be happy again?" When confronted with such questions, counselors may be able to help widowed persons see that although they will never be their "old selves" again, they can become reasonably comfortable "new selves."

Alternatively, other widows may express feelings such as "I'm tired of people feeling sorry for me. I guess I should be grateful, but I can't stand it when people talk to me as if my life must be over." A widowed friend recently explained, "Sure, I miss Joe, but I really do have a full life now, with many friends and interests."

Studies on widowhood report various findings regarding widowhood and social networks. For example, Utz et al. (2002) and Ha (2008) found an increase for widows in informal social participation with friends, neighbors, or relatives. These increases in support following widowhood were observed at an elevated level for 3 years before beginning to decrease to prewidowhood levels (Guiaux et al., 2007). Widowhood is a profound transition that influences social networks and interactions. The timing of this transition can bring different issues relating to family, friends, and social connections. For example, an 85-year-old client once described how difficult it was to have so many of her friends and relatives die in recent years. She stated, "Everyone is gone, and I never thought I would outlast everyone. … That's what's so hard about getting old." She found support in her grown children and grandchildren, yet these interactions were limited by work schedules and the fact that the grandchildren lived in different states and came to visit infrequently. Another woman lived near her children and grandchildren yet could not see them due to the children being in school during the pandemic and her need to be mindful of her underlying health conditions. Her adult children insisted that contact was not worth the risk and supplemented with FaceTime and phone calls. However, the loss she experienced while not being able to be with her family was significant.

Each of our clients comes in with unique personal histories, strengths and limitations, and supports related to becoming widowed. Worden (2009) concluded that, even though mourning tasks apply to all death losses, how an individual approaches and adapts to these tasks can be quite varied. He emphasized the importance of also understanding *the mediators of mourning,* referring to a wide range of behaviors and reactions. Differences among widowed persons may reflect not only their personal styles but also the social context in which they live. Comparative studies of widows in different communities in the United States and Canada revealed immense variation in social roles, support systems, lifestyles, and self-concepts (Lopata, 1987). A major role of counselors may be to listen carefully for information about those aspects of a widowed person's life. Such attention may provide clues, for example, as to whether the person's primary need is for self-esteem building, help in finding or utilizing informal supports, or referral to formal community resources.

Culture also plays a prominent role in the process of grieving, and although grieving may be similar across cultures, there can be striking differences. For example, a study was conducted on grieving Zulu widows in South Africa, and researchers found many similarities of these impoverished women with widows from economically developed countries. These widows found support, especially with the traditional norms in KwaZulu-Natal of sharing, so nobody goes hungry. However, it was also likely these widows would be avoided and feared as someone who performs witchcraft, thus making it harder to receive support (Rosenblatt & Nkosi, 2007). Although, as counselors, we may not have an opportunity to work with widows from South Africa, this example points to the prominence culture can have in the process of grieving.

Members of some social groups in the United States may effectively be deprived of services because they do not understand their availability and/or do not think it appropriate to ask for such assistance. In this situation, as in many others, counselors working with individuals from a different cultural group than their own need to educate themselves about that culture, refer the client to a counselor more familiar with that group, or else seek consultation. Also, unique barriers can be faced by same-sex partners who may experience increased feelings of isolation and exclusion, and existing models of partner bereavement may not provide frameworks when seeking to understand the experiences of widowed same-sex partners (Ingham et al., 2017).

Remarriage

For some widowed persons, particularly those who have spent many years in caregiving, the idea of remarriage holds no appeal. For others, it may be a primary goal or emerge as a surprising opportunity. Counselors may hear comments ranging from "I hate the thought of living the rest of my life alone, but how can a woman my age ever find another husband?" to "My wife has only been dead 3 months, but I really want to get married again. What will people say? What will the children think?" Divorced persons often talk about being "gun shy" or fearful of making "another mistake."

Gender differences with respect to remarriage are significant. A frequent finding in the literature on remarriage is that women are more likely than men to be widowed and are less likely to subsequently remarry. An explanation that has been proposed is the longer life span of women, along with a tendency for men to marry women younger than they are. This results in a larger pool of potential spouses for men. An alternative explanation is that marriage may benefit men more than it does women (Moorman et al., 2006). For many men, particularly those whose business responsibilities involve entertaining or whose ability or willingness to perform household tasks is limited, the thought of being without a wife may be too difficult to contemplate. Given the high ratio of widows to widowers among most social groups in this country, such men may be able to find another wife with relative ease. Women seeking remarriage may need to take more dramatic steps. One woman we know who was widowed in her 40s thought about where she had the best chance of finding a second husband and decided to take flying lessons. She was indeed the only woman in her piloting class, and her quests for a pilot's license and a husband were both successful.

In a study of 4,449 adults, aged 55 to 89, researchers in the Netherlands concluded that repartnering is a stressful life event that is incompletely institutionalized. They reported that more repartnered older adults choose unmarried cohabitation than remarriage. When these partners came together, their social networks expanded more than those of separated older adults. Yet the quality of the relationships with their children was negatively affected. Those who opted for unmarried cohabitation tended to have the weakest bonds with their children (De Jong Gierveld & Peeters, 2003). Although these findings may be informative of potential family issues, each family is unique regarding its assets and liabilities when adapting to changes within family relationships. Reactions of adult children may vary, both with cohabitation and remarriage.

A growing interest in the literature is the effect of remarriage on adult stepchildren. Clinical observations suggest an increase in the number of adults coming to counseling while they try to adjust to their parent's remarriage

Whether their clients are divorced or widowed, counselors may hear a variety of questions—logistical, emotional, and financial—relating to remarriage; for example, "How will we deal with all those children and grandchildren? How will we decide where to spend vacations and holidays?" "Do we live in his house, my house, or start all over?" "How do we deal with the 'exes'?" Sometimes, emotional and economic issues may be interwoven: "He says he loves me, but I'm worried he is really just interested in my money." "I'm not sure I love him but he could certainly support me and make the rest of my life more comfortable." "Will she think I don't trust her if I ask for a prenuptial agreement?" In many such discussions, counselors can help concerned clients explore their values, their resources, and their deficits. Discussions of the meaning of life may also come into play with respect to transitions involving a very different relationship, that of parenting.

Parenting Issues

Parenting, such as many other intimate relationships, can be a source of utter delight or unbelievable frustration. Counselors work with clients dealing with a host of issues, such as whether or not to have children, how custody should be arranged, or what child-rearing techniques are most effective. Parents of older children may have questions about how to encourage children to leave home or whether to allow them to return. Sometimes, parents wonder how to deal with their disappointment over nonevents, such as when children do not do what the parents expected.

All such decisions are complicated by the fact that many people and many dimensions of a person's life are affected. Consider the dilemma of a woman on the fast track at work who says, "My husband really wants to start a family, but I know I'd have to be the one to stay home when the baby is sick. I'm not sure I'm willing to sacrifice my career." These types of decisions have been a core stressor for many families when children are required to be learning remotely from home rather than attending school in person. As mentioned in an earlier chapter, more women than men have left the workforce to take on the additional roles at home. The long-term impact on women's careers is yet to be known.

Counselors may hear considerable talk about the ticking of the biological clock. Some couples, particularly those with professional careers, may postpone childbearing, but there comes a time when partners must face questions like, "Do I really want to have children, and if I do, how will it change my life?" "If I don't, am I letting my parents down? I know they are eager to become grandparents." "If I decide now not to have children, will I be sorry later?" Sometimes, the difficulty of the decision is masked with humor, "If we have a baby and then change our minds, can we return it to the store within 5 years?" The decision as to whether or not to have children may be one of the few irrevocable decisions many people ever make.

For some groups, the decision about parenting may be especially difficult. It is challenging for many people in the current socioeconomic context to make the commitment to having a child. For those who are unemployed or underemployed, the decision to postpone having children may be dictated by economic realities. Also, diverse couples may experience more complexity when making a decision to have children. For example, counselors working with gay or lesbian clients may hear statements like, "Just because I'm gay doesn't mean I wouldn't make a good parent," "I'm thinking about fathering a child for my lesbian friend who wants to be a mother," or "My partner and I really want to raise a child together. We're trying to decide whether one of us should be artificially inseminated or whether we should look for a baby to adopt. Apart from the logistics of how to do it, we wonder whether it would be fair to the child. What would its friends think?"

If an individual or a couple decides to have or adopt a baby, it is only the first of many transitions they will face. Kimmel (1990) summarized a number of studies on the impact of becoming parents and found such a step to be a profound transition, leading to changes in individuals' views of themselves as well as the couple's relationship. As clients approach the transition to parenthood, it is helpful to explore the changes that may affect the individuals and their relationship. Issues related to culture, gender roles, and expectations as parents can be addressed by exploring the unique context and impact on the couple's lives. As counselors, we must remain sensitive to individual reactions to the experience of pregnancy and becoming a parent. Although most children are born healthy, it is an unfortunate reality that some couples may experience a complicated pregnancy, a miscarriage, or even the death of their newborn child. These types of events are often unanticipated, and the transition itself can become a nonevent transition. Nonevent transitions are discussed more fully in Chapter 8, with suggestions for strategies and interventions.

Another area we address in our counseling offices is issues related to unmarried parents with children. According to the National Vital Statistics Reports (2018), nonmarital childbearing continues to trend downward. This could relate to overall lower birth rates; according to 2018 demographics, birth rates were down 2%, the fourth year of declining number of births. Teenage births rates, aged 15 to 19, also declined by 7%, with an overall decline of 58% since 2007. Also, the mean age of mothers at first birth was 26.9, which reflects a trend to women becoming mothers at older ages. The births to unmarried women also declined in 2018, with a percentage of 39.6%, the lowest level since 2007. Although these numbers provide helpful information, our clients present issues unique to their situations. Although we cannot make assumptions about our clients, it is important to recognize that many of the children of unmarried parents live below (or just above) the poverty line and receive little or no financial or emotional support from their nonresident parents. As counselors, we need to be informed about child-support policies and other legal issues that affect our clients and their roles as parents.

An issue often presented to counselors involves the legal custody of children. Most research has focused on the experience of single parents, and there has been increased attention to the plight of noncustodial fathers. Yet there is little research regarding a growing phenomenon of mothers who lose custody of their children due to separation and divorce (Kruk, 2010). According to Eicher-Catt (2004), the social context includes no parameters that legitimize noncustodial mothers as parents, and these mothers tend to be perceived by others and by themselves as an anomaly. A qualitative study (Kruk, 2010) was conducted as an exploratory inquiry, rooted in grounded theory and feminist practice principles. Each of the 14 women in this study had lost custody of their children to their former partners after separation. The primary theme across these women's stories was the impact of broken attachment to children and the resulting experiences of shock, denial, anger, and profound sadness. These mothers acutely felt the absence of their children in their lives and also were concerned about their children feeling abandoned by their mothers.

It is interesting that although these mothers were the subject of allegations of parental unfitness by their former partners, none of the allegations were substantiated. Yet they were judged harshly in court. Some were judged for fleeing a violent household with their children, whereas others were judged for remaining in the home and not doing enough to protect the children from an abusive partner. In some cases, mothers were considered too career-minded, spending too much time at work, and in other cases, mothers were seen as irresponsible for not working outside the home and providing for their children financially. Many of these mothers experienced the internalization of these judgments and a damaged self-concept in the face of the legal, medical, and educational systems' judgments of them as unworthy. This study highlights the painful stories that we often hear as counselors. This also speaks to the importance of advocacy for our clients as they grapple with institutional challenges with courts, laws, and systems. Although this study indicates the unfair and painful situation of women, this situation is not necessarily gender specific. For all clients required to relinquish their parenting roles, we must be available to sit with their pain while providing interventions to improve coping through bolstering their support and strategies. For example, an interesting newsletter designed for fathers addresses both custodial and noncustodial dads with support, advice, and general sharing (email Allan@dadvocacyconsultinggroup.com).

The myriad of child-rearing issues that arise for married couples, single parents, divorced couples, and extended families are beyond the scope of this book. Issues, such as finding appropriate day care, selecting schools, permitting dating, or fostering healthy sibling relationships, are often the subjects adults in transition most want to discuss. Counselors of adults are likely to hear about the triumphs and travails experienced by their clients in their role as parents, and, life not being tidy, such experiences undoubtedly affect other aspects of their clients' lives.

Grandparenting Issues

For most people, becoming a grandparent is an exciting and heartwarming experience. For others, however, it may be an unwanted confrontation with their own aging or a mark of their children's "problems." Becoming a grandparent serves as a reminder of the continuity of the generations and provides an opportunity, to varying extents, to again help shape a young life. Conversely, the realization that one will not become a grandparent may be a prime example of a ripple nonevent (Schlossberg & Robinson, 1993). When an adult child informs their parents about a decision not to or an inability to have children, this event can lead to unfulfilled expectations that alter the roles, relationships, and assumptions of the older person. A very disappointed "nongrandparent" may need to discuss this sadness.

Grandparenthood has become a focal point for researchers who have investigated its psychological dimensions, including social roles, legal rights following a divorce, and the impact of grandparenthood on mental and physical health. Some have described grandparenthood as a tenuous role that lacks clear, agreed-on behavior norms. Yet others have stated that grandparents typically have many preconceived ideas and expectations regarding becoming a grandparent and, furthermore, that younger family members have expectations of grandparents as well (Thomas et al., 2000). Grandparenting is especially interesting because it is one of the few roles for which people do not control the onset or timing (Reitzes, 2020). Reactions to becoming a grandparent may depend in part upon the ages and life situations of the newborn's parents as well as the life situation of the grandparent. For example, this may come at an ideal time, combined with more focus on family in retirement, or present an increase of responsibilities related to assisting with and/or raising grandchildren.

The clinical implications of grandparenthood were examined in several studies. Although increases in psychological well-being have been seen with grandparenthood in the traditional mode, grandparents may experience negative outcomes when they assume custody of grandchildren. This is a difficult transition, and these grandparents often experience ambivalence about the role along with conflicted dynamics with their adult child who has relinquished the parenting responsibilities. In fact, these grandparents have rates of depression that are higher than average. When their own children are abusive, incarcerated, or too ill to care for their own children, these grandparents' difficulties tend to multiply. Low-income grandparents are at particular risk of decreases in physical and emotional health (Thomas et al., 2000).

The phenomenon of grandparents raising grandchildren has captured the interest of the popular press and become the focus for support groups. *Family Circle* magazine frequently profiles "women who make a difference." One such profile (Waters, 1994) quoted a woman who captured the situation thus: "I felt guilty when some of my kids got on drugs. But now I'm gonna save my grandson." Across the United States, more than 2.7 million grandparents are raising grandchildren. Support is a definite need, with 33% of these grandparents not having graduated from high school, and one fifth having incomes that fall below the poverty line. More than 40% of children being cared for by a grandparent are with them due to at least one parent's substance abuse, and 28% of the children have been victims of abuse, abandonment, or neglect from their parents. Although this can be a long and difficult journey for all concerned, additional resources in the community are crucial for needed support (Father Matters, 2017).

Paradoxically, as more people become grandparents, the role becomes even less clear. Today's grandparents range in age from 30 to older than 100, and their grandchildren may be newborn or themselves retired. Some grandparents live with or very close to their grandchildren; others may be across the country or the world. One woman we know stopped complaining about her grandchildren being 300 miles away when she met a couple whose grandchildren were 3,000 miles away! Cherlin and Furstenberg (1992) identified three styles of grandparenting: companionate, remote, and involved. Companionate grandparents are affectionate but somewhat passive in their behavior. They clearly see the child's parents as "in charge." Remote grandparents are geographically distant and thus have difficulty establishing intimate relationships with their grandchildren. Involved grandparents, in their terminology, are those who engage in active parenting. This style tends to emerge at times of crisis or transition, such as after the child's parents' divorce. If the children's mother is forced to devote more time and energy to earning a living, the grandparent may take over more of the child-rearing responsibilities.

Not infrequently, grandparents may be asked by divorced children, usually daughters, if they may move back home. So-called "boomerang" children, with or without children of their own, clearly represent a lifestyle transition for all generations involved, and this may trigger a request for counseling. These types of living arrangements are likely sharply rising during the Covid-19 pandemic and may involve generations living together, whether divorced on partnered. Alternatively, fear of infection and desire to protect older parents/grandparents, has also led to *less* contact among grandparents and grandchildren. Add to this the difficulty or danger of travel and the fact that frequency of in-person contact has often been greatly diminished. Zoom is not the same as a hug.

Another issue that may bring grandparents to counseling is concern about losing contact with grandchildren. When parents divorce, grandparents on the noncustodial side, typically the father's parents, may find it difficult to maintain close relations with their grandchildren. After hearing rumblings about a separation or divorce in the family, a grandparent may tell a counselor, "I'm devastated for them, and from a selfish point of view I'm terrified I'll lose contact with my grandchildren." Myers and Perrin (1993) noted, "To the extent that grandparents are denied access to grandchildren as a result of divorce, they may experience difficulty in resolving their own developmental issues, feel a sense of dissatisfaction with their lives, or feel that some part of themselves is missing or incomplete" (p. 64).

Counselors may help grandparents concerned about losing contact with their grandchildren by suggesting legal assistance, support groups, or appropriate reading material. In recognition of legal battles that may arise, grandparent-rights provisions are written into some divorce settlements. Some self-help groups provide information and support for people who fear or experience a major interruption in their relationship with the grandchildren.

Counselors may hear of mixed feelings and value conflicts from people who become grandparents under nontraditional circumstances. One of our clients almost furtively showed pictures of a grandchild she yearned to hold but felt reluctant to visit because the child's parents were not married. On the other hand, there are grandparents who have a close relationship with the child of their gay son and a cordial relationship with the child's mother, who lives with her lesbian partner. In many families, grandchildren as well as their parents may be highly involved in elder care, an important relationship issue to which we now turn.

Eldercare

Caring for the elderly may involve *informal caregivers* (i.e., unpaid family member, friend, neighbor) or *formal caregivers* (paid care in a home or residential care facility). According to the The National Alliance for Caregiving (NAC), there has been an increase in the number of unpaid family caregivers in the United States, with an increase of 9.5 million caregivers from 2015 to 2020. The most recent report indicates that family caregivers now total 53 million, encompassing more than one in five Americans (NAC, 2020). For many midlife adults, the realization that they are or may soon be responsible for caring for their parents can constitute a major life transition. Often the realization is triggered by the parent's sudden illness, which typically comes as a shock. For example, a caregiver daughter was suddenly informed that her mother had broken her hip and an ambulance was on the way to her apartment, where she had been taking care of her husband after he experienced a series of strokes. To see her mother in the hospital in such a helpless situation was shocking, especially when she had previously been doing so well. As a result of the broken hip, other unanticipated ripple effects emerged, including a sharp decline in cognitive ability. Suddenly, this daughter became the principle caregiver for both her parents. Another whole arena of unexpected turns of events followed, often with the urgent need to learn about the physical, mental, and emotional repercussions that were facing her loved ones.

Becoming responsible for one's parents can radically change one's roles, responsibilities, and assumptions about oneself. Although most of us "know" that America is graying and that many older adults need some kind of assistance, it is very different when the older adult is "ours." In dealing with issues of eldercare, counselors are likely to hear a range of feelings, including love and concern for the parent, grief over the anticipated death of a parent, guilt over not being able to do enough, resentment over the interruptions in their own plans, confusion about where they need to invest their energies, or despair at realizing the situation may be out of their control.

Expectations about caregiving may be strongly influenced by the cultural background of both informal and formal caregivers. The training director of a large nursing home in an urban area talked of the difficulties that staff and family members have in understanding each other's values. The staff, who are primarily African American or foreign born, come from a culture that expects family members to take in "their" frail older adults. Therefore, they assume that the families of the residents "don't really care" or else they would have their relatives at home. Many of the family members, most of whom are middle class and White, think they are making a good choice to give their relatives the best possible care and opportunities for socialization.

The baby boomers in midlife are frequently part of two-income households, and added caregiving demands can create a values conflict for our clients. It has been estimated that the number of employees with eldercare responsibilities range from 2% to 30%, with 20% as the most often cited figure (Shoptaugh et al., 2004). Traditionally, the vast majority of caregivers to the old have been women, primarily wives and daughters, and daughters have provided even more long-term care than spouses. A prevalent and powerful theme in previous studies is that almost all daughters and daughters-in-law accept the idea that parent care is a woman's role and that they have been responsible for performing the instrumental, personal care, and nursing tasks that are needed. These women often feel responsible for the emotional well-being of the older people. Indeed, they often felt responsible for the happiness of everyone in their families (Brody, 2004). In collecting data on the strains experienced by caregivers, Brody interviewed 1,500 women, 300 of their husbands, and 150 of their siblings. She noted that the women's problems were exacerbated by the persistent myth that adult children don't take care of their elderly parents the way they used to in the "good old days." "It is ironic that many of the parent-caring women themselves believe that myth ... even though they do much more parent care than their counterparts in the past." Counselors who hear clients berating themselves for not doing enough may find it helpful to confront this misconception. Another salient issue, as mentioned earlier, is that of role conflict as women strive to balance their work roles with caring for their elderly family members.

Although most caregivers are women, Silverstone (1994) cautioned that we should not ignore the problems of male caregivers. Husbands and other male relatives may find themselves "odd man out" in terms of the provision of services. This can become more of an issue for *only sons*. For example, an elderly client was happy to be traveling back and forth from Michigan to Florida, determined by the seasons of the year. She had rented a lovely apartment in Michigan and enjoyed this lifestyle immensely. However, with the worsening conditions brought about by Covid-19, she made the decision to stay permanently in Florida. Her lease was up in Michigan, so this was perfect timing, but it also required her son to travel from another state to go pack up all his mother's things and arrange for movers to store her furniture until a later date. Although this example does not involve eldercare in the classic sense, it illustrates the responsibilities that may fall on an adult caring for their parent's needs.

Although children, particularly daughters, assume major responsibilities for eldercare, not all older adults have children. Special strains may come from caring for a frail relative who is not one's parent. Nieces and nephews, for example, may care for a childless relative largely out of loyalty to their deceased parents. Although older women in this country greatly outnumber older men, this is not true for all ethnic groups. Because many Chinese and Filipino men came to this country and either left wives at home or never married, there are large numbers of childless older men among these groups who have special needs and problems (Markides & Mindel, 1987). In helping clients with issues of eldercare, counselors may need to supplement their usual counseling techniques by providing case management services or making appropriate referrals.

Clients involved in caregiving may also be concerned about the impact on the rest of the family. Cutler (1985) talked about the spread of distress within a family and particularly the effect on grandchildren when an older family member has dementia. "The relationship between grandparents and grandchildren is often a close and special one, and when 'Grandpa' begins to be short-tempered and inappropriate, it can be devastating for the grandchildren" (p. 53). When a grandparent becomes incapacitated or dies, midlife adults may need to cope with their own grief as well as be a support to their children.

Death of a Parent

In terms of grief, counselors may find midlife adults surprised and confused by the extent of their reactions to the death of a parent. "Why am I so devastated when we knew it was coming?" is a common question counselors may hear. In a study of the impact of parent death, Douglas (1990) found that most of her sample reported that the death of a parent changed their outlook on life. They confronted their own mortality, and at the same time, they grappled with feelings of being alone and orphaned. Respondents also noted that the death of a parent was often a trigger for personal growth as it inspired them to look more closely at their own lives and appreciate the relationships they had.

The experience of grief depends on many factors, as discussed earlier. And as with any experience with grief, it is both uniquely personal and universal. How one moves through the grieving process is dependent on one's personality, the relationship with the deceased, the manner in which the deceased died, our life stage, and other contextual factors (Lichtenberg, 2017). When working with clients, we need to be mindful that meaning-making, a major component of coping, can be compromised by "off time" transitions, for example, when someone was "too young to die." And we can all relate to hearing the shattering news that a young parent has died. Support for the family and community is crucial, and yet, "clinicians should be wary of those who have experienced grief giving advice or telling others how healing occurs" (Litchenberg, 2017, p. 102).

The death of a parent often involves becoming a witness to the dying process. This can be an intensely emotional experience and most always involves learning about the process and understanding how to best care for a loved one. Hospice organizations provide much-needed education, support, and counseling to grieving families. Their nurses and social workers are invaluable in describing the symptoms and signs that indicate how close someone is to death. This helps one provide the best care, respond appropriately to the dying person, and also prepare oneself emotionally. Often the caregiver who is present must also be the conveyer of updates and information for anxious family members who cannot be present. Opinions may differ as to how to approach the situation. For example, one man could not accept allowing his father to "stay in place" when the hospice nurse informed him that his father had started the dying process. He stated that his father had always "done everything he could for his kids, and it is our turn to do everything for him, and get him to the hospital." The hospice doctor and nurse were patient and listened to this man's concerns, and although they understood his need to take action, also discussed the importance of respecting the dying process of the person and making them comfortable. The decision to stay in place came after a lengthy discussion, and his father died peacefully just 2 hours later that day. In our culture, we often prefer action over acceptance, something that we may hear about when talking with our clients. They may state that they did not "do enough" for their loved one, or ask "How could I not see how close he was to death?" Also, in the age of Covid-19, it can be heartbreaking when no loved one can be present to care for one's parent.

For many midlife adults, the death of the second parent may trigger much stronger feelings than the death of the first. Upon the death of the first parent, concern and attention are typically focused on the surviving spouse. But when the second parent dies, adult children may become increasingly aware of and free to pay attention to their own loss and orphaned status. Some orphaned adults may find their new responsibilities as the older generation daunting; others may view it as an opportunity to matter in a new way. In either case, they are likely to become the primary communication channels in the family, letting others know who needs help or who is to be congratulated.

The death of a parent may drastically alter sibling relationships. In some families, siblings become closer, realizing that they can no longer communicate through the parent. In others, if the family has stayed together only because of the parent, siblings may drift apart. Counselors are more likely to hear about the latter situation. Receiving support from friends who have experienced similar losses may be particularly helpful, along with more structured group counseling. With end-of-life issues, people may prefer to discuss their concerns with a pastor or chaplain, and we may also work collaboratively with our clients to explore their spirituality, beliefs, and experiences related to the unknown. It is often during such existential moments that spirituality becomes a salient issue, as well as a resource for coping.

Friendships

Although the well-known saying is "that's what friends are for," counselors may hear a wide variety of concerns regarding friends. Some adults who have experienced a major life transition worry about putting too much of a burden on their friends; others are disappointed in lack of support from friends. Some yearn for more and deeper friendships; others worry that the pressures of work and family prevent them from nurturing friendships, fearing that this neglect can have long-term as well as short-term negative effects.

In listening to clients' concerns about friendships, counselors need to be aware of gender differences that may affect the type and depth of friendships. Both research and conventional wisdom suggest that women do more self-disclosing and have more intimate relationships with same-sex friends than men. Rubin (1986) distinguished between male bonding, which arises from shared experiences and common physical or intellectual exploits, and male intimacy, which involves open expressions of thoughts and feelings. Male clients who do not understand this distinction may be surprised at their feelings of isolation, despite the presence of friends with whom they share interests.

Although the social ties across the life span may be different for men and women, it may also be the case for other areas of diversity (Ertel et al., 2009). This is especially important in considering differences relating to social networks based on race/ethnicity and socioeconomic status and how these factors intersect with life transitions and social integration (Antonucci et al., 2001). As we listen to our clients, we must be sensitive to the many aspects of diversity and how they relate to social ties and friendships. A client of one of the authors came from a large Lebanese family, and when asked about friendships, she stated that friendships with "outsiders" were discouraged. She had many siblings and cousins that she considered her friends. In the context of working with this client, the counselor explored the meaning of these relationships, both as family and as friends.

Different groups of the population may have different support and friendship patterns. For example, Lipman (1986) cited several studies showing that both older gay men and older lesbians have more friends than do heterosexuals of similar age. Such strong friendships may supplant or supplement traditional kinship support. These friendship circles may become *families of choice* and can be especially important when rejection from one's family brings a sense of isolation.

Another important factor regarding friendships is where our clients are developmentally. For example, the crucial role of peers in the lives of adolescents is both a developmental task and the bane of many parents' existence. To adults, friends are often the people with whom they can "be themselves." In his definition, Peter (1978) said, "You can always tell a real friend: When you've made a fool of yourself, he doesn't feel you've done a permanent job" (p. 206). Going beyond the humor, our friends are often the people who help us keep our lives in balance and our sense of perspective in place. Many transitions, however, can lead to drastic changes in friendship patterns. These types of transitions usually involve geographic moves, such as job changes, retirement, divorce, and widowhood. As people look at the balance between their resources and deficits, friends may move from one column to the other as they become harder to access.

Regardless of life stage, friendships can play an important role in coping. For example, Kidder (1993) studied residents of a large long-term care facility. He talked enthusiastically of Lou and Joe, two men who had been assigned as roommates and became great friends. Lou and Joe become "better friends every time I visit. They present an antidote to despair, which is connectedness, and for me, I learned it is only the connectedness of the human tribe that can hold despair at bay" (p. 55).

Sociologists have observed what they have termed a distinct new phase in the life course that relates to friendship and the transition to adulthood. This phase is characterized by movement in and out of independent living arrangements, including living with friends. Popular phrases have brought about newly coined terms such as *kidulthood* or *adultescence,* suggesting the blurring of youthful and adult roles. This shift has been attributed to the intensification of friendship networks among single people, including the greater significance of platonic (nonsexual) friendships. According to Pahl (2000), these friendships are increasingly part of the "social glue" of our contemporary society. He stated that these networks of friends act as a "social convoy" for support and self-identity into the 20s and 30s. As people continue to remain single for longer periods of time, friendship networks are taking on increased importance in their lives, often conceptualized as another example of *families of choice* (Heith, 2004).

Other studies suggest that friendships and partners meet different emotional needs. After studying couples who moved and individuals in "Parents Without Partners," Weiss (1976) concluded that both people with partners who have a limited network of friends and people with large support networks but no intimate partner can be lonely. People seem to need to be part of a social network to not experience social isolation; people need intimacy to avoid experiencing emotional isolation. When counselors hear about either kind of void, they need to listen carefully for what clients are saying, perhaps unconsciously, about themselves. Such statements may be a signal that it is time to explore one of the recurring themes of adulthood. It is again here that the Covid-19 pandemic has created difficulties for many. Saying safe can seem to be in conflict with staying connected. Technology helps, but one client complained, "I haven't touched a person in 6 months."

RECURRING ISSUES

Cassie, the client whose story started this chapter, expressed a number of concerns about herself and her situation. Her professional identity with aspects of self and her relationships regarding her needs for intimacy and belonging have been compromised. In fact, she may be overwhelmed with a sense of loss. She described this as "a well of grief." Each of the major issues embedded in her story—intimacy, belonging, and mattering—is discussed in the following text.

Intimacy

Intimacy is a major concern during the adult years. We may be intimate with a spouse, lover, parent, child, or friend as the term covers a wide range of close human relationships. *Intimacy* refers to a close and often affectionate relationship between individuals or within a group. Different people may describe intimacy differently, but the concept commonly involves relationships marked by strong caring, mutual support, openness, and a sense of being able to "be oneself" with another. Most people find a sense of intimacy to be an essential part of a complete life.

Concerns about intimacy—how to get it, keep it, or replace it—are issues frequently brought to counselors. We may see people who "glow" because of a new intimate relationship that adds warmth and color to their lives. Or we may see people whose lives look full but who experience a void because they do not have a special person or persons with whom they feel really close. Many different kinds of transitions can trigger issues of intimacy. For example, loss of a relationship through death, divorce, a move, or a change in commitment can cause adults a great deal of anguish. So can the realization that one is missing an important piece of a full life.

Adults experiencing similar transitions are likely to see very different options for themselves. An open discussion with three 60-year-old widows illustrated this. One said, "I don't care about men. It's finding a man or woman with whom I can be close. I figure I have more chances with women." The other two disagreed, saying they care about men. One said, "The demographics are against me. I'm miserable because I know I won't ever have another close relationship again." The other said, "I know I'll meet men—even if I have to run an ad in the local paper." Regardless of where they saw their options, all were discussing the pain of losing an intimate partner and were questioning how likely they were to be able to "reinvest" or replace their source of intimacy. Others may express doubt about whether a search for a replacement is worth the effort, saying, "I don't ever want to hurt that much again."

According to Erikson's stage theory, achieving intimacy (vs. isolation) is a developmental task of young adulthood (Erikson et al., 1994). Experience suggests, however, that concerns about intimacy, as with the other conflicts identified by Erikson, can surface or resurface at any stage of life. Hudson (1991) summed it up by stating, "In today's world, intimacy is a series of bonds and attachments, not merely a significant other" (pp. 11–12). The importance of close interpersonal relationships can hardly be exaggerated. To many people, the character of their relationships is what determines their level of happiness and/or life satisfaction. Many studies have found that married people have higher subjective well-being (SWB), and increasingly research is focusing on cohabitation and the differences in satisfaction between marriage and cohabitation. Although findings have limitations, there is some evidence that partnerships and SWB are not straightforward and are context specific (Perelli-Harris et al., 2019). However, close relationships have been found to be a significant buffer against the negative effects of stressful situations (Pearson, 1990). Parkes (1982) observed that people without significant attachment or intimacy are often considered at risk, whereas those who have such significant relations are better able to cope with transitions. Moreover, intimacy and attachment are often what add zest to a person's life.

There seem to be significant gender differences in the ability to form intimate relationships. In their longitudinal study of adults, Fiske and Chiriboga (1990) reported, "losing a spouse is often more traumatic for men, because men are less likely to have really close relationships with anyone but their wives ... men name their spouses as confidants far more often than women do" (p. 255). Thus, when a man's wife dies, he often loses his best friend along with the person who was responsible for his social life. Despite increased attention to "men's issues" and the formation of men's support groups (e.g., Bly, 1990), male friendships are often based on common interests and activities. However, Bergquist et al. (1993) reported: "By the time they reach midlife ... men find themselves increasingly concerned about connectedness rather than differentiation ... or the importance of intimacy and interpersonal commitment" (pp. 58–59).

Women's investment in establishing close relationships was documented in the research of Bergquist et al. (1993), who observed that women define themselves in a context of human relationships. Such relationships are clearly involved in a sense of belonging, another major theme of adulthood. It is important to also consider culture, especially with how people experience intimacy, cultural norms, and gender-role expectations.

Belonging

By the time we met Cassie at the beginning of this chapter, she belonged in many places; that is, she had established meaningful connections in her career, church, and family. She had apparently worked hard after her divorce to make sure she belonged in her community and as a small-business owner. However, due to the consequences of Covid-19, a lack of belonging had become a major problem. Consider the following statements that a counselor is apt to hear.

> I've joined a new church, but I don't really feel like I belong. It sure is different from the church in our old neighborhood.
>
> Joe and I belonged to a couples group that met once a month for dinner. We rotated from one house to another. After he died, I didn't know whether to stay with the group or not. A couple of people asked me to, but I wasn't sure they really meant it. Maybe they thought they had to. I went once and felt like a fifth wheel. I'm really more at ease when I'm with other widows or even just the wives. There is another dinner coming up next week and I just can't decide.

> I just moved out of my girlfriend's house, where I lived for 5 years. I really thought we'd get married someday, but it just didn't work out. Now I feel lonely and rudderless.
>
> The holidays are coming up and I don't know what to do. I wish I could get in bed and stay there for about a month. Before my son and his wife got divorced, they used to come to my house for almost all the holidays, and I loved it. Now my son is married to someone else. My stepdaughter is nice, but she has her own family. She asked me if I wanted to come for Thanksgiving, but I don't feel like I really fit.

The clients relating the preceding concerns seem to be questioning where they belong. Their transitions have placed them in an unclear situation between belonging and marginality or, stated differently, between being central or peripheral to a particular group. Every time individuals move from one role to another or experience a transition, they risk becoming marginal. The larger the difference between the old and the new roles and the less knowledge people have about the new role, the more marginal they may feel. Counselors who can discuss this phenomenon with their clients may help them better understand their concerns about not feeling "part of it." Counselors can also help clients realize that this sense of marginality may be only temporary.

Societal changes also can affect an individual's sense of belonging. For example, increasing mobility has meant that in many families, parents and children live far apart. The sense of not belonging experienced by many adults whose children have moved away is reflected in the title of an organization formed by an innovative religious organization. Members of the "Orphaned Parents Group" get together to discuss their concerns and provide support for each other and to hold group holiday celebrations so people have somewhere they belong.

Although the orphaned parents are meeting in one city, their children may be feeling equally lonely in another part of the country, where they, too, may be working to build friendship groups or families of choice with whom they can share holidays. Such groups may include courtesy "aunts and uncles," close family friends who are given honorary titles that may make them feel more a part of the family.

Societal changes can have a particularly negative effect on older adults. Difficulties may stem from a combination of internal and external factors. The pervasiveness and the debilitating effects of loneliness have been pointed out in research. The focus of this research tended to be on personality factors and/or social contacts (Rokach, 2002). For example, in a study of loneliness and adjustment to old age, Hansson et al. (1986) found that loneliness was related to both poor psychological adjustment and to dissatisfaction with family and social relationships. They noted that loneliness can stem from "an underlying lack of skill in living, perhaps including social skills, planning, and control over actions and internal thoughts … or loneliness may interfere with effective interpersonal functioning resulting in unpleasant and self-degrading emotional experiences" (p. 51). Loneliness has become an even more pervasive issue with the isolating factors related to Covid-19, and with so many people losing loved ones.

Social and spiritual isolation are growing issues for those aging in a society that places high value on autonomy and independence (MacKinlay, 2001). For example, in a cross-sectional study of depression in old age, loneliness was reported by 29% of the sample, and 16% felt lonely often. Frequent loneliness was reported as one of the strongest associations with pervasive depression. Women were 19% more likely to be lonely than men, and participants older than 82 years experienced higher rates of loneliness (Prince et al., 1997). In a study of the elderly in North America and Portugal, results indicated that cultural background influences the manner in which elderly people cope with loneliness. The North Americans reflected on, faced, and accepted feelings of loneliness. On the other hand, the Portuguese elderly were very rooted in and surrounded by their families, had less time to engage in solitary activities, and didn't consider reflection as a way to cope with loneliness. North Americans scored higher on both distancing and denial as coping mechanisms as well. An interesting finding was that the use of prayer and the sense of belonging felt through church services was a highly reported strategy of the North Americans, but not by secular people. Although the Portuguese elderly reported praying regularly, they did not consider it as a coping strategy but rather a familiar way of life (Rokach, 2002).

If counselors hear concerns about loneliness, they may want to help clients explore the basis for the loneliness and consider ways to find places where they belong or matter. Internal resources can also be a source of coping. Belonging and mattering are inherent needs related to being human, and the fulfillment of these needs exists to be met within our clients' cultural and social context. According to Chopra (2001), however, people most often look outside of themselves to convince themselves that they belong or matter, yet "going inward" can also be a strategy for meeting this need. We can help our clients to get in touch with what Chopra defines as the "true self" and move toward a greater awareness of all the realms where, in this world and beyond, we all are connected. The mere realization of these connections can then lead to choices resulting in reaching out to others. It is often helpful for clients to belong to a support group where they can make meaningful connections and support others. Oftentimes, becoming involved in helping others is the best approach to alleviating loneliness. This shift in perspective can be healing as it brings opportunities for fulfillment of our client's needs through reaching out to meet other people's needs within the context of their lives.

Mattering

Mattering, the need to be appreciated, noticed, and acknowledged, is a concern of people at all stages of life and can strongly influence behavior.

The late sociologist Morris Rosenberg coined the term *mattering* to describe a universal and overlooked motive. He pointed out how critical it is to believe that we count in other's lives and feel we make a difference to them. Mattering to oneself, others, and the world is the coordinating, although not single, issue that guides our understanding of ourselves: Do I know who I am? Do I appreciate myself? Do I feel competent? Are my inside and outside worlds congruent? Do *others* appreciate me? Do work and community worlds make me feel needed? Rosenberg's concept of mattering is a universal, lifelong issue that connects us all (Rosenberg & McCullough, 1981).

We need to look at ways people matter to others in their lives. One widow said, "I'll never be number one for anyone else again." Grandchildren whose parents are incarcerated or are addicted to drugs and who are often shifted between parents and grandparents do not know to whom they belong or to whom they matter. This is also the plight of children in the foster care system. And once they reach the age of 18, they are then on their own. Mattering is sometimes key to survival. For example, depressed people who think they matter to family and friends are less likely to commit suicide. A rationale for pet or horticultural therapy is that having responsibility for the care of a pet or a plant helps people know they still matter.

Mattering to others in relationships is not enough. For example, talk radio offers people an opportunity to express themselves, which results in the sense that they matter, that their views count, and that they are being heard. People who choose to become politically active can also find a venue to express their opinions and to possibly make a difference. Opportunities for expressing ideas and opinions have grown with technological advances, such as posting on social media or texting politicians to voice an opinion.

Individuals who are unemployed or underemployed often feel they are living in a neverland. Why are they not able to get jobs, feed their families, and live lives of dignity? Again, the need is to matter, to be treated with dignity, and to be noticed rather than shoved away. It is interesting that unemployment is now more prevalent among the young. A strategy when working with unemployed people of any age is to consider opportunities to invest their skills in areas with opportunities to matter. For example, a recent law school graduate decided that she would apply for an internship at a hospital, which involved raising money for the uninsured people treated there. She worked as an intern for a year and shared much enthusiasm about the meaningfulness of this work and her involvement with the development team at the hospital. Within that year, she interviewed and was hired as their main development officer. She was elated by this opportunity and also described with pride that she had raised $100,000.00 in grants for the hospital since becoming an intern. It mattered to her that most of these funds were for the children, most living in poverty with illnesses. This young woman found a path to mattering in her work as an attorney, and sometimes it may take an indirect path for people to find their way to mattering. Although some people find this through their careers, others may find this with their friends and family or through community involvement.

Cassie, the client described at the beginning of this chapter, may have mattered to others, both through her relationships and volunteer activities after her divorce and her transition to business owner. Her current transition is exactly the opposite. She is missing her connections and is concerned about how she will matter now that she has closed her business. She is also dealing with the paradox of mattering so much to her mother while not being allowed to be with her in person. Negotiating how she can still matter to her mother without being physically present would be important to address. Also, maintaining a sense of purpose, of mattering, would be central for Cassie as she navigates her changing relationships within the community. Mattering and meaning-making are especially relevant when relationships are changing and/or in flux and when processing losses, as with the death of Cassie's aunt.

The rejected lover may think, "If my former partner no longer cares about me, I may not matter to anyone." What has been called the *empty nest syndrome* is an example of a loss of mattering. Some people—men and women alike—feel that they are no longer important after their children leave home. Others view the emptying of the nest as a transition to a potentially exciting new stage of life. If adult children return home and refill the nest, it may be another example of mattering too much.

Mattering is clearly an issue outside of families as well as inside them. Employees who talk about constant put-downs and lack of appreciation at work as well as people who complain that their teachers do not listen to them may feel they do not matter. Schlossberg et al. (1989) gave examples of how adult learners might be helped to feel they matter to the school, basing their discussion on five dimensions of mattering identified by Rosenberg and McCullough (1981): attention, importance, dependence, ego-extension, and appreciation. For example, adult learners are more likely to feel accepted if they have a place to put their things and receive mail, e-mail, and messages. Adult learners may feel important if there is evidence that someone cares about what they want and notices whether they miss a class.

These same dimensions of mattering can be crucial to an adult facing a relationship transition. For example, a person who has lost a partner may experience lack of attention, feel unimportant, and think, "Nobody depends on me, is proud of my accomplishments, or appreciates what I do."

ASSESSING RESOURCES: LOOKING AT THE 4 S's

When counselors hear concerns about interpersonal issues, it should alert them to use the transition model to help clients analyze their resources for coping with the change in their lives. Each client brings to a transition a unique combination of situation, self, supports, and strategies. In discussing interpersonal transitions, clients typically talk first about the situations in which they find themselves. Counselors can then ask them to consider more carefully what they are saying about themselves. It is also important to hear what clients say about their support system and to learn something about the strategies they have used in the past.

Situations

Let us take another look at Cassie's situation.

In an article in *The New York Times*, Lewin (1993), referring to several studies on the impact of retirement, reported, "In many cases, husbands and wives find themselves troublingly out of sync as they approach retirement age. Husbands who have worked for 40 years may be eager to leave their job pressures behind, while wives who entered the workforce late find those same pressures exhilarating." Retirement often precipitates a renegotiation of marital roles, a situation that may bring one or both members of the couple to a counselor.

In terms of the facets to be considered when examining one's situation, the trigger for Cassie was the pandemic-related economic slowdown and the necessity of closing the store she loved. Her forced retirement was pushing her to reexamine all of the facets of her life, including the loss of relationships and the death of her beloved aunt. Her counselor could help her explore her internal resources for coping with change, along with processing her losses and sense of purpose.

Self

Many clients find it difficult to talk about, or even identify, their internal resources. These resources include the degrees to which they are optimistic or pessimistic in outlook, able to tolerate ambiguity, or inclined to act autonomously. Helping clients know themselves and clarify their values and assumptions about themselves is a key component of self-assessment. Cassie came for counseling to understand her feelings and to plan for this next phase of her life. She did not like how she was feeling and hoped that it could change. A counselor could help Cassie examine her work and family values, her sense of autonomy, her self-efficacy, and her spirituality. The counselor could also direct her attention to her support system and help her look at ways to use it more advantageously.

Support

As we listen to adults in transition talk about their relationships, support is often an integral part of the discussion. Indeed, providing emotional and instrumental support may be considered at least a partial measure of what constitutes a close relationship. However, such relationships can change over time. One older woman, whose close friends and relatives were suffering from many disabilities, told us in a weary tone, "My support group is no longer supportive. I still love them, but they're a drain now." Another woman joined a women's support group after her husband's death and found that she had trouble being heard in the group, which tended to focus on "male bashing." We heard very little about Cassie's support system. This leads her counselor to believe that a lack of support has resulted from the pandemic or has been lost with her retirement. She mentions her church but also says that without in-person contact, it feels less nurturing. She mentions former connections, such as the Humane Society, but gives little indication of their current place in her life. Cassie's pride in her independence may pose a challenge for her to be able to ask for needed support. However, if the counselor were to work collaboratively with Cassie, they may come up with ways that her friends from church could be supportive, along with how she might continue her connection with the Humane Society in meaningful ways. While Cassie may have decided that the support she found in her former life is no longer available to her, we would work with her to challenge these assumptions. Also, regarding the situation with her mother, more support could be made available. For example, if her mother qualifies for hospice, this would increase supportive services for both her mother and for herself. Grief counseling would be a helpful resource to process the loss of her aunt and explore her anticipatory grief around her mother's aging and decline.

Social support can be a major buffer enabling adults to cope with stressful situations. It can be provided by intimate relationships, family members, networks of friends, or by institutions. A paradox of support systems is that at the very time they may be most needed, during major transitions, such as divorce, widowhood, retirement, or a long-distance move, they may be most in jeopardy.

When helping adults cope with transitions, it is important to listen to their ideas of who and what serves as supports for them. Counselors may hear concerns not only about the presence or absence of supportive people but also about the way friends and family provide support. After finishing a trying course of radiation treatments, a colleague who had breast cancer wrote about what she most needed from her friends (White, 1992): "During a recent bout with cancer, I went through all the stages of grief. In the process, I relearned the importance of receiving helpful help, and that unhelpful help can actually hurt" (p. 7). She described the importance of her friends and family accepting the reality of her diagnosis, which encouraged her progress. She also emphasized what was unhelpful, such as friends who "discussed their own horror stories" of going through treatments or who "wanted to only talk of pleasant things" (p. 8).

Few clients are as clear and articulate about what they want from friends as this woman, but as helpers, we can encourage clients to identify and express their needs. This is important, as the needs of people in the same situation may vary considerably. Another coworker with breast cancer, for instance, wanted very different support from her friends. She chose to talk about her cancer with only a limited number of people and wanted her friends to keep her involved in social activities to the extent that her strength permitted.

Research findings support the concept that social support is one of the most effective strategies that people use to cope with stress. *Social support* has been generally defined as the experience of being loved and cared for and esteemed and valued, all within a social network of responsibilities, assistance, and communication. This social network may include immediate family members and other relatives, friends, and social or community links or owning a pet. The increased attention to the concept of social support is evident within the fields of counseling and psychology. Research findings support the positive impact of psychosocial support, which has been associated with resistance to stress, increased coping ability, and overall sense of physical and mental well-being. Support can include close attachments, social support, and money. These are considered key resources for people in that they may lead to higher levels of self-efficacy and optimism (Hobfoll, 2001).

All of these aspects of support have the potential to be compromised for people living through the pandemic, dealing with multiple transitions and losses. Although support is helpful in both nonstressful and challenging situations, the benefits are more obvious during highly stressful periods. Assisting a person in transition could include helping him or her to better comprehend the stressful event and to select the appropriate resources and coping strategies that could be implemented. It is important to note, however, that not all forms of social support are effective but rather are dependent on matching the support to the person's needs (Taylor, 2005).

Culture plays a role in social support as well. Individuals from cultures that prize interdependence view people as fundamentally connected, whereas Western cultures typically view people as independent and separate from others. For example, three studies of Asians, both in their home countries and in the United States, found that they reported less use of social support for coping with stress. It is likely that culture played a key role in this finding because of a concern with the possible consequences of seeking social support, which could include being criticized, losing face, making the situation worse, and disturbing the harmony of the group (Taylor et al., 2004). Another review of studies supported this view, in that the authors determined that support was beneficial to Asians and Asian Americans only if it does not involve explicit disclosure of personal events and/or feelings of distress (Kim & Sherman, 2008). These types of studies underscore the importance of considering the effects of both gender and culture when one is working with clients experiencing transitions.

Major transitions can affect not only receiving support but giving it. Pearson (1990) noted that "most long-standing support relationships are reciprocal in nature. Therefore, one of the issues a person may confront on the death or disability of a loved one is what to 'do' with the love, affection, companionship, and material assistance that had previously been expended on the lost one" (p. 31). Losing the ability to give can also stem from one's own disability. One woman, Millie, who lost a leg to complications of diabetes, became depressed over her inability to take care of other people as she had done all of her life. After listening to the woman and talking with various volunteer centers, her counselor was able to help her find a telephone job with a local hospital. She called newly discharged patients who lived alone at regular intervals to make sure they were all right. This was a win–win situation: Millie was helped, and the discharged patients felt that they mattered.

Cassie comes to the counselor seeing only her deficits—what she has lost. It is clearly important for her to be able to grieve those losses, but equally important for her to begin to plan how she will expand her current support system. In doing so, we would recommend that the counselor help her look at where she will give support as well as where she can get it. Some of the techniques described in Chapter 7 may be useful, including brainstorming, making a collage of the present and the desired future, and focusing on her short- and long-term goals for connecting—now and after Covid-19 restrictions have passed.

Strategies

A list of coping strategies can be found in Exhibit 5.1. It is important for counselors to help people identify the strategies they have used for coping with past relationship transitions. Counselors can ask clients how they made friends or dealt with past family tensions. By listening carefully to the answers, both counselor and client may learn about the client's decision-making styles as well as his or her experiences and feelings about intimacy, belonging, and mattering.

To help clients assess their coping strategies, counselors may wish to give them the Your Coping Keys Worksheet (Exhibit 5.1). This worksheet enables clients to identify strategies they currently use, as well as others they might include in their repertoire. They can ask themselves: Are there new strategies I can use to change or modify the situation, change the meaning of it for me, or change the way I manage my reactions to it?

In working with Cassie, for example, we could learn how she handled her divorce; how she related to her former husband, her friends and family; and also how she reached out to coworkers and customers as a source of friendship. We might ask what supports she drew on in opening her shop, emotional as well as instrumental. In looking at the meaning of her present situation, we might ask her how she imagines things would be in a perfect world (what is known as the *miracle question*). Another key area of exploration is sense of purpose and the meaning she is constructing from her current challenges and losses.

People like Cassie who are faced with a role change may find it useful to consider how they handled previous changes. For example, if they moved in the past, what did they do to integrate themselves into the social fabric of the new community? When they first became engaged, how did they relate to their partner's family? When they experienced a previous loss, how did they move through the grieving process? Counselors can ask questions like these to learn more about the relationships and coping skills of their clients.

EXHIBIT 5.1 YOUR COPING KEYS WORKSHEET

POSSIBLE COPING STRATEGIES	NOW USING	WILL TRY
Change/Modify Situation Through Problem-Solving	☐	☐
Negotiating	☐	☐
Taking optimistic action	☐	☐
Seeking advice	☐	☐
Asserting yourself	☐	☐
Brainstorming new plan	☐	☐
Taking legal action (if needed)	☐	☐
Change Meaning of Situation Through Reappraisal		
Applying knowledge of transition process	☐	☐
Rehearsing	☐	☐
Developing rituals	☐	☐
Making positive comparisons	☐	☐
Rearranging priorities	☐	☐
Relabeling or reframing	☐	☐
Selectively ignoring	☐	☐
Using denial	☐	☐
Using humor	☐	☐
Having faith	☐	☐
Manage Reactions to Stress		
Playing	☐	☐
Using relaxation, meditation, prayer	☐	☐
Expressing emotions	☐	☐
Doing physical activity	☐	☐
Participating in counseling/therapy/support groups	☐	☐
Reading	☐	☐

Other Strategies

____

____

____

SUMMARY

In this chapter, we have identified a number of relationship transitions involving role gains and role losses, discussed three major themes of adult development—intimacy, belonging, and mattering—and looked at ways to use the 4 S's of the transition model to listen more effectively to what clients tell us about how they handle relationship changes. Some people may have chosen to ignore or gloss over feelings generated by family transitions in the past; others may have always confronted them head on. People who cope effectively use a variety of strategies, and counselors need to listen carefully to their stories so as to help them identify and expand their repertoire of coping skills.

EXERCISES

1. In the first column of Exhibit 5.1, check off the items you are now using for your transition. In the second column, check off the items you'd like to try out. How might you try them?
2. Name three institutional supports that can be accessed by members of the clientele you see or hope to see. Provide their contact information.
3. Describe a relationship transition that you have experienced in terms of the 4 S's, describing the situation, yourself in that situation, the support you received or wish you had received, and the strategies that you used. What strengths did you develop from moving through this transition?

REFERENCES

Anderson, M. L. (2016). Supporting adaptation to new family roles in middle age. In C. L. Juntunen & J. P. Schwartz (Eds.), *Counseling across the lifespan: Prevention and treatment* (2nd ed.). Sage.

Antonucci, T. C., Lansford, J. E., Schaberg, L., Smith, J., Akiyama, H., Takahashi, K., & Dartigues, J. F. (2001). Widowhood and illness: A comparison of social network characteristics in France, Germany, Japan, and the United States. *Psychology and Aging, 16*(4), 655–665.

Bennett, K. M. (2005). Psychological wellbeing in later life: the longitudinal effects of marriage, widowhood and marital status change. *International Journal of Geriatric Psychiatry, 20*, 280–284.

Bergquist, W. H., Greenberg, E. M., & Klaum, G. A. (1993). *In our fifties: Voices of men and women reinventing their lives*. Jossey Bass.

Bly, R. (1990). *Iron John: A book about men*. Addison-Wesley.

Bonanno, G. A., Wortman, C. B., & Ness, R. N. (2004). Prospective patterns of resilience and maladjustment during widowhood. *Psychology and Aging, 19*, 260–271.

Bridges, W. (2004). *Transitions: Making sense of life's changes*. Da Capo Press.

Brody, E. M. (2004). *Women in the middle: Their parent-care years* (2nd ed.). Springer Publishing Company.

Bowlby, J. (1973). *Attachment and loss: Vol. 2. Separation: Anxiety and anger.* Basic Books.

Cherlin, C., & Furstenberg, F. F. (1992). *The new American grandparent: A place in the family, a life apart.* Basic Books.

Chopra, D. (2001). *The deeper wound: Recovering the soul from fear and suffering.* Harmony Books.

Clarkwest, A. (2007). Spousal dissimilarity, race, and marital dissolution. *Journal of Marriage and Family, 69*(3), 639–653.

Colgrove, M., Bloomfield, H. H., & McWilliams, P. (1991). *How to survive the loss of a love.* Prelude Press.

Currier, J. M., Holland, J. M., & Neimeyer, R. A. (2006). Sense-making, grief, and the experience of violent loss: Toward a mediational model. *Death Studies, 30,* 403–428.

Cutler, L. (1985). Counseling caregivers. *Generations, 10,* 53–57.

De Jong Gierveld, J., & Peeters, A. (2003). The interweaving of repartnered older adults' lives with their children and siblings. *Aging and Society, 23,* 187–205.

Didion, J. (2005). *The year of magical thinking.* Random House.

Douglas, J. D. (1990). Patterns of change following parent death in midlife adults. *Omega, 22,* 123–137.

Eicher-Catt, D. (2004). Noncustodial mothering: A cultural paradox of competent performance—Performative competence. *Journal of Contemporary Ethnography, 33*(1), 72–108.

Elwert, F., & Christakis, N. A. (2006). Widowhood and race. *American Sociological Review, 71*(1), 16–44.

Erikson, E., Erikson, J., & Kivnick, H. Q. (1994). *Vital involvement in old age.* W. W. Norton.

Ertel, K. A., Glymour, M. M., & Berkman, L. F. (2009). Social networks and health: A life course perspective integrating observational and experimental evidence. *Journal of Social and Personal Relationships, 26*(1), 73–92.

Family Caregiver Alliance. (n.d.). *Fact sheets.* https://www.fcsc.usc.edu/getting-help/family-caregiver-alliance-fca-fact-sheets

Father Matters. (2017). *Father Matters: Stronger fathers, stronger communities: 23 statistics on grandparents raising grandchildren.* Retrieved at: https://fathermatters.org/23-statistics-on-grandparents-raising-grandchildren

Fatima, M., Neto, L. M., & Marujo, H. A. (2010). We will be laughing again: Restoring relatinships with positive couples therapy. In Burns (Ed.), *Happiness, healing, enhancemet: Your casebook collection for applying positive psychology in therapy.* Wiley.

Fiske, M., & Chiriboga, D. A. (1990). *Change and continuity in adult life.* Jossey-Bass.

Guiaux, M., van Tilburg, T., & Broese van Groenou, M. (2007). Changes in contact and support exchange in personal networks after widowhood. *Personal Relationships, 14,* 457–473.

Ha, J. (2008). Changes in support from confidants, children, and friends following widowhood. *Journal of Marriage and Family, 70,* 306–318.

Hansson, R. O., Jones, W. H., Carpenter, B. N., & Remondet, J. H. (1986). Loneliness and adjustment to old age. *International Journal of Aging and Human Development, 24,* 41–53.

Hobfoll, S. E. (2001). Social and psychological resources and adaptation. *Review of General Psychology, 6,* 307–324.

Holland, J. M., Thompson, K. L., Rozalski, V., & Lichtenthal, W. G. (2013). Bereavement-related regret trajectories among widowed older adults. *Journals of Gerontology and Social Sciences, 69*(1), 40–47.
Howard, J. (1978). *Families.* Simon & Schuster.
Hudson, F. M. (1991). *Mastering the art of self-renewal: Adulthood as continual revitalization.* Jossey-Bass.
Ingham, C. F., Eccles, F. J., Armitage, J. R., & Murray, C. D. (2017). Same-sex partner bereavement in older women: An interpretive-phenomenological analysis. *Aging and Mental Health, 21*(9), 917–925.
Institute for Family Studies. (2019). *The U.S. divorce rate has hit a 50-year low.* ifstudies.org/blog/the-us-divorce-rate-has-hit-a-50-year-low
Kidder, T. (1993, October–November). Inside Linda Manor. *Modern Maturity,* 55–56.
Kimmel, D. C. (1990). *Adulthood and aging: An interdisciplinary developmental view* (3rd ed.). Wiley.
Kruk, E. (2010). Collateral damage: The lived experiences of divorced mothers without custody. *Journal of Divorce & Remarriage, 51*(8), 526–543.
Lewin, T. (1993, November 8). Conflict for working couples: When he retires, must she? *The New York Times,* pp. A1, B9.
Lewis, C. S. (1976). *A grief observed.* Seabury Press.
Lichtenberg, P. A. (2017). Grief and healing in young and middle age: A widower's journey. *The Gerontologist, 57*(1), 96–102.
Light, A., & Ahn, T. (2010). Divorce as a risky behavior. *Demograph, 47*(4), 895–921.
Lipman, A. (1986). Homosexual relationships. *Generations, 10*(4), 51–55.
Lobb, J. K., Krisjanson, S. M., Aoun, S., Monterosso, L., Halkett, G., & Davies, A. (2010). Predictors of complicated grief: A systematic review of empirical studies. *Death Studies, 34,* 673–698.
Lopata, H. Z. (1987). Widows and their families. In C. S. Chilman, E. W. Nunnally & F. M. Cox (Eds.), *Variant family forms* (pp. 133–149). Sage.
MacKinlay, E. (2001). Aging and isolation: Is the issue social isolation or is it lack of meaning in life? *Journal of Religious Gerontology, 12*(3–4), 88–99.
Mahmoodabadi, H. Z., & Zarei, F. (2018). The effect of divorce counseling based on Gottman's approach on the self-efficacy in divorce management of couples applying for divorce. *Social Behavior Researc & Health, 2*(2), 219–227.
Markides, K. S., & Mindel, C. H. (1987). *Aging and ethnicity.* Sage.
McDaniel, A., & Coleman, M. (2003). Women's experiences of midlife divorce following longterm marriage. *Journal of Divorce and Remarriage, 38*(3), 103–128.
Mikulincer, M., Bar-On, N., Shaver, P. R., & Tsachi, E. (2010). The pushes and pulls of close relationships: Attachment insecurities and relational ambivalence. *Journal of Personality and Social Psychology, 98*(3), 450–468.
Montenegro, X. P. (2004, May). Divorce experience: A study of divorce at midlife and beyond conducted for AARP The Magazine. *AARP,* May 2004.
Moorman, S. M., Booth, A., & Fingerman, K. (2006). Women's romantic relationships after widowhood. *Journal of Family Issues, 27*(9), 1281–1304.
Myers, J. E., & Perrin, N. (1993). Grandparents affected by parental divorce: A population at risk. *Journal of Counseling and Development, 71*(1), 62–66.
National Alliance for Caregiving. (2020). *Caregiving in the U.S.* https://www.caregiving.org/caregiving-in-the-us-2020
National Vital Statistics Reports. (2018). *Births: Final Data for 2018, 68,* 13. https://www.cdc.gov/nchs/data/nvsr/nvsr68/nvsr68_13-508.pdf

Neimeyer, R. A., Burke, L., Mackay, M., & Stringer, J. (2010). Grief therapy and the reconstruction of meaning: From principles to practice. *Journal of Contemporary Psychotherapy, 40,* 73–83.

Neugarten, B. L. (1968). The awareness of middle age. In B. L. Neugarten (Ed.), *Middle age and aging* (pp. 93–98). University of Chicago Press.

Pahl, R. (2000). *On friendship.* Polity Press.

Parkes, C. M. (1982). Attachment and the prevention of mental disorders. In C. M. Parkes & J. Stevenson-Hinde (Eds.), *The place of attachment in human behaviour* (pp. 295–309). Basic Books.

Pearson, R. E. (1990). *Counseling and social support: Perspectives and practice.* Sage.

Perelli-Harris, B., Hoherz, S., Lappegård, T., & Evans, E. (2019). Mind the "Happiness" gap: The relationship between cohabitation, marriage, and subjective well-being in the United Kingdom, Australia, Germany, and Norway. *Demography, 56,* 1219–1246.

Peter, L. J. (1978). *Peter's quotations: Ideas for our time.* Bantam Books.

Pew Research Center. (2019). *Millennial life: How young adulthood today compares with prior generations.* pewsocialtrends.ogg/essay/millennial-life-how-young-adulthood

Prince, M. J., Harwood, R. H., Blizard, R. A., Thomas, A., & Mann, A. H. (1997). Social support deficits, loneliness and life events as risk factors for depression in old age. The gospel oak project VI. *Psychological Medicine, 27,* 323–332.

Qu, L., Weston, R., & de Vaus, D. (2009). Cohabitation and beyond: The contribution of each partner's relationship satisfaction and fertility aspirations to pathways of cohabitating couples. *Journal of Comparative Family Studies, 40*(4), 587–600.

Reitzes, D. C. (2020). Catching up on grandparenting. *Gerontological Society of America, 91*(3), 1–2.

Rokach, A. (2002, June). *Loneliness in old age: The effects of culture on coping with it.* Paper presented at the 4th Biennial Convention of the Society for the Psychological Study of Social Issues, Toronto, Ontario, Canada.

Rosenberg, M., & McCullough, B. C. (1981). Mattering: Inferred significance to parents and mental health among adolescents. In R. Simmons (Ed.), *Research in community and mental health* (*Vol.* 2). JAI Press.

Rosenblatt, P. C., & Nkosi, B. C. (2007). South African Zulu widows in a time of poverty and social change. *Death Studies, 31*(1), 67–85.

Rossheim, B., & McAdams, C. R. (2010). Addressing the chronic sorrow of long-term spousal caregivers: A primer for counselors. *Journal of Counseling and Development, 88*(4), 477–452.

Rubin, L. (1986). On men and friendship. *Psychoanalytic Review, 73,* 165–181.

Schlossberg, N. K., Lynch, A. Q., & Chickering, A. W. (1989). *Improving higher education environments for adults.* Jossey-Bass.

Schlossberg, N. K., & Robinson, S. P. (1993). Non-events: Another name for heartbreak. *American Counselor, 2,* 21–25.

Silverstone, B. (1994, March). *You and your aging parent revisited: A 20-year retrospective on family caregiving.* Lecture presented at the 40th Annual Meeting of the American Society on Aging, San Francisco.

Stroebe, M., Stroebe, W., & Schut, H. (2001). Gender differences in adjustment to bereavement: An empirical and theoretical review. *Review of General Psychology, 5,* 62–83.

Taylor, S. E. (2005). *Health psychology* (5th ed.). McGraw-Hill.

Taylor, S. E., Sherman, D. K., Kim, H. S., Jarcho, J. J., Takagi, K., & Dunagan, M. S. (2004). Culture and social support: Who seeks it and why? *Journal of Personality and Social Psychology, 87,* 354–362.

Ternes, R. (1984). *Living with an empty chair.* Irvington.

Thomas, J. L., Sperry, L., & Yarbrough, M. (2000). Grandparents as parents: Research findings and policy recommendations. *Child Psychiatry and Human Development, 31,* 3–22.

Umberson, D., Thomeer, M. B., Rhannon, A. K., Lodge, A. C., & Minle, X. (2015). Challenges and opportunities for research on same-sex relationships. *Journal of Marriage and Family, 77,* 96–111.

Utz, R. L., Carr, D., Nesse, R., & Wortman, C. B. (2002). The effect of widowhood on older adults' social participation: An evaluation of activity, disengagement, and continuity theories. *The Gerontologist, 42,* 522–533.

Waters, R. (1994, October 12). Women who make a difference: Help for grandparents. *Family Circle, 106,* 17–18.

Weiss, R. S. (1976). Transition states and other stressful situations; their nature and programs for their management. In G. Caplan & M. Killilea (Eds.), *Support systems and mutual help: Multidisciplinary explorations* (pp. 17–26). Grune & Stratton.

White, B. (1992). "Me—the Helpee." Feedback (Newsletter of the Continuum Center, Oakland University), *20,* 7–8.

Worden, J. W. (2009). *Grief counseling and grief therapy: A handbook for the mental health practitioner* (4th ed.). Springer Publishing Company.

Yancey, G. (2007). Experiencing racism: Differences in the experiences of Whites married to Blacks and non-Black racial minorities. *Journal of Comparative Family Studies, 38,* 197–213.

Zhang, Y., & Van Hook, J. (2009). Marital dissolution among interracial couples. *Journal of Marriage and Family, 71,* 95–107.

6

Work Transitions

In this chapter, we consider a case study and relevant literature to understand using the transition model with work transitions. In looking at issues relating to self, we see that it is important to consider salience, balance, resilience, self-efficacy, and meaning-making. We also look at characteristics of the situation, support, and strategies.

Case Study

Sam Smith, a 40-year-old skilled carpenter, tells a career counselor the following:

> *I have always wanted to make things. When I was a child, my favorite activity was to play with Lego, doing more complicated sets as I got older. Then I really enjoyed making my own constructions, after I had built the one specified in the directions. I really liked both aspects of Lego, following complicated instructions and doing my own designs. In high school, I discovered that there were apprenticeships for carpenters. I went to the local vocational technical school and then was accepted as an apprentice to a master carpenter. It was a great fit for me and I was successful. After I became a master carpenter, I was able to get pretty steady work and I enjoyed it. Recently, however, the work has become less satisfying. I don't know why.*
>
> *My wife is a nurse, and she gets so much pride and pleasure from how she helps people who really need her. I enjoy building things, but it doesn't give me the pleasure it once did. I wonder whether I am too old to start again. During the recent pandemic, it seemed that the people in the health-care business were the most important. They were deemed essential, implying that what I did was nonessential. Somehow that bothered me. We have only one life to live, shouldn't we be doing something essential? I am hoping you can help me sort through all of this and decide*

whether I should be making a change. We live in a dense urban area. That was helpful before the pandemic as there were lots of jobs available. Now, however, so much is shut down. I am thinking I should keep doing what I am doing now as I do have work, but would like to use this time to plan for after things return to whatever the new normal turns out to be.

Sam Smith's issues are typical of those of many adults in a career transition. He is questioning not only what work he should do but also what is important to him as he enters midlife. The emotional fallout of the coronavirus Covid-19 pandemic is making him question what matters to him and how he wants to matter to society. He is in transition, and it is a very uncomfortable one.

To understand Sam's situation during his transition, it is important to look at the trigger, timing, source of control, concurrent stress, and his previous experience with a similar transition. Because he is successful at carpentry, this transition comes from an internal trigger.

As we use our transition model to analyze Sam's major issues relating to self, we see that it is important to consider salience, balance, resilience, self-efficacy, and meaning-making. Let us look at each of these from a broader perspective.

ISSUES RELATED TO SITUATION

Sam is not experiencing his transition in a vacuum. The world in which he lives had an impact on what is happening to him and on the possible outcomes of his transition. His personal history makes his situation unique, as each individual's does. As we write this chapter, the world is suffering from a global pandemic, predicted to last for an undetermined time. Many more people than usual face work transitions through job loss, impacting millions of people across the globe. Many people who had planned to retire find that they can no longer afford to, whereas others who planned to keep working are making the hard choice to retire early. Families are having to figure out how to navigate the uncertainty of a changing workplace, along with mandates to work from home and managing school closures that impact the work–life balance. Although this has been a historically unprecedented time, the following discussion is relevant for individuals experiencing work transitions. To consider such transitions, we address the situation factors identified in Chapter 3.

Triggers

When people experience a work transition, especially when it is unanticipated, they may come to counseling feeling that they are in crisis. Counselors may want clients to consider their values, interests, temperaments, and the like as they make new career decisions, but clients experiencing bad times may be too frightened to consider anything but their immediate needs for security. They may resist life planning as being more complex than they wish. The search for simple answers is a common one. Counselors have an obligation to explain the process and explain what makes decisions effective as opposed to merely efficient. In many cases, there may be what can be called an *unconscious conspiracy* between counselor and client to avoid ambiguity, short-circuit the process, and arrive at premature foreclosure. Clients often want their counselors to "fix everything," whereas counselors are trying to teach the clients self-directedness in their career decision-making.

As we began writing this fifth edition, the unemployment rate was the lowest it had been in decades. Unemployment was around 3% before the crisis, higher in urban "rust belt" cities and for people of color, especially Black men (in 2019, the unemployment rate for White men was 3.2% and for Black men was 5.4% (Bureau of Labor Statistics, 2019). Then, the pandemic hit. Updated figures are hard to come by but what we do know is that many millions of people are out of work, and those who still have jobs are often doing them in new ways, working from home, in particular. Past experience tells us that people of color and marginalized groups will take longer to recover from this crisis. For example, people with disabilities will also most likely suffer disproportionately. In order to better assist all clients, but particularly those whose cultural ethnicity puts them at greater risk, Arthur and Collins (2011) described the following four aspects of a culture-infused career counseling (CICC) model:

1. Gaining awareness of personal cultural identities: This may include questioning personal assumptions about achievement motivation, the egalitarian nature of the opportunity structure, or other culturally bound beliefs. Considering counselors' self-awareness regarding their own culture and identities is an excellent place to begin.
2. Gaining awareness of the cultural identities of other people: When working with our clients, an important concept is *intersectionality*, which recognizes that people have layers within their identities (Creshaw, 2017). For example, individuals may have aspects of diversity that can be seen, such as race and gender, or unseen, such as sexual orientation and some types of disabilities. Without careful questioning, we cannot know which aspects of diversity are most dominant or salient for a particular client. Another consideration is that although being *bicultural* may be viewed as a source of strength, negotiating dual group memberships can create problems for our clients (Sue et al., 2019). Counselor self-awareness of bias (conscious or unconscious) and cultural humility are necessary foundations for exploring these issues with our clients.
3. Understanding cultural influences on the working alliance: For example, one of the authors worked with older adults who preferred to call their interactions *consultation* rather than counseling, as in their age cohort, counseling implied mental illness with which they were not open to

identifying. This example illustrates that it is best to adapt our counseling styles and approaches to meet our diverse clients' sociodemographic characteristics (Sue et al., 2019). Similarly, the place of a counseling office or its décor may have positive or negative influences on the relationship. This includes the virtual environment that we create with telehealth as well, we must be aware of the importance of nonverbal messages we may convey.

4. Implementing culturally responsive and socially just career interventions: Blustein (2019) described an experience during whichhe, a middle-aged White professor, attempted to communicate about race and oppression with a group of ninth graders of color. "feelings of marginalization are are not always easy to talk about because they tap into a deep emotional well that feel too painful to discuss" (p. 136). This powerful quote underscores both the power and necessity of being deeply culturally responsive.

Considering generational and age-cohort influences, people in their 20s tend to change jobs more frequently than their older peers, regardless of ethnicity or education. It can be challenging to understand the different triggers related to these changes or to accurately define the true nature of the changes. For example, does this change mean they changed the nature of their work, or just changed the place of employment? However, what we do know is that there are an increasing number of work transitions for many. Feiler (2020) described what he termed as the *upheaval* in the current world of work, stating that the average worker today holds an average of 12 different jobs before they are 50, and those with higher education can expect to change jobs 15 times. He also shared that the typical job lasts for 4 years, and for those younger than 35, the average is 3years. He noted an alarming factor, stating that half of American workers are at risk of losing their jobs to automation, and four in 10 people have a *side hustle*. Career counselors often hear from clients a sense of urgency bordering on panic. One way to diminish that panic is to look simultaneously at immediate solutions, that is, a job right now, and long-term goals focused on work that fuels a sense of accomplishment. To recast the old adage, you must feed a man while teaching him to fish—you can't learn on an empty stomach. While dealing with the concrete problems, envisioning the future in anticipation of positive change can be powerful (McArthur-Blair & Cockell, 2018). More than ever today, people are striving to meet their basic needs and those of their families, and although short-term needs may take precedence for these clients, we also work to expand their future options.

Sam's transition stems from an internal trigger. He probably does not "have" to change careers to survive economically as might someone whose skills are becoming obsolete or whose whole industry is disappearing to offshore competition or technological change. But we are wise not to discount the urgency he feels. The pandemic spurred many to rethink their values, and Sam is not alone in wondering whether he would be happier doing something else or continuing his career differently.

Some other workers may be seeking increased responsibilities or better pay. They may love what they do but want to do it in another setting. We remember one client, a custodian in a large factory, who met her needs for mattering by becoming a custodian in a nursing home. There, her desire to help was met by informal interactions with residents as well as a sense of the importance of her work. There are many triggers—what they have in common is that they create change in the life of the individual.

Timing and Concurrent Stress

Two aspects of timing have an impact on Sam's transition—the state of the economy and the time of his own life. Sam is thinking about changing jobs at a time when the economy is in an uncertain cycle of recovery. He is responding to a future need, to have a more meaningful job, rather than a present emergency such as being laid off. One individual may have a good support system and few responsibilities; another may be a single parent living far from family and also battling a serious illness. Each of these timing and stress issues is mediated by the individual's perception of them.

We need to consider when a transition takes place in the life of the individual, but we also must look at the current context of the situation. It is far easier to cope with a work transition during economic "ups" than it is during down times. When there is full employment, jobs are easy to find—it is a "seller's market." During recessions, even highly skilled people may struggle to find new employment. We must also keep in mind that employment conditions vary greatly by locality. The ups and downs of the automobile industry are a classic example of this. The economic crisis of 2008 that continued for some time led to massive unemployment, 10% nationally and estimated to be as much as 30% in some areas. Latinx individuals had a higher unemployment rate than Whites, and Black Americans had an even higher rate. Also, unlike previous recessions, men were more likely to be unemployed than women. Because married men typically earned more money than their wives, this situation led to an even greater hardship for couples than if the female partner had lost her job. The coronavirus pandemic of 2020 created unemployment not seen since the Great Depression. Estimates of up to 30% of workers unemployed in certain areas were combined with tales of individuals whose lives were upended. Official estimates of unemployment often were accompanied by disclosures of their unreliability, given that many people who had been working and now were not were uncounted. Undocumented workers and gig workers are often left out of official unemployment statistics, and the many people who supplemented low-wage work with now-disappeared gig work are not included. We are certain that many books will be written about the world financial and human crises created by the pandemic. Suffice it to say here that there were innumerable lives disrupted and unwanted transitions forced upon the often most vulnerable populations. Ironically, people who are required to work, for example, grocery clerks and hospital cleaning staff, are among the lowest paid and are often disproportionally composed of women and people of color. For many of these people, issues of childcare and increased risk of infection were not within their power to navigate. They must work or lose their jobs. The pandemic also disproportionally affected women—indeed, some began to call it a *shecession*.

It is easier to contemplate "reskilling" or early retirement with support from an employer. For example, when an early-retirement package is offered, a joint union–management program prepays tuition, employers grant release time, or offer local free adult education programs, these can serve to ease the transition and provide needed support. These benefits, too, often reflect the state of the economy. Sam, apparently, has some time to make his decision. His current job is well paying, his wife is working, and his need for change is internally driven. As career practitioners, however, we should not minimize his need to change, even when some other clients are facing homelessness or doing without needed health care. This relates back to seeing the situation through the perspective of the client, exploring Sam's issues, including those related to both timing and managing the stress of his situation.

Control/Source

Stan Popovich was a successful tax attorney who wanted to help people as he had been helped when he had a substance abuse problem. He decided to go back to school and get a degree in counseling, specializing in addictions, planning to work in an inpatient setting in a hospital when he completed his degree. Jennifer Washington was another attorney facing a career transition, in her case, because she developed chronic fatigue syndrome and could not work the long hours her job required. For whom was the transition more difficult? We cannot answer that question without knowing a great deal more about both lawyers, but we can speculate that it was easier for Stan Popovich because the decision was his. It is the same with people who seek transfers, promotions, or new career areas: They are are likely to adjust more easily than those who have change thrust upon them, depending on their other resources.

Control can be achieved in ways other than being the source of the transition. People who can do two things will find it easier to find a new job than those who can only do one; those who can do three will find a new job easier than those who can do two, and so forth. Individuals who must change jobs have more control over the situation if they are adaptable. Similarly, they have more control over the transition if they have more education, have a good network, are healthy, and are not members of a group that has and continues to face longstanding and persistent workplace discrimination.

Many career counselors recommend that all of their clients have a "Plan B" (Schlossberg & Robinson, 1996) because in today's world, it is wise to be prepared for change. Clients who take that advice when faced with a career transition have more control than those who are unprepared. This type of preparation can generate a sense of hope: "Hope is about believing that no matter what the state is at this moment, the future is open to other possibilities" (McArthur-Blair & Cockell, 2018, p. 7). Sam's foresight places him in the optimal position of managing his own career transition and exploring his preferred options and possibilities.

Previous Experience With a Similar Transition

Ben Franklin is credited with saying, "Experience is a dear school." The lessons learned from experience may be hard, but they are valuable. Consider a 60-year-old man who worked for the same company for his entire working life and who lost his job due to a merger. Consider another 60-year-old man in this same situation who has held six different positions in his working life—losing the last three to similar corporate decision-making. We might say he was unlucky to have had to handle this sort of transition three times, but we could certainly credit him with expertise in making work transitions. Furthermore, he probably has more confidence in his ability to change than man number one. After all, he has done it before.

Transferable skills are usually described as being those skills that one can carry from one job to another, such as organizational or communication abilities or the ability to read a technical manual. Perhaps a critical transferable skill in today's global economy is knowing how to make changes. Just as with other transferable skills, the new task need not be identical to the old. A person can learn the skill of making changes by moving, by working in a variety of volunteer capacities, or by being involved in a workplace that is undergoing transformation. The trick is to recognize the learning and be able to apply it in the new situation. Sam has not told us about any previous experience with a similar transition. We do not know much about his process of moving along the continuum from apprentice to master carpenter. With judicious questioning, a counselor may find that he has had several job changes. It would then be useful to help him elaborate on how he made these changes, what supports and strategies he used, and how the changes affected his sense of self. On the flip side, this could be an area of particular challenge for Sam, who has been stable in his work for such a long length of time.

Summary

As you listen to your clients in transition, pay attention to what they tell you about what has triggered their transition, the timing of it in their lives and in the world situation, and the concurrent stress they are experiencing. All these will have an impact on the meaning of the transition as well as on your clients' ability to manage it. It is also useful to keep in mind the degree to which your clients make the choice, how much control they feel they have over the transition, and their past experience with similar transitions.

ISSUES RELATED TO SELF

The transition model encourages us to gather information about clients' internal worlds—their selves. We will now look at four self issues as they relate to work transitions.

Salience and Balance

Work is a major component of the lives of most adults, but clearly not the only component. The interplay of work, relationships, and leisure is what we mean by balance; the place of work in one's life has been called its *salience.* Super (1980) developed a widely cited life rainbow to graphically represent this idea. The rainbow includes the life roles of child, student, leisurite, citizen, spouse, homemaker, parent, pensioner, as well as worker. He postulated that one can ascertain the relative importance (salience) of work and other major life roles "in the life scheme of the client" (p. 19).

Let us consider how the rainbow might look for a young mother, aged 30, with two preschool children. The woman, an engineer, is on a fast track with her company, with the attendant demands of long working hours. One might speculate that her rainbow will have wide bands for work and parent, medium ones for spouse and homemaker, and narrow ones for leisurite and citizen. Let us look also at how the rainbow might look for a 60-year-old single female school teacher with three grown children and no grandchildren. Her widest bands are likely to be worker, leisurite, and citizen, with smaller bands for parent and homemaker. For both of these people, work is an important aspect of their lives. But what of a young man, father of three, doing occasional part-time work and staying home with his children while his wife works to support the family? How might his rainbow look? Clearly, it would have wide bands for parent and homemaker, a very small band for worker, and perhaps medium bands for citizen and leisurite. In his case, work is not a particularly salient aspect of life.

Using Super's (1980) rainbow concept, we can interpret Sam's current dissatisfaction with life as being primarily caused by his dissatisfaction with his work role. It is also important to look at his other life roles and help him assess both their current salience and his current comfort level in each. Is he in the process of reassessing his place in the community? With his relationships? It is not uncommon for people to seek a change in one life role even though the actual source of their discomfort arises out of another role. We often see this with clients who are progressing toward their educational goals, which can impact their relationships. For example, one client shared that she viewed education as a way out of poverty, became a teacher, married an attorney, and moved to the suburbs. A metaphor for thisemerged through the counseling process: She was *an immigrant* who traveled away from her family of origin; this metaphor captured her experience, especially the rejection ofher family, whose members did not choose to change their situation.

People frequently come to career counselors looking to change jobs, because it is "safer" to talk about career concerns than to face personal problems. A sensitive counselor needs to listen for this kind of displacement and help adults consider whether or not they really want to make a change, and if so, in what area of their lives—internal issues, relationships, work, or all three.

Counselors may also see clients who present with concerns about their relationships, using this to mask other issues. After appropriate trust has been established and after the counselors have had an opportunity to hear about the concerns, they may find that other issues underlie the stated problem or even replace it in importance. Some clients may be experiencing a fear of aging and think that a new job would cure all their problems. Some may be avoiding their spouse's confrontation of their alcohol abuse, or they may be unhappy at work and too afraid to face the implications of that unhappiness, "blaming" instead, an unsatisfactory relationship.

In their study of adults with orthopedic and soft-tissue injuries, Britnell et al. (1992) found persuasive evidence for the salience of work in the lives of many adults. These adults, whose average age was 35, typically wanted to and did return to work with significant pain, making necessary accommodations in their leisure and family time to do so. It is interesting to note that even though their injuries often resulted in lesser participation in their working roles, they did not result in a reduced commitment to that role. It is important to remember the distinction between participation and commitment when an injury or other external event forces reduced work time—when, for example, a client has to care for elderly parents or school their children at home. Counselors may hear such clients' frustration with their inability to act on the work salience they feel. They may hear hopes from some who will be able to return to full work participation in the future or expressions of grief for the permanent loss of such possibilities. It is crucial to remember, however, that some, for whom work is not particularly salient, may welcome the reduced participation. It is also important to remember that people with disabilities have historically been and are still subject to discrimination. Chan et al. (2020) remind us that these "cultural barriers … include work-place discrimination, negative attitudes, stigma, social isolation, biases, prejudices, and stereotypes" (p. 8) and that these barriers require active intentionality to advocate for and with this population.

As counselors listen to clients in career transition, it is important to remember that for some, work is a major life role, whereas for others, different roles are ascendant, such as home and family or leisure. Super and Nevill (1984) found that work salience was perhaps *the* important determinant of career adaptability. It is important to listen for values statements as clients describe their situations or the decisions they face. For example, clients may mention a desire to create something lasting, or to give back to their community. A transition may be a time to take a fresh look at values or to consider how current values may be better implemented.

In a "personal experience" article in *The New York Times*, Scofield (1993) described his own accommodation with the realization that he, in his mid-40s, probably would not get any more promotions, thereby offering him freedom from considering how each act would affect his job, freedom to speak his mind at work, and freedom to spend more time with his family. "Some would say I've lowered my goals to meet reality. I say I've exchanged career goals for a vision of life. I have never felt happier or more content. There's much more to my life today than just making a living" (p. 22). In other words, his work has become less salient, his family more so. Hansen's (1997) work on *Integrative Life Planning* is focused on this concept of looking at the balance of life roles.

Anecdotal evidence of changes in work salience in midlife is extensive. This change may be triggered by external events, such as plateauing at work, as described earlier, by the birth of children or grandchildren, or by the retirement of a spouse. Or it may be triggered by internal feelings of boredom with work or a need to be more connected with family and community, discussed elsewhere. A 60-year-old returning student said, "I have made enough money to be comfortable. I have proved I can be a success in business. Now I want to give back." This man returned to a career in teaching he had abandoned many years earlier. A woman we know whose older husband had retired many years earlier said, "It is time to spend more time with him, to be more available for my children and grandchildren, and to play more. So I am retiring from my job." This woman stayed active in her profession but gained the flexibility to choose her own activities and her own timetable.

Achieving balance between work and personal life continues to be a growing need in our country. The balance between family and work has become even more challenging when more people are working from home, and many are also involved with their children attending school online. These situations also fluctuate and change, requiring adaptability. Although some businesses continue to struggle for survival as a result of the pandemic and natural disasters, others are thriving. An example is that moving companies are overwhelmed as people are migrating away from areas impacted by climate change. Hospitals are also overwhelmed and dependent on their *essential* workers. Although many unemployed people struggle to maintain themselves and their families, others who are deemed essential are working longer hours, are under more pressure, and are looking for ways to manage their work and family commitments.

For Sam, his work as a carpenter has become less salient, less central in his life. But work as a whole still seems important. As he moves forward with envisioning his options, issues of work and family balance may become more prominent, as he has always maintained control of his work commitments. Although he needs to earn an income, he also wants fulfillment with meaningful work. Sam's dilemma may resonate with existential issues brought to light in a challenging broader context. Counselors often meet with clients as they seek to reappraise their commitments during difficult times, to understand what matters most, and to align their choices with their core values.

Resilience and Adaptability

The ability to bounce back, to weather changes without major personal turmoil, has been termed *resilience.* Another definition refers to the ability to successfully cope with difficult life situations. Self-factors of resilience would include flexibility, perseverance and hardiness, accepting challenges, effective coping skills, and a positive and hopeful perspective (Vos, 2018). These relate to the key goals we hold for our clients for increased coping while also promoting their overall well-being and resilience. Although we work with our clients toward achieving these goals, we must also consider the "contextual determinants" of well-being, For example, living in poverty adversely impacts well-being, especially in a society with increasing disparities and social inequalities (Pickett & Wilkinson, 2007). Sue et al. (2019) stated that although poverty does not constitute a cultural designation, this warrants consideration by counseling professionals. They emphasize that, especially for counselors from middle-class and more affluent backgrounds, it is crucial to be aware of the worldviews within *social class privilege* and the ways these are embedded within our psychological theory, research, and practice. Especially with the escalation of wealth inequality in the United States, and the financial crisis faced by increasing numbers in the current context, these are important factors to assess when working to foster resilience for our clients. Some of our clients, while striving to navigate work transitions, are also experiencing a scarcity of healthy food, safe communities, adequate health care, and face insecure housing situations. Although the self-factors of resiliency still apply, there may be added strengths needed to survive adverse situations. Banyard (2008) studied homeless women who were struggling to make decent lives for their children while also being stereotyped with classist, racist labels. Banyard reported that these women were not only surviving but demonstrated tenaciously creative survival strategies, problem-solving skills, and maintained a sense of hope. This brings us back to challenging biases, ours and others, along with our beliefs and our clients' beliefs regarding their potential for resiliency. Often, when we *see* this potential in our clients, they can come to also believe in their ability to overcome adversity.

Increasingly, career theorists have focused on context as an important component of career development. Watts (2004) suggested that we help clients develop a contextual awareness to understand how their personal transition fits into the world situation. He stated that we must remember "that all guidance services [must] reflect the economic, political, social, cultural, educational and labour market contexts—as well as the professional and organisational structures—in which they operate" (p. 3). For example, losing one's job may be a result of local, national, or international economic events or may result from personal activities such as a lack of keeping up with necessary technological advances. Valach and Young (2004) proposed that even within clients' action planning, there are three components at play: "manifest behavior, internal processes, and social meaning" (p. 65).

Context is a particularly important construct when one looks at people from diverse backgrounds, especially those from the nondominant culture. Whiston and Brecheisen (2002), in a review of the career development literature of 2001, summarized Constantine and Parker's (2001) assertion that "social constructionism emphasizes the importance of culture, language and socialization, which directly corresponds to the needs of African American women in transition" (p. 112). The Covid-19 pandemic, for example, has negatively impacted everyone across the globe. Yet it has disproportionately had an impact on communities of color, especially women of color. Women of color, in particular, play a vital role in maintaining the economic stability of their families and communities, yet due to longstanding discrimination on the basis of race, ethnic stereotypes, gender, and other forms of bias, they disproportionately work in low-wage jobs without access to opportunities for advancement or quality health care (Frye, 2020).

Self-Efficacy

As mentioned previously, Bandura (1982) proposed a construct to explain certain behaviors, such as persistence or the lack thereof in the face of obstacles. He called it *self-efficacy*, the belief that one's actions will have an impact on one's environment. He found that expectations of success or failure were important in determining motivation; there is much reason to try if you think you will achieve your goals, little reason if you think you will not. Lent and Hackett (1987) summed up self-efficacy research thusly: "With apologies to those with literary sensibilities, if you've got the skill, support, and desire, then 'thinking you can' could light your fire" (p. 377).

To bring this concept to life, let us imagine two 40-year-old women, both forced into early retirement by the new owners of their small plant, a pickle-bottling company. Both women were first-level supervisors, both had high school educations, and both had worked for the company since their graduation from high school. One of the women had overcome many obstacles in her personal life. She was married in her teens, was the mother of two by the time she was 20, was divorced at 25, and had been the sole support of both children since then. She also helped raise her younger sister, who was only 12 when their parents died in an automobile accident. She always believed that she could do whatever was necessary to get along. She trusted her coping abilities. In other words, she had strong self-efficacy beliefs.

The other woman had led a life with fewer challenges and fewer successes. She felt that she held her present position by virtue of luck and that, although she got good evaluations, she performed only minimally well. She lived at home with her parents and did not believe that she could manage on her own. She felt that nothing she did could make a difference and that she would only get new work if the job counselor found it for her. In other words, her self-efficacy beliefs were very weak. With respect to self-efficacy, the first woman has far better resources for coping with change than the second.

Counselors can add to their own efficacy by listening for and asking questions about clients' perceptions of their ability to make a difference in their world. Requests, such as "Tell me about past transitions and how you handled them," and questions, such as "How do you gauge your chances of being successful in finding work you enjoy?" will be helpful in assessing these perceptions.

Self-efficacy also seems to be related to salience. Layton (1984) found that for college women with high career salience, self-efficacy was an important determinant of choice, whereas that was less true for women with low-career salience. Similarly Mclennan et al. (2017) found that preservice teachers' self-efficacy mediated the relationship between career adaptability and career optimism. In a study of Latinx men and women, researchers found a relation between career decision self-efficacy and a higher endorsement of ethnic identity (Mejia-Smith & Gushue, 2017). Let us look at a woman with high self-efficacy beliefs who wanted to become an architect. She faced a demanding training program but was willing to put in the work because her career was important to her. Another woman who had also expressed an interest in architecture was not at all sure she could succeed (low self-efficacy) and was not willing to put in the time and effort because work did not matter that much anyway. She therefore chose an easier program of study.

Nevill and Schlecker (1988) found that women who had high self-efficacy expectations and who were assertive were more willing to choose nontraditional occupations. Yang (1991) stated, "Women who seek traditionally feminine roles operate from an external locus of control, but, conversely, women who consider nontraditional occupations tend to operate from an internal locus of control" (pp. 353–354). Clearly, if you feel independent of other's viewpoints, it is easier to plan involvement in a nontraditional activity. Undoubtedly, socialization and culture play roles here also (cf. Evans et al., 2002).

Self-efficacy also seems to have cultural determinants. Counselors need to be sensitive to cultural variations in the meaning of what they hear from clients whose culture is different from theirs. For example, achievement may be defined differently by those who prioritize relationships over individual successes. Similarly, we may view clients as lacking self-efficacy when they are reflecting a cultural imperative to appear modest, with a core value of humility over individual accomplishments. Although we most often relate self-efficacy to working with individuals, this can also be relevant at the collective level and involve large numbers of people pursuing shared objectives (Bandura, 1997). This focus has become more influential in recent times and can be applied to striving toward collective group efforts ((Lopez et al., 2015). Increasingly, we see many people coming together to influence change, especially as this relates to social justice and advocacy for causes all around the globe.

Meaning-Making

As we listened to Sam Smith's story, we heard that he was feeling pressure from inside to have work that is more meaningful to him—that meets his needs for more autonomy and more personal connections on the job. Men in midlife often become more interested in relationships with people, and women often become more interested in achievement—leading to greater balance in the lives of both. The term *affective men and effective women* is more than alliterative. It aptly describes this phenomenon.

As mentioned earlier, especially for midlife adults, meaning and purpose may become central concerns. As adults grapple with their mortal limits, death, and time to live, they frequently also come to a deeper awareness of their inner values and spiritual selves. Meaning in life usually comes from multiple sources, and a key source of meaning for many people is related to their spirituality.

Many discussions in the counseling field have focused on defining and describing the construct of spirituality as it relates to career development. Chiu et al. (2004) found that most researchers defined *spirituality using* an existential dimension, referring to the concepts of meaning and purpose and to the subjective, individual experience of meaning-making. According to Carlsen (2000), to search for meaning is to search for an organizing principle, a guiding ideal that helps to give significance to actions and to structure life purpose. Frankl (2006, 1963) stated in his classic work, *Man's Search for Meaning,* that striving for meaning is a primary force in life. While a prisoner in Auschwitz, he noted that those who lost faith in the future were doomed in that that they had lost the spiritual hold that sustained them. Frankl (1963) stated, "The way in which a man accepts his fate and all the suffering it entails ... gives him ample opportunity, even under the most difficult circumstances, to add deeper meaning to his life" (p. 76).

Psychologists in the realm of positive psychology have hypothesized that a deep understanding of ourselves and our lives is enhanced by our search for the sacred (Lopez & Snyder, 2009; Peterson & Seligman, 2004). Across research studies, findings point to the benefits of religion and spirituality in times of strife or when coping is necessary. For example, a study of participants dealing with low socioeconomic status indicated that those who are religious show better physical health and higher well-being than would be expected in their environments (Steefen, 2012). Spirituality has been associated with positive benefits across the aspects of wellness and is also acknowledged as a protective factor that promotes coping (Lopez et al., 2015).

The spiritual theme of *connectedness* relates well to Sam's issues. Bloch and Richmond (1998) stated, "Spirituality is the ability to find communion with that which is deepest within ourselves and the greatest outside ourselves" (p. 18). According to Bloch and Richmond (1998), we are all part of a system, something larger than ourselves. They stated that this system is one of believing and seeing that "enables us to learn our purpose, to discover our wisdom, to define and redefine ourselves, to connect and reconnect to our environment, and to create our future" (p. 7).

For Sam, meaning-making and spirituality might be directly related to his work situation. It seems that, as our social context has become more chaotic and unpredictable, people are seeking answers to questions that have historically been answered by spiritual traditions: "How do I live in uncertainty, unable to know what will happen next? … Where can I find the courage and faith to stay the course?" (Wheatley, 2002, p. 42). This turning to spirituality and/or the religious realms fits well with research that supports their positive relationship with hope, meaning, and optimism. Brewer (2001) asserted that the connection between work and spirituality relates to a personal sense of life's meaning, an unfolding sense of self, and purpose that is expressed and driven by action. Most of the writing about spirituality in the workplace addresses issues around the problem of meaning in work, both for the individual and for organizations, and a core concept related to meaning in the workplace is a sense of purpose. This connection between spirituality and work reflects a worldview of the workplace that is rooted in holism, interconnectedness, and authenticity. According to Savickas (1997), work provides the context for agency and union and is the forum for developing a sense of identity and social significance.

A related conceptual link between spirituality and work is the idea of *mission*. According to Bolles (2015), having a mission is a way of marrying our beliefs with our work, and these can work together to uplift each other. Hansen (2001) stated that people are increasingly considering their life mission, looking at what really matters, and exploring life purpose and meaning through their work. A sense of mission is relevant to questions about finding meaning within life: "What projects, relationships, and activities will bring me fulfillment? What path should I choose?" (Smith, 2017, p. 4). These are the types of questions that could work well with Sam, as he considers his sense of purpose and his choices.

In a study of corporate America, a unanimous agreement with the definition of *spirituality* was found among executives, managers, and workers at all levels in a variety of industries. This definition of *spirituality* had two components: a sense of connection to something beyond the individual, and a sense of meaning, purpose, and integration in life. Ashmos and Duchon (2000) found that corporate America is recognizing that meaningful work and connection to others is actually good for business, with the workplace offering its own kind of community as a key source of connectedness. In one recent *Harvard Business Review* study of 2,000 U.S. workers, on average, nine out of 10 workers stated "they'd be willing to forego 23% of their entire future lifetime earnings in order to have a job that was always meaningful" (Achor et al., 2018).

According to Ashmos and Duchon (2000), for many people, the inner life is about understanding one's own divine power and extending this to a more fulfilling outer life. They stated that this quest for meaning at work is not new and that workers are spiritual beings whose souls are either nurtured or damaged by their work. Research conducted by Lips-Wiersma (2000) found that, regardless of their diverse beliefs, people shared four purposes in the workplace: developing and becoming self, union with others, expressing self, and serving others. According to Lips-Wiersma, when these purposes are fully expressed, people are more likely to feel that their work is aligned with a bigger (divine) plan, and setbacks are thus reframed as opportunities for learning and development. The integration of spirituality into everyday work activities can be the spark that ignites meaningfulness and purpose within the workplace, both for individuals and for organizations (Looby & Sandhu, 2002).

Summary

The dimensions of salience, balance, resilience, self-efficacy, meaning-making, and sense of purpose are all critical aspects of a client's work transitions. Listening for and asking about these dimensions helps counselors gain a more complete picture of a particular client's experience and aspirations. These self-factors may reveal untapped inner resources, along with motivating influences for our clients moving forward. One could also think of them as the background of a picture, for which the client's own situation forms the foreground.

ISSUES RELATED TO SUPPORT

Counselors working with adults in transition often hear about a variety of available supports *and* the stressors that often go along with them. The following story illustrates this situation.

> *Laura O'Reilly is a 47-year-old White woman who is trying to balance her life as a parent, wife, child, and citizen. And perhaps even have some time for herself—for leisure. She has a job that seemed secure until recently. She is the executive assistant for a regional sales manager in the automotive parts industry. Recently, many parts are being made overseas and selling them to auto manufacturers is taking place more and more online. If her boss loses her job, Laura is out of work also. She is afraid of the future and afraid of how her losing her job could affect her family's financial security as her kids enter college. Her four children range in age from 10 to 17, so college expenses are coming up very soon. She and her husband have some savings for college expenses, but they are also trying to save for retirement.*
>
> *Laura's parents live nearby and until recently were an important part of her support system. They watched her children after school and during school breaks or teacher in-service days. Lately, they have been needing more support than giving it. As they get older, their energy seems to be diminishing. Her mother also seems to get confused occasionally. She*

doesn't feel comfortable leaving her children with her parents and is even thinking she may need to begin taking care of them, perhaps paying their bills, or making them some meals. She is glad that they live nearby, but her only other sibling, a brother, lives about an hour away and has not been of any help.

Laura's husband, who meets her needs for intimacy and love, is helpful when he can be, but he works long hours as a small-business owner and therefore cannot be as helpful on a day-to-day basis as either of them would like. Laura's friends are also in the so-called "sandwich generation" and she does find it helpful to share problems with them, but none of them are in a position to actually help, and she would not ask for financial help if she does lose her job. Laura has strong religious beliefs and is an active member of her church. She has talked to her priest, who encouraged her to join a support group for adult children of aging parents, but she does not think she can spare the time.

Laura has a potentially very effective support system, but she may not be using her access skills as well as she could. She also does not seem to be taking advantage of institutional support, such as agencies that might help her care for her parents.

Counselors often hear adults speak as Laura does, about needing to do everything themselves or not wanting to lean on others, appear needy, or "air their dirty laundry in public." Many racial and ethnic groups have their own version of this mindset. Keeping a stiff upper lip is not confined to those of Anglo-Saxon origin.

Goodman and Hoppin (1990) identified some support needs particularly relevant for work transitions. They included the following:

- feeling positive about yourself (provided by people who like you and know what you can do)
- encouragement (provided by people who expect you to succeed, can give you positive direction, and have an optimistic outlook)
- information (provided by people, books, and resource materials that teach job-hunting techniques and provide information on jobs and employers)
- referrals (provided by people and agencies who know of help like health care or financial support available to laid off or unemployed people)
- door openers (provided by people who are willing to make contacts for you); these may be harder to come by for people who are the first in their family to look for work in a particular setting
- practical help (provided by people who will babysit, loan money, provide transportation, or review and edit a letter or résumé)

The support systems of people from other cultures may be quite different. Martin (1991) listed the following traditional supports for American Indians: "the family, the tribe, religious beliefs, and the land itself" (p. 277). When working with marginalized populations, it is important to recognize sources of support unique to their culture. White counselors may not be cognizant of the historical trauma that influences our clients' experience and may not be aware of cultural support systems, rituals, and traditions that hold deep implications for healing. A profound example for overcoming historical trauma is the annual Dakota 38+2 Reconciliation Ride that began in 2005. This ride provides a communal effort to cope with the executions of 38 Dakota men, a hanging that took place on December 26, 1862. This was the largest mass execution in U.S. history, and afterward, two more Dakota men were also hanged. The significance of the reconciliation ride resonates with the trauma experienced by Native people in the United States. This event is viewed as a *sacred journey* that began with a dream by a Native spiritual leader, who dreamt of a spiritual journey by horse. This continues every year to promote reconciliation between American Indians and non-Native people and entails a 330-mile journey from South Dakota to Minnesota during the dead of winter. The horse is revered as a source of connection to nature and healing in Native cultures, and a riderless "spirit horse" is included as a symbolic presence on this journey, representing the ancestors and those who lost their lives in the executions. This example illustrates the importance of exploring the client's ethnic identity, tribal affiliation, and adherence to cultural values. Although a heterogenous group making up just 2% of the population, the Native American experience is unique from that of any other ethnic group. Thus, it is imperative to determine environmental contributors to problems, such as racism, discrimination, poverty, and acculturation conflicts (Sue et al., 2019).

Counselors often hear people describe very limited support—like Sam's. Unlike other people in the workplace, Sam has been working on his own. Although he likes meeting and working for his clients, these tend to be short-term and limited connections. This is unlike those who lose their jobs and also feel that they have lost much of their support system at the same time. Statements, such as "Most of my friends were from work. They can't help me; they've lost their jobs, too," are common. Clients often see support only in terms of individuals who can meet all of their needs—a rare breed indeed. Counselors should encourage clients to think about individuals who meet some of their needs as well as about nonpeople supports, such as job-training centers, online resources, their faith, being in nature, creative endeavors, or their pets. Support tends to be an area in which counselors hear little and can do much. Key aspects of support, as discussed earlier, relate to connecting our clients with resources that can come through sharing information, referrals, door openers, and practical help.

ISSUES RELATED TO STRATEGIES

What coping strategies are Sam and Laura using? Sam is tentatively beginning the process of exploring alternatives. Laura is using the coping strategy that has worked for her in the past—doing everything herself. Clearly, we have identified an area for further exploration and assistance. Counselors will want to make sure they hear about a person's past record of coping skills as well as about current strategies. Both Sam and Laura have wisely chosen the strategy of seeking help from a counselor, but their counselors are not hearing much about the strategies already underway.

Some of the strategies that counselors hear from other clients are listed in Exhibit 5.1, Your Coping Keys Worksheet.Counselors may also hear strategies designed to change or modify the situation through problem-solving, such as negotiating. They may hear strategies designed to change the meaning of the situation through reappraisal, such as developing rituals. And counselors may hear strategies designed for managing reactions to stress, such as implementing mindfulness practices, virtual support groups, and participating in physical activity.

MOVING IN, THROUGH, OUT, AND BACK (AGAIN) INTO WORK

Counselors listening to clients engaged in managing work transitions benefit from having a framework they can use to listen to and understand what their clients are experiencing. The model used in Exhibit 6.1 takes an individual

EXHIBIT 6.1 NANCY K. SCHLOSSBERG'S MODEL OF WORKLIFE TRANSITIONS

WORK TRANSITIONS	ISSUES FOR THE INDIVIDUAL
Moving in: New employees	**Expectations regarding:** Job Culture Explicit and implicit norms Marginality, at the edge
Moving through: Fast track Plateaued Caught in between	**"Hang in there, baby"** Loneliness and competence Bored, stuck Competing demands
Moving out: Reduction in force Retirement Career change	**"Leaving, grieving, striving"** Loss and reformation of goals Articulation of ambivalence
Trying to move in again: Unemployed and underemployed	**"Falling through the cracks"** Frustration Despair

through a work lifecycle. A newly employed person is said to be *moving in;* a person who is fast tracked or plateaued is said to be *moving through;* a person who has been laid off, retired, or is making a voluntary career change is said to be *moving out;* and an unemployed person is said to be *trying to move in again.* As counselors listen to clients' career concerns, they need to listen to:

- The focus of the career concern: Is the client trying to figure out how to *move into* a job or school? Is the client trying to hang in there and balance competing demands? Or is the client *moving out* of the job, school, or the workforce? In other words, where the client is—moving in, through, or out—influences underlying concerns.
- The way clients handle moving in, through, or out depends on their resources: What comprises the client's situation, self, support, and strategies?

What then do counselors hear from their clients during these times? In the following discussion, we examine these issues for individuals as they cycle, or recycle, through the various stages.

Moving In

When clients secure a new job, another transition must take place. Many employers fail to provide a true orientation to new jobs. Partly as a result of this failure to conduct good orientation and training, as many as 50% to 60% of all new hires leave their jobs within the first 7 months (Leibowitz et al., 1991). More recent, Jobvite (2018) found that 30% of new hires left within the first 90 days. Neither of these figures, which probably differ due to the economy at the time as well as the differing time spans in their research, are encouraging. The transition to a new job requires the worker to understand the expectations of peers, subordinates, and supervisors and also to learn the company's formal and informal norms. It often requires learning new skills and almost always requires learning new ways of using old skills. It can result in clients feeling marginal—the feeling that they are at the edge, on the fringe. For many bicultural individuals, of course, marginality is a way of life. Furthermore, many jobs in the 21st century are part of the gig economy or can be described as precarious. All of us, whether rich or poor, minority or majority, feel marginal when we move into new roles. We are not what we were, nor are we clear about who we should be and what is expected of us. This situation may be even more difficult for people belonging to racial and ethnic minorities, who often feel they must adapt to the majority White culture.

All of this comes at a time when both the individuals themselves and their families expect them to experience unadulterated joy at having a new position. One woman we know had finally moved to a long-sought-after position. She loved the new work and her new colleagues but was puzzled by her resistance to a new computer system. All of her feelings about the change had become displaced onto the unfamiliar machine on her desk. When she was finally able to recognize the magnitude of the change she had made, she was easily able to learn, and even embrace, the new system.

Moving Through

Moving through work has changed drastically in the past few decades. What was formerly a predictable series of stages (see Super's [1980], stages of establishment, maintenance, and decline), has become an unpredictable course, described by Gelatt (1993) as similar to the turbulent white water one encounters while river rafting.

Counselors may well hear clients' confusion and distress over navigation in the new white water and may also hear concerns about plateauing. Moving unpredictably is frightening for many, but many others are afraid of staying stuck in a dead-end job—plateauing. Bridges (1980) suggested two major strategies for helping employees through that confusing, conflicting middle period. "The challenge is how to provide an interim system of temporary policies, procedures, responsibilities, and authority structures to get people through ... creating temporary policies ... encouraging cohesion ... expecting old issues to surface" (pp. 62–63).

The issue of plateauing was also addressed by Land and Jarman (1992) in their book *Breakpoints and Beyond,* in which they look at the process of renewal for both individuals and organizations. The researchers described a cycle of change that begins with *forming,* a period of exploration, innovation, and invention. Using examples from the physical world, such as the transition of water to ice when the separate molecules forming the liquid "suddenly" line up and form a solid crystal, they postulate that after this phase, a massive shift occurs, which they call *breakpoint*. A person or organization then moves into a second phase, *norming*. This phase encompasses extending and improving what has gone before; the ice crystal grows but does not change its nature. It is in this phase that many get stuck, plateaued, one might say. If the individual or organization does not actively move into the next phase, *fulfilling,* the third phase will be a diminishment or a disintegration.

To move into a successful third stage, one must integrate the new and different. This results in a transformation that is necessary for successful fulfillment and leads to reinventing the future. If reinvention does not happen, and Land and Jarman argue that it usually does not, gradual decline is the norm. As an example, they remind the reader that the development of the airline industry was not done by the railroads, which were then at the height of their success and logically placed to be leaders in the new transportation industry. The railroad industry ignored the possibilities of the infant science of flight and was left in the dust as far as passenger travel was concerned.

The parallels for individuals at midlife are obvious. Counselors often encounter adults at the breakpoint between norming and fulfilling. What they hear is discomfort, distress, and a desire to cling to the comfortable norm even while the individual recognizes that it no longer serves its purpose. They hear confusion about what to do next and how to deal with changing demands. An understanding of the process of change itself may be useful to such clients for managing their transition, after which they will be in a better position to move back into work, at the same or a new job with renewed commitment.

Moving Out

As discussed in Chapter 2 and earlier in this chapter, moving out of a role can be a time of great distress. Liminality, the time on the threshold of change, is usually uncomfortable. In a classic study, Bridges (1980), conducting a workshop for people in transition, found that although the nature of their transitions varied widely, all the seminar members shared the basic experiences of (a) an ending, followed by (b) a period of confusion and distress, leading to (c) a new beginning, in the cases of individuals who had come that far. For work transitions, that ending, whether voluntary or involuntary, usually involved leaving the job.

Counselors frequently first hear about the grief that accompanies the moving-out phase. Even when a job change is voluntary, there is a process of mourning for the old ways. There may be ambivalent feelings that make it hard to acknowledge the sense of loss. When the change is involuntary, that is, when the worker is laid off, fired, or forced into retirement, the pain is often intense. A grief period can ensue, much like that identified by Kübler-Ross (1969) in relating to the death of a loved one.

In another classic study of men whose jobs were eliminated, Schlossberg and Leibowitz (1980) confirmed the notion that a transition can be an opportunity for either growth or deterioration. Reactions changed over time. They identified five phases—disbelief, sense of betrayal, confusion, anger, and resolution—as marking the movement in a transition process from disequilibrium following the transition to a new state of equilibrium. When the reduction in force (RIF) was first announced, many of the affected men reported feeling a sense of numbness and disbelief: "Why me?" One man said that when he was called into his supervisor's office, he thought that he was going to be commended for his work or else receive a challenging new assignment; the news of the RIF stunned him. Several of the men refused to accept and incorporate the loss. Instead, they felt an unrealistic hope: "Maybe it's not true."

A sense of betrayal often accompanied the initial disbelief. Most of the employees said they felt they had entered into a psychological contract with the organization, the terms of which were "If I am loyal and competent, the organization will take care of me." The RIF represented a breach of that contract, a "slap in the face," a "kick in the pants." One man, who was within 3 months of being a career veteran, was especially bitter about the betrayal: "If an RIF must be done, it should be based on a man's production."

Once they had recovered from the initial shock and their immediate sense of having been dealt with unjustly, the men began to accept the reality of the situation. At this point, many began to panic: "What do I do now?" They tended to be immobilized, waiting for some "magical" solution to occur. Around this time, a special program of career assistance was started, giving rise to some ambivalence. On one hand, the men were dismayed at being fired; on the other hand, they were grateful to the organization for the help and support it offered. They wanted to be able to put the blame somewhere but could not find a suitable object. Their emotions fluctuated from anxiety and anger to excitement and anticipation. Some men contradicted themselves in a single statement. For instance, one man began by talking about the problems created by the reduction in his income but then immediately after spoke with great excitement about his plans to move to Florida.

Among those employees who could not resolve their confusion, the natural progression was to *anger,* usually directed at themselves or at the organization. Often, the anger was expressed in inappropriate ways by "bad-mouthing" or "dumping on" the organization. In other cases, anger was directed elsewhere, for instance, at the veterans-preference provision in the Civil Service regulations or at the computer, which had been used to actually select the men to be fired. Sometimes the anger took a very concrete form: 14 of the 53 employees affected by the RIF filed formal grievance complaints against the employer. One man articulated his anger by saying, "I'm going to appeal this case and become a thorn in somebody's side."

By the time of the 3-month follow-up interviews of the 53 men, 19 had been reassigned to other jobs in the organization, nine had decided to retire, and the remaining 25 had found new jobs. In virtually all cases, they seemed to have resolved their reactions to the transition.

It is important to note that these positive reactions resulted from the fact that the men were all helped to obtain new jobs. This positive resolution was not as easily achieved at times, such as the present, when the increasing number of job losses is coupled with the decreasing number of jobs. Job loss during difficult economic periods often results in continued anger and increased depression. With today's enormous increase in unemployment, job loss has been increasingly linked to mental health issues. As puts it, "work plays a central role in the development, expression, and maintenance of psychological health."

Spencer and Adams (2002) provided a useful description of the grief process. They identified a series of stages that included losing focus, sinking into "the pit," and a search for meaning. Of particular interest to counselors working with the newly unemployed is the pit—a time when adults experience paralysis and even hopelessness of ever emerging from their despair. Counselors often hear tales of depression or inaction from adults in the midst of the job search that counter the logical expectations of maximum effort. Clients themselves may be as puzzled as their family members as to why they are not "looking harder." Some people may spend months in the pit. Counselors often find that all they can do for these clients is listen, be supportive, and help them begin to visualize an end to their pain. Developing job-search strategies is probably premature in this situation.

The study of Schlossberg and Leibowitz (1980) did not address the issue of making meaning of the pain caused by the RIF. Scofield (1993), who wrote the personal article in *The New York Times,* and the student who left his business to return to teaching are good examples of that search for meaning. Scofield found it in spending more time with his family; the student found it in doing work that he felt mattered. Sam, in reconsidering his career as a result of Covid-19, is exhibiting this search for meaning. Adults who tell counselors that they have used their involuntary leisure to develop closer relations with their families or who now volunteer their time to help other newly unemployed people illustrate this principle.

Moving out voluntarily was discussed in a special section of *The New York Times* (February 2, 2020) titled, "I Quit." This section invited a number of individuals to contribute essays on quitting. They ranged from quitting use of an I phone to quitting giving a damn. In the essay on quitting a job, Veronica Chambers described leaving a job where she, as a Black woman, was told she would never be promoted and become a full-time writer. She describes her decision as "reclaiming the self-esteem that unlocks a world of possibility" (p. 4).

Moving In Again

Families of the unemployed may also develop useful strategies for coping with job loss. In one family in which the husband had been unemployed for 18 months, the wife used three major coping mechanisms. First, the family kept trying to modify the situation by continuous, systematic job hunting. In fact, their phone bills soared, indicating that the husband was working on networking and contacts. Second, they tried to control the meaning of the problem. They joined a support group, made up of others with the same problem, which focused on the economic aspects of structural unemployment as well as job-search strategies. They also identified the positive aspects of the situation; for example, the father was now able to be involved with the children on a more regular basis. In this way, they took the blame away from themselves personally. Third, they used responses that helped to manage stress by keeping busy with a rental property, running, and gardening. Obviously, moving out raises many issues for counselors to attend to. What about moving in?

When we examine moving in again, we can benefit from research done by Sampson et al. (2013) on the needs of career decision makers: The readiness of clients to use career resources effectively is influenced by their personal characteristics and circumstances; knowledge of self, options, and decision-making; and prior experience with career interventions.

Sampson et al. (2013) found that some clients who came to their center were decided—that is, they knew what they wanted to do and only needed help in knowing how to get there. Those people would tell counselors that they needed academic advising, job-search assistance, résumé writing, and so on. For those students who needed instrumental assistance and information, workshops could be offered to address specific needs. A series of workshops on job search, for example, might include networking, writing a cover letter, writing a résumé, identifying job openings, learning how to "ace" an interview, and learning follow-up techniques.

Another group of students was undecided. They talked about the pros and cons of various possibilities and wanted assistance in sorting out their priorities, interests, and values. These students could also be served in a group format through a structured career development program. The group discussion could focus on identifying values, interests, and temperament; learning about the world of work and labor market information; looking at lifestyle choices; learning decision-making strategies; and developing an action plan.

A third group, most challenging for counselors, consisted of those who were indecisive. These students presented more complex issues and often had personal issues that blocked their ability to make decisions. They may have been in too great turmoil to focus appropriately on career decision-making. For these students, individual counseling was usually the treatment of choice. Each student had to be helped to work through individual issues before they could move to make career decisions. A successful outcome of counseling for those students might be to move into group one or two.

Gender Differences

Many researchers have looked at gender differences and work, considering differences in such variables as attitudes toward job and career, drive to achieve, and work-related behavior. Often such approaches involve analyzing these differences on the basis of early socialization patterns. These ongoing socialization experiences affect women's self-perceptions and can include learning to prioritize the needs of others by taking on the role of nurturer and caregiver (Sue et al., 2019). This has had a profound impact during the pandemic, with many women dropping out of the workforce to care for their children and be at home to oversee their online learning. Also, many women are balancing family caretaking responsibilities and work commitments.

When working with our female clients, an important consideration is the pervasiveness of sexism and discrimination, both in social and professional settings. According to the Pew Research Center (2015), nearly two thirds of women believe that their gender is a source of discrimination. As a counselor educator, one of the authors can attest to the number of female students sharing experiences with sexual harassment and microaggression in the workplace. Students in the careers class were asked to write down an experience with discrimination that they have had or observed in the workplace.

This was done anonymously and distributed to read aloud. Although each group of students expected to hear of microaggressions against minorities, it was consistently surprising how many women who shared adverse experiences related to their gender.

Other broad issues can also have a negative effect, for example, societal pressures to measure up to stereotyped standards of beauty, which are promoted through advertisement, film, and music industries, often contributing to girls' internalization and feelings of low self-esteem (Sue et al., 2019). Although these influences may not be universal among people of differing cultures, these are relevant to women, both in their personal and professional lives. Also, many women come to be inculcated by the vicarious achievement ethic first identified by Lipman-Blumen and Leavitt in 1976. Such women define their identities not through their own activities and accomplishments but through those of the dominant people (usually men) in their lives: at first, their fathers; later, their husbands; and still later, their children. As a corollary of this tendency, many women perceive themselves primarily in roles such as wife, mother, and homemaker; even those with jobs outside the home may devalue or deemphasize their role as worker. Men, on the other hand, are governed by the direct achievement ethic and tend to base their identities on their career achievements. They are "success objects," whose value as human beings is measured by their ability to provide for their families.

There has been increasing attention in recent years on women's career development; however, issues may still relate to earlier research discussed by Gutek and Larwood (1989). They summarized the following reasons why women's careers are different from men's:

- There are differential expectations for men and women regarding the appropriateness of jobs for each gender.
- Husbands and wives are differentially willing to accommodate themselves to each other's careers, with wives more willing to move or otherwise adapt to a husband's career needs than vice versa.
- The parent role is differentially defined for men and women; the mother role requires substantially more time and effort than the father role. Compared with men, women face more constraints in the workplace, including discrimination and various stereotypes detrimental to career advancement.

Women also face unique barriers, especially with organizations that continue to operate under a value system that emphasizes power and control over relationship skills (Sue et al., 2019). When working with our clients, we often hear about barriers to success in work, both external and internal. Although the situation is improving, women do not yet receive pay equal to that of men for comparable jobs. On average, women earn 80 cents for every dollar their male counterparts earn, but for many women of color, the average is much lower. When broken down by race, Asian women earn 85 cents, White women earn 77 cents, Black women earn 61 cents, Native American women earn 58 cents, and Latinx women earn 53 cents compared with White men (American Association of University Women [AAUW], 2019). Many people remain unaware of the extent of this discrimination. Over a 16-year period, college students, although aware of the existence of the gender pay gap, were unaware of its magnitude (Beyer, 2018). Neither is there yet full access to certain occupations or certain levels of responsibility—the so-called glass-ceiling effect. In a Pew research survey on women and leadership (2018), there were wide gender gaps in views about women in leadership. Although seven in 10 women said that there are too few women in political offices and executive business positions, only about half of the men said the same. However, recent developments are hopeful, with more women being elected to political positions, including the vice-presidency of the United States.

Some of these patterns were reflected in a classic study of women in middle management and top executive positions (Hennig & Jardim, 1977). Most of the women in the sample had made their career decision (defined as "a conscious commitment to advancement over the long term") 10 years later than is generally true for men. For some of these women that decision was in a certain sense a passive one, something that "just happened" when the woman suddenly realized that she was probably going to be working for the rest of her life. These managerial women were inclined to attribute their success to luck or to the kindly intervention and encouragement of a superior. Nonetheless, most of them believed that further advancement would come about through their own efforts at self-improvement and their development of competence on the job. What these women lacked, according to Hennig and Jardim, is "a sense of the organizational environment—the informal system of relationships and information sharing, ties of loyalty and of dependence, of favors granted and owed, of mutual benefit, of protection—which men unfailingly and invariably take into account" (p. 12). Discrimination clearly also plays a part. We know of one attorney who had to sit outside the door at attorney staff meetings because the partners chose to hold them in a venue that did not allow women in its dining room.

This difference is attributed in part to men having learned early in their lives to play games, such as football, that involve teamwork, the long-range goal of winning, and the use of short-term strategies with a view to reaching that goal. Although this is changing, women often have less exposure to such team sports, concentrating instead on activities, such as swimming, tennis, and gymnastics, that focus more on the display of individual competence and do not involve working with team members. Women's failure to recognize the team-sport aspects of the managerial career may lead them to behave in certain ways that decrease their chances of success in the organization. However, key issues also include cultural boundaries that emphasize a "good old boys network" and the fact that women receive less frequent and effective mentoring (Sue et al., 2019). These issues relate to a sense of belonging at work, which can be even more complex for Black women and their career trajectories, which are inextricably related to structures based on race, gender, and power in organizations and society at large (Mccluney & Rabelo, 2019).

Hennig and Jardim (1977) specified the following behavioral differences between men and women in management. First, the genders interpret "risk" differently: Women may see only the immediate negative aspects (the danger of failure), and men may see not only negative but also long-range positive aspects (the opportunity for success and advancement). Second, in deciding on what style to use in playing the role of subordinate helper, follower, junior colleague, equal, friend, men are more aware of the expectations of others, especially the boss, and choose a style that will satisfy those expectations, whereas women may be more inclined to adopt a take-me-as-I-am attitude. This can, however, feel like walking *a tightrope,* as two thirds of women report having to "walk a fine line between being seen as 'too feminine' to be competent and as 'too masculine' to be likeable" (Sue et al., 2019, p. 495). In addition, nearly two thirds of women with children shared that they faced assumptions that motherhood would reduce their competence and commitment to work (Sue et al., 2019).

Although older studies may serve to reinforce general stereotypes, these are salient issues to explore with our female clients, which relate to aspects of self as discussed earlier, along with the realities that women continue to face in the workplace today. Clearly, women are individuals and many defy these categorizations. Law school and medical classes tend to be about 50/50 in their gender makeup, but there still seem to be differences in career sequencing between women and men. Goodman and Waters (1985) described it as the out-of-sync career commitment curve. We must recognize that gender differences are critical in understanding the transition process.

SUMMARY

We have presented a multiplicity of issues related to the kinds of experiences, thoughts, and feelings that have an impact on adults engaged in work transitions. We have discussed what counselors might hear from the perspective of the 4 S transition model and have added to that the proposition that all transitions involve moving in, through, out, and back in again. We hope you keep these examples in mind as you read Part III, What Can We Do With What We Know and Hear?

EXERCISES

1. Work transitions, even when voluntary, involve losses as well as potential gains. List all of the losses other than income you can think of that someone might experience with the loss of a job, for example, loss of routine or colleagues.

2. Contextual awareness is an important part of managing a work transition. Find three sources of information about the labor market in your local area. How might you explain these to clients and which might you teach them to use independently?
3. What are your primary work values, for example, achievement and recognition? What are some other work values that might be important to your clients? How will you manage empathizing with clients whose values are different from yours?

REFERENCES

Achor, S., Reece, A., Kellerman, G. R., & Robichaux, A. (2018). 9 out of 10 people are willing to earn less money to do more meaningful work. Harvard Business Review. https://hbr.org/2018/11/9-out-of-10-people-are-willing-to-earn-less-money-to-do-more-meaningful-work?utm_source=facebook&utm_medium=social&utm_campaign=hbr

American Association of University Women. (2019). The simple truth about the pay gap. https://www.aauw.org/resources/research/simple-truth/

Arthur, N., & Collins, S. (2011). Infusing culture in career counseling. *Journal of Employment Counseling, 48*(4), 147–149.

Ashmos, D., & Duchon, D. (2000). Spirituality at work: A conceptualization and measure. *Journal of Management Inquiry, 9*, 134–145.

Bandura, A. (1977). Self-efficacy: Toward a unifying theory of behavior change. *Psychological Review, 84*, 191–215.

Bandura, A. (1982). Self-efficacy: Mechanism in human agency. *American Psychologist, 37*(2), 122–147.

Banyar, V. (2008). *Welfare queens or courageous survivors? Strengths of women in poverty.* University of New Hampshire Scholars Repository. https://scholars.unh.edu/discovery_ud/34/

Beyer, S. (2018). Low awareness of occupational segregation and the gender pay gap: No changes over a 16-year span. *Current Psychology, 37*(1), 373–389. https://doi.org/10.1007/s12144-016-9521-4

Blustein, D. L. (2008). The role of work in psychological health and well-being: A conceptual, historical, and public policy perspective. *American Psychologist, 63*(4), 228–240. https://doi.org/10.1037/0003-066X.63.4.228

Blustein, D. L. (2019). *The importance of work in an age of uncertainty.* Oxford University Press.

Bolles, R. N. (2015). *What color is your parachute?* Ten Speed Press.

Brewer, E. W. (2001). Vocation souljourn paradigm: A model of adult development to express spiritual wellness as meaning, being and doing in work and life. *Counseling and Values, 45*, 83–93.

Bridges, W. (1980). *Transitions: Making sense of life's changes.* Addison-Wesley.

Britnell, E. S., Madill, H., Montgomerie, I. C., & Stewin, L. L. (1992). Work and family issues after injury: Do female and male client perspectives differ? *Career Development Quarterly, 41*, 145–160.

Bureau of Labor Statistics. (2019). *The employment situation, May 2021.* htpps://bls.gov.news.release/pdf/empsit.pdf

Carlsen, M. (2000). The sustaining power of meaning. *Generations, 23,* 27.

Chan, C. D., Love, C. A., Wright, G., Rowe, J., Ford, Jr., D. J., & Childs, J. R. (2020). Affirming diversity and disability in career development: Multiple perspectives, issues, and constituencies. NCDA Career Developments, Spring, 6–9, 24.

Chiu, L., Emblen, J. D., Julia, D., Van Hofwegen, L., Sawatzky, R., & Meyerhoff, H. (2004). An integrative review of the concept of spirituality in the health sciences. *Western Journal of Nursing Research, 26*(4), 405–428.

Constantine, M. G., & Parker, V. F. (2001). Addressing the career transition issues of AfricaAmerican women: Vocational and personal considerations. In W. B. Walsh, R. P. Bingham, M. T. Brown & C. M. Ward (Eds.), *Career counseling for African Americans* (pp. 99–112). Erlbaum.

Evans, K. M., Rotter, J. C., & Gold, J. M. (2002). *Synthesizing family, career, and culture.* American Counseling Association.

Feiler, B. (2020). *Life is in the transitions: Mastering change at any age.* Penguin Press.

Frankl, V. (2006, 1963). *Man's search for meaning.* Beacon Press.

Frye, J. (2020). *On the frontlines at work and at home: The disproportionate economic effects of the coronavirus pandemic on women of color.* Center for American Progress. https://www.americanprogress.org/issues/women/reports/2020/04/23/483846/frontlines-work-home/

Gelatt, H. B. (1993). *Career development in organizations.* Paper presented at the California Career Conference, San Diego.

Goodman, J., & Hoppin, J. M. (1990). *Opening doors: A practical guide to job hunting* (2nd ed.). Continuum Center, Oakland University.

Goodman, J., & Waters, E. B. (1985). Conflict or support: Work and family in middle and old age. *Journal of Career Development, 12,* 92–98.

Gutek, B. A., & Larwood, L. (1989). *Women's career development.* Sage.

Hansen, S. (2001). Integrating work, family, and community through holistic life planning. *Career Development Quarterly, 49,* 261–274.

Hennig, M., & Jardim, A. (1977). *The managerial woman.* Doubleday.

Jobvite. (2018). *Job seeker nation study.* https://www.jobvite.com/wpcontent/uploads/2018/04/2018_Job_Seeker_Nation_Study.pdf

Land, G., & Jarman, B. (1992). *Breakpoint and beyond: Mastering the future today.* HarperCollins.

Layton, P. L. (1984). *Self efficacy, locus of control, career salience, and women's career choice* [Unpublished doctoral dissertation). University of Minnesota.

Lent, R. W., & Hackett, G. (1987). Career self-efficacy: Empirical status and future directions. *Journal of Vocational Behavior, 30,* 347–382.

Leibowitz, Z., Schlossberg, N. K., & Shore, J. E. (1991). Stopping the revolving door. *Training and Development Journal,* 43–49.

Lipman-Blumen, J., & Leavitt, H. J. (1976). Vicarious and direct achievement patterns in adulthood. *Counseling Psychologist, 6,* 26–32.

Lips-Wiersma, M. S. (2000). *The influence of "spiritual meaning making" on career choice, transition and experience.* DAI 61, no 14A. University of Auckland.

Looby, E., & Sandhu, D. (2002). Spirituality in the workplace: An overview. In D. Sandhu (Ed.), *Counseling employees: A multifaceted approach.* American Counseling Association.

Lopez, S. J., Pedrotti, J. T., & Snyder, C. R. (2015). *Positive psychology: The scientific and practical explorations of human strengths.* Sage.

Lopez, S. J., & Snyder, C. R. (2009). *Oxford handbook of positive psychology*. Oxford University Press.

Martin, W. E., Jr. (1991). Career development and American Indians living on reservations: Cross-cultural factors to consider. *Career Development Quarterly, 39*, 273–283.

McArthur-Blair, J., & Cockell, J. (2018). *Building resilience with appreciate inquiry: A leadership journey through hope, despair, and forgiveness*. Berrett-Koehler.

Mccluney, C., & Rabelo, V. (2019). Conditions of visibility: An intersectional examination of Black women's belongingness and distinctiveness at work. *Journal of Vocational Behavior,* 113, 143–152. https://doi.org/10.1016/j.jvb.2018.09.008

Mclennan, B., Mcilveen, P., & Perera, H. (2017). Pre-service teachers' self-efficacy mediates the relationship between career adaptability and career optimism. *Teaching and Teacher Education, 63*, 176–185.

Mejia-Smith, B., & Gushue, G. (2017). Latina/o college students' perceptions of career barriers: Influence of ethnic identity, acculturation, and self-efficacy. *Journal of Counseling & Development, 95*(2), 145–155. https://doi.org/10.1002/jcad.12127

Nevill, D. D., & Schlecker, D. L. (1988). The relation of self-efficacy and assertiveness to willingness to engage in traditional/non-traditional career activities. *Psychology of Women Quarterly, 12*, 91–98.

Perosa, S. L., & Perosa, L. M. (1985). The mid-career crisis in relation to Super's career and Erikson's adult development theory. *International Journal of Aging and Human Development, 20*, 53–68.

Pew Research Center. (2015). *Women and leadership: Public says women are equally qualified, but barriers persist*. http://www.pewsocialtrends.org/2015/2015/01/14/women-and-leadership/

Pew Research Center. (2018). *Women and leadership 2018: Wide gender and party gaps in views about the state of female leadership and the obstacles women face*. https://www.pewsocialtrends.org/2018/09/20/women-and-leadership-2018/

Pickett, K. E., & Wilkinson, R. G. (2007). Child wellbeing and income inequality in rich societies: Ecological cross sectional study. *British Medical Journal, 335*(7629), 1080–1086.

Sampson, J. P., McClain, M.-C., Musch, E., & Reardon, R. C. (2013). Variables affecting readiness to benefit from career interventions. *Career Development Quarterly, 61*(2), 98–109.

Savickas, M. (1997). The spirit in career counseling: Fostering self-completion through work. In D. P. Bloch & L. J. Richmond (Eds.), *Connections between spirit and work in career development: New approaches and practical perspectives* (pp. 3–25). Davies-Black.

Schlossberg, N. K., & Leibowitz, Z. B. (1980). Organizational support systems as buffers to job loss. *Journal of Vocational Behavior, 18*, 204–217.

Schlossberg, N. K., & Robinson, S. P. (1996). *Going to plan B: How you can cope, regroup, and start you life on a new path*. Simon & Schuster.

Scofield, M. (1993). About men: Off the ladder. *The New York Times Magazine*, p. 22.

Smith, E. E. (2017). *The power of meaning: Crafting a life that matters*. Crown.

Spencer, S. A., & Adams, J. D. (2002). *Life changes*. Impact.

Steefen, P. R. (2012). Approaching religiousity/spirituality and health from the Eudaimonic perspective. *Social and Personality Psychology Compass, 6*, 70–82.

Sue, D. W., Sue, D., Neville, H. A., & Smith, L. (2019). *Counseling the culturally diverse.* Wiley.

Super, D. E. (1980). A life-span, life-space approach to career development. *Journal of Vocational Behavior, 16,* 282–298.

Super, D. E., & Knasel, K. G. (1979). *Development of a model, specifications, and sample items for measuring career adaptability (vocational maturity) in young blue collar workers.* National Institute for Careers Education and Counselling, and Ottawa, Ontario, Canada, Canada Employment and Immigration.

Super, D. E., & Knasel, E. G. (1981). Career development in adulthood: Some theoretical problems and a possible solution. *British Journal of Guidance and Counselling, 9,* 195–201.

Super, D. E., & Nevill, D. D. (1984). Work role salience as a determinant of career maturity in high school students. *Journal of Vocational Behavior, 25,* 30–44.

Valach, L., & Young, R. A. (2004). Some cornerstones in the development of a contextual action theory of career and counseling. *International Journal for Educational and Vocational Guidance, 3,* 61–81.

Vos, J. (2018). *Meaning in life: An evidenced -based handbook for practitioners.* Springer Nature.

Watts, A. (2004). *Career guidance policy: A report on the OECD, EU and World Bank Review.* Address delivered to an International Symposium on "International Perspectives on Career Development," the International Association for Educational and Vocational Guidance, and the National Career Development Association, San Francisco.

Wheatley, M. (2002). Spirituality in turbulent times. *School Administrator, 59,* 42–46.

Whiston, S. C., & Brecheisen, B. K. (2002). Practice and research in career counseling and development— 2001. *Career Development Quarterly, 51,* 98–154.

Yang, J. (1991). Career counseling of Chinese American women: Are they in limbo? *Career Development Quarterly, 39,* 350–358.

III

WHAT CAN WE DO WITH WHAT WE KNOW AND HEAR?

7

Individual Counseling

The transition model provides a framework, a conceptual lens if you will, for counselors to use as they help their adult clients look within themselves, look at their relationships, and their work. Our approach is simple: Help clients enhance their resources for coping by assessing their situation, self, support, and strategies.

Levinson (1978) provides a case example of John Barnes, a biologist. He tells us about a man who has changed his view of himself from the one he had when younger. He has accepted himself as a capable, albeit flawed, adult man:

> He felt privileged to be able to do work he enjoyed, and he was content to make a modest social contribution as parent, concerned citizen, scientist, teacher, and mentor to the younger generation. He had a sense of well-being. (p. 277)

How can we help other adults in transition achieve the same peace? Cormier et al. (2017) presented a particularly useful road map for counselors to follow when helping clients work through problematic transitions. We clearly cannot, in one chapter, present all that you need to know to become a counselor, but the following overview should provide a way to tie your counseling knowledge to the framework of the transition model.

A SIMPLE COUNSELING MODEL

Cormier et al. (2017) describe a simple counseling model that owes its roots to Rogers (1957), based on the premise that the counseling relationship is developmental in nature. Although each of their four stages is not truly discrete from the others, and clients and counselors may move back and forth among the stages, the process can be described in a linear fashion. The stages are (a) establishing an effective therapeutic relationship, (b) assessment and goal setting, (c) strategy selection and implementation, and (d) evaluation and termination. We discuss each of these stages briefly and then concentrate our attention on what we call the action stages—assessment, goal setting, and strategy-selection interventions.

Relationship Building

The first stage, relationship building, occurs when the counselor develops rapport with the client. This stage requires the counselor to demonstrate what have been called the *core conditions* of empathy, genuineness, and unconditional positive regard or respect (cf. Rogers, 1957). It has been said that the counselor's goal is to demonstrate respect and the client's goal is to build trust. Respect should be a given; trust has to be earned. Most theorists, even if they are not proponents of Rogerian person-centered therapy, agree that these conditions are useful in developing a positive relationship with the client. The client–therapist relationship has been shown to be one of the common factors that most influences change (Ronnestad & Skovelt, 2013).

To demonstrate these conditions and in general to help clients see that you are interested in them and able to help them, you need to use certain skills. It is in the relationship-building stage of counseling that we must pay particular attention to the issues of cultural diversity.

For example, eye contact, considered a necessity of communication in Western middle-class society, is regarded as intrusive by some groups. Comfort with physical proximity varies greatly among cultures. A handshake that may be expected by some is considered intrusive by others. The pandemic and its requirement for most practitioners of seeing their clients by way of telehealth has upended many of these considerations. New ways of connecting in separate physical spaces are being forged. For many, the lack of in-person contact is troublesome, but others have found that some clients find the distance allows a sense of safety that encourages deeper sharing.

Hackney and Cormier (2005) stated that counselors must "consider the cultural factors in *all* client–helper interactions" (p. 47). These cultural factors include the client's ethnic and cultural sense of self, as well as other aspects of the client's life experiences that have shaped his or her worldview and his or her wish to change. We would add that even seasoned counselors must stay alert for multicultural issues, especially when their clients are from a group with whom they have had little experience. It is particularly important to be aware of the client's experiences with oppression, especially if you are a member of the majority culture. All counseling relationships depend on the following behaviors:

1. *Demonstrate empathy*: Counselors can use nonverbal attentiveness, verbal attentiveness, paraphrasing and reflecting client messages, and reflecting client feelings.

2. *Convey genuineness*: Counselors can use supporting nonverbal behaviors such as direct eye contact, smiling, an interested facial expression, and leaning toward the client while seated. Counselors can also use congruence, openness, and self-disclosure.
3. *Convey positive regard*: Counselors can use nonverbal behaviors similar to those used to convey genuineness. Again, it is important to be cognizant of the client's cultural background to ensure that the message communicated is the one you want to send. The authors give as an example the fact that different cultural groups vary in their degrees of comfort with silence. Counselors must therefore not only be sensitive to these differences but also perhaps discuss them with their clients. After all, who is more expert about a client's culture than the client?

Assessment

The second stage, problem assessment, makes use of the techniques of clarifying questions— both open-ended and closed. Some of the information that one might want to acquire in an intake interview includes identifying data, the range of problems, current life setting, client worldview, cultural identity, family history, and personal history—medical, educational, military, vocational, sexual, and marital. Be careful not to act as an interrogator, with one closed question followed by another. Your questions should provide information necessary to lead into a problem-definition analysis that includes (a) components of the problem—feelings, cognitions, behaviors, physical or somatic complaints, and interpersonal relationships; (b) patterns of contributing events; (c) duration of the problem; and (d) client coping skills, strengths, and resources (Cormier et al., 2017). It is important to remember the possibility of misunderstandings arising from cross-cultural differences as you use assessments, which may be minimized by using narrative and informal assessments along with more formal types. It is interesting to note here that some research has shown that increased exposure to a diverse clientele improves cultural sensitivity (Arthur & Januszkowski, 2001; Wihak & Merali, 2007).

Because assessment can have positive and negative effects on clients, it is important to use care and sensitivity during the assessment portion of the counseling interview. If assessment is done well, clients feel understood, relieved, hopeful, and motivated. If assessment is not well done, clients feel anxious, interrogated, vulnerable, and evaluated. Counselors can avoid some of these negative reactions by taking care to intersperse relationship-building techniques such as reflecting thoughts and feelings and by being sensitive to the client's reactions during the assessment phase.

Although assessment remains a key aspect of this phase of counseling, we do not view it as an initial discrete responsibility of the counselor. Rather, assessment is an ongoing process throughout the counseling relationship and is best approached in a collaborative manner with the client. Transitions involve adjustment and the assimilation of life changes, and ongoing collaborative assessment keeps both counselor and client mindful of the process. Working with the client in this way provides ongoing opportunities to adjust the focus of counseling, affirm the client's strengths, and work with liabilities. As clients change during the counseling process, and during the time during which counseling evolves, it is important to continually reassess both the client and their goals for counseling. As we described in Chapter 1, identity renegotiation (Blume, 2010) is an ongoing process and necessitates renegotiating goals and objectives of counseling.

Goal Setting

The third stage, goal setting, responds to counselors' and clients' need to know where they are heading. Goals have motivational, educational, and evaluative functions. Agreeing on the desired outcomes of counseling can keep the sessions on track; agreeing on how the counseling will proceed is an appropriate aspect of entering into any therapeutic relationship. The ideals of integrative life planning (Hansen, 1997) lend credence to the cross-cultural necessity of having a road map for counseling, that is, goals, while recognizing the need to change the goals as counseling proceeds.

Both outcome and process goals may change during counseling. As counselors help clients deepen their understanding of themselves and their situations, they may abandon earlier goals and set new ones. The important point is to make these changes as explicit as possible. Often the client's stated goals—the so-called presenting problem—are a way for clients to test the counselor and the process. The stated goal is usually real but not always the most important. This phenomenon is particularly common when clients come to counselors with career issues. This "safe" topic often gives way, after trust is established, to concerns about relationships or the clients' own internal feelings. Changing or deepening of goals may also occur in situations in which the counselor's culture is different from that of the clients. In that situation, the question "Can I trust you?" may be especially salient. When setting goals, counselors may also use the techniques of confrontation, imagery and visualization, and role enactment. Language work that includes completing sentences such as "I want ..." or "I do not want ..." may also be useful at this stage.

Interventions

Cormier et al.'s fourth stage—interventions—is clearly the heart of the counseling process. The selection of appropriate interventions reflects the counselor's theoretical orientation. Let us express a hope here that you will be flexible in choosing interventions, basing your choice on your client's needs as well as your own predilections and that you will consider your client's culture, learning style, and the characteristics of the problem as well as your own experience and comfort level. Most counselors adhere to one of the following four major theoretical orientations. The first, *affective interventions*, was designed to help clients focus on feelings. Some strategies used by affectively oriented counselors include listening for and reflecting feelings, focusing (cf. Gendlin, 1981), and helping clients integrate or change feeling states. Some other techniques that may be used come from the Gestalt literature, for example, the empty-chair technique or dream work.

The second, *cognitive interventions*, was designed to help clients change their belief system—their thinking. Strategies include (a) Ellis's (e.g., 1984) ABC process for challenging irrational beliefs, (b) transactional analysis (cf. Berne, 1964), (c) postponement strategies, and (d) cognitive restructuring—shifting from self-defeating to coping thoughts. A noted researcher in this area is Aaron Beck (1976, 1996) who promoted cognitive restructuring as a treatment modality. The main idea behind this is that if clients *choose* to use this modality, they can learn to alter their thoughts and core beliefs and therefore change their behavior.

The third, *behavioral interventions*, was designed to help individuals replace a maladaptive behavior with a more desirable one. Some strategies include social modeling; role play and rehearsal, systematic desensitization as well as self-management techniques, for example, self-monitoring, self-rewards, or self-contracting. And the fourth, *system interventions*, was designed to change the system in which individuals find themselves. These are based on the beliefs that (a) all elements in a system, for example, a family, are interrelated; (b) change in any part of a system, for example, in an individual, will lead to alteration of the entire system; and (c) systems have inertia and therefore resist change. This leads to the conclusion that it is difficult for individuals to change without a concomitant change in the system in which they are involved, usually their family. Systems interventions, or family therapy, are beyond the scope of this book, but they are often appropriate for people in transition, especially if the transition is one that involves the family, such as a job loss or the birth of a child. Some systems interventions include altering communication patterns, role-playing, altering family structure, and using the family genogram. (For more information on systems interventions, see Haley & Richetort-Haley, 2003; McMahon & Patton, 2019; Minuchin & Fishman, 1981.) For a discussion of cultural diversity and systems theory, see James et al. (2018).

Another type of intervention key to the counselor's role involves *advocacy*. Especially when working with clients who are marginalized, poor, or dealing with oppression, advocacy can be an important component of the counseling process. We discuss counselors as advocates in Chapter 10.

Termination and Follow-Up

Stage 5, termination and follow-up, is a process that begins when either the counselor or the counselee decides that the counseling relationship will end soon. Reasons for termination vary widely, ranging from a projected move, to lack of funds, to dissatisfaction with progress, or to such satisfaction with progress that there is a lessening need to continue. Regardless of the etiology of the decision, progress should be assessed by the client and the counselor and generalized when possible into other areas of life. Follow-up should be planned and should include referral if necessary. Finally, the relationship should end.

An alternative termination strategy uses the metaphor of the periodic check-up. Goodman (1992) suggested that the "dental model," with its expectations of regular check-ups and routine maintenance, is an analogy that can be applied to counseling. In the more traditional format, we, as counselors, often distinguish ourselves from many of our mental health colleagues by saying that we use an educational rather than a medical model. Instead of diagnosis, treatment, and cure, counseling emphasizes teaching students and clients the necessary skills for developing satisfying and productive lives.

The premise behind the dental model of counseling is regular check-ups, closer together at first, but lengthening eventually, to see how things progress. In those meetings, counselors and their clients will check out the effectiveness of the maintenance activities they had agreed upon, for example, mood-altering exercises or support utilization. They would make a determination about the effectiveness of current levels of functioning and work together to plan the future. In this model, final termination would be a rare event; rather, each check-up would include decisions about future sessions.

Counselors' behaviors during the relationship-building and termination stages of counseling are not likely to vary, regardless of the area of the transition model being addressed. In relationship building, counselors strive to build rapport—to get to know their clients better. During termination, counselors strive to help their clients evaluate their progress and make plans for their futures. However, counselors can enhance their work in the assessment, goal setting, and intervention stages by using their understanding of the 4 S's of the transition model. Suppose that a counselor is at the *intervention* stage of counseling with an adult who, during the *assessment* stage, identified the *self* as an area of need and, during the *goal-setting* stage, expressed a desire to return to a *sense of equilibrium*. You might use the intervention of a *positive asset search* to help that adult rediscover strengths and identify internal resources to use in coping. The balance of this chapter provides more detail about using the standard counseling assessment, goal-setting, and intervention stages with each of the components of the transition model—situation, self, support, and strategies.

ASSESSMENT

The goal of the assessment phase is to help both counselors and clients gain a better understanding of the issues that brought the client to counseling in the first place. During this phase, they jointly assess the clients' balance of resources and liabilities. It is important to keep in mind that assessment is ongoing throughout the counseling process because this continues as a collaborative process with our clients, checking with them, adjusting accordingly, and reassessing for the balance of strengths and liabilities.

Assessing Situations

To understand a client's situation during a transition, a counselor must explore the transition's triggers, timing, source, control, role change, and duration; the client's previous experience with a similar transition; and concurrent stress. These describe aspects of the transition that are particular to the individual. As mentioned, a dozen adults experiencing the same transition, such as getting divorced, all operate in a context that makes each of their situations unique. These areas should be discussed with clients as you work jointly in the initial assessment phase of counseling, bringing about a greater understanding of the nature of their transition. Let us look at two divorced women to examine how clients facing similar transitions can differ.

Shu Fen Lee, a 40-year-old Chinese American homemaker, recently divorced her husband of 20 years. She worked as a receptionist in a law firm for 3 years after graduation from high school and then married and worked as a stay-at-home momraising her five children, who now range in age from 7 to 18. Although she is receiving child support, she must return to work to support herself and help support her children.

In working with her to assess her situation, Shu Fen's counselor helps her to look at the context in which the transition is happening. On the positive side, she is staying in the family home, which she now owns without a mortgage. Her ex-husband is reliable about paying his child support. Her health is good. Her elderly parents live with her, and her mother can help with childcare for brief times, if necessary. On the negative side, her ex-husband hardly sees his children, her father's health is rapidly failing, her mother will probably soon need help in caring for him, and her secretarial skills are out of date. She has never touched a computer.

Ivana Wilson, also newly divorced, came to this country 2 years ago to marry her husband, whom she met when he was working in Hungary. She speaks very little English, has never worked in the United States, and is still waiting for her citizenship papers. Her parents are dead, and the rest of her family is scattered, with none living near her. Ivana did not want the divorce. Ivana's situation is clearly very different from Shu-Fen's.

Counselors can use an environmental scan as a strategy to help clients assess their situations. This scan is often referred to as *developing contextual awareness*, that is, being aware of the context in which one lives (A. G. Watts, personal communication, June 2000). Bluestein (2006), discussing work, pointed out that context includes "economic trends, cultural beliefs about work and wealth, relationship factors, historical issues, and political frameworks" (p. 65).

In a classic work, Locke and Parker (1994) identified five areas of cultural assumptions and values for counselors to think about as they work with clients. They are as follows:

1. Activity: How do people approach activity? How important are goals in life? Who makes decisions? What is the nature of problem-solving?
2. Definitions of social relations: How are roles defined? How do people relate to those whose social status is different? How are gender roles defined? What is the meaning of friendship?
3. Motivation: What is the achievement orientation of the culture? Is cooperation or competition emphasized?
4. Perception of the world: What is the predominant worldview? What is the predominant view on human nature? What is the predominant view on the nature of truth? How is time defined? What is the nature of property?
5. Perception of self and the individual: How is self defined? Where is a person's identity determined? What is the nature of the individual? What kinds of persons are valued and respected? (pp. 42–43)

We suggest that you keep these questions in mind as you read the rest of this section. Be aware that you do not need to know all the answers; often the best way to find out your clients' values is to ask them. Given the variety of values within even the dominant culture, it may be important to ask such questions of all clients, as the answers may affect the meaning of their transitions. Ratts et al. (2019), focusing on career counseling, provided a rationale appropriate for all counseling. "Multicultural and social justice career counseling has many benefits. [It] … ensures that client problems will be viewed with a wider lens that includes the social milieu, thus providing … a more comprehensive understanding of the issues with which clients present" (p. 112).

Some clients may need to be taught how to look at the environment in which they find themselves. They may need to be encouraged to watch the news on television, listen to it on the radio, or read information on the internet or in the newspaper, with an eye on issues related to the one they are facing. Often "news magazines" on air, online, or in print supply the in-depth coverage that provides this kind of awareness. Others may gain an awareness of the world around them by listening to friends, acquaintances, and coworkers discuss their lives, again listening for information that will help them understand the context of their personal transition. Maintaining a skeptical stance may also be helpful, as information may not be accurate or may not be applicable to the client's situation.

It is important to remember that clients' cultural environments are also a part of the context. People have differing ways of looking at goals and decision-making, defining roles, viewing the world, or valuing competition or cooperation. Both counselors and clients need to understand the implications of these cultural mediators as they strive to assess their transition situations.

For transitions related to the individual, the environment may include others engaged in similar searches for meaning. The women's and men's movements are good examples of this. Knowing that others are experiencing transitions like one's own provides a kind of emotional support. As we look at relationship issues, the relevant context may be a family situation, including the changing customs of society. Consider, for example, the difference between 1950 and 2020 in how someone might react to the transition of becoming a grandparent via an unwed daughter. In 1950, many people lied to the neighbors and refused to acknowledge the child and a few even severed relations with the daughter. In 2020, most would come to terms with the situation and maintain close ties with both daughter and grandchild. For others, it may not even require "coming to terms" but may seem natural and normal. Another important example relates to the way sexual orientation is viewed. In 1950, a person who was gay or lesbian, nonbinary or transgender was most often "in the closet" at work and even with friends and neighbors. In 2020, they are much more likely to be open and be accepted by others for who they are, although homoprejudice certainly still exists.

Ivana and Shu Fen share the overall environment of the United States, but they may be in different minienvironments created by where they live or the belief system of their cultural group. Contextual awareness may help laid-off workers avoid shame at their plight and increase understanding of the societal forces that caused the company to reduce its size, go out of business, or move to another state or offshore. In all of these examples, contextual awareness may also lead to political action, empowering clients to change their context. As we discussed, the recent sociopolitical context continues to ignite group actions, such as the large protests across the United States drawing attention to needed changes and social justice. The Black Lives Matter movement, which was triggered by George Floyd's death, brought out people from across all races and ethnicities, uniting people in unprecedented numbers, young and old, men and women, coming together with a clear purpose.

As counselors help clients assess their environments, it is important to help them develop a reality base—approaching their situations as they really are, not as they perhaps wish or fear. We are reminded of a client who had lost her ability to drive because of failing eyesight. She determined that asking friends for rides was her only option, a position she found extremely demoralizing. Her counselor was able to help her discover both public and private transportation designed for physically challenged people. Because she was able to accept herself as being "one of them," she was able to expand her view of the environment in which she was now operating.

Traditional assessment techniques may also be used in examining clients' situations. In assessing Mike Suarez's situation (see Chapter 4), for example, the counselor could have Mike describe his family and community obligations and have him begin to learn about the world of work and opportunities for education and training. The technique of information interviewing (see Azrin & Besalel, 1980) is an effective way for many adults to conduct this exploration. Others may find it helpful to read about occupations on the internet or in publications such as the *Occupational Outlook Handbook* (2020) that is available free on the internet at www.bls.gov/oco as well as in most libraries.

Assessing the Self

We believe that the most effective way to assess clients' internal resources is by listening as clients tell their "stories." This narrative approach to counseling, as described by Savickas (2005, 2019) and others, has been shown to elicit rich and detailed client histories. By using the basic counseling skills of attending, reflecting thoughts and feelings, and asking open and closed questions, we get to hear these stories from the client's perspective. In the discussion that follows, we will first examine some methods of assessment, and then we focus on three particular areas of the self: hardiness, spirituality, and self-efficacy. For any one individual, we want to target certain areas of the self. In Mike's case, for example, one might give him an interest inventory or an ability test. These would help Mike expand his knowledge about what he likes and what he can do. Further, these kinds of instruments often tie interests and abilities to job titles, so Mike might be able to consider a wider range of opportunities. Or one might help him use a card-sort technique to identify occupations of interest while recognizing the need to set priorities and make choices. Particularly since Mike has indicated that he would like to change areas of occupation and consider one that has more meaning to him, this phase of counseling is especially important.

A career counselor could have Mike compose a work autobiography to observe his transferable skills and his past decision-making and problem-solving approaches. Systematic assessment instruments are also helpful. For example, counselors may use The Salience Inventory (Super & Nevill, 1986) to help understand the importance of work in an individual's life. They might use Krumboltz's (1991) *Career Beliefs Inventory* to help individuals become aware of and confront beliefs that may be blocking their progress. An inventory designed to create a format for discussion with a counselor and connected to Hansen's (1997) integrative life planning is Reile's (2010) Career & Lifestyle AIM* Aspirations In My Life.

Informal assessment techniques offer a nonthreatening and often enlightening way to assess clients' aspects of self. Creative art techniques, such as creating a collage representing the present and the future, can bring to light many aspects of a client that formal assessments miss. The processing of these types of projects can enrich the counseling sessions with deeper held meanings, values, and dreams of the client. Other informal techniques include creating a lifeline or the aforementioned genogram.

A lifeline provides a visual graph of the client's life story with a graphic detail of life's ups and downs. Working with a lifeline can help clients tell their stories in greater detail, and the counselor can reflect the strengths and life lessons the client has gained through past experiences. The life story can be divided into chapters with each chapter given a title. The overall story may have a title and a motto as well. Processing these types of informal assessments may deepen the client–counselor relationship while empowering clients to have a clearer vision of their imagined futures. Clients often experience these as creative outlets, and they may help clients give voice to what may not be as easily conveyed verbally during the counseling session. Hansen's (1997) Circle of Life is another technique that is useful in helping clients explore what is meaningful in their lives.

A genogram is often used by those who apply a family systems approach and can be a valuable tool in assessing the self. For example, clients can explore internalized family messages and family influences by using the genogram. Cultural values are often brought to the forefront when a genogram is processed, especially as these relate to gender, educational, and career expectations. These types of informal techniques allow for both personal and culturally held meanings, values, spirituality, and role expectations to be part of the assessment process.

Some computer-aided career development programs are particularly geared to the needs of adults. They provide a way for clients to integrate their interests, values, and preferred work environment with job titles and descriptions and to gain information on required training or education for each. (It is beyond the scope of this book to describe these instruments and programs in depth; for more detailed information, see books such as *A Comprehensive Guide to Career Assessment* 7th edition by Stoltz & Barclay, 2019, or *Using Assessment Results for Career Development*, 9th edition by Osborn & Zunker, 2015.)

Hardiness. As we begin assessing an individual's ability to manage the transition at hand, we might consider looking at hardiness, a concept that provides a way of looking at an individual's stress resistance—the way people view themselves and their situations (Maddi, 1999, 2002). He says that "hardiness seems to decrease the tendency to appraise events or circumstances as stressful. … [it] seems to motivate coping with stressful circumstances in a transformational (solution oriented) rather than regressive (avoidance oriented) manner" (p. 85). Dailey (n.d.), expanding on this work, described several dimensions of a hardy person, including openness to change, commitment, control, and confidence. Let us discuss each in turn.

1. *Openness to change*: Looks to the future rather than to the past, sees opportunity rather than barriers, and accepts and perhaps even enjoys challenge. The simplest way to assess openness is to ask individuals questions such as the following: "What do you fear and what do you look forward to as you think about the future?" and "What positive consequences can you see coming from this transition?" It is important not to devalue clients' suffering if the transition is painful; rather, the goal is to help them see that there is a future for them, albeit a different one from what they had anticipated. A new widow usually does not see her

transition as positive, but she can be helped to see that her future may still contain happiness.

2. *Commitment*: Sense of purpose, sees meaning in their own actions, feels connected to social goals. Clients who feel that they matter to individuals and to society usually have a stronger sense of purpose than those who do not; clients with unambiguous goals are often better able to focus on the future than those who wait for events to happen to them. Perhaps the clearest way to define commitment is to say that it is related to the amount of energy the client is willing to invest in achieving goals. Counselors can assess commitment by considering factors such as whether clients keep appointments or do assigned "homework" or whether they seem willing to experience some pain in exploring and gaining understanding of their internal world. Counselors can help clients achieve commitment by identifying incentives or rewards for achieving counseling goals. Rewards can come from adding something positive to life, for example, developing talents or minimizing something unpleasant, such as reducing pain.
3. *Control*: Believing that one has control over how one will respond to life events is the opposite of a sense of powerlessness. One may still express deep feelings; we do not believe that keeping "a stiff upper lip" is always, or even often, the best course to follow. One may control one's response by choosing to grieve deeply and publicly over a loved one, crying (or raging) frequently, and allowing oneself to feel and express all of one's pain. Another person may, however, choose to express his or her grief by maintaining a dignified quietness, by using the energy of grief to work for cancer research, or by becoming involved in action-oriented groups such as Mothers Against Drunk Driving, Black Lives Matter, or by supporting gun control legislation.
4. *Confidence*: Feels personally valuable and believs that rejection does not mean worthlessness. Although we should never underestimate people's insecurities, confident people approach transitions with a distinct advantage. We can assess global confidence in a variety of ways: with formal self-esteem measures, by asking our clients how confident they feel, and by looking at their nonverbal behavior and making our own estimation of confidence. We can also ask them questions that reveal how accepting they are of others, knowing that confident people accept their own imperfections and therefore tend to be more accepting of the imperfections of others. When judging confidence, we must be aware of cultural differences in how confidence may be expressed or hidden. Many cultural groups have taboos against speaking positively about oneself; others have taboos against eye contact or assertive speech patterns. It would be a mistake to assume that people who have these taboos lack confidence because their behavior differs from the patterns of the White Western male. In addition, people often hide their lack of confidence under an attitude of bravura; counselors need to be able to see beneath such surface presentations. Not all lack of confidence is internally based and therefore "curable" through

> attitudinal change. A person may be reacting realistically to a situation that is indeed discouraging and perhaps beyond their ability to fix. Oppression exists, and individuals in discriminated-against groups must manage this, often on a daily basis. A. G. Watts (personal communication, June 2000) stated that counselors have an obligation to help clients learn about the relevant sociopolitical–economic causes of their transition so that they can separate their own responsibilities from those things over which they have little or no control.

In a related vein, we are encouraged to think about Seligman's (2006) definition of optimistic and pessimistic persons. In the assessment phase, we need to listen for "half-full/half-empty" viewpoints. Seligman provides a "test" of optimism that clients can take if additional evidence is needed to determine where they fit on this dimension. We hope this is an area that can be improved throughout the assessment process.

Spirituality: Another way to assess individuals' ability to handle the transition they are facing is to learn about their spiritual beliefs. Jung (1933) incorporated the spiritual dimension into his theory of human development and conceptualized spirituality as a process of *achieving wholeness.* According to Jung (1933), life is a journey, and particularly in the second half of life, life can become a spiritual process. He viewed the spiritual search for meaning as an integral part of midlife. He believed that, as people reach this stage of development, they become increasingly centered and more deeply connected to their spiritual selves. We might hypothesize that this development is encouraged by the myriad transitions faced by most adults in midlife. (It is important to state here that although spirituality may include organized religion, it is not necessary to our understanding of the concept.)

Spirituality has been defined as "the pursuit of meaning and purpose in life, often individual to clients, including the influence of their belief system and worldview and their values as they face the challenges of life events" (Robert & Kelley, 2015, p. xiii). Spiritual coping has been seen to positively influence the amelioration of distress and to play a central role in coping with stress. Studies have found that the more vital a person's spiritual health is, the more numerous are his or her coping skills (Graham et al., 2001). Graham et al. stated that "spirituality may involve something beyond tangible resources ... spiritual health may include finding meaning and purpose in one's life, relying on a higher power; experiencing peace, or feeling a connection with the universe, the world, or nature" (p. 7). This statement brings attention to the many personally held meanings that spirituality can have for our clients. Understanding these may help them to more effectively use their inner resources. Cormier et al. (2017) stated that spirituality taps into multiple healthy behaviors, including "fostering a sense of meaning or coherence, ... and locating people in support networks who tend to be responsive toned" (p. 431).

Spirituality has been correlated with the experience of resilience and the ability to overcome and succeed in times of distress and challenge (Walsh, 2008). Resilience has also been found to correlate with positive emotions.

Cohn et al. (2009) found that "participants who experienced frequent positive emotions became more satisfied not simply because they were enjoying themselves, but because they built resources that help deal with a wide range of life's challenges. Positive emotions predicted growth in ego resilience, a psychological resource that has proven useful in dealing with both mild and severe stressors" (p. 366). Henderson et al. (2010) studied displaced older adult survivors of Hurricane Katrina and found that "Positive thinking, modified thinking, staying busy, and spirituality were categories that emerged from the qualitative analysis of 119 participants and explained coping" (p. 48).

All of this leads us to the conviction that as we help clients assess their internal resources, we need to include an assessment of their spirituality and resilience. These areas of assessment must be culturally sensitive, and as counselors, we invite, rather than force, exploration of these issues. It is beneficial to discuss spirituality, which may be part of a person's cultural identity, as a potential source of strength. Similarly, self-efficacy beliefs form a part of clients' internal resources.

Self-efficacy: Bandura (1982, 1997) found that expectations of success or failure were important in determining motivation. The phrase *self-fulfilling prophecy* reflects a commonsense understanding of the relationship of self-efficacy to helping adults in transition set goals and plan their futures. Clients who believe that their own actions can influence their environment will be more motivated to set goals and work toward them than those who doubt their effectiveness.

To assess self-efficacy, we may ask clients whether they believe that they can influence their world, their situation, or their fate. Do they feel that most of the control for what happens to them comes from themselves? Do they feel capable of meeting the challenges that they face?

Assessing Supports

How do we help clients assess this area of their life? We need first to ask them to describe, or list, the external resources they have available to them. Who is "in their corner"?

The people in our clients' support systems may also be the same ones who create stress for our clients. We are reminded of the dualistic concept of nourishers versus drainers. This concept is perhaps best described by using an analogy that compares our emotional sense of satisfaction to the water level in a bathtub. If we imagine life's nourishers as filling our "tubs" with water, and life's drainers as allowing the water to flow out, we can see that for our clients to be "full," they need to have or create enhanced flow in (nourishers) and diminished flow out (drainers). This may mean avoiding situations that are confidence draining, avoiding people who are negative or pessimistic, and spending more time in positive situations and with positive, encouraging people. In the assessment phase of counseling, we can determine how full our client's tub is and who and what are the nourishers and the drainers.

We may also want to assess clients' abilities to add to their support system, to make connections. This skill has been identified with hardiness, as people who know how to access support are more able to do so in times of stress. Getting a "reading" on clients' abilities to make connections will help counselors decide what strategies they may need to teach.

Assessing Strategies

Many adults have experienced prior transitions that they navigated successfully. The strategies they used then may be expanded. This is what might be called *a base for growth.* Helping clients remember past useful strategies can be accomplished in a variety of ways, some of which depend on whether you, as counselor, are primarily affectively, cognitively, or behaviorally focused. An affectively oriented counselor, for example, might ask Terry Walker, the overcommitted client, to describe when she felt more in control of her life. A cognitively oriented counselor might encourage her to think about the irrational beliefs that led her to think she must take care of everybody and make them all happy. A behaviorally oriented counselor might encourage her to keep track of how many times each day she says yes to her family members and to try saying no to each of them twice a day.

Pearlin and Schooler (1978) delineated three coping responses that represent a systematic way to examine strategies for managing transitions:

1. Changing the situation through negotiation, optimistic action, advice-seeking, and exercise of potency.
2. Controlling the subjective meaning of the situation by positive comparisons, selective ignoring, and substitution of rewards.
3. Managing the stress of the situation by emotional discharge, self-assertion, and passive forbearance.

We must always consider, however, those strategies that were successful in the past but that no longer are in the client's best interest. A classic example comes from the Adult Children of Alcoholics literature (e.g., Black, 1987; Wegscheider-Cruse, 1989). A child may have become the "good kid" to help survive in a chaotic alcoholic family. That good kid may have hidden all feelings, especially negative ones, eventually not being even aware of them. Virginia Satir (1972) used the dramatic phrase, "brave response for survival," for strategies that helped one cope in childhood with difficult situations. For example, one might have learned to repress feelings to cope with the pain of being abused by an alcoholic mother. The response may no longer be useful, and the conditions that spawned it no longer in existence. Similarly, people raised in a tough neighborhood may have had to be ready to fight at all times; that pugnacious attitude is probably not helpful as they face adult transitions. Sorting out useful strategies already in our clients' repertoires from those that may be counterproductive is therefore another useful assessment arena.

GOAL SETTING

If we agree that a primary goal of assessment is to help the client have a basis for goal setting, then we can see clearly that the self-appraisal fostered by the strategies listed earlier is an essential starting place. Let us look then at goal setting in light of the transition model.

Goal setting helps the client discover a scenario for a better future. Cormier et al. (2017) stated that goals "are a direct response to one or more of the following questions: Where do I want to be?, Where do I need to be?, Where do I want to be?" (p. 252). Each aspect of the 4 S model can be considered in assisting clients in setting goals.

Goals Related to the Situation

Clients working with internal transitions may set a variety of goals—goals that help them to have a different cognitive understanding of the situation, goals that relate to a deeper understanding of their own psychological dynamics, or goals that relate to changing their behavior. Clients may set goals that change the way they perceive a particular situation, or they may want to change the situation. We call this *modifying the environment.* Clients struggling with transitions involving relationships may set goals that help them redefine the relationship, change the ways they relate to significant others in their lives, or grieve for lost relationships. Clients involved in work transitions may want to enter a particular work situation or may be forced to leave it; they may want to plan changes within a work situation, or they may have goals related to formal or informal education or training. Or they may want or have to choose an entirely new occupation.

Goals Related to the Self

Even when a transition is desired or well accepted, we often still want our feelings to "return to normal." Sometimes, we just want to come to peace with the transition. *Talking it out* is the commonsense phrase for what helpers know is an important process of expressing rather than suppressing feelings. Frequently clients will use a transition experience as a spur to pursue other therapeutic goals. Unresolved conflicts from earlier times in life may be addressed; longstanding problems, such as depression, may be brought to the counselor's office. Behavioral issues, such as phobias, may be confronted.

Transitions, be they events or nonevents, or of short, long, temporary, or permanent duration, create a disequilibrium. In more idiomatic terms, they *upset the applecart.* Psychologically as well as physiologically, human beings share with the rest of the physical world the tendency to return to homeostasis, to return to equilibrium. Clients express this tendency when they say things such as "I wish things could just stay the same," or "I wish things could go back to the way they were." Often dynamic self-understanding is the first step to a return to equilibrium.

An impetus for personal growth, what has been called the *teachable moment,* sometimes occurs during times of disequilibrium. It may be expressed by questions such as "What did I do to get myself in this mess?" "How come I always get involved with alcoholics?" or "I seem to be overqualified for every job I get. Am I doing something wrong?" These questions help clients set goals for change. Goals related to the self then usually involve a search for emotional relief or personal growth, in counseling terms, dynamic self-understanding. Mike Suarez from Chapter 4 expressed this when he said he was glad that his wife's divorce request had motivated him to seek counseling, whichhe could use to address his general malaise.

Goals Related to Support

Generally, people in transition find that their support systems either have diminished or have been overwhelmed by the new demands placed on the members of the system. These people need then to *enhance* or *increase support.* Terry Walker exemplified an important exception. Terry, you will remember, mattered too much to too many people. What might be viewed as her support system was actually functioning more as a stress system. Terry needed to get support by adding other sources. She needed to add nourishers and to find ways to protect herself from drainers.

Former supports often fail to meet an individual's current needs. For example, many newly divorced or widowed people find that the couples who were an important part of their support system while they were a part of a couple are no longer interested in being a part of their new life. And even when they are willing, the support they used to provide may no longer be what the newly single person needs. Similarly, new parents may find that old friends, if childless, do not understand the complexity of their lives. These friends may have trouble understanding the need to plan all social events well in advance and to never be sure they will not have to change plans at the last minute.

Goals Related to Strategies

Clients often come to counseling because the strategies they have been using in the past are not successful now. Furthermore, they are often at a loss about what else to do. Helping them develop more, or better, strategies is often an important immediate goal of counseling. In reality, clients often wish to move directly to strategizing, and counselors have to "slow them down" to look at other issues before they move to action. *Developing an action plan* is an appropriate goal, after enough self-understanding has been created to make the plan likely to be a success.

Case Study

Let us use an example to make some of the preceding discussions come to life.

Chuck Danto, a 33-year-old, single, recovering alcoholic, finds himself flooded with feelings he does not know how to handle. He stopped drinking 2 years ago with the help of the Alcoholics Anonymous (AA) 12-step program and thought that after 2 years of nondrinking he was "home free."

Suddenly he finds that he is reacting to everything—his family, friends, and colleagues say that he is overreacting. He sometimes feels out of control emotionally. He will react with rage to a minor irritation, and he finds himself crying at little things. The irony in all of this for Chuck is that, as far as he remembers, he never "fell apart" like this while he was drinking. Chuck's goal is to *return to the equilibrium* he has recently been feeling, without returning to drinking. His counselor helps him articulate another goal: to develop a *dynamic self-understanding,* in other words, to get a better handle on what's happening to him. The counselor tells Chuck that it is common for drinking to be used unconsciously or consciously to stifle feelings and assures him that the flooding emotions he feels now are also common. As Chuck develops an understanding of the family patterns and personal predilections that led to his drinking, he will be able to better manage these unaccustomed emotions.

Chuck also decides to set a goal of changing some of the places and people with whom he spends time—*modifying the environment.* He is finding that his increased sensitivity makes his job as an assistant principal in a junior high school more difficult. Specifically, he finds himself empathizing too much with the students and finds that he is less comfortable imposing discipline on them. He decides to add career decision-making to his list of counseling goals. He also realizes that although he stopped seeing his drinking buddies when he joined AA, and although he still attends weekly AA meetings, he has not developed new friends. This has meant relying on his family for most of his social life, a situation that is not satisfying for him. *Increasing support,* then, has become another of Chuck's goals, meaning, in his case, looking for new relationships.

As all of these goals are developed and agreed upon, Chuck and his counselor recognize that the final step will be to *develop an action plan* that will enable him to master strategies such as reframing, selective denial, and developing hope and optimism. Using these strategies will help him complete his transitional journey.

At this point, you have worked with your clients to assess their current status and you and your client have set mutually acceptable goals for counseling. What do you do next? Your interventions will vary, reflecting both your own preferred counseling approach and the needs of your particular client.

INTERVENTIONS

Individuals often need help in identifying options. The story of a 36-year-old man who became a paraplegic as the result of an automobile accident illustrates this point. After the initial physical battle to survive, he became preoccupied with how to live. Not surprising, at first he saw no options. Before the accident, he had been a construction worker. Clearly, he would be unable to continue that activity. His first attempt to build a new life was aborted when his application to law school was rejected. After exploration, it became clear that this application had been a response to the influence of his mother, who was a lawyer. A year after the accident and before he clarified his vocational goals, he wrote his mother, "I want to share with you the perspective I now have on my future. Because of your love and support, I am facing the future with courage, hope, and curiosity." The word *curiosity* showed that on a deep level he was going to make it, that he was going to create options, and that he was going to be in control. And, in fact, soon afterward, he applied and was accepted to a school of architecture, which continued his interest in building and took account of his disability. He created an option.

Fifty clerical workers at the University of Maryland (Charner & Schlossberg, 1986) were asked to identify a significant transition. The transitions fell mostly in the family category, followed by a geographical move and work change. When asked, "Generally, in change situations, how do you perceive options?" Ninety-four percent saw more than one. However, when asked, "For this transition, how many options did you perceive?" Thirty-four percent saw only one. This indicates that individuals in transition usually see options, but under stress or when in the midst of a transition that has significantly altered their lives, they often "freeze" and can see only one option.

The concept of options also explains the difference between those who have a midlife crisis and those who experience a midlife transition. Everyone has a midlife transition, that is, a time when he or she begins to see time until death instead of time from birth. But only a few run off, as did Gauguin. Those having a "crisis" probably see limited options.

In the interventions stage, we see the greatest differences among counselors who take different theoretical stances. Following is a discussion that is organized around types of interventions—affective, cognitive, and behavioral—that will illustrate how those approaches can be used in helping clients work with situation, self, support, and strategy issues.

Affective Interventions

Affective interventions are often the most appropriate for those issues relating to identity, autonomy, and meaning-making. The *active listening* techniques used in establishing a relationship are useful in beginning the process of helping clients identify and clarify their feelings. Strictly client-centered therapists may use these techniques almost exclusively throughout their counseling sessions. Often the discomfort that arises from transitions involving the self stems from the fact that a person is not aware of why they are feeling ill at ease. Labeling the feelings and discovering their normality may provide relief. Some clients, however, will find it difficult to identify any feelings; some will be blocked only on some categories of feelings. Although it is an overgeneralization, we have found it useful to be alert for women who have trouble identifying angry feelings and men who find it difficult to recognize their frightened or sad feelings. Early socialization messages, such as "Nice girls don't get mad" and "Big boys don't cry," do carry forward into adult life. These prohibitions are often so strongly internalized that the adult is not even aware of having them, let alone willing to express them.

Narrative approaches (e.g., Maree, 2019; Savickas, 2011, 2015) are frequently used by affectively oriented counselors. The modernist search for human truth is being replaced with the concept of socially *storied lives*. This constructivist-oriented technique, sometimes called *the storied approach* (Brott, 2019), centers on the exploration of the client's world through three phases of story development. The phases include the following: co-construction, deconstruction, and construction. The process involves the co-construction of the client's life stories with the counselor, disassembling the stories by looking at them from various perspectives to deconstruct them. Reconstruction of the stories can then take place through the process of reauthoring the stories. This approach is future orientated in that in reauthoring of the story, the client is empowered to make new choices.

Many other techniques have been developed to help people recognize and express feelings. These include bibliotherapy, focusing, and Gestalt techniques. Some affectively oriented helpers believe in delving into childhood experiences to explore sources of current feelings. These explorations may lead clients to change the way they feel about current events or situations.

One man experienced acute anxiety as he faced his 50th birthday. His wife encouraged him to begin financial planning for retirement, which he resisted mightily, calling it the "R" word, and refusing even to discuss it. As he explored the meaning of this birthday, he found that he felt well physically, was at a comfortable place in his career, and was looking forward to the easing of the family's financial burdens when his youngest child completed college in 2 years. His anxiety was a puzzle to him.

His counselor encouraged him to think back to his childhood and how he viewed 50-year-old men at that time in his life. He then "remembered" that his father, in his early 40s when our client, an only child, was born, had a major stroke a few weeks after his 50th birthday. His father lived as an invalid for many years after this time, and the family never expressed its grief for its loss of a healthy father and husband. The young boy came to be referred to as the "man of the family" and indeed took on many responsibilities much earlier than he otherwise would have.

This awareness enabled the client to do several things. He began to grieve for his father and for his own "lost" childhood. In the process of doing that, he was able to learn to feel and express other emotions, a development that greatly enhanced his sense of well-being and improved his relationships with his wife and children.

In addition, he now could separate his own life from that of his father, understand the care he took of his health, exercising and eating sensibly, and give credence to his doctors when they said he was at a low risk for a stroke. He could plan for the future with some confidence that he would live to have one. His anxiety was diminished, and he faced the future "with optimism."

Ivey et al. (2014) described one affective intervention—a positive asset search. The purpose of this intervention is to identify and emphasize client strengths. They indicated that this process is useful for clients to accept and acknowledge their own strengths and to establish a positive base from which clients can grow.

Using active listening skills as a base, the counselor conducts a positive asset search by asking questions such as "What went on this week that you feel good about?" Some clients respond well to a checklist of strengths (cf. Goodman & Hoppin, 1990) or to looking at transferable skills. Reframing, discussed later, can also be a useful tool in identifying positive assets, particularly when your clients see themselves primarily in negative ways.

An important function of affective interventions for people in transition is that of validating and clarifying their feelings. Adults often feel alone with their feelings, especially their fears. Adults in transition often think that the people around them "have it all together" and that others know what they want and how to get there. Tentative efforts to express their concerns to friends or family members may be met with sympathy, or they may be brushed off. Many of these others may be uncomfortable with feelings in general and, if they are family members, may in addition be afraid to see weakness in someone they depend on. They may feel anxiety about a transition that could or already is affecting them.

For instance, Mike Suarez's wife (from Chapter 4) may not be sympathetic to Mike just because of what his potential change may mean to *her.* Mike, however, may find relief by having a counselor truly listen to him and help him understand what he is feeling. Terry, who we met earlier in this chapter, likewise, may find it helpful to list the positive aspects of her situation and look at her own strengths in that context. She may then be able to articulate her feelings to her husband in a way he can hear, but first she must be clear herself about their origin. She needs to separate out her expectations for herself from what she perceives as his and the children's expectations.

Cognitive Interventions

Many counselors find cognitive interventions to be a useful way of helping adults navigate transitional experiences. We do not mean to imply that the distinctions are always clear. Often cognitive work is combined with affective and/or behavioral work.

Reframing can be described as the process of looking at a situation from a different point of view. The oft-used example of seeing a glass as half empty is an example of a situation ripe for reframing. The goal in this case would be to help the client see it as half full.

Consider the following example. A 40-year-old woman has recently been left by her husband of 20 years. After she took some time to ventilate some of her fear, anger, and grief and after the counselor had gained some information about the marriage, she was asked, "Could you imagine yourself thinking that he did you a favor?" As her life progressed and she began dating, she was finally able to reframe what she had seen as desertion and relabel it as a chance for her to create a new and happier life. Her counselor had helped her to reframe the events and therefore change their meaning.

Instilling hope has often been described as an essential component of good counseling. Without a belief in the possibility of change for the better, it is difficult to muster up energy to take action on one's own behalf. Niles et al. (2019) outlined what they termed *hope-action theory*. They stated that it "incorporates the following attitudes and behaviors needed for creating and sustaining hope: self-reflection, self-clarity, visioning, goal setting and planning, and implementing and adapting" (p. 283).

Hof (1993) described a process of instilling hope and optimism. He said that counselors should use their full range of skills in doing this but added suggestions for some specific hope-fostering techniques. Although geared to couples, they offer useful ideas for counselors working with anyone in transition. Five of his suggestions are presented here:

1. Counselors can provide support, nurturing, and empathy. They can also help clients see that "It is okay and normal to learn/change in steps or stages" (p. 225). Helping clients understand what they can and cannot control can be a very powerful intervention indeed. Consider an unemployed aerospace worker who was laid off because of a reduction in the defense budget. Before this person can complete the grieving process and move on in life, the frustration around being fired must be "let go" and focus placed on what is controllable—personal decisions and planning.
2. Hof's second technique, relabeling and reframing, can be used to turn negative views around and correct client's cognitive distortions. This may include helping clients see positive aspects of their situations, silver linings if you will. Not all events, however, have positive interpretations. For example, a man adjusting to the death of his wife and son in an automobile accident would be hard-pressed to see anything good in this tragic event. Helping him gain hope that he can still have a positive future is appropriate; telling him that there is a silver lining would be cruel. However, a physician who had a similar experience, losing his wife and daughter in an automobile accident, said that the only thing that enabled him to cope was realizing the many lives that were saved when he donated their organs for transplantation.
3. A positive asset search (see Ivey et al., 2014) is designed for the purpose of implementing Hof's third technique, "identifying ... strengths and the expression of them, or of positive potentials" (p. 226). People undergoing

work transitions may also find it helpful to look at their technical and transferable skills (see Bolles, 2020; Goodman & Hoppin, 1990).

4. Helping clients identify and use their spiritual or transcendent beliefs, values, and resources is Hof's fourth technique. Because many religions, life philosophies, or ethical creeds offer encouragement and hope in times of trouble, the use of those beliefs, values, and resources can infuse some hope in a time of difficulty, pain, or even despair. Shame and guilt cause many individuals and couples to turn away from their religious and spiritual supports, just when they need them the most (Hof, 1993). Spirituality is often enhanced or embraced for the first time in midlife. This phenomenon makes Hof's suggestion even more appropriate for counseling adults in transition.
5. Hof's fifth technique involves using absurdity, humor, and laughter. Hope can be increased when clients recapture or learn for the first time child-like playfulness and creativity. The physiological effects of laughter can be healing in themselves; psychologically, humor can help clients keep their problems in perspective.

Amundson (1996) proposed 12 reframing strategies for clients struggling with unemployment. These approaches, divided into looking at the past, present, and future, include normalization, looking at accomplishments, transferable skills, and attitudes, positive affirmation, externalizing the problem, and limiting negative thinking, which are all designed to help clients "attain new perspectives on themselves and the labor market" (p. 161).

Seligman (2006) contended that optimism, too, is learnable. Blind optimism might be a mistake, but choice is the goal. For example, a risk analysis can help one determine whether optimism is the right course. If the risks are too great, one should perhaps be careful. (We do want our pilot to be pessimistic and deice the plane one more time!) But in navigating a transition, counselors can help their clients learn to choose when to take an optimistic stance—when to have hope.

Ellis (1984) proposed a step-by-step process for challenging a client's view of a situation. The process, often known by its acronym A-B-C-D-E, includes (a) discovering the Activating event, (b) identifying the client's Belief system, (c) identifying the emotional Consequences of the event, (d) Disputing the client's existing beliefs, and (e) arriving at new Effects. This A-B-C-D-E process is geared toward changing clients' thinking about events, beliefs, and consequences. A key element in this approach is the disputation or confrontation of irrational beliefs.

Using the analysis developed by Ellis (1984), Seligman (2006) proposed that people use one of the following techniques to change irrational beliefs:

1. *Distracting oneself*: Some ways to do this are the following:
   a. *Think of something else*: Counselors can help clients plan ready substitutes for disturbing thoughts, and clients can learn to use them. For example, one might ask newly laid off workers to practice thinking,

"I am worthwhile" whenever they start to think, "I am useless." Thought stopping, closely akin to thought substitution, focuses on not thinking about a particular person or event (see *How to Survive the Loss of a Love* [Colgrove et al., 1991]).

   b. *The imaginary umbrella stand*: This technique involves leaving one's worries in an imaginary umbrella stand at the door of one's home or workplace. The premise is that it is easier to let go of troublesome ideas if they can be reclaimed when convenient. A related technique is to list disturbing thoughts to think about later.
   c. *Physical reminders*: Many people find it helpful to have a concrete reminder, for example, a rubber band around the wrist that can be snapped as a reminder when one starts to think troublesome thoughts.
2. *Disputation*: With this technique, clients are taught to argue with their own beliefs and, we hope, win the argument. A recently divorced woman who wanted to date again but believed she was too unattractive to interest any man kept a log of any compliments she received or heard about herself. She enlisted a few trusted friends to help her and soon had a satisfyingly long list. These "facts" effectively disputed her beliefs, and she soon was able to change, or at least modify, her beliefs.
3. *Looking for alternative explanations:* It was said that the great actress Helen Hayes always felt sick to her stomach before a performance. Clients who experience nausea when anxious about an upcoming event, a job interview, for example, can tell themselves that they are preparing for a performance in the same way a great actress did.
4. *Decatastrophizing:* Going off a diet one evening does not mean being out of control forever. Nor does one bad grade mean flunking out of school. Many people need help in becoming aware that their catastrophic expectations are unlikely to materialize. Suppose, for example, you are trying to help a woman who moved across the country with her newly transferred husband. She is having trouble settling in and making friends. She says, "The neighbors are all snobs. I called on the woman across the street and she never even called me back. I know I'll never make any friends here." Assisting her to identify her irrational beliefs can help her to reopen her efforts at making friends.

Or take the adult who begins a session with her career counselor with, "This time I want to make the right decision. I want to get training in a field that I am sure will have opportunities for me and that I will enjoy and be able to stay with for the rest of my working life." Waiting for that kind of certainty—a near impossibility—could paralyze the client. Challenging the irrational belief may help the individual engage in effective career planning.

Cognitive restructuring is another thought-based approach in which an analysis of self-defeating thoughts and behavior is used as the precursor to changing how one deals with the world. Cudney (1980a, 1980b) proposed a system in which he invited clients to examine their self-defeating behaviors and to choose between what he called the *life road* and the *death road*—metaphors for ego-affirming and ego-destroying feelings, thoughts, and actions. Times of transition seem to call forth a particular need to rethink one's thought patterns, as previous ones may no longer fit new circumstances.

Networking, often touted but rarely taught, is another method clients can use to manage their need for support during work transitions, based on the fact that approximately 80% of jobs are found through some personal contact. In networking classes, clients are taught how to identify potential contacts, write a script, rehearse telephone calls, develop a record-keeping system, and follow-up on commitments. (cf. Shortland [2015], for an extensive look at networking, including issues faced by women and diverse clientele.) Learning how to network results from a cognitive intervention; actually networking is a behavioral change.

Meichenbaum (1977) used cognitive analysis to develop behavioral interventions. His stress inoculation training is based on the belief that people will cope more effectively if they understand the situation they are in and if they know and use techniques to reduce their anxiety. Ritter (1985) used Meichenbaum's concepts to help clients develop and rehearse a repertoire of self-statements designed to help them prepare for, confront, and cope with stressors. Counselors can help clients formulate statements such as the following:

- You can develop a plan to deal with it, don't worry.
- Don't try to eliminate the fear entirely; just keep it manageable.
- Take one step at a time.
- Relax, you are in control; take a slow deep breath.
- Keep the focus on the present; what is it you have to do?
- It worked; you did it; it wasn't as bad as you expected.

Behavioral Interventions

Behaviors can be defined to include thoughts, but here, we focus on overt actions. We believe behavior change is important and also that there are occasions when affective and cognitive change occur as a *result* of behavioral change.

Modeling, Role Play, and Rehearsal

These closely related techniques provide ways for clients to see others or see themselves performing desired behaviors. Imagine that you are working with a 40-year-old man who is having difficulty adapting to a new marriage. After his parents were divorced, he had little contact with his father. Twenty years of living on his own have made him unsure about how to be part of a couple. He tends to make unilateral decisions about activities and is then puzzled at his wife's resentment. His counselor suggests the following strategies:

1. Watch other couples and observe what the husband does, particularly in regard to decision-making about how they will spend their time (*social modeling*).
2. Act out with the counselor a situation in which he is not sure how to behave. He will play his wife and the counselor will play him (*live modeling and role play*).
3. Act out the previous scenario playing himself (*role play*).
4. Act out a real situation that he expects to face in the near future (*rehearsal*).

When using each of these interventions, the counselor needs to provide feedback about specific details of what is being done. It is also helpful to begin with easier behaviors and move up to more difficult ones. In the case just described, we might want first to have our client practice asking his wife's advice before he makes dinner reservations and eventually discuss with her his career plans and long-term goals.

Imagery Training

A special kind of rehearsal, imagery, allows people to mentally practice handling situations. Commonly used by athletes and performers, imagining oneself successfully behaving in the desired manner can be helpful in actually attaining the desired behavior. It has several advantages over rehearsal: It can be done alone, at any time; it applies in situations for which rehearsal is impractical; and it encourages clients to become self-directed, not depending on the counselor to play other roles or provide feedback.

Many people need practice in imagining a specific situation, but keep in mind that even though for the majority of people imagery is visual, for many, it is auditory or kinesthetic. Ideally, it combines all three elements. Thus, a person preparing for the first day on a new job may want to "walk through" the day beforehand, imagining preparing for work, arriving there, seeing the worksite, hearing its sounds, feeling its atmosphere, performing the job duties, managing breaks and lunch, and ending the workday. Additional elements may be added as necessary and appropriate. When helping people with poor work records, for example, you may want to encourage them to imagine all the barriers that might prevent them from getting to work or completing the assigned tasks. Strategies for overcoming these barriers can then be identified and rehearsed.

Assertion Training

One way of helping clients change their situations is by teaching them some assertiveness skills—communication techniques that provide for the rights and dignity of others while maintaining one's own rights and dignity. Being assertive is an alternative to being passive or being aggressive. Counselors can help their clients integrate assertive approaches by examining the socialization messages they received as children. Many people heard things from their parents that they interpreted, rightly or wrongly, as "You don't count" or "What you want doesn't matter." Or they may have heard "rules" such as "Don't make waves!" "Don't make trouble!" or "Don't draw attention to us!" People in vulnerable positions, for example, women and members of some ethnic minorities, may have had such "rules" foisted on them even more firmly. People who received these kinds of messages tend to be passive more often than is useful to them. On the other hand, some people heard messages such as "The squeaky wheel gets the grease" or "Might makes right." These people may tend to use an aggressive communication style.

Adult children of alcoholics often hear strong messages concerning keeping family secrets. Being truly assertive may require telling the truth about another's drinking or other "skeletons in the closet." It may be difficult for such clients to recognize that they have as much right to help as their family member has to the secret. In this case, assertiveness training may be a necessary prelude to any other helping interventions.

For assertiveness training to be useful, it must be translated into behavior. Clients are typically given an opportunity to practice difficult behaviors during the counseling sessions using role play and rehearsal and then are given "homework" that requests them to practice the behaviors in real situations. They then return and discuss what went right and what did not and perhaps practice again and try again in "real life." Most people who need assertion training are too passive, but there are some clients who are too aggressive and can also benefit from it. These people, too, need new interaction skills and behaviors. Because of the increased potential for feedback, assertiveness training is often particularly effective in a group format.

Anxiety-Reduction Techniques

Affectively oriented counselors may ask nervous clients about their feelings during anxiety-producing experiences. Cognitively oriented counselors may ask nervous clients about their thoughts. Behavioral counselors generally identify symptoms and focus on reducing the physical manifestations of anxiety or fear, often relying on progressive relaxation and systematic desensitization to help clients experience less anxiety. Although it is beyond the scope of this book to give instruction in implementing these behavioral strategies, they are often a useful beginning to any intervention in which anxiety is debilitating or blocking other change. We have found progressive relaxation often to be a useful beginning to a counseling session, allowing the client to be more fully present.

Another intervention relates to mindfulness, sometimes presented as an adjunct to mediation. Research on mindfulness continues to demonstrate that it can reduce stress, anxiety, depression, and pain resulting from medical conditions (e.g., Kabat-Zinn, 2003; Segal et al., 2002). Mindfulness can be viewed as simply bringing one's attention into the present moment (e.g., Langer, 1997; Langer & Moldoveanu, 2000). Kabat-Zinn (2003) described mindfulness as "the awareness that emerges through paying attention on purpose, in the present moment, and nonjudgmentally to the unfolding of experience moment by moment" (p. 145). He stated that mindfulness, as a practice rooted in Buddhism, was an unfamiliar concept in Western culture until recently. However, mindfulness has become increasingly popular as a practice independent of religious and cultural underpinnings, especially as an intervention for stress reduction (Baer, 2003). Detailed instructions for using mindfulness in counseling are provided by Cormier et al. (2017, pp. 473–484). Engagement in mindfulness can take a variety of forms, from formal meditation practices, to informal strategies aimed at cultivating a greater awareness of the present moment within the activities of daily living. Mindfulness interventions may be a helpful strategy for helping clients manage their stress while attending to the present moment rather than ruminating about the past or worrying about the future.

Combination Interventions

Few counselors adhere strictly to one type of intervention. Client needs differ and counselors must be able to vary their approach accordingly. Some interventions we find particularly helpful with adults in transition do not fit neatly into any of the categories previously described.

Problem-Solving Interventions

Force-field analysis, originally developed by Kurt Lewin in 1943, provides a method for analyzing the steps needed to reach a goal. The steps include (a) stating a goal or desired outcome, (b) identifying all of the pathways or methods you now know to reach the goal, (c) identifying all the actual or potential barriers that may prevent you from reaching your goal, (d) picturing the pathways and barriers as forces or vectors operating in opposite directions, and (e) discussing ways to increase the pathways or reduce or overcome the barriers. Many clients find this to be a helpful way to approach an action plan or solve a problem. And, as mentioned earlier, identifying barriers makes it more likely that a person will have the resources to manage them if and when they arise.

This approach was very successful with a rural displaced homemaker, Marie. She wanted to be a nurse's aide, but the community college was 60 miles away. Although she had a grant to attend school, was sure of her career goal, and very much wanted to be self-sufficient, all she could see were problems in attaining the goal. She listed innumerable barriers, including external barriers such as no childcare if her children were home sick from school, potential bad weather in the winter that might make driving difficult, and no private place to study at home. She also identified several internal barriers such as fear of failure, occasional bouts of depression, and a history of not following through on commitments.

Force-field analysis allowed Marie to visualize these barriers on paper. She then added, with the help of her counselor and a positive asset search, her ability to learn new things, her genuine delight in helping others, a new maturity, and a determination to make this change a successful one. She identified a few new barriers also, including lack of funds for books and materials and a sister who thought she was nuts to work so hard and told her so frequently. She was then able to do the following: (a) make contingency plans for the external barriers, for example, find a neighbor who could handle childcare in a pinch, (b) learn some assertion techniques to get her sister "off her back," (c) identify a person in her displaced homemaker support group to call when she got depressed or anxious, (d) investigate further grant funds from the college to help pay for books and materials, and (e) set aside a small corner of her bedroom for a private study place. Although new problems may well arise for her, she has learned a way of analyzing them.

Many people find other problem-solving strategies useful. For some, concrete, sequential, decision-making activities fit their personal style. DECIDES, the easily remembered acronym for the step-by-step approach developed by Krumboltz and Hamel in 1977, has become a classic. They suggest that clients:

1. Define the problem: What is the decision to be made?
2. Establish an action plan: How will I make this decision?
3. Clarify values: What is most important to me?
4. Identify alternatives: What are my choices?
5. Discover probable outcomes: What is likely to be the result of following each alternative?
6. Eliminate alternatives systematically: Which alternatives won't fit my values and situation? Which have the least probability of success?
7. Start action: What do I need to do to make my plans a reality?

Other people suggest more intuitive decision-making approaches. H. B. Gelatt's (1991) positive uncertainty theory posits that if you wait to be sure, you will never decide; if you decide too firmly, you won't be flexible enough to change as needed. His plan was based on two attitudes: (a) accepting the uncertainty of the past, present, and future, and (b) feeling positive about that uncertainty. It includes four paradoxical principles: "(1) Be focused and flexible about what you want. … (2) Be aware and wary about what you know. … (3) Be objective and optimistic about what you believe. … [and] (4) Be practical and magical about what you do" (p. 12). Gelatt has continued to update and expand this theory in his blog.

Solution-Focused Brief Counseling

Another problem-solving strategy is based on the premise that maintaining a solution focus helps clients avoid playing "ain't it awful?" (Berne, 1964) and move to looking for new thoughts, feelings, and behaviors. Clients (a) identify what they want, stating their goals in positive terms; (b) discuss what is working—exceptions to the current unproductive behavior; and

(c) identify what could be hypothetically happening—if a miracle occurred. It is often compared to motivational interviewing and can be used to manage resistance in counseling and therapy. (See, for example, Cormier et al., 2017, pp. 336–378.)

Play Therapy, Humor, Metaphors

Typically considered an intervention for children, Frey (1993), however, made a case for using play therapy with adults. It is especially effective for adults who did not play much as children or for those who have reached some sort of therapeutic impasse. Because play is naturally illogical, it frees people to break away from the way things have been and see what could be. Perhaps it taps into different parts of the brain than other approaches do. Regardless of the mechanism, it seems to work with many clients. Much has been written about using humor in helping, a technique closely related to play therapy (e.g., Mosak, 1987). Humor, too, used with delicacy, can help adults in transition see their problems in a new light. There is considerable evidence of the usefulness of humor as a means of enabling communication, fostering relationships, easing tension, and managing emotions (Kean & Major, 2018). In a similar vein, the use of metaphor has been found to be a useful adjunct in counseling adults during transitions (see, e.g., Amundson, 2019). Clients often present us with metaphors of their situation, such as "being stuck in the middle of the lake without any oars" or "feeling adrift" in their situation. Metaphors can be developed collaboratively as well. A client, a talented artist, created a metaphor of her situation. She depicted a dark hole, surrounding by bricks, and with a chained butterfly trying to fly out of the hole. This became a useful metaphor throughout the therapeutic process, with "taking one brick down at a time" and the instillation of hope that the butterfly represented.

Developing Rituals

Certain transitions, for example, weddings, births, or retirement, come with attached rituals that ease the passage. Others, such as divorce, job loss, chronic health problems, or failing to get a promotion, are ignored. Furthermore, the rituals that often were a part of life before the transition may be accessible no longer. For example, three couples who were all married on the same date, in different years, developed a tradition of celebrating their anniversaries jointly, making it a special event. When one of the couples got divorced, the tradition continued with the other two. Not only did the former husband and wife lose a cherished celebration, but they also felt left out of an important ritual.

A ritual can help with the "betwixt and between period" to connect you to your former roles, assumptions, relationships, and routines, and to move you to your new ones. Myerhoff (1984) discussed the importance of rituals in helping people deal with marginal periods when they are shifting from one phase of life to another, that is, when they are in transition. Housewarming parties are a commonplace example of this. Originally these events provided a way for people to acquire the goods necessary to set up housekeeping; for most people today, they are a ritual to connect old friends with one's new locale.

Nonevents, in particular, are rarely ritualized. Counselors can use Myerhoff's suggestions to help clients develop new rituals. For example, a couple who has decided not to have children may celebrate the decision with the purchase of fragile glassware and invite their friends for an "exhibition." A man who has realized that he will never be promoted to upper management may take his family on a vacation to "celebrate" the lessened work commitment that results from this awareness.

SUMMARY

The foregoing has been an attempt to summarize some of the techniques you might use in helping an adult client cope with transitions using the Hackney–Cormier and transition models in combination with other techniques. We have discussed counselor techniques to be used in the assessment, goal setting, and intervention stages of the model as appropriate, in helping individuals increase the balance of deficits to resources in the areas of situation, self, support, and strategies. We have also indicated how counselors from different theoretical orientations might use this framework to help their clients.

EXERCISES

1. How might you learn about a client's situation in the relationship-building portion of your counseling sessions? If you follow narrative techniques, how might this be different than if you followed cognitive restructuring techniques?
2. Elucidate three ways of helping clients apply their past experiences to their current transition.
3. In assessing a client's support system during counseling, what questions might you ask? How would you help a client learn support-access skills?

REFERENCES

Amundson, N. E. (1996). Supporting clients through a change in perspective. *Journal of Employment Counseling, 33*(4), 155–162.

Amundson, N. (2019). Active engagement: Answering the call for imagination. In N. Arthur, R. Neault & M. McMahon (Eds.), *Career theories and models at work: Ideas for practice* (pp. 1–7). CERIC.

Arthur, N., & Januszkowski, T. (2001). Multicultural competencies of Canadian counselors. *Canadian Journal of Counseling, 35*(1), 36–48.

Azrin, N. H., & Besalel, V. A. (1980). *Job club counselor's manual: A behavioral approach to vocational counseling*. University Park Press.

Baer, R. (2003). *Mindfulness training as a clinical intervention: A conceptual and empirical review*. American Psychological Association.

Bandura, A. (1982). Self-efficacy: Mechanism in human agency. *American Psychologist, 37*(2), 122–147.

Bandura, A. (1997). *Self-efficacy: The exercise of control*. Freeman.

Beck, A. T. (1976). *Cognitive therapy and the emotional disorders*. International Universities Press.

Beck, A. T. (1996). Beyond belief: A theory of modes, personality, and psychopathology. In P. Salkovskis (Ed.), *Frontiers of cognitive therapy* (pp. 1–25). Guilford Press.

Berne, E. (1964). *Games people play*. Grove.

Black, C. (1987). *It will never happen to me*. Ballantine Books.

Bolles, R. N. (2020). *What color is your parachute?* Ten Speed Press.

Brott, P. E. (2019). Narrative career counseling: The storied approach. In N. Arthur, R. Neault & M. McMahon (Eds.), *Career theories and models at work: Ideas for practice* (pp. 73–82). CERIC.

Charner, L., & Schlossberg, N. K. (1986). Variations by theme: The life transitions of clerical workers. *Vocational Guidance Quarterly, 34*, 212–224.

Cohn, M. A., Frederickson, B. L., Brown, S. L., Mikels, J. A., & Conway, A. M. (2009). Happiness unpacked: Positive emotions increase life satisfaction by building resilience. *Emotion, 9*(3), 361–368.

Colgrove, M., Bloomfield, H. H., & McWilliams, P. (1991). *How to survive the loss of a love*. Prelude Press.

Cormier, S., Nurius, P. S., & Osborn, C. J. (2017). *Interviewing and change strategies for helpers* (8th ed.). Cengage.

Cudney, M. R. (1980a). *Instructors guide for the book for eliminating self defeating behaviors*. Life Giving Enterprises.

Cudney, M. R. (1980b). *Workbook for eliminating self defeating behaviors*. Life Giving Enterprises.

Dailey, R. J. (n.d.). *The stress resistant personality*. Unpublished workshop handout. Continuum Center, Oakland University.

Ellis, A. (1984). *Rational-emotive therapy and cognitive behavior therapy*. Springer Publishing Company.

Frey, D. (1993). Play therapy can be a tool in working with adults. *National Psychologist*, 21.

Gelatt, H. B. (1991). *Creative decision making: Using positive uncertainty*. Crisp.

Gendlin, E. T. (1981). *Focusing*. Bantam.

Goodman, J. (1992). The dental model for counseling. *American Counselor, 1*, 27–29.

Goodman, J., & Hoppin, J. M. (1990). *Opening doors: A practical guide to job hunting* (2nd ed.). Continuum Center, Oakland University.

Graham, S., Furr, S., Flowers, C., & Burke, M. T. (2001). Religion and spirituality in coping with stress. *Counseling and Values, 46*, 2–13.

Hackney, H., & Cormier, S. (2005). *The professional counselor: A process guide to helping* (5th ed.). Pearson.

Haley, J., & Richeport-Haley, M. (2003). *The art of strategic therapy*. Routledge.

Hansen, S. (1997). *Integrative life planning: Critical tasks for career development and changing life patterns*. Jossey-Bass.

Henderson, T. L., Roberto, K. A., & Kamo, Y. (2010). Older adults' responses to Hurricane Katrina. *Journal of Applied Gerontology, 29*(1), 48–69.
Hof, L. (1993). The elusive elixir of hope. *Family Journal: Counseling and Therapy for Couples and Families, 1*, 220–227.
Ivey, A. E., Ivey, M. B., & Zalaquett, C. P. (2014). *Intentional interviewing and counseling: Facilitating client development in a multicultural society*. Brooks Cole/Cengage.
James, A. G., Coard, S. I., Fine, M. A., & Rudy, D. (2018). The central roles of rce and racism in reframing family systems theory: A consideration of choice and time. *Journal of Family Theory and Review*, https://doi.org/10.1111/jftr.12262
Jung, C. J. (1933). *Modern man in search of a soul*. Harcourt Brace.
Kabat-Zinn, J. (2003). Mindfulness-based interventions in context: Past, present, and future. *American Psychologist*, 144–156.
Krumboltz, J. D. (1991). *Career beliefs inventory*. Consulting Psychologists Press.
Krumboltz, J. D., & Hamel, D. A. (1977). *Guide to career decision-making skills*. Educational Testing Service.
Langer, E. J. (1997). *The power of mindful learning*. Addison-Wesley.
Langer, E. J., & Moldoveanu, M. (2000). The construct of mindfulness. *Journal of Social Issues, 56*(1), 1–9.
Levinson, D. J. (1978). *The seasons of a man's life*. Ballantine.
Lewin, K. (1943). *Field theory in social science* (pp. 43–59). Harper.
Locke, D. C., & Parker, L. D. (1994). Improving the multicultural competence of educators. In P. Pederson & J. Carey (Eds.), *Multicultural counseling in schools: A practical handbook* (pp. 39–58). Allyn & Bacon.
Maddi, S. (2002). The story of hardiness: Twenty years of theorizing, research, and practice. *Consulting Psychology Journal: Practice and Research, 53*, 175–185.
Maddi, S. M. (1999). The personality construct of hardiness: Effects on experiencing, coping, and strain. *Consulting Psychology Journal, 51*(2), 83–94.
Maree, J. G. (2019). Career construction theory and its application. In N. Arthur, R. Neault & M. McMahon (Eds.), *Career theories and models at work: Ideas for practice* (pp. 217–226). CERIC.
McMahon, M., & Patton, W. (2019). The systems theory framework of career development: Applying systems thinking to career development theory and practice. In N. Arthur, R. Neault & M. McMahon (Eds.), *Career theories and models* at work: Ideas for practice (pp. 237–248). CERIC.
Meichenbaum, D. H. (1977). *Cognitive-behavior modification: An integrative approach*. Plenum.
Minuchin, S., & Fishman, H. C. (1981). *Family therapy techniques*. Harvard University Press.
Mosak, H. H. (1987). *Ha ha and aha: The role of humor in psychotherapy*. Accelerated Development.
Myerhoff, B. (1984). Rites and signs of ripening and intertwining of ritual, time and growing older. In D. Kertzer & J. Keitch (Eds.), *Age and anthropological theory* (pp. 305–330). Cornell University Press.
Niles, S. G., Amundson, N., & Yoon, H. J. (2019). Hope-action theory: Creating and sustaining hope in career development. In N. Arthur, R. Neault & M. McMahon (Eds.), *Career theories and models at work: Ideas for practice* (pp. 283–291). CERIC.
Osborn, D. S., & Zunker, V. G. (2015). *Using assessment results for career development* (9th ed.). Brooks/Cole.

Pearlin, L. I., & Schooler, C. (1978). The structure of coping. *Journal of Health and Social Behavior, 19,* 2–21.

Ratts, M. J., Santos, K. A. T., & Greenleaf, A. T. (2019). Career counseling without borders: Moving beyond traditional career practices of helping. In D. Capuzzi & M. D. Stauffer (Eds.), *Career counseling: Foundations, perspectives, and applications.* Routledge.

Reile, D. M. (2010). *Career & Lifestyle AIM* Aspirations In My Life.* Self-published.

Ritter, K. Y. (1985). The cognitive therapies: An overview for counselors. *Journal of Counseling & Development, 64,* 42–45.

Robert, T. E., & Kelley, V. A. (2015). *Critical incidents in integrating spirituality into counseling.* American Counseling Association.

Rogers, C. R. (1957). The necessary and sufficient conditions of therapeutic personality change. *Journal of Counseling Psychology, 21,* 95–103.

Ronnestad, M. H., & Skovholt, T. M. (Eds.). (2013). *The developing practitioner: Growth and stagnation of therapists and counselors.* Routledge.

Savickas, M. (2005). The theory and practice of career construction. In S. D. Brown & R. W. Lent (Eds.), *Career development and counseling: Putting theory and research to work* (pp. 42–70). Wiley.

Savickas, M. L. (2011). *Career counseling.* American Psychological Association.

Savickas, M. L. (2015). Career counseling paradigms: Guiding, developing, and designing. In P. Hartung, M. Savickas & W. B. Walsh (Eds.), *APA handbook of career intervention, Volume 1, Foundations.* American Psychological Association.

Savickas, M. L. (2019). *The career construction manual.* Author.

Segal, Z. V., Williams, J. M. G., & Teasdale, J. D. (2002). *Mindfulness-based cognitive therapy for depression: A new approach to preventing relapse.* Guilford Press.

Seligman, M. (2006). *Learned optimism.* Knopf.

Shortland, S. (2015). Networking. In P. J. Hartung, M. L. Savickas & W. B. Walsh (Eds.), *APA handbook of career intervention, Volume 1, Foundations.* American Psychological Association.

Stoltz, K. B., & Barclay, S. R. (2019). *A comprehensive guide to career assessment* (7th ed.). National Career Development Association.

Super, D. E., & Nevill, D. D. (1985). *The salience inventory.* Consulting Psychologists Press.

Walsh, F. (2008). *Strengthening family resilience* (2nd ed.). Guilford Press.

Wegscheider-Cruse, S. (1989). *Another chance: Hope & health for the alcoholic family* (2nd ed.). Science and Behavior Books.

Wihak, C., & Merali, N. (2007). Racial/cultural identity: Transformation among school-based mental health professionals working in Nunavut. *Canadian Journal of Education, 30*(1), 291–322.

8

Helping Clients Deal With Nonevent Transitions

Nancy K. Schlossberg

Counselors hear stories about what might have been, about what should have been, and about what did not happen. Yet much research and counseling advice has been focused only on marker events such as marriage, childbirth, changing jobs, divorce, or being fired. Most of these events are observable; many have rituals and celebrations attached to them. Counselors have enormous power to help clients exchange heartbreaks for mended hearts. There are many ways in which they can work with clients—individually, in groups, in workshops, and at brown-bag lunch discussions. Whatever mode they use to help people deal with lost dreams in their lives, they need to be aware of special characteristics associated with these heartbreaks.

The study of nonevents—what they are, how they change lives, and the ways they can be transformed—is new and needed. To that end, a team of researchers at the University of Maryland, College Park, conducted two studies. In the first study, they examined nonevents using multidimensional scaling. This method uncovered the dimensions that differentiate one nonevent from another. Just as we can all tell the difference among cars, such as Fords, Jaguars, and Cadillacs, they felt it would be important to identify the dimensions that differentiated between the disappointed mother and the disappointed doctor. To do that, Schlossberg et al. (1992) collected accounts of nonevents from graduate students, training directors from business and industry, and returning students. From these, they developed eight prototypical nonevents for use in the multidimensional scaling study.

Armed with the findings of this early research, they began searching for additional answers. They arranged interviews with a random sample of

45 men and women aged 55 years and older who served as retired volunteers in the Office of Experiential Learning at the University of Maryland. Other interviews of adults aged 20 to 55 were added to broaden the perspective. These interviews allowed them to hear firsthand what the nonevents of these adults were, how they changed their lives, and what they did to cope.

Combining qualitative and quantitative data allowed the research team to learn about the drama of the unseen, the unlabeled, and the heartbreaks that occur in all our lives. This research resulted in a book written for the general public by Schlossberg with Robinson (1996) titled *Going to Plan B.* But more is needed. Counselors need to help clients deal with nonevents. Thus, this chapter focuses on specific suggestions and strategies for counselors to use with their clients.

I suggest a three-step program for counselors to use as they help clients work through their nonevents. The three steps that the counselors need to use are:

Step 1: Understand the concept of nonevents as a way to listen with a third ear.
Step 2: Develop specific strategies for clients to use as they cope with nonevents.
Step 3: Teach lessons for life literacy.

STEP 1: UNDERSTAND NONEVENTS

The following discussion of nonevents illuminates their role in the lives of adults and helps counselors listen with a new sensitivity to what did not happen in the lives of their clients. Here are some examples of this phenomenon from the lives of people who were interviewed:

- I gave up my career to stay home and raise my children, but they did not turn out as expected. I had a picture of them with sweaters tied around their shoulders and going to Eastern colleges. Instead, one, who had to go to a special school, now works in a grocery store. Another dropped out of school and hasn't made a comeback. The third is a janitor. There is nothing wrong with them or what they are doing. I just spend my life expecting something different. I am so jealous when I read about other families in which the children moved up and made something of themselves. Why do I walk around feeling depressed?
- I always expected to be a parent. I love children and feel I have a lot to give. My wife and I discovered that we can never have children, and my wife refuses to adopt. Am I going to spend the rest of my life being angry at my wife and feeling cheated about not having children? I am really struggling with what to do now.
- My father never realized his dream of becoming a physician. Instead, he sells pharmaceutical supplies and is a chronically unhappy individual.

> The problem is that his lost dream has affected our whole family—my mother, my sister, myself. You wouldn't think someone else's lost dream would affect so many lives. We walk around him as if on egg shells. Is there a healthier way for our family to function?

People often ask, "Am I alone in wondering what might have been?" The answer is no. In fact, these stories, in a sense, are everyone's stories. Each of these people has experienced that sense of what might have been, the earnest expectations that were not met, the dreams that somehow got lost along the way. It is true that some nonevents might seem more significant than others perhaps, but who is to say? Does a thwarted beauty queen feel less pain than a childless man? And how might these adults deal with their pain and give new shape to the future?

Where Do Unmet Dreams Reside?

The researchers found that their respondents' nonevents fell into the following domains: relationships that did not materialize; family problems, such as internality or not becoming a grandparent; career issues, such as not getting a job, not being promoted, or missing an educational opportunity; and issues related to self, such as not shedding those extra pounds. In other words, their subjects and people in general dream about love, family, success, legacy, and self-image.

We recognize that life is not tidy—what starts out as a dream about career can impact dreams about self and family. The woman who discussed her father's career disappointment—not becoming a doctor—noted how it has influenced the family. His depression affected his wife. His disappointment in himself projected onto his adult children. He expected them to perform, perform, and perform some more.

What Triggers Nonevents?

Some triggers can be external, such as a colleague getting promoted while you are still in the same job; others are internal, such as some highly personal reminders that an expectation may never be realized. Whether internal or external, the underlying issue relates to feeling "off time."

Nonevents are triggered when people feel that the events they expected should have occurred and they are woefully behind. Despite what we know about variability in timing of transitions in adulthood, people still hold onto a picture of age-appropriate expectations.

Maria cried the night before her 27th birthday: "I don't give a damn about a career. I want a baby and family. It has not happened, and I am beginning to believe it is never going to happen. I don't want to celebrate my birthday." For several reasons, Maria has decided that her timetable has not been met.

She is Hispanic with a family-oriented cultural heritage, and her sense of timing has triggered a feeling of great loss.

At the same time, another single woman of Maria's age might be delighted that no family responsibilities interfere with her desire to advance her career. Clearly, what is a nonevent and off time for one person might be a desired state of affairs for someone else.

What Types of Nonevents Exist?

Generally, four types of nonevents can be identified: personal, ripple, resultant, and delayed.

1. *Personal nonevents* refer to individual aspirations and might include not having a baby, not being promoted, or never marrying. For example, a person who has been in the same job for 20 years might present an example of nothing happening externally, yet everything changes internally; that is, the person's assumptions about competency and identity are gradually shaken. The expected job change never occurred, altering that person's assumptions.
2. *Ripple nonevents* refer to the unfulfilled expectations of someone close to us, which in turn can alter our own roles, relationships, and assumptions. The parents of two young adults who were interviewed described their children to friends as "just fine." Yet they are upset because neither child has married. The parents are in their late 60s and are not the grandparents or in-laws they expected to be. What is not happening to the adult children means that certain expected events are not happening to the parents. As we examine such disappointments more closely, we see that a nonevent for one person may ripple significantly into another's life.
3. *Resultant nonevents* start with an event that leads to a nonevent. Take the example of the mother who gives birth to a child with multiple disabilities. From this traumatic event may come the resultant nonevent of never being able to have another child. Or consider a rejection from medical school: The resultant nonevent is failing to become a physician. The events themselves have a beginning and an end. Not being a physician can last a lifetime.
4. *Delayed events* are paradoxical. In their interviews, the research team found that adults keenly felt the loss of their dreams, the fear of never realizing a cherished expectation. Yet they can be convinced that possibly their losses are merely delayed events. During the middle years, whenever they come, people begin to face the possibility that they are experiencing nonevents and not delayed events. They begin to give up hope and lose confidence that they can make the dream come true. The question of when an unrealized dream becomes a nonevent rather than a delayed event is not clear-cut.

Are All Nonevents the Same?

Schlossberg et al. (1992) found that nonevents differ in three critical ways: They can be *hopeful* or *hopeless, sudden* or *gradual,* or *in* or *out of one's control.* The most crucial way in which these nonevents differ is in terms of the degree of hope surrounding them. One man, a political exile, gave up all hope of ever returning to his country because of his political standing. And though his sadness remains, he has refused all offers of help. For him, the situation is without remedy, and he is stuck in his private despair. Infertility, not having grandchildren, and rejection from a professional school are also viewed as hopeless. Absence of marriage, surprisingly, was not seen as hopeless. As long as there is breath, our respondents felt, there is a chance to meet the mate of one's dreams. Nonevents perceived as hopeless will have the greatest impact on the adults who contend with them.

Some disappointments seem to broadside us suddenly. Ralph returned to college at the age of 50, a hopeful turn after a sudden resultant nonevent. He wrote on his nonevent questionnaire: "I was groomed from childhood to someday run the family company. That was cut short when my father suddenly sold the business. After some agonizing, infuriating months, I have gone back to graduate school to study gerontology." Ralph faced a number of events: his father's sale of the business and his subsequent return to school. But what is often overlooked is the lost dream. Ralph wrote: "The nonevent for me was that I had been groomed since childhood for a certain career. All my adult life, the company and its demands had been given first priority. This determined my relationship to friends, suppliers, employees, friends, wife, and family. My father's precipitously selling the business—a definite event—caused me to no longer have the role for which I had been prepared."

In a follow-up interview a year later, Ralph said, "When your pencil is broken, you find out very rapidly who your real friends are. At home, it was confusing to my children. I suddenly went from being the provider to a period of uncertainty and then, for want of anything better, I became a student. It was hard to suddenly have no office, no base. It also changed the way I saw myself. For years, I had been the customer, not the vendor. I had no idea how difficult it is to sell oneself. But mostly, I had expected to peak in my business career by the age of 50. Instead, I am embarking on a new career. I am glad you are doing this study. Failure of a long-expected event to materialize can create more change in lifestyle, attitudes, and social support than the occurrence of the event." Some nonevents are out of our control, such as infertility or not having grandchildren. But even career and personal nonevents can be beyond our power, no matter how hard we strive to achieve them. One woman told us: "In 1977, when I entered the Jesuit School of Theology at Berkeley, California, I thought that I would be one of the first women to be ordained as a Roman Catholic priest. The papacy became more conservative; the U.S. bishops weakened, and repression of forward-thinking church people was rising. It was out of my control. It was part of the structure and system of the church. It's strange. I look the same to all my friends; I am doing the same thing that I have always done, yet I feel so different. I am a perfect example of nothing happening but everything inside changing." Asked how this thwarting of her vocation changed her life, she used words, such as *betrayed, angry,* and *powerless,* to describe her initial feelings. Over time, she mobilized her anger and founded an organization that helps women who feel oppressed. She also entered a doctor of philosophy program, preparing to become a therapist.

Exercise 1: Listen With a Third Ear

1. The counselor should listen for the heartbreak. For example, John talks about the physical aspects connected with multiple sclerosis.
2. It is important for the counselor to listen for what John does not discuss: his dreams for his life that never materialized. John had started law school but did not have the physical stamina to continue. He is experiencing both events—multiple sclerosis—and nonevents—the life he cannot live.
3. The counselor needs to identify the impact this has on others: John moved back to his parents' home. He discussed his feelings of dependency, anger, and gratitude. Counselor is aware of how John's life is impacting his parents.
4. The counselor needs to listen for the future. Is there hope? What is in John's control? John's condition was gradual but now is very debilitating. At first, he had hope that his condition would not interfere with his career plans. Later, because of the severity of his condition, he had to withdraw from school and move home. He feels out of control of much of his life but in control of his attitude about what has happened to him.

STEP 2: DEVELOP SPECIFIC STRATEGIES FOR CLIENTS TO USE AS THEY COPE WITH NONEVENTS

Just as there is no magic coping strategy, there is no magic counseling strategy. It is impossible to present a formula to use that works with all clients. It is important, however, for counselors to continually examine current research as a basis for helping themselves listen and act with new sensitivity. Theory and practice must continually inform each other.

In analyzing how people cope with nonevents, Heiser (1991), in one study, and Schlossberg and Robinson (1996), in later conceptualizations of the work, identified four major ways that people cope with nonevents: discovering, grieving, refocusing, and reshaping.

Coping with nonevents may demand special strategies, because most nonevents are hidden, most are losses, and there is usually no rehearsal for them. Although many go through a process that includes discovering, grieving, refocusing, and reshaping, each person's story is unique. Each person goes through a process, not necessarily in the same order and not necessarily covering every part of the process. This is a process that takes time. People often ask, "How long will it take?" It would be great to provide a definitive answer, but the amount of time depends on the person, the particular nonevent, and the supports the person has.

Discovering

Usually, the first step is to discover the nonevent and give it a name. This has the double effect of diluting the power a nonevent can have and of helping an individual to take control of the situation. Strategies that give a nonevent clarity include acknowledging it, making meaning, labeling it, telling a story about it, and using metaphors to describe it.

When first interviewed, Betty said she thought that the study was interesting but that it did not apply to her—she was in the midst of too many events, not nonevents. She had just started a business and had two young children and a husband. Betty called back the next day asking for another interview. The realization had hit her: No, she had not experienced any nonevents overnight, but she realized that her father's lost dream, his nonevent, had significantly influenced her life. She felt that he was pressuring her to be a superb wife and mother while achieving great success in her business. Living with a depressed father and a disappointed mother had not been easy. Their nonevents had rippled unhappily into her life. She said that just hearing the term *nonevent* had helped her greatly to become aware of what had been going on in their family. The awareness of the concept enabled her to articulate what her parents' problems were and how they influenced her.

Louis, who experienced a career nonevent—he was passed over for promotion for 7 years—did not know how to deal with this blow. Alternately, he felt anger, humiliation, and even guilt that he should have performed better at work. His reactions were confusing and unsettling. Fortunately, he talked with his company's human resource person, who helped him take a reality check. He realized that he was in a dead-end situation. He began talking about his career nonevent and his emotional reactions to it. This enabled him to stop blaming himself and focus his energies on career planning. He also developed a story to tell his friends. His new mantra became "It's time for a change."

The biggest difference between events and nonevents relates to the fact that nonevents are undercover. Therefore, it is particularly important for clients to listen for what did not happen. Was the lost dream one that rippled from someone else, one that resulted from an event, or one that was solely the individual's? Is it a delayed event rather than a nonevent? Encourage clients to tell a story about the nonevent; the story will then demystify the experience. The question of how to acknowledge your nonevents to others is very important. People do not usually go around saying: "Let me tell you about my career nonevent, or the job offer that never came." Unless you let others know you are experiencing a painful nonevent, they will not know how to comfort you or even that you need comforting. So telling a story, making your pain explicit, can also help mobilize others to mobilize you.

Exercise 2: Tell Your Story

1. Have the client tell the story of the nonevent as if the client were to blame for it. (I'm no good; that's why I was not promoted.)
2. Have the client retell the story attributing a different cause. (Times are bad in my field. What happened is inevitable.)
3. Ask the client to now tell the story that could be told to friends. (Things are at a dead end at work, so I am rethinking my career. Any ideas?)

Grieving

Many respondents reported the need to grieve for the loss of a dream. For example, it is easy to recognize the grief that accompanies the death of a significant person in one's life. But most people do not recognize the grief that persists over never finding a companion or significant other. To ease this loss, respondents sought support, wrote in journals, talked about their faith, and, of course, invoked humor.

People are expected to grieve over events such as a death or rejoice over events such as a promotion. But how do we help others to deal with their grief over what did not happen—a baby that was never conceived, a book that was never published, or a relationship that never materialized? Grieving for nonevents is difficult because the reason for the grief is unrecognized by others. Once the nonevent or loss is acknowledged and named, then coming to terms with it can occur.

This is where the counselor can play a critical role. The counselor is someone to whom a person can moan about nonevents, who can arrange support groups of others with the same issues so that they can share their losses, and who can encourage the person to keep a journal, chronicling the reactionsover time to the nonevent over time.

Doka (1989) described a disenfranchised grief—a special kind of grief that is not recognized by society. This type of grief is particularly applicable to nonevents, because they are not public. For them, grieving is disenfranchised. There are no wakes, no chicken soup. The sadness is intensified: There is the loss of a loved one or dream and the loss of recognition from others. Labeling the grief and sharing it with others who have similar issues can be very helpful.

Counselors can start nonevent support groups. For example, a support group for those sharing the loss of a dream can provide an opportunity for each person to state the particular lost dream and comfort others regarding their loss. It is easier to share with others experiencing similar pain, even if the lost dream is different, than to bury the emotions and try to go on. We need "good grief" before we can move on.

Exercise 3: Sharing the Loss of a Dream With a Group

1. Each person tells the story of the lost dream. (I never had the baby I wanted; my child is a disappointment to me, etc.)
2. Group members identify ways to help each other grieve.
3. Group members suggest ways to initiate help from friends and family outside the group.

Refocusing

The next part of the process can be difficult because it requires letting go of old expectations and reframing the nonevent. People often have difficulty changing their perceptions of themselves and the world and moving to a new vision. However, shifting focus is necessary as we shape new goals by reframing our future selves and forcefully identifyi a new dream, a new vision, or a new self.

A major way to assist this transformation is through the use of rituals. Myerhoff (1984) discussed the role of rituals, ceremonies, or rites of passage as a way to help people separate from the past and move into a new place. Rituals help people make sense out of the contradiction and paradox of many transitions—the paradox being that there is no single truth; there are many truths and individuals are not only part of the past but also of the future. Myerhoff described the three stages of any ritual: First, the individual is segregated as in a graduation ceremony; second, the ritual acknowledges the somewhat bewildering phase during which the individual is between the old and the new; and third, the ritual helps the individual move into a new identity.

Unfortunately, nonevents are too often bereft of rituals, and nonevents need rituals even more than events. Yet how to develop them is a bit more difficult. However, through an article in *Ms.* magazine, we begin to see the endless possibilities for developing nonevent rituals. The following announcement says it all:

Alice and Carl Hesse
are pleased to announce their daughter
Susan A. Hesse
is settling into
joyous old maidhood
after which she shall cease
looking for Mr. Right

and begin giving
scintillating dinner parties and soirees.
To help celebrate this wonderful occasion,
gift place-settings
are available at
Macy's Department Store.

Counselors can help clients develop nonevent rituals by using the form in the following exercise as a guide.

Reshaping

Shifting focus is necessary as we shape new goals by reframing our future selves and forcefully identify a new dream, a new vision, and a new self. This shift includes taking stock, regaining control, and transforming the dream by imagining another, more possible, self.

Exercise 4: Developing a Nonevent Ritual

1. Name your nonevent. Example: A 17-year-old adolescent announced to her parents that she was not going to college and was moving out of their home and into an apartment with a roommate and going to work as a waitress. The parents' nonevent was their disappointment with their daughter's plans. Their expectation, based on their own experience, was that their daughter would be like all their friends' children and move from high school to college as expected.
2. Identify your emotional reaction to the nonevent. Example: They were embarrassed, disappointed, and even angry.
3. Design a ritual to help clients grieve for the past that might never have been and move them closer to the future, keeping in mind that the ritual needs to be a shared activity with an opportunity for acknowledging and naming the past and rehearsing for the future. Example: To ease their pain, they invited another family (the daughters' godparents) over for a special dinner—a shared activity. They then made a speech to their daughter, giving her the money to install a phone but then saying she would have to pay the monthly bills. They also acknowledged her need to follow her own muse, stating that they would support any kind of future education or training when she was ready. *Note:* Their daughter eventually went to college, but the use of the ritual enabled the family to avoid the usual screaming fights that can attend such a decision. The ritual also helped the family define this transition as a positive, not a negative, transition.

Margy's 30th birthday was approaching. She refused to let her parents plan any celebration; in fact, she dreaded her birthday. She felt that her life was nowhere. She had always expected to marry, have children, live on a farm, and produce her art. Instead, she lived in a condo in a suburban area and had no prospects of marriage. She did have a job she liked, but the celebration of a birthday was not where she was; rather, she wanted to grieve for unmet dreams. Instead, Margy went to the beach with a friend. When she returned, she announced to her parents that she realized that she was focusing on the total dream. She was willing to have a piece of the dream and control the part she could. She put her condo up for sale; it took 9 months to sell. She searched and finally bought a farmette with a historic house on it. The house was in terrible shape, but Margy realized that she would spend the next 10 years fixing it up. Actually, she is still teaching and is now raising angora goats, free-range chickens, and produce. She still has no husband or child and sometimes grieves deeply about that. Although she has not given up hope, she moved on to live a life that incorporated some of what she wanted.

Counselors can help clients examine their lost dreams and make proactive decisions about what to do. Counselors can help clients make decisions about whether the nonevent is in the client's control, when to give up hope and move on, and when to hold onto the dream and keep trying to make it. Hope and control are critical dimensions differentiating one nonevent from another. For example, the immigrant man who gave up hope of ever returning to his homeland or seeing his family again differed from the woman who wanted a baby and was not married but had not given up hope. If Helen Santmyer, the author of the best seller *And Ladies of the Club* (1982), had given up, that book would have gone unpublished. She kept on working and hoping. It was published when she was in a nursing home. The dilemma is when to hold on to hope using new strategies or when to reshape the dream all together.

The following exercise may help clients figure out how to move ahead despite their sadness.

Exercise 5: Reshaping Your Dream

1. Your lost dream. Example: Daniel expected to write musical comedies. He enrolled in a music school on the GI Bill. However, his wife became pregnant. He then dropped out of music school, followed in his father's footsteps by going to law school, and became a labor arbitrator.
2. Is there any hope? Example: Daniel gave up hope. He now regrets giving up a music career and thinks he should have stuck with it longer.
3. If so, what can you still do to make the dream come true? Example: Daniel plays the piano and writes musical comedies for his church. His nonwork life is devoted to music.
4. If not, the choice is yours. Do you want to modify the dream or put the dream to bed and develop a new dream? Example: Daniel gave up the dream for his vocation but held onto the dream as an avocation.

STEP 3: LESSONS FOR LIFE LITERACY

Lessons for life literacy can be learned through individual or group settings and with professionally trained counselors, support groups, or just plain living. Whatever the format, the lessons are the same. They are lessons that can help clients as they face the ups and downs of living.

Lesson 1: Always Have a Plan B

Because life does not follow a preordained script, it is important to have backup plans. For example, Mike Wallace interviewed Oprah Winfrey on television. During the interview, he showed a videotape of their first interview just as Oprah was beginning her show. Wallace asked her what she would do if the show were not a success. Her answer was that she did not know, but she was more than her show and would develop something else. Quite different was the response of one of the women in the movie *Waiting to Exhale* when asked what she was going to do now that her husband had left her for another woman. She said, "I don't know. I never had a Plan B."

All of us will have scripts for our lives that are interrupted and do not go according to plan. All of us have surprises—some positive and others negative. We cannot count on life just following a neat, arranged, linear script. Part of life is having alternative plans—from A through Z.

Lesson 2: Challenge Assumptions About "Age-Appropriate Behavior"

Many individuals catastrophize about what it will be like to get old—having less fun, less sex, and less power—but rarely take into account the fact that each age offers new possibilities. We often identify each decade as offering less than the last. Yet we can probably all think of people in their 70s and 80s who fall in love, start new relationships, and pursue new volunteer or business possibilities. It is true that there are losses, but one must remember there are gains also. Newer research on the emergence of wisdom confronts negative attitudes about aging.

The MacArthur Foundation sponsored a series of studies on midlife. The conclusion was that midlife is a benign period with endless possibilities. The *midlife crisis* is an artifact of the media.

Lesson 3: Explore Options Even If You Think There Are None

Jim, a stockbroker, lived a double life: the life in his head he lived outdoors, roughing it, and the life he lived in business suits and fancy offices. He had seen no way to reconcile these two lifestyles. Finally, he broke out of his it-can't-be-done mode. He convinced his company to let him open an office in Bozeman, Montana. He goes to work in boots, lives an outdoor life, and keeps in touch with clients by email, fax, and phone. He could have spent his whole life not living out the dream. Instead he created options.

Of course, that is easier for some to do than others. The person working for McDonald's does not have the same options as a stockbroker. And the goal is not to dream the impossible. But we find that there are often opportunities to think in new ways about our lives. Sometimes, there are seemingly more barriers than one can overcome. Who would have ever thought that Christopher Reeve could still produce and act in movies after the accident that left him a paraplegic? Another example is the film *My Left Foot* in which the protagonist is a person with physical handicaps who came from an impoverished family created new options for himself.

Lesson 4: It Is Never Too Late to Put Meaning Back in Your Life

McMurtry (1999), in the book *Duane's Depressed,* described the sudden shift in one man's life. Responding to the death of a neighbor, Duane wondered about his life and felt deep regret for all the things he never accomplished. The book chronicles Duane's struggle to put meaning back into his life. And that is something we can help our clients do—put meanings back in their lives. To quote Gayle King, assistant pastor of St. Bonifice church in Sarasota, Florida, "You can have it all, but maybe not at the same time." And remember the Latin phrase *"Carpe diem"*—Seize the day.

Exercise 6: Practice Lessons for Life Literacy

1. Have the client identify a cherished goal. Then, ask the client to think of a Plan B if the goal is not realized. Example: "I had always planned to have lots of children. I am not married, I am 40, and I will either adopt a hard-to-place child or become a foster parent."
2. Challenge assumptions about what you cannot do. Example: "I can't start a doctoral program. I am 53 years old." Think of those who started such programs. Aina enrolled in a doctoral program at 55. Now, at 65, she has completed her work and has embraced a new career as a licensed therapist.
3. Have clients who say it cannot be done begin to brainstorm options. Example: Marcy, a manicurist, began lying and saying she was an interior designer. When confronted by her counselor about this discrepancy and challenged to begin training as an interior designer, Marcy explained all the reasons that was impossible. Over time, Marcy did find an evening program and is beginning her training.

SUMMARY

Be aware that what looms as a lost dream for one person might not be an issue for someone else. Clients' expectations and feelings guide both the professional counselor and the client in seeking solutions for these silent forms of heartache. In the long run, we are all looking for hope to outlast the broken dreams and for a promise to ease the sorrow of defeat. By giving nonevents their place in adult development, professional counselors can offer that brighter reality—and even redirect our own lives as well.

REFERENCES

Doka, K. J. (1989). Disenfranchised grief. In K. J. Doka (Ed.), *Disenfranchised grief: Recognizing hidden sorrow* (pp. 3–11). Lexington Books/D.C. Heath.

Heiser, L. (1991). *Summary of data on coping strategies for non-events research* [Unpublished paper].

Myerhoff, B. (1984). Rites and signs of ripening and intertwining of ritual, time and growing older. In D. Kertzer & J. Keitch (Eds.), *Age and anthropological theory* (pp. 305–330). Cornell University Press.

Schlossberg, N. K., Lissitz, R., Altman, J., & Steinberg, L. (1992). *Non-events: Describing a new construct* [Unpublished manuscript].

Schlossberg, N. K., & Robinson, S. P. (1996). *Going to plan B: How you can cope, regroup, and start your life on a new path.* Simon & Schuster.

9

Group Counseling

This chapter focuses on group counseling as a useful modality for facilitating transition work with our clients. Groups are complex, requiring counselors to combine individual counseling and group-leadership skills. We begin this chapter with some general information about the unique value of groups and discuss factors that are relevant to group work, including therapeutic factors, cultural diversity, and multicultural competencies. We also illustrate the different types of groups designed for adults who are experiencing various types of transitions. We then turn to an examination of the value of groups in helping people assess their assets and liabilities in each of the 4 S areas.

GROUP COUNSELING AS A MODALITY

Groups have been around since the beginning of humankind and across all cultures. People have historically gathered into groups to create, achieve, and resolve matters that would be otherwise impossible (Gladding, 2019). Besides the potential to accomplish tasks, groups are sources of meaning and belonging, meeting needs for personal contact and interaction (Burn, 2004). A key question that many people ask regarding group and individual counseling is "Which is better?" Experts agree that group counseling is not for everyone, yet they also agree that most people may benefit from group counseling. Sometimes, a combination of both individual and group counseling is considered beneficial, and for some clients, the group modality is determined to be the better option. For example, specific types of issues may be best addressed by members talking with one another, giving feedback, and receiving input from others (Jacobs et al., 2012). Within these types of groups, members can learn from one another and help one another gain perspective on their issues, along with benefitting from emotional support. Groups provide an efficient way to provide help, where members can learn new approaches for moving through transitions, and the group experience includes valuable opportunities for mutual responsibility and accountability among members (Conyne, 2014).

Since group counseling was first introduced in the 1940s, group treatment modalities have evolved to meet the numerous changing issues of a diverse society. In fact, Yalom and Leszcz (2005) stated that "the multiplicity of forms is so evident today that it makes sense to speak of 'group therapies' rather than 'group therapy'" (p. xi). Formal groups are often designed to treat specific issues, and these span the spectrum from groups for treating anxiety or caregiving for the elderly to groups for treatment of early sexual abuse or personality disorders. Another growing area is the many informal self-help groups that take place "in person" or "online" to help with various issues. Although there are too many of these groups to list all of them here, they include specialized groups for addressing issues such as bereavement; adjusting to divorce; and dealing with disease (i.e., HIV, cancer), disorders (panic disorder, bulimia), or addictions (alcohol, narcotics, gambling, sexual addictions, overeating). Other topic-focused groups may center on growth and development, such as groups for healthy living, creative expression, and positive strategies for wellness.

Groups are often a helpful intervention for adults experiencing transitions, and it is tempting to say that the key to success in working with adults in transition is support, support, and support. Whether the transition is a temporary one or a permanent one, whether it represents a role gain or a role loss, and whether it comes "on time" or "off time," people experiencing major changes in their lives often benefit from a better understanding of what they are going through and from realizing that "I'm not the only one who's experiencing this" and "I don't have to handle it alone." Stated differently, adults in transition need information and support, both of which can often be provided most effectively through group counseling. Another key aspect of group counseling is the therapeutic factors that emerge among group members throughout the process.

Therapeutic Factors in Group Counseling

Let us consider how Yalom's (1985) discussion of the therapeutic factors in group therapy applies to adults in transition. He identified 11 therapeutic factors: instillation of hope, universality, imparting information, altruism, corrective recapitulation of the primary family group, development of socializing techniques, imitative behavior, interpersonal learning, group cohesiveness, catharsis, and existential factors. The underlying assumption is that the interpersonal process must take place, in the here and now, in order for these factors to become active. The distinctions among these factors are arbitrary, in that they are actually interdependent, and they operate to greater or lesser degrees depending on the particular group involved. Participants in the group will vary as well regarding which factors are the most helpful to them (Yalom & Leszcz, 2005).

Instillation of Hope

People in a group who have "been there," that is, people who have experienced a similar transition and are further along in the process of moving through it, can instill hope in people who are moving into the transition. The same therapeutic factor can operate whether the group is designed for returning learners, dislocated workers, or people who have just learned they are HIV positive. People who are reeling from the impact of the transition can benefit from seeing people who have begun to cope with it or who have integrated the transition as part of their lives. For example, people who fear losing their sight or have been told that they will lose their sight can receive tremendous inspiration from watching people who are blind function. A major strength of many of the 12-step programs, such as Alcoholics Anonymous, is that at each session people who have experienced the particular problem and are in the process of "recovering" tell their stories to inspire others. Group members can serve as beacons of hope to one another; another example is a group for women combatting breast cancer. These women were able to share about their coping strategies, along with providing hope through their approaches to meaning-making and steps moving forward after the diagnosis.

According to Yalom and Leszcz (2005), hope is activated through connection with others, and it is flexible in that it continually redefines itself throughout the life of a group. The group leader can nurture this sense of hope by making observations of members' improvement. As group members bring this factor to one another, the leader also brings hope through a belief in the efficacy of group counseling (G. Corey, 2016). A metaphor often used by one of the authors of this book is that of a lighthouse on the shore. The client may feel that they are in a little boat in stormy weather, yet through the hope and belief of the counselor, there is a lighthouse visible on the shore. The stormy weather of a transition may continue for some time, but the lighthouse remains a steady, guiding beacon of hope.

Universality

As they move into or out of any particular situation, adults can benefit from discovering their commonalities and realizing that they are not alone. Such a realization, referred to by Yalom (1985) as a sense of universality, typically comes when people in a group learn that many others have shared similar experiences and feelings.

A group of older adults, meeting at a senior center, arrived at such an awareness in an unusual way. One member of the group reported on his discomfort as he reflected on the large holiday dinner at his daughter's house the previous week. "I don't understand," he said, "why I always feel so much more comfortable when our daughter comes to our house than when we go to hers." As other members of the group reported a similar preference for being hosts rather than guests, they realized that they were seeing relocation of the holiday dinner as a signal of decreasing abilities. It became a metaphor for their fears about becoming dependent on their children. As they discussed this with their counselor, several members of the group realized that while fear of becoming a burden was an understandable and shared concern, it was counterproductive to let those fears—that anticipation of a possible future transition—interfere with current pleasures.

Considering the factor of universality, counselors need to be mindful of multiculturalism and the diversity in their groups. Members bring various aspects of diversity to the group, some easily recognized and others that remain hidden until disclosed. Areas of diversity may relate to race, ethnicity, culture/worldview, gender, age, disability, and/or sexual orientation, and some members may have a combination of areas where they feel different from other members in the group. Paying attention to issues of diversity is crucial in forming trust in the group. Yalom and Leszcz (2005) stated that although it is important to address the issues related to diversity that arise among members, it is also imperative to move the group past these differences to the transcultural, universal factors of human situations and reactions. G. Corey (2016) puts this another way in stating that although we each have a unique multicultural identity, members share a common goal—the success of the group. Becoming a culturally skilled group leader requires an understanding of diverse cultural worldviews and the potential impact on relationships, behaviors, and the willingness to participate in the group (DeLucia-Waak & Donigian, 2004). Rapid demographic changes continue to underscore the need for sensitive practice in all professions and the ability to listen to diverse members and see the world through their eyes (Basso et al., 2010). Yalom (2002) described this as "looking out the other's window" (p. 18) and emphasized that this takes place in the immediate present of the therapy experience. The key point he makes is that we cannot assume that the clients and therapist have the same experience in the sessions.

Imparting Information

We can hardly overestimate the value to clients of gaining information about the transition they are experiencing or anticipating. Regardless of whether that transition involves confronting a change in family status or a career change or whether it is an event or a nonevent, obtaining information about the change helps individuals gain some sense of control. Yalom (1985) noted that information often "functions as the initial binding force in the group until other curative factors become operative" (p. 11).

Many groups include a didactic component. This is especially true of groups for specific types of transitions and/or specialized topics. Group members learn about the issues that bring them together, and the leader may bring in experts and/or information relating to the topic. An example would be a group for women who have experienced domestic violence. The leader could teach members about the cycle of abuse, using a diagram depicting this cycle. Members could also discuss this cycle in terms of their situation, which would move the group back to group process. All groups are a combination of content (members' statements, information) and process (what is transpiring between members in the group). Leaders shift focus from content to process, keeping the members' needs in mind. For adults in transition, both information and group process are helpful components.

Altruism

Helping each other relates to Yalom's (1985) fourth therapeutic factor, altruism. He observed that clients benefit "from the intrinsic act of giving. ... They offer support, suggestions, reassurance, insights, and share similar problems with one another" (p. 14). When people experience major transitions, their self-esteem often plummets. The opportunity to be helpful to others by providing support and/or information may help to reverse the downward slide in self-esteem. Group leaders may take notice of altruistic moments between group members, keeping in mind that these acts of unselfish giving are also benefitting the giver in an indirect way. Reaching out to support someone else helps clients realize that they can be helpful to others, which in itself increases confidence and self-esteem. Consider the case of an international student, who may be experiencing the challenges of adapting to life in the United States. She may be experiencing language barriers and feel isolated, without meaningful relationships in a new setting, while also missing family and the culture from her home country. If she is able to reach out to another international student to ease the transition through connection with her, this in a powerful factor in seeing herself as worthwhile and as a valued guide for another student navigating the transition. According to Yalom and Leszcz (2005), group therapy is unique in providing these opportunities for clients to both receive and give help to others.

Corrective Recapitulation of the Primary Family Group

In Yalom's (1985) view, a major value of therapy groups is that they help patients relive and correct problems stemming from their original family groups. As group members interact with leaders and other members, they often find themselves falling into similar patterns and behaviors learned as a child and used with parents and siblings. These roles need not be discussed explicitly regarding families of origin yet can be explored in helping clients to develop new, adaptive behaviors (Yalom & Leszcz, 2005). Leaders can work with members to relate their patterns of behavior and reactions to how these either serve or limit reaching their goals. Early issues, such as sibling rivalry, can also surface and become topics of discussion. Although such a "correction" can be very valuable for certain clients, most groups for adults in transition do not spend time reviewing early experiences in the family. When such assistance seems necessary, a referral for individual or specialized group therapy may be appropriate.

Development of Socializing Techniques

Groups can serve as a meaningful laboratory in which to learn social skills. Some groups may focus on social skills directly, with interventions, such as role plays, designed for this purpose. Most groups, however, offer an indirect benefit regarding social skills, with members receiving feedback and increasing their awareness of their impact on others through the group interactions (Yalom & Leszcz, 2005). Through the group process, members can better understand how they relate to others and how others react to them, and they can also practice new behaviors within the safety of the group. Ideally, these new behaviors would be taken back outside the group. Consider, for example, the widower who relied on his wife to make social engagements with friends and nurture family relationships. His actual or feared ineptness in such situations may keep him from reaching out for the sociability and intimacy he now needs. In getting feedback from other group members about how they perceive him, he can develop "outsight" as well as the insight that can come from individual counseling. The group can help him identify and acknowledge the social skills he does have as well as help him develop additional strategies that he can apply in his life outside of the group. A powerful reinforcer is when group members practice new behaviors within the group, take these outside the group, and then come back to share their experience and perceptions with the group. Another example was a group member who had the realization that he wanted to quit his job, yet he was hesitant to tell his boss about the workplace issues that led him to his decision. After processing this within the group, he made the decision to talk with his boss. He was happy to report to the group after confronting his boss, that not only did he talk about the situation, he was also able to switch departments within the company, which made all the difference.

Imitative Behavior

In groups, members have an opportunity to model themselves after the group leader and/or other members. They also can learn vicariously as they observe interactions between the counselor and other group members as well as among members themselves. An example of this factor is a group for grandparents raising their grandchildren. An increasingly common role for grandparents is the parenting role, and many may feel ambivalent and unsure as to how to approach these new responsibilities. In transitioning to this expanded new role, grandparents are faced with a myriad of tasks on a daily, weekly, and monthly basis.

The counseling group provides an excellent format for grandparents negotiating the many tasks related to meeting the needs of their grandchildren, along with the challenges and adversities regarding their adult children. Through the group format, members may share their strengths and wisdom, and as they observe others in that role, members may develop a more optimistic picture of the future. For example, in a group designed for grandparents raising grandchildren, a grandmother described her role as a way to demonstrate love and concern to her adult child when she could not help in any other way. Within this group, members had the opportunity to draw on one another's life experiences, strengths, and resourcefulness (Newsome & Kelly, 2005). This therapeutic factor was evident as members observed others in their approach to their new role, along with how they went about implementing practical strategies in caring for their grandchildren. This example also highlights how the therapeutic factors may intersect and overlap, as with imitative behavior and the installation of hope that were activated in this particular group.

Interpersonal Learning

Yalom and Leszcz (2005) contended that interpersonal learning is the unique keystone of the group modality. Through interpersonal learning, people can become aware of their patterns of relating to others, along with their blind spots, within the context of relationships within the group. As these relationships are jointly constructed among members, the group becomes what Yalom (1985) referred to as a *social microcosm*. As clients come together and display their interpersonal behaviors, they can learn from these interactions by receiving feedback from the other group members. Such feedback can facilitate learning for people who are trying to adapt to life changes. For example, a 48-year-old divorced man in a group continued to berate himself for losing his relationship with his adult children after the divorce. The group helped him identify his patterns of behavior in relating to his children, which included a condescending attitude along with extensive advice giving. Several group members pointed out times within the group when they had experienced this attitude and advice-giving from him as well. Through this feedback and work within the group, he was able to explore new patterns of relating to his grown children as adults. Group leaders can facilitate interpersonal learning among members by working to identify the various interpersonal patterns within the group (Yalom & Leszcz, 2005). These interactions tend to be multifaceted as group members form relationships, interact with one another, and receive feedback. Leaders can increase the opportunities for growth and learning through a focus on the interpersonal factors that emerge throughout the group process.

Group Cohesiveness

Cohesion refers to the "groupness" or "we-ness" of the group and can be considered how members find the group to be attractive. This concept is similar to what is considered "good rapport" in individual counseling, and facilitating cohesiveness can be considered as a precondition in order for the therapeutic factors to operate (Yalom & Lesczc, 2005). Members of cohesive groups are accepting of each other and tend to be more supportive and more likely to self-disclose. Such cohesiveness can be encouraged by skilled leaders who help people share about their transitions and give each other constructive feedback. Capuzzi and Gross (2002) suggested, "The actual benefit of self-disclosure and feedback relates to how these processes generate empathy among members. Empathy, or the actual experience of being understood by other members, is what catalyzes personal growth and understanding in the context of a group" (p. 19). Being part of a cohesive group can also supply the support and motivation that people in transition need to take constructive action on their own behalf.

Appropriate humor can add to group cohesiveness. Sometimes humor involves using a paradoxical approach. For example, a counselor can ask group members to brainstorm strategies that will guarantee that the transitions they are contemplating will lead to disaster. A paradoxical instruction might be: "Think of as many ways as possible to 'not listen' to friends, family, and coworkers!" or "What could you do to turn off people in your support system?" People who have recently assumed a management position can be asked what they could do to make staff meetings as dull as possible. Once the laughter subsides, the group can often help members develop appropriate strategies.

Another example was provided by Bergman (n.d.). He described some of the efforts he made, including returning to school, becoming a writer, taking up dancing, and traveling to Europe by himself. Paradoxically, one of the major actions that helped Bergman cope with the transition of being widowed was embarking on several other transitions. The support and encouragement he received from the group seemed to inspire these new directions.

Catharsis

Many people experiencing transitions have a lot to be angry, sad, or frightened about. Yet they may be reluctant to express their feelings to their family or friends for fear of further burdening them. Similarly, people experiencing some transitions may be reluctant to let work associates know of the situation, or their feelings about it, for fear that they may be considered less valuable as an employee. Groups provide a safe and supportive environment in which people can disclose such concerns and, as these are shared and validated, achieve catharsis.

Group counselors must constantly make decisions about how to handle such sharing of concerns. Some members may have difficulty expressing emotion and suppressing and denying their feelings, while others may have easier access to discussing their feelings as they arise. Depending on the member and the goals of the group, leaders must decide how to respond to cathartic moments in the group. It is important to remember that, although catharsis can be helpful, it is the processing and acceptance of the group that are the therapeutic factors. For example, in a group for women in transition, many of the women shed tears as they told their stories of failed marriages, lost jobs, and lost dreams. The leader validated the feelings expressed, and members identified with one another, often with similar stories and tears. Through this acknowledgment and shared commonalities, the leader linked the members and the themes of the group and moved members on to defining the goals of this particular group based on what had been discussed.

Existential Factors

Acknowledging that the term *existential* is hard to define, Yalom (1985) related it to "the central features that make us human—that is purpose, responsibility, sentience, will, values, courage, spirit" (p. 94). Such concepts may be helpful to adults in transition even when they are not discussed directly. Yalom and Leszcz (2005) related the existential factors to how people address ultimate concerns of being human (death, isolation, freedom, and meaningless). The existential factors can be powerful among group members as they experience the presence of one another. For example, Yalom and Leszcz (2005) discussed a comment made by a group member: "One of my members put it elegantly when she described herself as a lonely ship in the dark. Even though no physical mooring could be made, it was nonetheless enormously comforting to see the lights of other ships sailing the same water" (p. 106).

For some people contemplating or experiencing difficult transitions, the realization of their own ultimate responsibility for their lives may be both reassuring and challenging. Leaders can work toward activating existential factors by forming authentic relationships within the group, along with helping members to make choices to live more fully and take responsibility for their decisions. According to Yalom (2002) the group therapy format offers a particularly powerful leverage for taking responsibility, with the group's emphasis on feedback and processing within the here and now of the group. When confronting the realities of life and claiming the *response-ability* to make decisions, group members benefit most by a combination of both challenge and support. This balance varies with the stages of the group, along with being tailored to the unique situation of each group member.

Cautions About Group Counseling

Although group work can be extremely valuable, participation in group counseling also comes with potential risks. Clients often express concerns around confidentiality and the possible repercussions of telling others of their struggles. As members approach a new group situation, many feel anxiety regarding trusting the other members. For many, other previous group experiences are brought to the surface, which challenge their ability to participate. Such concerns underline the importance of group counselors being well trained in group leadership as well as in counseling skills. These cautions also argue for a carefully thought-out selection and orientation process for group members. As part of that process, Corey (2016) suggested that group leaders inform prospective members about particular risks. For example, members should be made aware of the possibility that participation in the group experience (or any other therapeutic endeavor) may be disruptive to their lives. Corey noted that even changes that are constructive in the long run may create crisis and turmoil along the way. As Yalom (2020) pointed out, the majority of individuals seeking therapy may have some fundamental problems in their relationships, and the group is a social microcosm. In other words, the interpersonal challenges that people experience will be played out within the group. While taking a *here-and-now* approach addresses these dynamics and promotes interpersonal learning, there are also risks that come with the interactions intrinsic to the group process.

Another major risk of group counseling is that confrontation may be misused. It is important to be mindful that intrusive interventions, overly confrontive leader tactics, and pushing of members beyond their limits often produce negative outcomes (Corey, 2016). Corey stated that skillful confrontation requires that the leader truly care about the person and that the member needs an ample opportunity to consider and respond to what is being said. Rather than avoid confrontation, Corey recommended that leaders model effective and nonjudgmental behavioral feedback. Although confrontation may have negative connotations, if carried out with sensitivity, this can be a very effective intervention, especially when offering authentic feedback. An example of the need for confrontation was seen in an experiential training group for counselors-in-training. A White male student continued to exhibit his unawareness of his impact on group members, especially with his comments and reactions to both marginalized and female colleagues. The group leader artfully prompted group members to share how they were being affected by his reactions to them, as these occurred within the group. Although confrontation may be misused, intentionally managing group member feedback can provide meaningful growth opportunities. The importance of realizing blind spots and/or areas of unawareness cannot be overstated, especially for counselors-in-training.

It has been well established that group therapy is an effective form of treatment (Kivlighan et al., 2019); however, Gladding (2019) observed that research on group counseling is less sophisticated than evaluations of individual counseling. He summarized some of the methods that can be used to assess group members' progress on a variety of dimensions. Evaluation continues for the duration of the group and is an ongoing process. Leaders must not only appraise the movement and direction of the group but must also teach the participants how to evaluate themselves and the group outcomes (Corey, 2016). Because groups are not the treatment of choice for all clients, we strongly urge practitioners to build evaluation procedures into their programs whenever possible. Discussing the progress of the group may be facilitated within the group setting and also assessed with regular member evaluations, along with reflective journals submitted to the group leader. These methods of evaluation can be useful for the group leader(s) to stay informed with how members are experiencing the group and assessing the effectiveness of group interventions.

When considering clients for group membership, it is important to keep in mind that most clients could fit into *some* type of group, depending on the focus and goals of the particular group. Although some lists have been made of the types of clients who are poor candidates for group counseling, it is more helpful to consider the major guidelines in selecting members for group counseling. Yalom and Leszcz (2005) summarized general guidelines, stating that "clients will fail in group therapy if they are unable to participate in the primary task of the group, be it for logistical, psychological, or interpersonal reasons" (p. 234). They also outlined more specific guidelines, which include being able to self-disclose, a willingness and capacity to examine their interpersonal behaviors, and an ability to give and receive feedback. Prescreening through an individual session is a helpful practice, both to assess for fit in a group and to inform potential group members of expectations and norms. An orientation session is also very useful in providing an opportunity for the group counselor and each potential member to make an informed decision about the appropriateness of the group and lay the groundwork for participation.

Types of Groups

There are different types of groups, each requiring both general established competencies and advanced competencies for particular areas of specialization. Training standards have been developed for four types of groups, which include guidance/psychoeducation, counseling/interpersonal problem-solving, psychotherapy/personality reconstruction, and task/work groups (Association for Specialists in Group Work, 2019). Corey et al. (2017) identified four types of groups: *task-facilitation* groups, which include task forces, committees, and planning groups; *psychoeducational* groups, comprising well-functioning people who may need information in a certain area; *counseling* groups, in which the focus is the resolution of specific short-term issues; and *psychotherapy* groups, in which work is done to remediate in-depth psychological problems. All the types of groups can be helpful to people anticipating or experiencing transitions if there is a good match between their needs and the content and process of the group. As stated previously, thoughtful prescreening and informing of group members are key aspects of laying the groundwork, which is conducive for any type of group experience.

To illustrate the different types of groups, we may consider the need of adults in transition for stress -management skills. Addressing this need can be provided by any of the group formats mentioned, depending on the orientation of the group. For example, a stress-management program that focuses on explaining the sources of stress and giving information on stress-management techniques would be considered psychoeducational. A group that combines provision of information about stress with opportunities for group members to practice stress-management techniques with each other and to give and receive feedback would be group counseling. If the goal of the group is to "uncover" the reasons why members experience various events as stressful and to implement psychodynamic interventions, the group would be more therapeutic in nature. Laypeople meeting to discuss their concerns about reducing stress would be considered a self-help group.

Cultural Diversity

Although many cultures function in groups and value participation in them, what actually occurs in these groups may be quite different from the expected behaviors and norms of traditional counseling groups. For example, some members may be hesitant to become active participants or share personal information in a group counseling situation. Many cultures prohibit the sharing of personal information that will bring shame on the individual and more important, on the family (DeLucia-Waack & Donigian, 2004). It is important, however, that counselors not assume that there are no differences among group members from the same ethnic, racial, or other diverse groups. Although group members may come from similar ethnic groups, for example, Chinese American and Japanese American, these members may have significant differences based on historical and political experiences, culture, language, food, level of acculturation, histories of conflict, and beyond (Chung, 2004).

Group leaders must always consider the different cultural factors that influence group members and their interactions within the group (Jacobs et al., 2012). Cultural identity directly influences the way a person interacts with others as well as group process factors such as proxemics (emotional and physical distance), unconscious behavior, emotional intensity, and silence as a form of communication (DeLucia-Waack & Donigian, 2004). Working with culturally diverse clients requires that group leaders have the awareness, knowledge, and sensitivity toeffectively deal effectively with the concerns these clients bring to a group. It is not ethically possible for counselors to ignore their own or their clients' cultural background or cultural context (Corey et al., 2017).

Cultures are not static, and an example of a culture undergoing dramatic change is China, which opened its doors to the outside world in the 1970s. In China, group work has been embraced as a tool for solving a variety of social problems. For example, there has been a growing demand for group services to assist workers and students to identify the kind of future work and education that fits them and the needs of their society. Counselors working in this setting must be mindful of the dominant philosophical traditions of Taoism and Confucianism, which guide behaviors and relationships with others and with nature. It is evident that working with different cultures demands skillful and sensitive interventions. For example, sufficient time must be allowed to process what happened within the group and, especially, what those events meant. Processing and understanding meanings can be challenging in these types of settings, in which there are language differences as well as cultural differences (Conyne et al., 2000).

While discussing groups and cultural diversity, we must recognize that all groups are, in fact, diverse. DeLucia-Waack and Donigian (2004) have proposed a model to systematically incorporate multicultural awareness into the group-work process. This includes activities that explore cultural heritage, worldview, and background, along with confronting racism and prejudice. They also recommend a series of steps that group leaders can take to work toward multicultural group-work competency. These steps include the following:

- Examine your own cultural and ethnic values and racial identity to understand who you are as a person.
- Examine your beliefs about group work and assumptions inherent within the Eurocentric view of group work.
- Learn about other cultures in terms of what they value and how this may affect their relationships in group work.
- Develop a personal plan for group work that emphasizes and uses cultural diversity.

Personal and professional growth in the area of diversity is an ongoing process. Addressing and honoring diversity is a challenging as well as an enriching aspect of the group counseling experience. Developing cultural competence is a lifelong process, and counselors may experience profound emotions as they encounter the challenges of group work and lean into this experience. According to Sue et al. (2019), undertaking the journey to cultural competence and cultural humility, while a monumental task, provides profound rewards when being able to encounter diverse points of view and engage in honest diversity conversations. Facilitating groups at this level can make for the most meaningful learning opportunities among members, and for the group leader as well.

Culturally competent leaders continue to work on their own self-awareness regarding their culture, attitudes, and biases, and they display a great sensitivity when working with their clients. The Association for Specialists in Group Work (ASGW) developed a set of guidelines, *Principles for Diversity-Competent Group Workers,* that outline multicultural competencies for group leaders (ASGW, 2019). This document was then updated to become *Multicultural and Social Justice Competence Principles for Group Work* (2012), which emphasizes a broader perspective of unique worldviews and "recognizes that the issues of multiculturalism and social justice affect group process and dynamics, group and individual outcomes, facilitation, training, and research" (p. 1). Effective group leaders must continue to develop these competencies through seeking out coursework, workshops, readings, and life experiences that serve to broaden their understanding (Jacobs et al.,

2012). It is crucial to be knowledgeable and yet to also approach clients from a "not knowing" position. Members are the experts on their own lives and can teach us if we are open to learning.

Characteristics of Effective Groups

Regardless of the specific focus of the group, whether this is educational, career, social, or personal, all group work emphasizes interpersonal communication within a here-and-now context. To facilitate an effective working group, leaders use both verbal and nonverbal techniques along with structured exercises. The purpose of these techniques is to facilitate the interaction among group members, helping them to learn from one another, establish specific goals, and translate their work in group to their lives through concrete actions toward desired change (Corey, 2016).

Effective groups are characterized by the productivity of the work done by members as they move to become more independent and less dependent on the leader. Although the characteristics of specific groups may vary, Corey (2016) has outlined some key factors of effective working groups. These factors include a here-and-now focus, clearly identifiable goals, members taking responsibility for reaching their goals, members feeling included in the group, and members' continuous assessment of their level of satisfaction with the group, along with taking the steps to change matters that they determine need changing. This type of productive work relates directly to the therapeutic factors outlined earlier in this chapter that emerge throughout the life of a group. Group leaders facilitate this productive work by challenging and supporting group members in communicating in the here and now, sharing their perceptions of group process, and discussing their reactions and feelings of satisfaction or dissatisfaction with the group.

ILLUSTRATIVE GROUPS FOR PEOPLE FACING TRANSITIONS

A variety of intrapersonal, interpersonal, and/or career transitions bring people to group counseling, and specific groups have been designed to meet the needs of clients experiencing various transitions. For example, groups have been designed especially for engaged couples; for widowed, separated, or divorced persons; for families; and for adults in career transition, to name a few. To describe the many types of groups is beyond the scope of this chapter, and the possibilities seem endless. However, recurring themes across these transitions reflect concerns around intimacy, belonging, and mattering.

For example, immigrants moving from one country to another may experience serious emotional as well as geographic dislocation, clearly related to issues of belonging. Moving often takes people away from close friends and extended families. Although not as dramatic a change, people who move from one part of the country to another or from one neighborhood to another may also experience feelings of marginality. The need for support is lifelong, yet an individual's existing support system can often be one of the "casualties" of a major life transition. Ironically, we may have most need of a support system as we are moving into or through a transition that may disrupt that very system. Frequently, this is true in cases of a geographic move. The same problem may arise when a job change, retirement, or illness takes us away from coworkers who were close friends and colleagues.

Especially in the current economic context, counselors are providing groups for adults experiencing work-related transitions—looking for jobs, changing jobs, being promoted or laid off, not securing a desired job, or retiring. In most such situations, clients may have to let go of dreams or expectations and establish new goals. As they do this, the line between career transitions and other parts of an individual's life often blurs. Career-related changes, whether made by choice or necessity, are apt to raise concerns about mastery, competency, balance, and identity. These recurring themes can be addressed through groups that combine providing career-related information with opportunities for group support. Although group work may be provided virtually throughout for the duration of the pandemic, the therapeutic factors, information, and support remain key aspects of an effective group. And more than ever, the sense of belonging, of mattering is crucial.

Regardless of the type of transition, the need for support can become enormous. Adults making life/career transitions frequently benefit from opportunities to talk to others who are "in the same boat" or further along in the process. As many people who navigate relationship or career decisions are reluctant to ask friends and coworkers for assistance, their usual sources of support may be cut off. Therefore, the support of group members becomes particularly important and may serve as a model encouraging people to seek support from others.

As we have discussed, transitions are sometimes internally triggered, stemming from a person's desire to initiate a change. At other times, a transition may be thrust upon the individual. The context in which transitions arise determines the type of group experience that is most helpful. For example, counselors working with people who are angry about being laid off or forced to take an early retirement must attend to the anger before they can expect group members to begin career planning or a job search in earnest. Although not comprehensive, the following examples of groups are included to highlight some types of group interventions that may be implemented for adults experiencing various types of transitions.

Groups for Wellness

Although wellness-focused groups may be considered preventative, when experiencing transitions, people may choose to focus on wellness as a way to increase coping. *Wellness* has been defined by Myers et al. (2000) as "a way of life toward optimal health and well-being, in which body, mind, and spirit are integrated ... to live life more fully within the human and natural community" (p. 252). The Wheel of Wellness (Witmer & Sweeney, 1992, 2008) depicted key areas of wellness, such as spirituality, self-direction, love, friendship, and work. Each of these areas include tasks related to aspects of self: Creative Self, Coping Self, Social Self, Physical Self, and Essential Self. Their model fits well with Bronfenbrenner's (1977) Ecological Model, with both of these models considering the impact of the different social and ecological contexts on the individual.

Although beyond the scope of this chapter to discuss in detail, these are helpful models for designing group interventions and promoting well-being and balance across the areas depicted. Attention to the different aspects of wellness works well when tailoring interventions to the individual member's needs, and/or the overall focus for the group. For example, a group on spiritual health could include mindfulness practices as part of the group structure. Activities to enhance creativity and processing existential issues could also be incorporated into this type of group. Ohrt et al. (2019) discussed applications of the Wellness Model as a holistic approach and stated that change in one area can lead to positive changes across other areas of wellness. Thus, wellness groups could benefit from using an integrated approach, as members work on their different aspects of wellness. As with any group, goals can be explicit, yet the group process can provide a catalyst for change. It is also important to be cognizant of the importance of the group leader *practicing what they preach*. This includes modeling group interactions for members and also being a role model with their own overall health, wellness, and life balance.

Any changes in health involve transitions, and positive gains may result in improvements related to a person's identity and sense of self-efficacy. Groups provide an ideal setting for affirmation of progress, along with accountability for movement toward established goals. Some newer developments in group work include what has been termed *EcoWellness* (Reese & Myers, 2012), which provides a framework for incorporating the therapeutic aspects of the natural environment. Recent studies have demonstrated the potential benefits of nature-based interventions, integrating psychoeducation and purposeful contact with nature within the EcoWellness framework, with increased positive outcomes and group connection (Reese & Gosling, 2020). Wellness groups, in various formats, may also be a useful follow-up intervention for those recovering from illness who are on the road to recovery.

Groups for Persons With Particular Illnesses

Coping with a major illness is obviously a significant transition. Several studies have examined the effects of peer-support interventions for adults with diabetes and cardiovascular disease risk factors, especially as this support comes from people with their own experiences with these conditions and self-management skills (Patil et al., 2018). An earlier study by Livneh and

Sherwood-Hawes (1993) discussed the value of group counseling for persons who have had heart attacks and suggested cognitive, affective, and behavioral goals for participants. Cognitive goals include using information about cardiac impairment to realistically assess their strengths and limitations; affective goals focus on provision of support, relief of tension, and reduction of depression; and behavioral goals include development of skills to promote independent functioning, utilize appropriate exercise and relaxation techniques, and access interpersonal and community resources. They suggested that groups be conducted in an inpatient setting so that members can "practice strategies for coping with problems, and achieve a less complicated transition from the hospital or rehabilitation center into the external community" (p. 57). The authors recommended groups that are educationally based and focus on coping skills rather than on development of insight alone.

A special challenge with this population is that persons who have had a heart attack may deny that they have heart disease or acknowledge the presence of the disease but deny its seriousness. Three strategies that may be used to undermine the impact of denial are the raising of awareness, mild confrontation, and the inclusion in group meetings of successfully coping veteran participants. Some participants may have moved beyond any sense of denial and may benefit from a group focused on the existential issues related to their health crisis. This could be a follow-up group in an outpatient setting, and prescreening would be important inpreparing group members for this type of group experience.

Another area of illness relates to breast cancer patients. Numerous studies have examined the efficacy of supportive group therapy for decreasing depressive symptoms for women with breast cancer (Geise-Davis et al., 2011). Research has supported the theory that group therapy is effective in reducing mood disturbances and anxiety while enhancing the quality of life and potentially extending survival time. Groups have been successful in improving the psychological, social, and physiological well-being of these women as they undergo the necessary medical interventions for breast cancer (Goodwin, 2005). As demands for genetic counseling for cancer have increased, group counseling may be an option for high-risk clients and their families. In a pilot study of a group for genetic counseling (Ridge et al., 2009), researchers found that in the initial phases, there were challenges with meeting the diverse needs of women participants, indicating the need for individual follow-up sessions. The later phases of the group were composed of women with a similar health history and this commonality better met the needs of the individual participants. However, across phases of the group, the benefits of the shared experience and support were observed and reported by participants. The authors discussed both the advantages and the disadvantages of using a group format and suggested that more research is needed to determine whether group counseling is an acceptable alternative to individual genetic counseling. This example serves to highlight the importance of evaluation of the effectiveness of group modalities when providing specialized services for clients.

Life-Review Groups

Since Robert Butler first articulated the concept, life-review groups have become increasingly popular as a counseling intervention with older adults (Capuzzi et al., 1990; Waters & Goodman, 1990). Although people of all ages periodically take stock of their lives, often at times of transition, this activity has special meaning in old age, a sensitive period of the human life span, especially among the institutionalized elderly (Damirchi, et al., 2017). During this time of life, people reflect on their lives and may ask questions, such as "Who am I?" "Who have I been?" and "How did I do?" The answers to these questions may affect how people feel about themselves in terms of integrity versus despair, as identified by Erik Erikson (1950, 1997, p. 230) as the Eighth stage/crisis of development in old age. Joan Erikson (1982) extended this version of the life cycle by adding what as she described as the Ninth Stage. According to Joan Erikson this final stage experienced by the "oldest old" brings new demands and reevaluations, along with daily difficulties. She suggested recognizing the unique challenges of this stage, along with the strengths of wisdom and humility necessary to traverse this last stage of development. A question she would ask, "Suppose you have learned that knowing yourself is true wisdom and opens your ears and eyes. How does that knowledge alone prepare you for the last long trek to death's door?" (p. 116). Having discussions around these types of questions in a group setting underlines the value of the existential therapeutic factor identified by Yalom (1985). As when working with any specific population, it is crucial to recognize the heterogeneity and variations among participants. After many lived experiences, those in their elderly years tend to be more different from one another than at any other time during the life span, and disparities for marginalized populations can be intensified with increased risk factors such as health and social isolation (Vach-Haase & Aeling, 2016). Beyond age, individual challenges and risk factors are important to assess for assets and liabilities.

Life-review groups may provide protective factors for the elderly as people are confronted with the realities of their aging process. According to Joan Erikson (1982), people may feel an uncertainty about their changing status and roles. She stated that "you may be confused about what role, what position you are supposed to take in this period when older values are suddenly vague and crumbling" (p. 110). In a study to investigate the effectiveness of life-review group therapy on well-being and life expectancy of elderly women, Damirchi et al. (2017) concluded that potential benefits include increased autonomy, environmental mastery, personal growth, positive relationships with others, sense of purpose, and self-acceptance. They also stated that group therapy would be highly recommended to enhance both psychological well-being and increased life expectancy.

Counselors can trigger life reviews in many different ways, depending on the needs of particular clients and groups. As Yalom (2002) described, these group approaches use "unfreezing" techniques, which are the first stage of the exercises, and he emphasized the importance of debriefing and processing the experiences. For example, group counselors can ask participants to think about various periods of their lives and to identify the people and activities that were most important to them at each stage. Counselors can then encourage participants to think about how their support system has changed over time and what they did to access support in the past. In guiding a life review, counselors can help group members gain a sense of pride from looking at the people they have influenced and the crises they have weathered. This also relates to the concept of *mattering*, which was discussed by Schlossberg (2009) as applied to older retired populations. Such recollections may also serve as an excellent vehicle for encouraging people to identify past coping strategies and to consider how they can be adapted to fit new transitions.

Although most life reviews involve talking, a variety of props, such as old magazines and newspapers, political buttons, greeting cards, or photographs, can be used to stimulate memories and discussions. People whose transitions involve a reduction in cognitive functioning may find such stimulation valuable. Music works particularly well in such cases. In many long-term care settings, older adults who have difficulty with conversations may be seen singing and dancing to songs from the past. This kind of successful experience may help to strengthen the coping resources of people whose balance of assets to deficits is declining.

Groups for Couples and Families

Couples' groups may be targeted to engaged couples, married couples, or couples in other sorts of living arrangements, whether of traditional or newer composition. Some religious groups require that couples receive counseling, often from a member of the clergy, before they can be married in the Church. Corey et al. (2017) described a number of exercises they use in couples' groups. For example, group members may be asked to complete sentences such as "The thing I'd most like to change in myself or my spouse is … " or "My greatest fear concerning our relationship is … " (p. 266). The stimulus for couples to enroll in couples' counseling groups may be an event that occurred, such as one partner's thinking about or having an affair, or nonevents, including a general feeling that the relationship could be better.

When working with families in transition, "family" may be understood as a very specialized type of group, and many aspects of group therapy apply to family therapy as well. Some unique aspects of working with families include the generational differences seen among members, the ongoing (lifetime) nature of relationships, the intensity of involvement over time, and the power of the family in fostering primary attitudes toward life, including the needs and expectations among members (Wadeson, 2010). It is crucial to be sensitive to many different forms that family can take, acknowledging that for some clients, families may not be related by blood but rather are *families of choice*. Also, many families coming to counseling are navigating the transition of becoming a blended family or stepfamily, which presents unique challenges and issues for family members. Today, it is increasingly common for families to include multiple generations, sometimes living within one household. Clients may be experiencing distress regarding changing relationships and various transitions across these generations. Sometimes, counselors work with families in coming to terms with the reality of their family situations, especially as compared to previously held expectations (Anderson, 2016).

Creative techniques are often helpful when working with families. Expressive art therapy has made contributions as a vehicle for family members sharing their perceptions, and this is especially helpful if some family members tend to be more verbal than others (Wadeson, 2010). For example, when some members are more withdrawn or have difficulty articulating verbally, art interventions can be useful in allowing all the family members to express themselves. These types of techniques can be especially helpful when working with families with young children.

Rituals and metaphors can also be useful in family counseling to help some families move through transitions. Family rituals are the events that give family life texture and meaning, and these may include daily rituals, holiday traditions, and rites of passage that create memories and define individuals as part of the family and the community (Imber-Black et al., 2003). It is important for counselors to be sensitive to cultural norms in creating rituals with family, and generally, it is helpful to cocreate these with family members in order for them to be relevant and meaningful.

An example of a family intervention was provided by Sand-Pringle et al. (1991), as they described the use of gardening activities as a ritual to help a family allow a son to leave for a halfway house. He planted some seeds in the family planter to symbolize his continuing place there and took a separate planter with him to his temporary home. The mother, who needed to be empowered in the family, was cast as the master gardener. In this case, the family was the group with many of Yalom's (1985) therapeutic factors operating. The plants symbolized hope, the joint efforts led to some cohesiveness, and family members were able to express some of their pent-up feelings. In the typology of groups, this is an example of a psychotherapeutically oriented group.

Another ritual designed especially for stepfamilies is called the *Remarriage Box Ritual* and allows the participants to give voice to their feelings, which might otherwise be acted out destructively. The purpose of this intervention is to provide a constructive way to achive mutual understanding, and family members are asked to gather objects that represent their feelings regarding what they may be gaining or giving up as the result of the remarriage. Family members then take turns placing their objects in a large box and telling others what the items symbolize. In conducting this ritual, it is important that participants are respectful of one another, with one person speaking at a time. As with other types of rituals, family members must agree to participate and have an opportunity to modify the activity to suit their needs (Meyerstein, 2000). Another adaptation of this exercise (Yalom, 2002) would be to use strips of paper, giving several trlips of paper to each family member with the instructions to write "Who am I?" and indicating different aspects of their roles within the family on each strip of paper. This could provide a springboard for each person to discuss the issues this evoked for them. This could also open discussion about mattering, and how family members are important to one another.

Groups for Caregivers

As people live longer, older adults often need caregiving from spouses, adult children, friends, and/or paid caregivers. The mix of love and frustration that often accompanies having major responsibilities for a parent or other older adult is well documented. Fortunately, the need for help is becoming more widely recognized, and groups for caregivers are springing up at hospitals, nursing homes, senior centers, family service agencies, religious organizations, libraries, and community centers. For example, cohort models have provided an ideal context for family caregiver interventions, with the potential for participants to "hold genuine compassion for one another while empathizing and identifying with other's circumstances and struggles" (Off et al., 2019, p. 7). Both information and support are important resources for caregivers.

Counselors who work with caregivers need to be familiar with a variety of community resources, which can serve as formal supports. Counselors also need to understand the feelings of caregivers, who may be emotionally drained and physically exhausted—sometimes by family conflicts as well as by their caregiving responsibilities—and yet are often reluctant to use external resources. In dealing with people suffering from severely disabling illnesses, particularly dementia, caregivers may find that "the mourning process may be even more debilitating when the lost loved one is still alive" (Dobson & Dobson, 1991, p. 188). Research shows a high prevalence of distress and disruption to the lifestyle of family caregivers, who have been identified as "hidden patients" at risk of poor health outcomes (Gopinath et al., 2017). Gopinath et al. (2017) discussed the effects of age-related macular degeneration, which is a leading cause of blindness and low vision among the elderly. They had previously conducted a cross-sectional survey of caregivers that revealed significant sacrifices made to meet the needs of their loved one, along with feelings of sadness, frustration, and isolation, identifying difficulties that can worsen over time. They discussed the advantages of a multimodal support service program for family caregivers to improve their coping strategies, enhance self-efficacy, and increase their ability to access social and financial support. They emphasized that early intervention, awareness programs, and community resources could be helpful in alleviating caregiver distress. These suggestions illustrate the importance of programs and resources for people experiencing challenging transitions.

Johnson (1990) developed a useful concept that helps caregivers understand the difference between giving up and letting go, distinguishing between situations that can and cannot be controlled. In all situations, these caregivers need to decide whether or not to take action. If the decision is one that can be controlled and they take action, then they are achieving mastery; if they do not, they are giving up. For example, if an older person wishes to stay in their home and assessment indicates that this is possible with appropriate support, then the caregiver is achieving mastery if they arrange for adult day care and appropriate home care. A challenge with situations that require decisions is that family caregivers may differ in their opinions as to what is best for the elderly person, along with various levels of commitment and investment of time and energy in the tasks of caregiving. An example: A woman in her 60s is caring for her aging parents and understands better than her siblings their need for assisted living. The parents were also resistant to moving, and after a time with some assistance with in-home care, eventually all agreed to make the move for more round-the-clock care—never an easy decision.

On the other hand, there are situations that cannot be controlled. For example, if a parent resides in a nursing facility shut down to visitors during the pandemic, that can cause significant distress for adult children. With assistance from the counselor, group members can help each other process this situation, one out of their control, and work toward "letting go" of the guilt around not being able to be with their loved one. With the largest death tolls from Covid-19 occurring in the elder population, not being present for the death of a parent can be particularly painful. Group counseling can be helpful in processing the unique aspects of the grieving process, especially as members share their experiences and realize that they are not alone in grappling with their feelings and striving for a sense of closure.

Career Exploration and Planning Groups

As with other work focused on transitions, career counseling is most effective when it takes into account the various contextual and cultural influences at play (Swanson & Fouad, 2015). In the world of work, "changing demographics, multiple worldviews, and cultural plurality influence the career development intervention process" (Niles & Harris-Bowlsbey, 2017, p. 99). According to Niles and Harris-Bowlsbey (2017), there is ample evidence that women, people of color, persons with disabilities, gay men, lesbian women, and transgender people continue to face tremendous obstacles in their career development. Designing career interventions, therefore, must be grounded in a social justice perspective. Failure to do so could, in essence, result in promoting a cycle of economic and social disempowerment for unemployed people and their families (Bhat, 2010). Designing groups for those who are not from the dominant culture should include a focus on empowerment through promoting skill building for the changing workforce and implementing multiple levels of interventions that include social advocacy (Blustein et al., 2008).

Over the past two decades, Blustein and his colleagues have promoted their *psychology of working theory* (*PWT*) to provide a more inclusive approach relevant to career practitioners, advocates, and researchers (Blustein et al., 2019). In essence, rather than focusing on how people can adapt to their circumstances, the theory builds on a systemic change mission and social justice movements in counseling and psychology. PWT was founded on the core assumption that work is an essential aspect of positive human functioning and is a basic human right. They emphasized that decent work leads to fulfillment, general well-being, and satisfaction of basic needs. According to Blustein et al. (2019), work is inseparable from the context of the worker, which includes individuals' cultural background, family context, and social/class identities. They also acknowledge the importance of unpaid work, along with the disparities that systems perpetuate based on social identities and economic privilege. They conclude that as the needs of society are changing, approaches also need to transcend the more traditional focus on career choice, development, and adjustment issues. Practical suggestions for group counseling include strategies that fit both individuals and systems. Although beyond the scope of our discussion here, key applications of PWT include assessing individuals' needs, optimizing coping, and mobilizing support. All of these initiatives lend themselves well to group work, along with strategies relevant to Schlossberg's 4 S model.

In a group designed for long-term unemployed adults, Bhat (2010) incorporated a job-club model with interventions to facilitate personal awareness, empowerment, and career self-efficacy. The central purpose of this group was to help the group members find jobs, and job clubs are based on the premise that people who are looking for work benefit by *doing* rather than by listening or taking a more passive stance. The group had a highly structured format, with members learning and practicing specific job-search skills such as writing résumés and cover letters, making calls to employers, responding to advertisements, handling interviews, and following up after an interview. Simulation activities, such as role -plays, were used, and group members were given extensive feedback, including video feedback. Group facilitators tended to be active and directive, supporting and encouraging members and fostering an environment in which members support each other. The group leader also worked with an employer liaison to advocate for the group members within the community in achieving employment. This group was significantly different from traditional career counseling groups and serves to underscore the need for group counselors to be creative and proactive in meeting their clients' needs in the current economic context. This is especially crucial when members face the internal and external barriers related to oppression and long-term unemployment. According to Bhat, mobilizing local involvement is vital in preventing the ripple effects of unemployment in the entire community. She stated that making unemployed clients feel visible and valued also helped the group members move through a difficult phase of the transition to becoming employed.

Group Interventions for a Challenging Social Context

It is a challenge for counselors to meet diverse clients' needs when facing increasingly complex problems. An example of an unfortunate complex reality relates to the increase in displaced people and homelessness in the United States and throughout the world. With unemployment on the rise, an increasing number of people are experiencing home foreclosures, high medical costs, and poverty. Many are losing their homes and living in shelters or on the streets (Erlenbusch et al., 2008). Although many factors continue to contribute to the increased homelessness rates, group counseling provides a framework for homeless clients to reevaluate the context and history of their experiences, take responsibility for change, and renew a sense of personal empowerment. Althoughhomelessness is an especially challenging situation, as individuals are given an opportunity to share their personal narratives, they may positively influence themselves, one another, and their communities (Brubaker et al., 2010).

A group created for the homeless included a critical analysis of the members' lived experiences, and these group members experienced the therapeutic factor of altruism, as described by Yalom and Leszcz (2005). As the members supported one another, their influence extended beyond the group into the wider community. The fact that they spoke as *insiders* rather than *outsiders* gave them the ability to speak to their living conditions with credibility. A powerful symbol was created by this group, a painting that challenged racial stereotypes in a message to the community. The painting was of two sets of hands reaching out to one another, intentionally painted in multiple, rich colors and titled *Blind to Color*. This large painting was prominently displayed and became a source of power, energizing people to help one another. The authors (Brubaker et al., 2010) stated that groups like these may choose to take on a direct role in political activism, and this illustrates an alternative format to traditional group counseling models.

Models of group intervention have also been developed for people who have experienced disasters, and the need for these types of groups has increased in recent years. Within the past decade, people worldwide have experienced disasters such as hurricanes, earthquakes, floods, fires, mudslides, and cyclones. The results of these events have left many people displaced from their homes, with shortages of shelter, food, water, sanitation, and healthcare. Traditional Western approaches to group and mental health counseling have been challenged by these events, especially as many marginalized and disenfranchised communities have been underserved or not served at all (Chen et al., 2007). It is crucial for counselors to be mindful of the needs of people in these extreme situations, adapting group objectives toward promoting a sense of psychological and physical safety and creating space for group members to grieve, reconnect with themselves and others, and share their trauma in order to validate and normalize their experience (Bemak & Chung, 2011). Although a full description of these types of group interventions is beyond the scope of this chapter, the need for group work is imperative in helping people cope with the uncertainty, chaos, and aftermath of disaster. Reconsidering established group counseling models is essential, and counselors are encouraged to better understand the needs of these populations through further reading, training, and supervision.

When working with people in extremely challenging situations, group counselors may design interventions to strengthen members' coping by tapping into their own stories. Westwood and Ewasiw (2011) proposed an integrated approach to group work that combines two complementary group-based interventions: guided autobiography and therapeutic enactment. The autobiography provides a narrative framework for the client to construct a life story. The group members then narrate, witness, and receive feedback from others in the group. As the members share their life experiences, they gain awareness and insight for a strengthened self-concept, personal integration, and meaning. The focus is on the experiential process of reviewing their life stories, especially as critical events emerge. According to Westwood and Ewasiw (2011), these critical events are pivotal in recognizing and addressing unresolved issues. These events then provide the bridge to the second phase, which is implemented through one-on-one interviews with group members to explore these events further. Group members then complete this second phase through enacting the continuation of their story in the group.

USING THE 4 S MODEL WITH GROUPS

When working with groups as well as with individuals, counselors can integrate the Hackney–Cormier (2005) counseling model with the transition model. This integrated model, as discussed in Chapter 7, fits well with the group stages as depicted by Corey (2016). Corey described groups as moving through the pregroup, initial, transition, working, and ending stages of the group counseling process.

During the initial stage, counselors help members get acquainted and begin to assess their problems and formulate goals in relation to their life changes. In the transition stage, members may address their resistance as they begin to move to action. In the working stage of groups, counselors intervene to help members develop new coping strategies. Whether working with individuals or groups, counselors should view the termination stage as the appropriate time to assist clients in evaluating their progress and making a commitment to follow up.

In almost any groups designed for people considering, anticipating, or experiencing a transition, the first step is to encourage them to describe their transitions. What happened or may happen? After that, the major focus of group counselors is to encourage group members to assess and improve their resources for coping in each of the four areas of the transition model.

Although we talk about the 4 S's separately in the following discussion, it is important to remember that the lines among them blur. In some ways, the situation of any individual includes aspects of the other three S's. Each individual's personal environment is unique. Thus, four women in the same job-seeking group may have very different resources in terms of their socio-economic situation, support systems—friends, extended family, work colleagues, spiritual resources—and coping strategies. An effective group can help each member identify and enhance unique available resources.

For example, a woman who has lost her job and is feeling helpless in terms of finding another may get useful feedback from other group members who help her realize how successfully she has weathered other transitions. The group may also help her see her network of supportive friends and her ability to take care of herself as assets in her present situation. A group can help one woman who is financially able to be unemployed for a short time see that this as an asset in that it enables her to be more selective about other jobs. At the same time, the group may be able to persuade another woman, whose financial situation is tenuous, that it is appropriate to accept government assistance to tide her over.

Situation

In groups, members can explain how, from their point of view, the context in which they operate affects the impact of the transition. They can also discuss the extent to which the transition alters their lifestyle, what we have earlier called their *roles, relationships, routines,* and *assumptions.* As the other group members offer feedback, each of the group members can realize that although they may all be experiencing a similar transition, their individual situations differ.

Self

Under skilled leadership, a group may be particularly valuable in helping members assess self factors. For example, individuals concerned that they do not have the psychological resources to cope with major losses may be reassured to learn from other members that their degree of turmoil is normal. They may also profit from hearing ideas as to how people experiencing similar transitions gained some measure of control over their lives. Many transitions, particularly those involving role losses, lead to a drop in self-esteem. People who feel they are no longer needed can benefit just by having group members who are glad to see them each week. When members share resources, their ability to contribute to someone else may positively affect their view of themselves.

One activity, which is part of a job-seeking workshop developed by Goodman and Hoppin (1990), illustrates the value of group feedback. To demonstrate the concept of transferable skills, the leader asks one member to come to the front of the room and write the title of a recent job on a simulated theater marquee. The marquee has the words "Star of the Cineplex" at the top. The "star" explains the job and, with the help of other group members, lists as many skills as possible involved in that job. Then, the group discusses ways in which the skills and personal characteristics of the group member can be transferred to other jobs and settings. Frequently, "stars" leave with a more positive view of their skills and abilities and a more optimistic outlook about finding another position. This activity also helps members prepare for their job search, with positively identified skills they may have taken for granted.

Group counselors can maximize the effectiveness of feedback by encouraging interaction and humor. For example, to enliven the discussion of transferable skills, the counselor can tell the story of a man who, with no background in the field, got a job in labor relations. He convinced his employer that as a former basketball referee he knew how to make quick decisions and take the heat.

Support

By their very nature, well-functioning groups provide support. In addition, they can encourage members to explore and enhance their individual support systems. Regardless of the type of transition, clients need to consider who or what has been supportive of them in the past and how they have accessed that support.

Pearson (1990) developed a model for using social support-oriented concepts and procedures in counseling practice. The first step is to identity the strengths and deficiencies in an individual's support system. If this assessment indicates that client-based barriers, such as withdrawal, ineptness, and alienation, are the major causes of the problem, then the task of the counselor is to help the client make some changes. Depending on the theoretical orientation of the counselor, client-based interventions might focus on restructuring attitudes or changing behaviors through modeling and communications skills training. Opportunities to practice new skills in a group can be particularly valuable.

Using Pearson's (1990) model, a useful group activity for the assessment stage is to have people evaluate their own support systems. The idea of a support system can be explained to most clients with words such as *people who are there for you* or *people who are in your corner*. To facilitate self-evaluation, counselors can use a worksheet listing needs, such as acceptance, self-esteem, peers, guidance, and role models. Next to each need is a brief description of the type of support provided. For example, to meet our need for acceptance, we need people who like us, and to meet our need for peers, we need people who *are* like us. In a blank column on the worksheet, clients fill in the name of the person or group who supplies that type of support to them (Waters & Samson, 1993; see also the surveys in the appendix of Pearson, 1990). There are many strategies that can generate discussion regarding support, and creative group leaders can devise multiple ways to approach this topic. As stated so often throughout these chapters, it is imperative to be mindful of cultural norms and factors when working with group members, being careful not to overlay expectations from the dominant culture.

If the initial assessment suggests that the barriers lie more with other individuals or the larger social context in which the person operates, then interventions must focus outside the individual. These can range from counselor contacts with the client's network to political advocacy. Sometimes this involves linking informal supports with formal ones. This linking may be particularly important with some of the caregiver groups discussed earlier. A relevant activity is to have group members list the names of people whomthey trust and then check off the different characteristics of these people. Oftentimes, this brings an awareness of how supports may be expanded beyond the usual comfort zone. For example, people may realize they rely mostly on people from their own age cohort or gender. However, in situations involving systems, working in a larger context may mean that the counselor moves to specific actions focused on advocacy. More is written on advocacy strategies in Chapter 10.

Strategies

Throughout this book, we have mentioned three types of strategies for coping with a transition: those aimed at modifying the situation, those designed to change the meaning of the situation, and those serving to help individuals manage the stress of change. Groups can help in all three areas. Strategies are tailored to the specific needs and focus of the group and the possibilities are far too numerous to list here. However, we can emphasize that it is key to be collaborative with group members, flexible to the needs of the group, and creative with designing interventions to achieve the goals of the group. Conyne et al. (2008) discussed specific steps to take when selecting techniques for a group: (a) Identify the group type and purpose, best practice area, and developmental stage; (b) analyze the presenting situation by applying ecological concepts; (c) review possible group techniques, considering focus and level; (d) select a best fit technique; and (e) implement and evaluate how well the technique worked. These authors discuss each of these steps, and their implicit message is that strategies and techniques should be intentional, well-thought out, and evaluated after implementation.

Group leaders need strategies also. There are many useful resources for finding activities for group work. For example, for activities related to career development, an excellent resource is the book by Pope et al. (2011) *Experiential Activities for Teaching Career Counseling Classes and for Facilitating Career Groups, Vol. III.* Also, the American Counseling Association lists 50 resources related to group counseling (counseling.org/store).

SUMMARY

In this chapter, we discussed the value and limitations of groups for adults in transition, highlighting the benefits of the therapeutic factors that enhance the group process. We also described examples of counseling groups, along with applications of the transition model in group settings. In groups, clients have opportunities to explore their situation, strengthen the aspects of self, and increase the support needed to take steps forward through their transitions. Especially in an increasingly challenging social context, group counseling provides a useful modality. Throughout this chapter and the book, we have emphasized the importance of cultural and contextual factors when working with our clients. A central goal when counseling adults in transition is increased coping, which is inherently influenced by factors related to the individual, group, and larger contexts. Another key aspect of our counseling role is advocacy, a focus of the next chapter.

EXERCISES

1. List some facts about a special population in your community. What type of group would best address their needs? Consider group interventions you would implement across the 4 S model (situation, self, support, and strategies).
2. What counseling skills do you possess that will help you as a group leader; what new skills might you need to acquire? List some specific steps you can take to further your professional development.
3. Imagine that you are a school counselor and have been asked to conduct a counseling group for children newly in a blended family. What resources could you use to plan for the group? How would you determine which children would be appropriate for the group and how would you prepare students for the group experience?

REFERENCES

Anderson, M. L. (2016). Supporting adaptation to new family roles in middle age. In C. L. Juntunen & J. P. Schwartz (Eds.), *Counseling across the lifespan: Prevention and treatment*. Sage.

Association for Specialists in Group Work. (2019). *Multicultural and social justice competence principles for group workers*. American Counseling Association.

Basso, R., Pelech, W., & Wickham, E. (2010). Diversity in group work: Interdisciplinary perspectives. *International Journal of Interdisciplinary Social Sciences*, *5*(4), 135–144.

Bemak, F., & Chung, R. C.-Y. (2011). Post-disaster social justice group work and group supervision. *Journal for Specialists in Group Work*, *36*(1), 3–21.

Bergman, G. (n.d.). Fresh currents in the stream of life. *Gray Panther Network*. The Gray Panthers Newsletter.

Bhat, C. S. (2010). Assisting unemployed adults find suitable work: A group intervention embedded in community and grounded in social action. *Journal for Specialists in Group Work, 35*(3), 246–254.

Blustein, D. L., Kenna, A. C., Gill, N., & DeVoy, J. E. (2008). The psychology of working: A new framework for counseling practice and public policy. *Career Development Quarterly, 56*, 294–308.

Blustein, D. L., Kenny, M. E., Autin, K., & Duffy R. (2019). The psychology of working in practice: A theory of change for a new era. *The Career Development Quarterly, 67*(3), 236–254.

Bronfenbrenner, U. (1977). Toward an experimental ecology of human development. *American Psychologist, 32*(7), 513–531.

Brubaker, M. D., Garrett, M. T., Rivera, E. T., & Tate, K. A. (2010). Justice making in groups for homeless adults: The emancipatory communitarian way. *Journal for Specialists in Group Work, 3*(2), 124–133.

Burn, S. M. (2004). *Groups*. Wadsworth.

Capuzzi, D., & Gross, M. D. (Eds.), *Career counseling: Foundations, perspectives, and applications*. Pearson.

Chen, A., Keith, V., Airriess, C., Li, W., & Leong, K. (2007). Economic vulnerability, discrimination, and Hurricane Katrina: Health among Black Katrina survivors in Eastern New Orleans. *Journal of the American Psychiatric Nurses Association, 13*, 257–266.

Chung, R. C.-Y. (2004). Group counseling with Asians. In J. L. DeLucia-Waack & D. Gerrity (Eds.), Citizens for better care (pp. 200-212). Sage.

Conyne, R. K. (2014). *Group work leadership: An introduction for helpers*. Sage.

Conyne, R. K., Crowell, J. L., & Newmeyer, M. D. (2008). *Group techniques: How to use them more purposely*. Pearson.

Conyne, R. K., Wilson, F. R., & Tang, M. (2000). Evolving lessons from group work involvement in China. *Journal for Specialists in Group Work, 25*(3), 252–268.

Corey, G. (2016). *Theory and practice of counseling and psychotherapy* (10th ed.). Brooks Cole.

Corey, M. S., Corey, G., & Corey, C. (2017). *Groups: Process and practice* (10th ed.). Cengage.

Damirchi, E. S., Ghomi, M., & Valoii, F. E. (2017). Effectiveness of life review group therapy on psychological well-being and the life expectancy of elderly women. *Iranian Journal of Ageing, 12*(3), 312–325.

DeLucia-Waack, J. L., & Dongian, J. (2004). *The practice of multicultural group work: Visions and perspective from the field*. Brook/Cole-Thompson Learning.

Dobson, J. E., & Dobson, R. L. (1991). Changing roles: An aging parents support group. *Journal for Specialists in Group Work, 16*, 178–184.

Erikson, E. H. (1950). *Childhood and society*. W. W. Norton.

Erikson, J. (1997). *The life cycle completed*. W. W. Norton.

Erlenbusch, B., O'Connor, K., Downing, S., & Phillips, S. W. (2008). *Foreclosure to homelessness: The forgotten victims of the subprime crisis*. National Coalition for the Homeless. http://www.national homeless.org/housing/foreclosure_report.pdf

Gladding, S. (2019). *Groups: A counseling specialty* (8th ed.). Pearson.

Goodman, J., & Hoppin, J. M. (1990). *Opening doors: A practical guide to job hunting* (2nd ed.). Continuum Center, Oakland University.

Goodwin, P. J. (2005). Support groups in advanced breast cancer. *Cancer, 104*, 2596–2601.

Gopinath, B., Craig, A., Kifley, A., Liew, G., Bloffwitch, J., Van Vu, K., Joachim, N., Cummins, R., Heraghty, J., Broady, T., Hayes, A., & Mitchell, P. (2017). Implementing a multi-modal support service model for the family caregivers of persons with age-related macular degeneration: A study protocol for a randomised controlled trial. *BMJ Open*, https://doi.org/10.1136/bmjopen-2017-018204

Hackney, H., & Cormier, S. (2005). *The professional counselor: A process guide to helping* (5th ed.). Allyn & Bacon.

Jacobs, E. E., Masson, R. L., Harvill, R. L., & Schimmel, C. J. (2012). *Group counseling: Strategies and skills* (7th ed.). Brooks/Cole.

Johnson, R. P. (1990). The Serenity prayer. *Group Networker, 6*(1), 2.

Kivlighan, D. M., Adams, M. C., Obrecht, A., Kim, C., Ward, B., & Latino, C. (2019). Group therapy trainee's social learning and interpersonal awareness: The role of cohesion in training groups. *Journal for Specialists in Group Work, 44*(1), 62–76.

Livneh, H., & Sherwood-Hawes, A. (1993). Group counseling approaches with persons who have sustained myocardial infarction. *Journal of Counseling and Development, 72*, 57–61.

Meyerstein, I. (2000). Case studies: The remarriage box ritual: Helping stepfamilies differentiate between fear and reality [Document ID: 671603021]. *Family Therapy Networker, 24*(4). (Document ID: 671603021).

Myers, J. E., Sweeney, T. J., & Wittmen, M. (2000). The wheel of wellness, counseling for wellness: A holistic model for treatment planning. *Journal of Counseling and Development, 78*, 251–266.

Newsome, W., & Kelly, M. (2005). Grandparents raising grandchildren: A solution-focused brief therapy approach in school settings. *Social Work With Groups, 27*(4), 65–84.

Niles, S. G., & Harris-Bowlsbey, J. (2017). *Career development interventions*. Pearson.

Off, C. A., Griffin, J. R., Murray, K. W., & Milman, L. (2019). Interprofessional caregiver education, training, and wellness in the context of a cohort model for aphasia rehabilitation. *Topics in Language Disorders, 39*(1), 5–28.

Ohrt, J., Clarke, P., & Conley, A. (2019). *Wellness counseling: A holistic approach to prevention and intervention*. American Counseling Association.

Patil, S. J., Ruppar, T., Koopman, R., Lindbloom, S. G, Elliott, S. G., Mehr, D. R., & Conn, V. S. (2018). Effect of peer support interventions on cardiovascular disease risk factors in adults with diabetes: A systematic revew and meta-analysis. *BMC Public Health*, 18, 398–418. https://doi.org/10.1186/s12889-018-5326-8

Pearson, R. E. (1990). *Counseling and social support: Perspectives and practice*. Sage.

Pope, M., Minor, C. W., & Lara, T. M. *Experiential activities for teaching career counseling classes and for facilitating career groups, Vol. III*. National Career Development Association.

Reese, R. F., & Myers, J. E. (2012). EcoWellness: The missing factor in holistic wellness models. *Journal of Counseling & Development*, 90, 400–406. https://doi.org/10.1002/j.1556-6676.2012.00050.x4

Reese, R. F., & Gosling, M. (2020) The group ecowellness wodel of change: A conceptual framework for facilitating groups in nature. *Journal for Specialists in Group Work, 45*(4), 331–352. https://doi.org/10.1080/01933922.2020.1799465

Ridge, Y., Panabaker, K., McCullum, M., Portigal-Todd, C., Schott, J., & McGillivray, B. (2009). *National Society of Genetic Counselors, 18*, 87–100. https://doi.org/10.1007/s10897-008-9189-5

Sand-Pringle, G., West, J. D., & Bubenzer, D. L. (1991). Family counseling rituals: A case study. *Journal of Mental Health Counseling, 13,* 500–505.
Schlossberg, N. (2009). *Revitalizing retirement: Reshaping your identity, relationships and purpose.* American Psychological Association.
Substance Abuse and Mental Health Services Administration. (2001). *Summary of findings from the 2000 NHSDA.* Author.
Sue, D. W., Sue, D., Neville, H. A., & Smith, L. (2019). *Counseling the culturally diverse.* Wiley.
Swanson, J. L., & Fouad, N. A. (2015). *Career theory & practice: Learning through case studies.*
Wadeson, H. (2010). *Art psychotherapy* (2nd ed.). Wiley.
Waters, E. B., & Samson, J. (1993). *Strengthening your team: A training program for volunteers and staff who work with older adults.* Continuum Center, Oakland University.
Westwood, M. J., & Ewasiw, J. F. (2011). Integrating narrative and action processes in group counseling practice: A multimodal approach for helping clients. *Journal for Specialists in Group Work, 36*(1), 78–93.
Wuthnow, R. (1994). *Sharing the journey: Support groups and America's new quest for community.* Free Press.
Yalom, I. (2002). *The gift of therapy.* HarperCollins.
Yalom, I. D. (1985). *The theory and practice of group psychotherapy* (3rd ed.). Basic Books.
Yalom, I. D., & Leszcz, M. (2005). *The theory and practice of group psychotherapy* (5th ed.). Basic Books.

10

Consultation, Program Development, and Advocacy

When we hear the word *counseling*, most of us envision a professionally trained helper working face-to-face with one or more people considered clients. Indeed, individual and group counseling is what we are trained to do and what most of us like to do. But this is not the whole story. Increasingly, counselors are being called upon to act in other ways to assist adults in transition. As we consider the four pillars of the transition model, we need to think about how we can be of assistance to adults working on each of the components. With advocacy, for example, we usually focus on changing the situation and/or the supports available to our clients. But in teaching advocacy skills, we are also intervening in our clients' repertoires of coping responses—their strategies—and usually increasing their self-efficacy and self-confidence as we do so. Similarly, consultation and program planning can address all of the aspects of the model.

Some counselors now work in the corporate world, and others are community organizers; some counselors design programs for colleges and universities, whereas others develop workshops for senior centers; some walk the halls of legislatures as lobbyists, whereas still others talk about mental health on talk shows, on their own or others' blogs, on Twitter, or other internet sites and social media. For some counselors, these broadened roles represent an exciting challenge; for others, they are an intrusion or a necessary evil.

As part of their training, counselors are taught to be supportive, encouraging, and accepting. In contrast, advocacy and legislative efforts may involve controversy and adversarial relations. In a random sampling, mental health counselors expressed limited interest in learning how to lobby more effectively or provide psychoeducational services to clients (Wilcoxon & Puleo, 1992), probably because such activities take counselors out of their comfort zone. On the other hand, the Legislative Institutes sponsored by the American Counseling Association (ACA) draw a number of counselors each year who are eager to learn advocacy skills, albeit sometimes nervous about their capabilities.

No longer can counselors be merely good listeners. As consultants, trainers, advocates, and program developers, counselors have opportunities to make organizations and systems more responsive to the needs of our clients. If clients are to look for available supports in the community, those supports must be there. And counselors can play a role in putting them in place. In some cases, counselors' efforts can help create structures that favorably tip the ratio of resources to deficits for adults in transition. For example, a counselor might help to create a chapter of PFLAG (Parents, Families and Friends of Lesbians and Gays; http://community.pflag.org). Parents who discover that a child is gay may experience several event and nonevent transitions, including perhaps anticipating not having the grandchildren they have dreamed of, changing their beliefs about what is right, and changing their life from politically inactive to activist. A counselor who helps create a PFLAG chapter is providing a support structure for these clients.

It is our opinion that although counselors should not impose their own values on their clients, counselors should act on their own values to bring about needed societal changes. In this chapter, we talk about a variety of ways counselors can do these things, including consulting, developing programs, and advocacy.

WORKING AS ADVOCATES

An advocate is an individual who supports a person or cause through their speech, writing, and actions. Social scientists talk about functioning as change agents, but, in lay terms, we may think of advocacy as standing up for what you believe in. Whatever the definition, in this discussion, we are talking about counselor efforts to make life fairer to and more supportive of adults in transition. Sometimes, those efforts involve working to empower adults so they can act on their own behalf. In other situations, counselors may need to intervene on a broader level, urging organizations and systems to be more responsive to the needs of adults. Kazan and Bluestein (2020) investigated counseling psychologists who were trained in social justice advocacy from the perspective of implementing change. They found that those trained in social justice advocacy maintained their commitment to change, even with the challenges they faced in "real-world" settings. They suggested that simply training during graduate programs is not sufficient, but ongoing training and support would make advocacy achievements more likely. Watson et al. (2004) suggested that counselors become advocates when they recognize that clients can be helped by effecting change in their environments as well as within themselves. They provide a list of four, "extrapsychic targets for counselor intervention: (a) the primary group, such as the family, couples and close friends; (b) associational groups, such as classes clubs, or a dormitory; (c) institutions, such as community mental health programs, alcohol and drug treatment programs, and a department of corrections; and (d) the community at large" (p. 291). As we consider these environments, we can refer back to Bronfenbrenner's (1977) ecological model for areas of intervention.

Counselors also need to be sensitive to the fact that clients are not on a level playing field as far as resources and barriers to empowerment. We can, as counselors, unconsciously make assumptions that could be detrimental to our clients. Advocacy is related to a conscious realization regarding the socioeconomic realities and barriers facing many of our clients. The 2020 Covid-19 pandemic and the Black Lives Matter movement have underlined the disparities faced by people of color and people in poverty. The unemployment faced by many during the pandemic has had a disparate effect on women and minorities. As noted earlier, the economic downturn has been called a *shecession* by many because of its disparate effect on women's employment as a result of the need for childcare whileschools are only attended remotely.

Toporek and Daniels (2018) updated the original advocacy competency model developed by Lewis et al. (2005; Figure 10.1) for the ACA. These competencies address client, community, and public arenas from the perspective of acting with and acting on behalf of clients. They help the counselor-advocate move from the micro to the macro level, using the appropriate advocacy skills for each circumstance. They were developed in response to a perception that many counselors want to advocate for their clients but do not know how to be effective. The competencies were designed to help counselors operationalize the necessary skills. The competencies were also operationalized in a book (Ratts et al., 2010) that includes applications across populations, settings, and specialty areas. The new model adds the dimensions of client involvement and the focus of counselor energy.

Let us look at some of the competencies. In the category of client empowerment, the authors recommend identifying potential allies—a support system using the terminology of Schlossberg's theory. When they approach

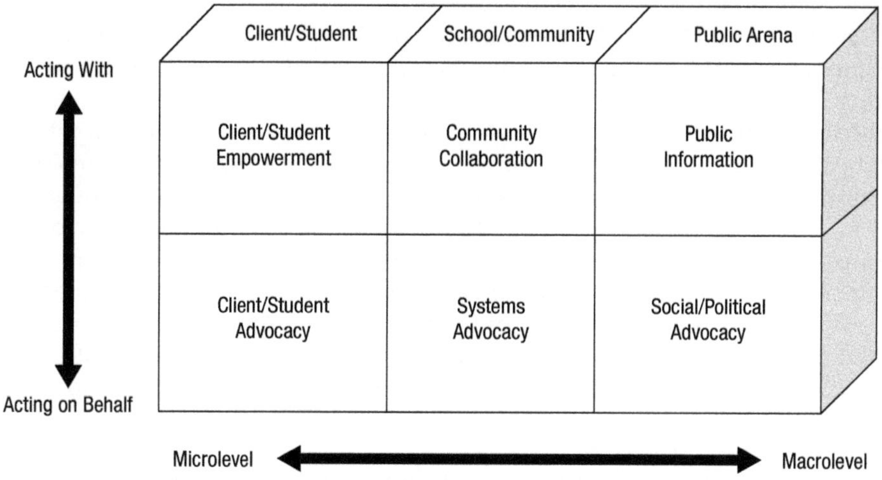

FIGURE 10.1 Advocacy competency domains.

Source: The American Counseling Association website, http://www.counseling.org/Resources/. Reprinted with permission. No further reproduction authorized without written permission from the American Counseling Association.

advocating at the community level, they discuss finding groups already involved in the same or similar efforts and suggest that counselors join those efforts. In those and other advocacy efforts, they suggest that counselors contribute their particular expertise in communications, training, and research. Similarly, the competency suggestions encourage counselors to use their existing skills in listening, identifying strengths, and knowledge of human development. Goodman (2009) used a metaphor to describe these levels of advocacy that she called *starfish, salmon,* and *whales*. Starfish are used to represent advocacy at the individual level, referring to the parable of the man saving starfish on the beach by throwing them back in the ocean after they are stranded by the tide. When the man is questioned about the utility of this, given how many millions of starfish are stranded around the world, he replies, "It matters to this starfish." Salmon are endangered because of a combination of community actions like logging in the Pacific Northwest dams, fish farming that poisons the water, and similar activities. To help the salmon, one must act at the community level. Saving whales requires a worldwide effort, as whales migrate for thousands of miles. Advocates for whales must enter the broader political arena.

A number of suggestions for advocating for older adults were provided by Goodman (2010). These suggestions follow the original ACA advocacy model levels (Lewis et al., 2002). For the individual level, counselors might monitor the physical environment in their office, for example, painting white lines on the front of steps or improving lighting. For the community level, the counselor might advocate with area agencies on aging to provide more mental health services in community settings or to provide counseling to older adults who are making a transition to assisted living. For the public arena level, counselors might testify before governmental agencies about the needs of older adults in transition.

Toporek and Daniels (2018) make the further point that although it may be important for clients to learn advocacy skills and be empowered by advocating for themselves, this position represents a particular, culturally determined, worldview. They argue that there are many circumstances in which advocating for clients is appropriate and indeed necessary. This position is supported by the ACA ethical standards (2014) as they state in standard A.7.a. Advocacy: "When appropriate, counselors advocate at individual, group, institutional, and societal levels to examine potential barriers and obstacles that inhibit access and/or the growth and development of clients" (p. 5). They also state in A.7.b. Confidentiality and Advocacy: "Counselors obtain client consent prior to engaging in advocacy efforts on behalf of an identifiable client to improve the provision of services and to work toward removal of systemic barriers or obstacles that inhibit client access, growth, and development" (p. 5).

This affirmative ethical responsibility requires that counselors, to best help their clients, be aware of institutional or societal barriers and take steps to change those barriers. To illustrate this further, consider this case example.

Case Study

Paulina Juarez worked at a job-placement center near her home on the south side of Chicago. Her center was always busy helping people find jobs, but during the Covid-19 pandemic and resulting economic downturn, she "saw" an unusual number of job seekers. Many she saw remotely, but she did go into her office 1 day a week to meet with clients who did not have access to the internet. She wore her mask and stayed 6 feet away but always felt uneasy on that day. Nevertheless, she saw her job as essential and carried on with trying to help. One of her clients was Takesha Williams, a 20-year-old African American woman who, until the recent downturn, had managed to support herself as a waitress while attending community college in a liberal arts transfer curriculum. She was experiencing challenges related to transferring to a 4-year college to study general accounting. Takesha had moved back in with her parents, and they did not have internet access. She had done her schoolwork at the restaurant where she worked but now that had closed and she was not only without income but without a place to use the tools she needed to manage her remote classes.

As Paulina considered how to best address Takesha's issues, she was aware that using her regular list of employers was pretty much useless during this time as many of the small businesses who hired her clients had closed, temporarily or permanently, and even those still operating had reduced staff. Her usual tactic was to encourage clients to set short- and long-term goals—the short term relating to survival and the long term to career decision-making. She had developed a comprehensive list of resources and was usually able to connect her clients with some sort of assistance while they figured out how to survive. Now though many of these resources had been tapped out and she felt very frustrated at her inability to "fix things" for her clients.

Paulina's sense of worth at her job derived from her success in helping people find work or manage until they did, and she was feeling extremely depressed at her inability to do that during the present crisis. She no longer had a sense of self-efficacy and dreaded her time at work, both remote or in person. It came to her attention from a client that a local pastor was trying to organize a ride-sharing program so some local residents could get to job sites in the suburbs and in Indiana that were still hiring. Paulina asked her whether they could meet, and she became an enthusiastic supporter of the program. These work sites represented alternatives for her clients that had not been possible with the public transportation most of them relied on.

Being able to do something concrete helped Paulina counter her sense of helplessness and reenergized her determination to help her clients. She developed a good working alliance with the pastor that also opened up other areas of advocacy. She began to redefine her job to include advocating for her clients as well as helping them advocate for themselves. As she continued working with her clients, she also made others in her work setting aware of the need to provide training in advocacy skills. From her efforts, several experts were invited to design webinars for her and her colleagues. Attendance was voluntary and participation served to boost the morale in her workplace and promote further community collaborations.

Advocacy as Empowerment

In our quest to be supportive of various groups of adults, we must be careful not to take over for them. The ACA advocacy model provides that we act with as well as act on behalf of clients and client student empowerment is the cornerstone of level one. Teaching clients to advocate for themselves is a critical component of applying the transition model. As we have discussed elsewhere in this book, strengthening one's self and having effective strategies to use are important to the successful navigation of a transition.

In many situations, counselors need to operate on more than one level. In terms of the transition model, counselors can help clients develop more effective *strategies*, and counselors and clients can work together to improve available institutional *support*. For example, counselors in college and university settings may be able to empower returning students through workshops that build self-esteem and teach assertive skills and effective study techniques. At the same time, these counselors can encourage their educational institutions to offer evening advising hours, offer financial aid for part-time students, and generally be more supportive of the needs of returning learners. Liu (Liu & Hernandez, 2010) noticed that he was frequently advocating on behalf of his clients at a homeless shelter with the same agencies: The Veteran's Administration, the local hospital, the city police, and others. In order to begin the process of educating these agencies about the needs of his clients as well as about each other's services, he invited representatives of all of them to a fundraiser at the homeless shelter. "Shelter residents were included in the event, some … honored for their own educational, vocational and life-changing accomplishments. These new collaborators saw they would be part of a larger network of help givers and that their services would be recognized" (p. 47).

As another example, the University of Maryland, College Park, has a returning student fund that offers grants to adult learners experiencing financial emergencies. These grants, ranging from US$100 to US$500, have enabled a number of students to stay in school and continue to provide for their families. Several of the recipients spoke of the grants as a tremendous source of motivation, in part because they made the students feel they really mattered to someone.

To assess the degree to which adult learners feel they matter to their institutions, Schlossberg et al. (1991) developed "The Mattering Scales for Adult Students in Higher Education." These easily administered scales give students an opportunity to record their perceptions about their educational environment in five different areas: administration, advising, peers, multiple roles, and faculty. Questions deal with issues such as the degree to which students feel appreciated or missed when they are not in class and the degree to which they find the policies of the institution cognizant of the competing demands in their lives. Data from the scales provide information for change. Administrators and student development educators can pinpoint the areas in which adult learners feel they do not matter and then take appropriate action to create a more hospitable environment.

Counselor–advocates can also work to make nonprofit agencies more user-friendly for their adult clients. At one employment office, an official of the U.S. Department of Labor heard many unemployment counselors talking among themselves about how "their hearts ached for the people who had to stand in line to collect their checks and wait to talk with them." After looking over the office, the official suggested several changes to make the environment more supportive. He recommended that people take numbers and be able to sit down while retaining their place "in line." He also recommended changing the physical environment so that clients could sit in chairs rather than lean over a counter when talking with counselors (Robinson, 1994).

Acting at the Local, State, and National Levels

When one is working with an individual client, advocacy often takes the form of "running interference," often as part of the referral process. Operationally, that means you do not just give your clients the name of an agency that might provide the services they need, but you call the agency yourself, verify the services they offer and the hours they provide them, and perhaps alert them to your clients' special needs. Also, adults who are apprehensive about negotiating a transition, whether it be returning to school, attending the first meeting of a widowed persons' group, or looking into Alcoholics Anonymous, may need the name of a particular person to look for, or perhaps a "buddy" to accompany them. You can be of help there.

Clients may also need help in coping with bureaucracies. The thought of going for the first time to an employment (or unemployment) office, admissions office, Social Security building, or senior center can appear daunting to many adults in transition. Counselors can help by walking clients through the process, literally or with an in-office rehearsal. To make appropriate referrals, counselors need to be knowledgeable about local resources. The process of helping adults with such practical concerns may also build trust and open the door to dealing with their emotional problems as well.

Dealing with bureaucracies can pose additional problems for people in certain ethnic or minority groups. Non-English-speaking adults may have particular problems if the agency staff speak only English and if the forms they must fill out are only in English. Counselors can advocate by encouraging the agency to provide translators or multilingual staff members.

A major transition for adults may come when they need to deal with the criminal justice system for the first time. Whether they are the victim of a crime or the family member of a perpetrator, the thought of going to the police can seem overwhelming. This may be particularly true for adults who come from groups that historically have experienced adversarial relationships with the police. Counselors can intervene both to help clients reframe their views of police as potential helpers and to work with police to help them become more receptive to clients from diverse ethnic backgrounds. A major transition is experienced when an individual leaves prison, whether after 3 years or 30 years. A number of halfway houses and other programs have arisen to assist with this transition (cf. Gopnik, 2020).

Middleton et al. (2010) discussed advocacy on behalf of clients with disabilities as an aspect of multicultural counseling. They summarized needs for advocacy at all three levels of the ACA model and reminded readers that important targets for advocacy efforts are counselor educators, who have an important influence on new practitioners. Describing advocacy efforts within rehabilitation settings, they suggested that underrepresented groups are often shortchanged even more than other clients in need of vocational rehabilitation.

The ACA Legislative Affairs Unit encourages counselors to get involved politically. They stated ACA members make a big difference in ACA's efforts to advocate for counseling. "Legislators pay attention when they hear from their constituents. If they don't hear from anyone about issues that affect counseling, they may not pay attention to those issues" (ACA, 2021).

There are a host of issues involving every aspect of a person's life that can be addressed legislatively at the local or national level. Counselors' students and clients encounter these challenges daily. They may include minority oppression, disability rights, LBGTQ rights, healthcare, funding for schools at all levels, security and portability of pensions, and community-based programs to provide assistance to adults experiencing temporary crises or long-term difficulties, and many others.

As discussed earlier in this chapter, counselors can advocate in many different ways. For example, they can represent the interests of adults to community organizations and educational institutions. This may mean recommending that colleges and universities schedule supportive services at convenient hours for adults, testifying at a local hearing of a planning agency about the need for additional transportation services for persons with disabilities, or urging libraries to establish in-home services.

Some advocacy efforts are best done by counselors acting individually, whether in their professional roles or as private citizens. Politicians do pay attention to letters and phone calls from constituents. Other times, counselors can maximize their effectiveness by working with an advocacy group representing their point of view. For example, Citizens for Better Care (CBC;

http://cbcmi.org/) is an advocacy organization monitoring conditions in nursing homes. When counselors are aware of CBC's findings, they can help families locate dependable facilities with a well-trained staff and avoid those where CBC has found instances of mistreatment. When counselors have this information, they can make appropriate referrals and perhaps ease the transition of placing a family member in a nursing home. Increasingly, professional associations of counselors are becoming involved in advocacy efforts.

Two noted organizations whose members see their primary role as advocacy are Counselors for Social Justice (CSJ) and Psychologists for Social Responsibility (PsySR). The stated purpose of PsySR (2020) is to ethically use psychological research and practice to support social justice and peace, acknowledging the importance of diversity in addressing economic, gender-based, and racial injustice. Some of the organization's priorities include promoting global environmental sustainability, universal human rights, and mutual understanding through collaboration.

CSJ (2005), a division of the ACA, is described as "a community of counselors, counselor educators, graduate students, and school and community leaders who seek equity and an end to oppression and injustice affecting clients, students, counselors, families, communities, schools, workplaces, governments, and other social and institutional systems."

CSJ is committed to:

- challenging oppressive systems of power and privilege;
- implementing social action strategies, including the Social Justice Advocacy Competencies through collaborative alliances with other ACA entities, counselor education programs, and N–16 schools and community organizations
- disseminating social justice scholarship about sociopolitical and economic inequities facing counselors and clients/students in schools and communities
- maintaining an active support network online and in person for engaging in social justice activities in schools and communities
- providing lively professional development to enhance counselor, counselor educator, and graduate student competency in social justice advocacy via ACA annual conference programs (Day of Action/Day of Learning), branches, regions, counselor education programs, N–16 schools, and community agencies; and
- maintaining social justice advocacy resources online (Mission 1).

The ACA's Government Relations Committee, composed of association members as well as professional staff, advocates for the interests of both clients and counselors. The Committee's mission is to identify and initiate proactive and reactive positions on public policy issues confronting professional counselors, human development professionals, and those whom they serve.

The Committee urges its members to contact their legislators on a wide range of human service needs, to provide the lawmakers with information and to express appreciation when their actions are in line with the interests of clients and counselors. Counselors can support advocacy efforts by joining these and similar organizations as well as by their personal advocacy efforts.

Another major benefit of counselor advocacy has been the move toward counselor credentialing. As of 2011, all 50 states and the District of Columbia have a counselor licensure law. Certification and licensure serve as a way for counselors to indicate their commitment to professionalism. Certification also makes it easier for adults in transition to identify qualified counselors. Many advocacy activities can have considerable impact on the opportunity structure for adults. In our view, that is a major reason for counselors to be involved beyond their office doors.

It is our opinion that although counselors should not impose their own values on their clients, counselors should act on their own values to bring about needed societal changes. In this chapter, we talk about a variety of ways counselors can do this, including consulting, developing programs, and advocacy. A special issue of the *Journal of Counseling and Development* (Singh & Nassar, 2020) was devoted to looking at multicultural and social justice competencies together. Articles in that journal will be useful to anyone looking to advance their advocacy skills.

CONSULTING WITH ORGANIZATIONS AND THEIR EMPLOYEES

Recent events have thrown the conflict between police and minority communities into sharp focus. Counselors can both advocate for minority clients and also offer their services to police departments as consultants to find ways to ameliorate this conflict. Consulting gives counselors a chance to have an impact on adults' everyday environment. Consulting can take many forms. In their introduction to two special issues on consultation of the *Journal of Counseling and Development*, editors Kurpius and Fuqua (1993a) noted that there is no universally accepted definition of *consulting*. However, most agree that "consultation is a process for helping individuals, groups, organizations, and communities function more effectively and efficiently, with greater satisfaction" (p. 596). When counselors are involved as consultants, they have an opportunity to assist adults in transition indirectly rather than directly.

A major difference between consulting and counseling is that consulting is triadic. Counselors work directly with clients; consultants work with consultees who, in turn, serve a client system. The consultee may be an individual, a group, or an organization. The form of the consultation can be varied, but, at the broadest level, writers distinguish between expert consultation and process consultation. Consultants function in the expert role when they have knowledge or experience needed by the consultee. Although this can be a satisfactory arrangement, Dougherty (2014) noted the danger that individuals or organizations may get used to having somebody else perform the service and not develop their own problem-solving abilities.

Process consultation casts consultants in a less directive and more interactive role with the consultee. The consultant helps the consultee examine how problems are being addressed, rather than focusing on what the problems are. "The expert mode includes heavy responsibility for the consultant for the design, implementation, and success of an intervention. The process mode emphasizes shared responsibility between consultant and consultee and provides for the consultee to internalize planned change process as an acquired capability" (Kurpius & Fuqua, 1993b, p. 599). Counselors can function as consultants in either mode if they have the required skills.

Summarizing the skills that are integral parts of every counselor's repertoire, Dougherty (2014) concluded that effective counselors have the interpersonal skills and communication skills that we associate with effective counseling, including the so-called core conditions (Rogers, 1957) of empathy, genuineness, and unconditional positive regard. He also stated that effective consultants need problem-solving, organizational, and group skills, skills in dealing with cultural diversity, and skills to be able to practice ethically and professionally. The 2005 American Counseling Association Code of Ethics specifically addresses counselors' role in consultation in Sections B8 and D2. These sections include statements on consulting agreements, including confidentiality and its limits, as well as respect for privacy. They also include the responsibility of the counselor as consultant to have appropriate training and to refer to others as necessary. The guidelines remind counselors of the need to have clear goals shared with the client organization, written and verbal statements of rights and responsibilities, and clear statements of potential risks and benefits. They also address the issue of cultural competence and the limits of confidentiality.

The issue of confidentiality can be particularly tricky. One of the authors, Goodman, was involved in consulting for a healthcare organization that was struggling with some internal communication problems as they transitioned to a different system of scheduling patient visits. After working with some of the staff on being more assertive and less aggressive in dealing with each other, the management wanted a report on how individuals were progressing and how they saw the issues. After discussion with the trainees, it was decided that the consultant would present management with a summary of the outcomes of the training and also present some requests for support from staff to management. Management would have preferred more specific accounting but was content with what was provided. Goodman learned that next time, what would be shared and what kept confidential should be negotiated at the beginning of the contract.

It is important to remember that multicultural issues arise during consultation, just as they do in counseling. Jackson and Hayes (1993) provided suggestions for the consultant encountering client organizations whose members or some of whose members are different culturally from the consultant. The first suggestion is that the consultant either have a familiarity with the culture of the consultees or learn about it from the clients or from others, and the second is that the consultant acknowledges the differences and his or her own lack of information as appropriate. They suggested that the consultant pay particular attention to verbal and nonverbal expressions, location of consultation, written versus verbal agreements, and time assumptions. They pointed out that it is important to understand and pay attention to high-context or low-context cultures and the implications of this dynamic. If this is not done, they suggest that the outcome may be "(a) lack of mutual goals . . . (b) frustration, and (c) disappointment" (p. 145). They concluded that "to continue down the existing training and consulting path using monocultural philosophies and strategies, consultants, along with the profession of consultation, will be seen as ineffective, nonresponsive, and potentially identified as nonessential" (p. 147). These are strong words, and we hope that readers will therefore be motivated to enhance their multicultural competencies. An interesting example of how multicultural issues may be more broad reaching than race and ethnicity is given by Barack Obama (2004) in his book *Dreams From My father.* Obama described an experience from his community-organizing job in Chicago. At the time, Obama was a college graduate and had lived in many places, including Indonesia and Hawaii. He was very cosmopolitan. He had invited the mayor of Chicago at that time, Harold Washington, to an event that was held to promote better services for Chicago's South Side. When Washington came to visit, Obama's less sophisticated colleagues were so starstruck that they forgot their assignment to lobby the mayor and the need to "stay on message." Obama and his co-organizers were African American but had greatly different life experiences.

Dougherty (2014) developed a generic model of consultation that included four stages: (a) entry, (b) diagnosis, (c) implementation, and (d) disengagement. At all stages, consultant and consultees work together. During stage 1, the consultant enters the organization and explores organizational needs. In stage 2, diagnosis, the focus is on gathering information, defining the problem, setting goals, and generating possible interventions. Stage 3, implementation, is the action stage of a consultation. Consultants and consultees choose an intervention and then formulate, implement, and evaluate that plan. Stage 4, disengagement, requires evaluating the consultation process and planning for necessary follow-up. These stages relate closely to the stages of counseling identified in the Cormier et al. (2017) model, described in Chapter 7, that is, (a) rapport and relationship building, (b) problem assessment, (c) goal setting, and (d) initiating interventions and termination and follow-up.

As part of the action or implementation stage of a consultant relationship, counselors can teach administrators and managers about the transition model. Managers who understand the significance of adult transitions will be more understanding of their employees' behavior and better able to provide support. Sargent and Schlossberg (1988) directed the following remarks to managers to demonstrate this aspect of consultation:

> As a manager, you need to know that people in transition are often preoccupied and a little confused, even if the transition is a desired one. For example, a promotion to a first supervisory job can

> be exciting, yet the new supervisor—whose roles, relationships, assumptions, and routines have been altered—will be disoriented while he or she figures out what is expected in the new role. In addition, the isolation from friends who were colleagues and who are now subordinates can be upsetting. . . . When adults start new jobs, for example, they find themselves suspended awkwardly between their old role and the new one. During that period, they need special help, such as new employee orientation and the rapid development of support systems. . . . The move from incompetence to competence can be tortuous. Managers can help by acknowledging the rough transition rather than denying it, and by offering support and specific strategies to learn new competencies. (pp. 58–60)

Consultants may also be able to help organizations set up a transition-management program. Some of the transitions in private business and industry organizations that lend themselves to the assistance of consultants include diversity and multicultural evolution, restructuring of a workforce (which often includes downsizing or outsourcing employment), team building, and mergers or divestitures. Management of nonprofit organizations, governmental agencies, and nongovernmental organizations may wish to use counselors and consultants when they develop strategic missions, change the focus of their services, or change—voluntarily or by necessity—their sources of funding.

Counselors who want to be more involved in the business world get experience outside of their usual environment, read business journals as well as counseling journals, and attend meetings of organizations such as the American Society of Training and Development. They also need to talk with other consultants and trainers and watch them work. The business section of most daily papers, whether read on paper or online, provides much valuable information for counselors wanting to enter this arena. Kai Ryssdal has a daily program on public radio, *Marketplace*, that can be listened to live or as a podcast that includes up-to-date news on events related to business (http:/ marketplace.publicradio.org).

Many counselors work with profit and nonprofit companies to provide outplacement services for workers in transition. Companies provide such services, partly out of concern for their employees and partly because they have found that if former employees make a smooth transition from one job to another, it saves money in severance pay and avoids possible legal actions. Workers who remain with the company are also reassured when they see that their former coworkers have been helped. For those individuals who do not have company-provided services, or for whom those services have extended their time limit, other structures have arisen to meet their needs. The Adult Career Counseling Center is one such place (http://www.oakland.edu/?id=10213&sid=1) that has been offering services for more than 25 years. In addition to the supervision provided to the students provided by the faculty sponsor, an experienced career counselor meets with the students individually weekly to assist them in better serving their clients. This is another form of consultation that overlaps with supervision.

Noel (1993) stated that many organizations do a much better job with those they are firing than with those who are staying, those who, in our terms, have experienced a nonevent transition. He used the term *layoff survivor sickness* to describe an illness characterized by a variety of feelings, including fear, anger, depression, guilt, and betrayal. In his view, "only compelling multilevel interventions can affect the pathology of layoff survivor sickness" (p. 2). Toward that end, he designed a model, including interventions, that clarifies the process, facilitates grieving, breaks some existing patterns, and creates new systems.

Many of those interventions are based on skills that counselors can use either directly or as consultants to company employees. The examples just discussed illustrate the use of expert consultation skills. The following case study shows how a counselor used process consultation skills to help a group deal with the need to lay people off.

A Consultation Case Study: Transition Model in Action

The designer of the transition model used in this book, Nancy Schlossberg, had an opportunity to consult with a group of six nurse managers and a professor of nursing in a Canadian city. Nursing supervisors had been "ordered" to dismiss almost half of their trained nurses. As each spoke, the situation began to sound hopeless: The nurses had to be fired, they would never get other jobs in the field, it was unfair, but the supervisors had to carry out the orders.

The consultant's first step was to listen to what the clients were saying and reflect it back. She heard a sense of catastrophe and no hope. Therefore, the goal of the consultation became (a) to help the nurse managers put this negative transition in perspective and (b) to provide skills so they would feel competent to help those they fire learn how to negotiate transitions.

Addressing the feelings of the nurse managers was critical to helping them take control of their role as "messengers of bad news." If they felt hopeless, they would communicate this to those they had to fire. After discussing their feelings, they began to see that although the situation was negative, it was not a disaster. Joblessness can be a defeat and leave one hungry and homeless, or it can be an opportunity to think about getting different training and reshaping goals. Once they could begin to redefine it as a challenge, albeit a negative one, they were on their way.

In addition to feeling guilty about having to fire people, the managers were concerned that they did not have the skills to do it. As they were dealing with transitions, and actually creating transitions in other people's lives, they needed to learn how to help people negotiate transitions. So the consultant helped them learn to teach others how to (a) approach change, (b) assess their resources for coping with change, and (c) develop action plans to take control of the change.

She suggested that in discussing ways to approach change, the managers give all those being fired an opportunity to express their views of the transition. For example, do they see it as positive, negative, or neutral? If the firings were being discussed in a group, group members might be able to suggest alternate ways to view the situation to each other. Perhaps some will see it as an opportunity to do life planning, rethink their careers, or start over.

To help the managers assist the fired nurses in assessing their resources, she taught them how to explain the 4 S's model. Managers were to help nurses identify their resources and deficits with respect to their situation at the time of their job loss, their self, their support at work and at home, and their strategies. In teaching the managers to help nurses develop an action plan, she suggested the use of group discussions to encourage the nurses to identify resources they could strengthen.

In describing this consultation, the counselor noted that three groups needed attention—the supervisors who had to convey the bad news, those being fired, and those not being fired. In this situation, as in many others, "survivors" may be preoccupied with a fear of impending doom. Consultants must remain aware of the needs of all three groups, rather than just the person or group they are with.

Many organizational development consultants come from the ranks of counselors. They may be hired to implement a career development program. In that case, they would work with the management to understand the advantages to the company of employees who are satisfied as well as satisfactory, to use the words from work adjustment theory (Dawis & Lofquist, 1984). Often one level of management is interested in the contracted-for consultation, but others need to be "brought along" to see the advantages of investing time and money in the process. Often managers fear that if employees receive career decision-making assistance and skills training, they will take their skills elsewhere. A persuasive argument used by one CEO was to point out that if other companies did not want his employees, why should he?

In other cases, counselors are hired to improve the organization's multicultural competency. Many of these consultants start with the ACA's (2015) multicultural competencies and also use the companion operationalization guidelines (AMCD Professional Standards and Certification Committee, 1996). These are organized as follows:

- I. Counselor Self-Awareness;
- II. Client Worldview;
- III. Counseling Relationship; and
- IV. Counseling and Advocacy Interventions.

In this endeavor, consultants are asked to help organizations consciously create a transition to a more multiculturally competent entity. This transition is one that often creates resistance, as exemplified in *Who Moved My Cheese?*

(Johnson, 1998). In his best-selling book, Johnson presented an allegory of mice that resist change to the point of starvation and compares them to mice that accept change and move on. The lessons learned by the "resilient" mice are (a) change happens, (b) anticipate change, (c) monitor change, (d) adapt to change quickly, (e) change, (f) enjoy change, and (g) be ready to quickly change again and again. The underlying message is that not only is change constant but also that one must embrace change and see it as leading to more positive outcomes. It is beyond the scope of this book to describe the transition of an organization to a more multicultural one, but it is certainly fruitful ground for counselor consultants.

Another transition that may be addressed by counselor consultants occurs when organizations engage in strategic planning. Whether this takes the form of strategic visioning or the more traditional detailed planning, carrying out the vision or plan will lead to both big and small transitions for the people who work in or connect to the organization. Whenever counselors engage in consultation roles, they find that their counseling skills are necessary precursors to developing the relationships that facilitate effective consultations. Counselors can also assist individuals and organizations manage transitions by designing and delivering programs and workshops.

DEVELOPING PROGRAMS AND WORKSHOPS

Another way that counselors can expand their impact on adults in transition is through designing and presenting structured workshops and acting as program developers. We define a *program* as an array of services offered by an organization, and a *workshop* as a short-term educational or growth experience. Thus, the program of any organization may include several workshops as well as other activities.

Obviously, a competent counselor can be extremely helpful to an individual suddenly conscious of being middle-aged, to a divorced person, or to a job seeker. The same counselor, however, can reach many more people by offering a workshop on midlife changes, divorce, or job-seeking skills. And the workshop may add the bonus of group support. In addition, some adults who are reluctant to seek counseling may find it easier or more socially acceptable to attend a workshop. Another option is to provide webinars for virtual attendance. Participation in workshops and/or webinars may be enough to help some people through the transitions. Others may find that they are now more comfortable with the idea of individual or group counseling.

Counselors involved in designing workshops or programs may find it useful to follow Caffarella and Daffron's (2013) description of program planning as a process that consists of a set of interacting and dynamic components. They described three interconnected and related subprocesses: planning, design and implementation, and evaluation and accountability. Flexibility in program planning is particularly important in programs for adults in transition because the needs of participants may change as they learn more about *themselves* and their *situations* and see a need to develop new sources of *support* and alternative *strategies*.

Designing Programs

Setting up a comprehensive program is a complicated procedure. It requires that program planners look broadly at the environment and consider the needs of the individuals to be served, as well as those of the organization and the community. Typically, designing a program requires identification of specific tasks and a timeline.

The National Occupational Information Coordinating Committee (1989) developed the useful three-stage model for program design shown here (Kobylarz, 2005):

Stage 1. Planning (0–6 months)

- Form committees.
- Conduct needs assessment.
- Establish program standards.
- Initiate evaluation planning.

Stage 2. Development (7–12 months)

- Direct committees in program development.
- Review the current program.
- Revise the plan.
- Design the evaluation.
- Identify staff development needs.

Stage 3. Implementation (13–24 months)

- Involve committees in program implementation.
- Conduct staff development.
- Monitor program implementation.
- Evaluate and use results for program improvement.

Because formative evaluation is a continuous process used to improve program design, discussion of evaluation procedures continues throughout the process. Committees are also involved in all stages. When committees are broadly based and include community representatives, they can assist in marketing and recruiting as well as program design.

Reentry students are the target group for a variety of college and university programs. Jacoby (1991) developed a model for serving adult students. The four components of the SPAR model—services, programs, advocacy, and research—can be a useful guide for counselors. According to her definitions, services are performed *for* students and must be scheduled to accommodate their multiple roles. Programs are carried on *with* students, often through adult student organizations. Advocacy on *behalf* of students is designed to see that the policies and practices of educational institutions are responsive to student needs. Research helps counselors and other professionals better understand the needs of adult students and evaluate existing programs.

Designing and Presenting Workshops

By virtue of their training and experience, counselors already have many of the communication skills necessary to conductworkshops. Typically, counselors know how to listen to workshop participants, ask clarifying questions to make sure that participants understand the information, "read" the group's nonverbal language, and promote group interaction.

Effective workshop leaders must also know how to present information clearly and use examples that are appropriate for particular individuals and groups. Counselors can learn these skills. A study of training needs of career development facilitators revealed a significant interest in learning how to train both clients and other career development facilitators. The authors recommended that "train-the-trainer sessions emphasize training skills and that only experienced, effective trainers be used to train other personnel" (Hoppin & Splete, 1994, p. 85).

Counselors interested in designing effective workshops may find Loesch's (1985) seven-step procedure helpful. The seven steps—define your goals, profile the participants, profile the setting, design your agenda, prepare your resources, prepare yourself, and practice—can be applied to almost any workshop. If, for example, you have been asked to design a workshop for dislocated workers in your community and you know the workers are concerned about their ability to look for jobs, your goals might be to provide practical information about job-search techniques and labor-force projections, as well as to build worker confidence. In designing the agenda, you might want to consult both local employers and a list of competencies needed by job seekers, such as that contained in Goodman and Hoppin (1991).

In planning workshops, it is important to think of who, what, where, and when. Who and what need to be carefully coordinated so that the content and manner of presentation fit the needs of a particular clientele. Thus, a workshop for adults who have recently learned they have attention deficit disorder should not be done in a straight lecture format. A variety of activities, many experiential, should be included. The leader of a workshop for returning learners needs to inform students about resources at the college or university and give them an opportunity to express some of their concerns about their new role.

Workshop planners also need to consider the cultural background of their participants. After investigating the self-esteem of Arab adults studying English as a second language, Klee (1994) urged counselors and teachers to cooperate in tailoring programs for their special needs. She suggested that single-gender workshops might be more appropriate for this population and also recommended that workshop participants have "opportunities for cultural and linguistic interactions with native English speakers outside of the classroom . . . [possibly through] field trips, 'pot lucks,' forums, guest speakers, or language exchange partners" (p. 31).

The time at which a workshop is offered also affects who can come. Workshops for displaced homemakers with young children can be offered during the day if childcare is available. If a business wants spouses to attend a retirement planning seminar, it usually needs to be an evening program so spouses do not have to take time off from their own jobs. Workshops for older adults often have to be scheduled when transportation is available. Safety issues are also important. In their publicity, sponsors may want to mention secure, lighted parking if that is apt to be an issue. Having representatives of the targeted population involved in the planning process increases the likelihood that the right questions about who, what, where, and when will be asked. Many of these issues have been resolved by virtual workshops, seminars, and webinars, which can reach more people and fit with their various schedules and responsibilities.

A Sampling of Programs and Workshops

Earlier in this chapter, we identified a number of topics that could be the focus of support groups for people experiencing individual, family, and work-related transitions. Many of those topics lend themselves to a workshop format, if a more educational focus is desired. This section contains ideas for workshops counselors can conduct or promote and descriptions of a few we considered innovative.

Sometimes, the approach of community-based counseling represents a blending of the stated desires of adult clients with the perceptions of counselors as to their needs. In conducting career decision-making groups, counselors typically want their clients to engage in a comprehensive decision-making process. Adult clients, on the other hand, particularly those adults whose career change is not voluntary, want help in finding a job. Goodman (2006) described this circumstance as an "unconscious conspiracy" (p. 69) between the counselor and the client to look for short-term solutions to deeper problems.

A National Career Development Association-commissioned Gallup poll (Miller, 2000) found that one tenth of Americans stated that they needed assistance with career planning in the past year. Furthermore, 69% said that if they were starting over, they would seek more information and more assistance than they had during their first occupational decision. The data also indicated that career assistance was not available to everyone equally. Minority individuals and youth received substantially less help than the population in general (Herr et al., 2004). A number of powerful suggestions for career counseling for diverse populations are provided by Pope and Pangelinan (2010). Their suggestions include some that are important for all clients and some that are specific to certain populations. For example, they suggest that counselors directly address occupational discrimination and provide assertive communication training to all clients from diverse groups. They suggest including the family in counseling, and/or discussing the ramifications of going against family expectations for people from collectivist cultures (see pages 211–213). Programs, such as the Adult Career Counseling Center at Oakland University (Goodman & Savage, 1999) and the One Stop Career Centers around the nation, are designed to address both immediate needs and the need for comprehensive planning.

An innovative career-counseling program, Operation ABLE, provides classroom-based training and self-paced instruction in a variety of computer applications, as well as offers a "Career Resilience Center" for older workers who need assistance with employment and career decisions, resume development, interview preparation and coaching, and job-search assistance (Nationalable.org., n.d.). The Resilience Center also offers skills and aptitude testing and professional career counseling. Classes are also offered in basic skills such as reading, math, and grammar.

Job Link targets food stamp recipients who do not have dependents. The program provides job skills training and placement services to help its clients find job placements. Employment Link works with homeless individuals referred by Med-Link and provides job skills training and placement services to help them find job placements. Work Connect helps hard-to-place individuals with histories of incarceration, substance abuse, and other obstacles to find jobs. Skills remediation and employment services help them successfully enter the job market.

An innovative program was developed by the Ball State University Center for Peace & Conflict Studies (www.bsu.edu/peacecenter). They compiled a list of acts of kindness and peace done during the 2020 Covid-19 and racism pandemic to address the feelings of frustration and sadness experienced by many counselors and other helpers. They gathered good news stories weekly and sent them to everyone on their email list. CNN and other news sources have done something similar with weekly "good news" news blasts (TheGoodStuff@newsletters.cnn.com., downloaded November 2, 2020).

Although designed for teens, an antibullying movie, *Surviving Lunch* (surviving lunch.com) is an example of looking at nontraditional ways to advocate for clients. Educational experiences do not always take place in classrooms. In San Francisco, a vacant lot turned into an urban garden was the site of an innovative program for people being released from prison. People experiencing this transition may find that their preprison support system is no longer intact, and their previous strategies for coping with their lives are no longer appropriate. The Garden Project, founded in 1991, was a model project designed to help recently released ex-offenders reenter their communities, learn new skills, and avoid the temptations of the street.

A press release about the program, undated and simply titled "The Garden Project" noted, "To help achieve personal goals, 'students' in the program also fulfill requirements to participate in alcohol and drug rehabilitation programs, as well as pursue continuing education studies." An article about the project in *The New York Times* characterized the fruit and vegetables of the garden as "metaphors for what went wrong in a prisoner's troubled past. . . . The simple process of weeding is a good place to start re-examining a life gone wrong. The weeds are whatever got in the way: smoking crack or whoring or stealing" (Gross, 1992). In addition to the metaphorical value of planting, cultivating, and weeding, gardeners are paid for their efforts from the revenue earned by the produce. Local businesses supported the project with-their purchases and several foundations have supplied additional income.

Another San Francisco garden program, Fresh Start Farms, hired homeless people to work as organic gardeners. According to an article in the *San Francisco Examiner*, homeless workers were driven to the garden. They were paid minimum wage while working and given a generous bonus after a year of working to assist them in finding unsubsidized work after this experience. Some were also offered pay to train others (Nakao, 1993). Although these projects are not typical workshops for adults in transition, they represent innovative efforts for which counselors can advocate.

Another program planning model was developed by the Kellogg Foundation. Termed *the logic model*, it suggests that planning proceed by examining what you plan to do, that is, your inputs resources, and activities, and what you hope to accomplish, that is, the outputs, outcomes, and impact. By separating the immediate or short-term outcomes from the long-term impact, the model encourages planners to look beyond the immediate activities, and thus fits well with the advocacy efforts described in the following.

A 40-year-old displaced worker who decided to return to school might benefit from individual and/or group counseling. We, as supportive counselors, can help him explore his situation. For example, we might find it important to evaluate his financial resources by asking him questions about whether his previous employer will cover any educational expenses, whether he has a working partner, and whether the family has health insurance. Our counseling would also provide an opportunity for him to express his feelings about two major role changes: (a) being laid off and (b) returning to school.

Before helping him set realistic goals, we, as counselors, could also help him explore the self resources he brings to the transition. What is his attitude toward change and his general outlook on life? Answers to questions about both situation and self might be important in determining whether to refer him for financial aid and in helping him decide how many courses to take the first semester.

If we were serving as consultants to the school, we might encourage the administration to engage in a self-study and work with faculty and staff to help them become more sensitive to and supportive of the needs of returning students. We might help them establish a returning student center, help them design programs to meet the special needs of nontraditional students, and/or consult with existing campus offices to add or modify services to serve this population. As advocates, we could testify before the state legislature to urge additional funding to support the establishment of special programs for students as well as retraining for faculty and staff. As advocates we might also work with university administrators to understand the need for evening hours for campus services such as the bookstore, career advising, and even childcare. We might even advocate with campus life staff or student activities officers to encourage them to reach out to nontraditional students.

If, on the other hand, our client is a 54-year-old grandmother suddenly faced with the task of raising grandchildren, she might need counseling to help her deal with her changing roles, relationships, responsibilities, and assumptions about herself. Her life plan has probably changed dramatically. We might work with a local hospital to offer parenting classes designed for grandparents, or, in what might be considered a role reversal, work with local adult education programs to design workshops for teenagers being raised by grandparents.

In our role as consultants to school districts, we might encourage teachers and counselors at the schools attended by the grandchildren to participate in in-service training to familiarize them with appropriate ways of handling this special group of youngsters and their grandmothers. As advocates at the state or federal level, we could argue for policy changes that would provide better financial benefits for grandmothers raising their grandchildren. As advocates at the local level, we might suggest that schools change standard notes and/or emails from "Dear parent" to use more inclusive terminology. We might encourage those in charge of "parent–teacher associations" to broaden their reach as well and provide suggestions to them.

We hope these examples underline what we have been saying throughout the chapter and the book.

SUMMARY

Counseling adults in transition is an exciting and challenging job that gives us an opportunity to function at many different levels. Advocacy, consulting, and program development are three ways that we can assist our clients with their transitions—through changing the situation, enhancing their sense of self, developing more supports, and increasing the strategies available to them.

EXERCISES

1. Imagine that you work in an outreach center for LBGTQ youth. Even though there seems to be increased acceptance on a societal level, your clients are concerned on a personal level about how their parents, friends, and teachers will react if they come out. Many have been subject to bullying and fear it will increase if they are open about their gender expression or sexual orientation. What steps might you take to address these concerns? Please consider steps beyond working with your individual clients.

2. As the only school counselor in your rural high school, you have been asked to consult with the administration and staff about how they can work more smoothly together. There has been much friction of late, and this has led to a tense atmosphere in the school that has been commented on by students and parents. How might you proceed?
3. Your government-funded career center has been charged with educating local employers about your services, in particular the support you can offer if they hire persons with disabilities. How would you go about planning the workshop?

REFERENCES

American Counseling Association. (2014). *2014 code of ethics*. https://www.counseling.org/docs/default-source/ethics/2014-code-of-ethics.pdf?sfvrsn=2d58522c_4

American Counseling Association. (2021). *Take action*. https://www.counseling.org/government-affairs/actioncenter?vvsrc=%2FRegister%2FPrivacyPolicy%3Fpartial%3Dtrue

Bloom, B. S., Engelhart, M. D., Furst, E. J., Hill, W. H., & Krathwohl, D. R. (1956). *Taxonomy of educational objectives: The classification of educational goals. Handbook I: Cognitive domain*. David McKay.

Bronfenbrenner, U. 1977. Toward an experimental ecology of human development. *American Psychologist, 32*(7), 513–531.

Caffarella, R. S., & Daffron, S. R. (2013). *Planning programs for adult learners: A practical guide* (3rd ed.). Jossey-Bass.

Cormier, S., Nurius, P. S., & Osborn, C. J., (2017). *Interviewing and change strategies for helpers* (8th ed.). Cengage.

Dawis, R. V., & Lofquist, L. H. (1984). *A psychological theory of work adjustment: An individual differences model and its applications*: University of Minnesota Press.

Dougherty, A. M. (2014). *Psychological consultation and collaboration in school and community settings* (6th ed.). Brooks/Cole.

Goodman, J. (2006). Toward a holistic view. In D. Capuzzi & M. D. Gross (Eds.), *Career counseling: Foundations, perspectives, and applications*. Pearson.

Goodman, J. (2009). Starfish, salmon, and whales: An introduction to the special section. *Journal of Counseling and Development, 87*(3), 259.

Goodman, J. (2010). Advocacy for older adults. In M. J. Ratts, R. L. Toporek, & J. A. Lewis (Eds.), *ACA advocacy competencies: A social justice framework for counselors* (pp. 97–106). American Counseling Association.

Goodman, J., & Savage, N. (1999). Responding to a community need: Oakland University's adult career counseling center. *Career Development Quarterly, 48*, 19–30.

Gopnik, A. (2020, November 16). Coming home. *The New Yorker*, pp. 18–24.

Gross, J. (1992, September 3). A jail garden's harvest: Hope and redemption. *The New York Times*, Section A, p. 16.

Hoppin, J., & Splete, H. (1994). *Training needs of career development facilitators*. Career Development Training Institute at Oakland University.

Jackson, D. N., & Hayes, D. H. (1993). Multicultural issues in consultation. *Journal of Counseling & Development*, 72, 144–147.

Jacoby, B. (1991). Today's students: Diverse needs require comprehensive responses. In T. K. Miller & R. B. Winston, Jr. (Eds.), *Administration and leadership in student affairs* (pp. 281–307). Accelerated Development.

Johnson, S. (1998). *Who moved my cheese?* Putnam.

Kobylarz, L. (2005, June). *National career development guidelines overview.* Paper presentedat the meeting of the National Career Development Association, Orlando, FL.

Kurpius, D. J., & Fuqua, D. R. (1993a). Introduction to the special issue. *Journal of Counseling & Development, 71,* 596–597.

Kurpius, D. J., & Fuqua, D. R. (1993b). Fundamental issues in defining consultation. *Journal of Counseling & Development, 71,* 598–600.

Lewis, J., Arnold, M., House, R., & Toporek, R. (2005). *Advocacy competencies.* Retrieved from http://www.counseling.org/counselors.

Liu, W. M., & Estrada-Hernandez, N. (2010). Counseling and advocacy for individuals living in poverty. In M. J. Ratts, R. L. Toporek & J. A. Lewis (Eds.), *ACA advocacy competencies: A social justice perspective* (pp. 43–53). American Counseling Association.

Middleton, R. A., Robinson, M. C., & Mu'min, A. S. (2010). Rehabilitation counseling: A continuing professional imperative for multiculturalism and advocacy competence. In R. K. Conyne & E. P. Cook (Eds.), *Ecological counseling: An innovative approach to conceptualizing person-environment interaction* (pp. 173–183). American Counseling Association.

Miller, J. V. (2000, Summer). Career trends: The fourth NCDA/Gallup national survey of working America. *Career Developments.* http://www.multiculturalcounseling.org/index.php?option=com_content&view=article&id=205:amcd-endorses-multicultural-and-social-justice-counseling-competencies&catid=1:latest&Itemid=123

National Occupational Information Coordinating Committee. (1989). *The national career development guidelines (Trainer's manual).* Author.

Noel, D. M. (1993). Leadership in an age of layoffs. *Issues & Observations, 13,* 1–5.

Obama, B. (2004). *Dreams from my father.* Crown Publishers.

Pope, M., Pangelinan, J. S., & Coker, A. D. (Eds.). (2011). *Experiential activities for teaching multicultural counseling classes and infusing cultural diversity into core classes.* American Counseling Association.

Psychologists for Social Responsibility. (2020). *Our mission.* https://psysr.net/our-mission/

Ratts, M. J., Toporek, R. L., & Lewis, J. A. (2010). *ACA advocacy competencies: A social justice perspective.* American Counseling Association.

Robinson, J. (1994, August). *Making informed labor market choices: The right tools, the right times.* Presentation at the national conference of State Occupational Information Coordinating Committees, Danvers, MA.

Rogers, C. R. (1957). The necessary and sufficient conditions of therapeutic personality change. *Journal of Counseling Psychlogy, 21,* 95–103.

Sargent, A. G., & Schlossberg, N. K. (1988). Managing adult transitions. *Training and Development Journal, 41,* 58–60.

Schlossberg, N. K., Lassalle, A., & Golec, R. (1991). *The mattering scales for adult students in higher education.* University of Maryland.

Singh, A. A., & Nassar, S. C. (July, 2020). Integrating the multicultural and social justice counseling competencies into ractice, research, and advocacy [Special issue]. *Journal of Counseling and Development, 98,* 233–347.

Toporek, R. L., & Daniels, J. (2018). *American Counseling Association advocacy competencies*. Counseling.org.

Watson, A. L., Collins, R. L., & Correia, F. C. (2004). Advocacy and social action in the context of ecological counseling. In R. K. Conyne & E. P. Cook (Eds.), *Ecological counseling: An innovative approach to conceptualizing person-environment interaction* (pp. 289–313). American Counseling Association.

Wilcoxon, S. A., & Puleo, S. G. (1992). Professional development needs of mental health counselors: Results of a national survey. *Journal of Mental Health Counseling, 14*, 187–195.

INDEX

Lightning Source UK Ltd.
Milton Keynes UK
UKHW021151140921
390561UK00006B/56

9 780826 135469